APPLEWOOD'S
AMERICAN FRONTIER
SERIES

Sketches of Louisiana

Historical and Descriptive

Major Amos Stoddard

APPLEWOOD BOOKS
Carlisle, Massachusetts

Sketches of Louisiana
was originally published in
1812

ISBN: 978-1-4290-4582-7

APPLEWOOD'S AMERICAN FRONTIER SERIES

Thank you for purchasing an Applewood book. Applewood reprints America's lively classics—books from the past that are still of interest to modern readers. This facsimile was printed using many new technologies together to bring our tradition-bound mission to you. Applewood's facsimile edition of this work may include library stamps, scribbles, and margin notes as they exist in the original book. These interesting historical artifacts celebrate the place the book was read or the person who read the book. In addition to these artifacts, the work may have additional errors that were either in the original, in the digital scans, or introduced as we prepared the book for printing. If you believe the work has such errors, please let us know by writing to us at the address below.

For a free copy of our current print catalog featuring our bestselling books, write to:

APPLEWOOD BOOKS
P.O. Box 27
Carlisle, MA 01741

For more complete listings, visit us on the web at:
www.awb.com

Prepared for publishing by HP

SKETCHES,

HISTORICAL AND DESCRIPTIVE,

OF

LOUISIANA.

BY MAJOR AMOS STODDARD,

MEMBER OF THE C. S. M. P. S. AND OF THE NEW YORK HISTORICAL
SOCIETY.

.... *Altius omnem*
Expediam primâ repetens ab origine famam. VIRGIL.

Præcipuum munus annalium reor, ne virtutes sileantur; utque pra-
vis dictis, factisque, ex posteritate et infamiâ metus sit. TACITUS.

PHILADELPHIA:
PUBLISHED BY MATHEW CAREY.

A. SMALL, PRINTER.
....
1812.

DISTRICT OF PENNSYLVANIA, TO WIT:

{Seal.} BE IT REMEMBERED, That on the third day of September in the thirty seventh year of the Independence of the United States of America, A. D. 1812. Amos Stoddard of the said district, hath deposited in this office the Title of a Book the right whereof he claims as author, in the words following, to wit:

"Sketches, Historical and Descriptive, of Louisiana. By Major Amos Stoddard, Member of the U. S. M. P. S. and of the New York Historical Society.

................*Altius omnem*
Expediam primâ repetens ab origine famam. VIRGIL.

Præcipuum munus annalium reor, ne virtutes sileantur, utque pravis dictis, factisque, ex posteritate et infamiâ metus sit. TACITUS.

In Conformity to the Act of the Congress of the United States, intituled, "An Act for the encouragement of Learning, by securing the Copies of Maps, Charts and Books, to the Authors and Proprietors of such Copies during the times therein mentioned."—And also to the Act, entitled "An Act supplementary to an Act, entitled " An act for the Encouragement of Learning, by securing the copies of Maps, Charts, and Books, to the Authors and Proprietors of such Copies during the Times therein mentioned," and extending the Benefits thereof to the Arts of designing, engraving, and etching historical and other Prints."

D. CALDWELL, *Clerk of the District of Pennsylvania.*

By transfer
5 Ja 1907

CONTENTS.

PREFACE.
CHAPTER I. *Historical Sketches of Louisiana,*   1
      II. *Of the Floridas,*   111
      III. *Extent and Boundaries of Louisiana,* 131
      IV. *New Orleans.——The Delta, &c.*   151
      V. *From Chafalia to Arkansas, &c.*   177
      VI. *Upper Louisiana,*   205
      VII. *Land Titles, &c.*   243
      VIII. *Government and Laws,*   269
      IX. *Commerce and Manufactures*   293
      X. *Learning and Religion,*   307
      XI. *Character of the Louisianians,*   319
      XII. *State of Slavery,*   331
      XIII. *Antiquities,*   345
      XIV. *Of the Rivers of Louisiana,*   353
      XV. *Mineral Riches,*   389
      XVI. *Aborigines,*   409
      XVII. *A Welsh Nation in America,*   465

PREFACE.

IT fell to my lot, in the month of March 1804, to take possession of upper Louisiana, under the treaty of cession. The high civil trust confided to me in that country, drew my attention in the first instance to the jurisprudence, in the second to the principles of the French and Spanish colonial governments, and in the third to the civil history and geography of those regions. The records and other public documents were open to my inspection; and, as it was my fortune to be stationed about five years on various parts of the lower Mississippi, and nearly six months on Red river, my enquiries gradually extended to Louisiana in general.

That country, even at this day, is less known than any other (inhabited by a civilized people) of the same extent on the globe. While it was in possession of France and Spain, at least till near the close of the American revolution, it was almost inaccessible to us; nor were we influenced by motives of interest or curiosity to visit it. The entrance of our vessels into its ports was either interdicted, or its commerce too unimportant to incite maritime adventures; and the mountains and uninhabited wilderness on our frontiers, presented strong barriers to enterprise over land. The Spanish government, in particular, was always actuated by a dark and intricate policy; it was careful to exclude strangers from its dominions; to prohibit surveys and discoveries, except for the benefit of the cabinet, and to place the seal of malediction on whatever was calculated to awaken the curiosity or envy of other nations.

No wonder then that Louisiana at the time of the cession, was so little known to the United States. They had suddenly and unexpectedly acquired a territory of which they knew not the extent; they were equally unacquainted with its climates, soils and productions, the magnitude and importance of its numerous rivers, and its commercial and other natural advantages. I therefore indulge the expectation, that the subsequent SKETCHES, however inaccurate or erroneous, will not prove wholly unacceptable to the public; particularly as no one before me, to my knowledge, has attempted an history and description of this territory.

Historians have but partially noticed that country; none of their works seem to embrace, in regular detail, any considerable number of years; they are extremely barren of events, and unfortunately contain many chasms. These are in part supplied from some ancient manuscript journals, and other documents, to which I gained access; yet it is to be regretted that materials are still wanting to exhibit even the prominent historical features of Louisiana. The writings of missionaries at least those I have seen, and the accounts published by French officers who were employed in the country during part of the two last centuries, are mostly of an uninteresting nature. I am, however, much indebted to both dead and living authors; and if I have been less solicitous to acknowledge my obligations to them, than to collect and arrange the substance of their labors, it was because I relucted at marginal and other references.

These are some of the obstacles in the way of a regular and correct civil history of Louisiana. Those opposed to a complete geography and natural history of that country, are still more insuperable. All the old maps are extremely defective. The one prefixed to the work of Du Pratz, is unquestionably the best. No detailed accounts of the interior are to be found in the records of Louisianian literature: On Indian traders, and other transient persons, we are obliged in most instances to rely for what limited information we possess. They present us indeed, with an exuberant mass of materials, but extremely crude, confused and contradictory; and it requires no small share of patience and attention to distinguish truth from fiction. I am indebted to some fugitive and other publications relative to particular portions of Louisiana; and to the authors of them I am proud to pay my acknowledgements. Respectable men, in most of the districts, furnished me with such local and other information as they possessed, and I have made the best use of it in my power. My own excursions in that country were extensive, and I have endeavored to describe what fell under my own observation with as much fidelity as possible. The notices of the Floridas are partly derived from the valuable work of Bernard Romans, and partly from an equally valuable manuscript of an itinerant friend.

These are some of the materials on which the subsequent SKETCHES are founded; and yet it is believed that few or none more accurate or authentic are at present in existence, except those in possession of our late western travellers; time and enterprise are necessary to afford the world a just conception of Louisiana. The paucity of veracious materials, forbade the hope of an entire and complete work, and therefore SKETCHES only have been attempted. That there are many omissions and errors, is more than probable; but who is able at this early period, to supply the first, or fully to correct the second?

The avocations of military men are seldom favorable to literary pursuits; their studies are usually desultory, and more multiform in their nature than is consistent with labored disquisition. During the progress of the ensuing work, I was wholly secluded from the literary world, and the aid of literary friends, destitute of books, and most of the time afflicted with the endemics of the climate. This will in some measure account for occasional aberrations of manner and style; imputable in part, perhaps, to the rugged service of eighteen years, "in the tented field." I am fully apprised of the danger to which I expose myself in this literary attempt. I expect not the approbation of scientific men, though I hope to escape their censure. If they cannot think favorably of my genius or erudition, I trust they will at least commend my industry and motives. I worship not in the temple of science; my devoirs are limited to its humble vestibule.

Persuaded I am, that, when Louisiana is accurately known, when the advantages it affords are manifested and felt, not an enemy to the cession will remain. No doubt much of the opposition to it (perhaps, in some measure, stimulated by the prejudices of party) arose from the want of information, which dictated caution. It requires no great penetration to perceive that, if the arbiters of Europe, and indeed of the world, had spread themselves over that country, the tranquility of the United States would have been disturbed, and perhaps their liberties jeopardized. Whatever may be my speculative opinions on political subjects, I have felt no disposition to yield to them; solicitous as a public servant to avoid the exacerbations of party; steady in the pursuit of truth.

AMOS STODDARD, Major,
Fort Columbus 1812.   Corps United States' Artellerists.

HISTORICAL SKETCHES OF LOUISIANA.

CHAPTER I.

THE Spaniards and the French discovered and settled Florida and Canada long before Louisiana was known. These early events have a direct bearing on the subsequent affairs of those nations in the new world; and hence a concise detail of them will not be deemed foreign to the design of these Sketches, particularly as they serve to throw much light on the policy pursued by both in the establishment of their Colonies.

After the Spaniards landed on the Islands, nearly twenty years elapsed before they attempted any new discoveries. During this period they collected immense quantities of gold, especially in Cuba and Hispaniola. They first deprived the natives of their treasure, and then condemned them to seek for more in the bowels of the earth, or among the rocks of the mountains. These people were unable to satiate the avidity of the Spaniards. Millions of them perished, and the remainder were doomed to ignominious slavery. No sooner were the Islands exhausted of their wealth than the Spaniards turned their attention to other regions. They penetrated to the isthmus of Darien, and attempted to form settlements in the bay of Campeachy.

Perhaps they became acquainted with the discoveries of Sabastian Cabot along our coast in 1497. Ponce de Leon, a celebrated Spanish adventurer, was induced to discover and explore the continent from a singular motive. The Caribbees informed him, that a fountain existed in that quarter, whose waters were calculated to transform the aged into youth. He landed in the month of April 1512 in N. Lat. 30 deg. 8 min. (some say N. Lat. 38 deg. 8 min.) and the country he named Florida, because he found it in full bloom at that early season of the year. He made a fruitless endeavor to discover the fountain; and great numbers of his followers probably perished in the wilderness, as they never returned to their companions. He even made a second voyage, which proved as unsuccessful as the first, and chagrin and disappointment drove him back to the Islands. The name he gave the country was extended to all North America, and was attached to it till 1586, when it was restricted to a territory of inconsiderable extent to the northward of the gulf.

These adventurers convinced the Spaniards of the existence of other unexplored regions, and they readily conceived them to be filled with the precious metals. They determined to realize what their imaginations painted in such fascinating colours. Accordingly a body of them under Grijalva landed on the coast of Florida in 1518. The Indians gave them a friendly reception, and presented them with pearls, silver, and gold. When they were about to retire, they ungratefully seized a number of these innocent people, and reduced them to slavery in the Islands.

Providence seldom permits such acts of cruelty and injustice to remain long unpunished; and the injuries inflicted by the Spaniards drew on them, in a variety of instances, the vengeance they merited. Their evil genius led them to pay these people another visit in 1520, when the manner of their reception induced them to make a precipitate retreat from the country. Not discouraged at this repulse, they again landed on the same coast in 1522, when two hundred of their men perished by the hands of the natives.

Florida was now of sufficient importance to attract the notice of the crown. Francis de Geray obtained the first grant or patent of that country about the year 1524; but he did not long survive this mark of favor, and was succeeded by de Allyon, who visited his province.

The Spaniards for some time were confounded at the vigorous opposition of the natives; they did not perceive, that the inhabitants of the continent were more resolute and hardy, more independent and lofty in their sentiments, than those of the Islands, whom they had enslaved. They at last concluded, that the country abounded in the precious metals, and that the natives were possessed of immense wealth, which they were determined to defend with their lives: On no other principle were they able to account for the numerous obstacles opposed to their progress. These conceits served to swell their prospects, and to urge them on to new exertions. Accordingly in 1528, Pamphilo Narvaez, on whom the province had devolved, landed in Florida with a considerable body of Spaniards. The Indians made use of a stratagem to draw them into the interior. They presented some gold to them, and at the same time intimated, that this treasure abounded in the Appalachian mountains. The Spaniards marched directly into the wilderness, extremely delighted with the prospects before them. But how great was their surprise, when they found themselves in an ambuscade, and vigorously attacked by several nations! The contest was long and bloody. Narvaez perished with many of his men. The remainder attempted to regain their ships. Their provisions were soon expended, which reduced them to the painful necessity of feeding on the carcasses of their dead companions.

This disaster checked for a while, but did not damp the ardor and perseverance of the Spaniards; nor did it serve to restrain their ambition and avarice. On the death of Narvaez, that celebrated adventurer, Ferdinand de Soto, succeeded to the Government of Florida. This man was of a temperament not to be intimidated by the misfortunes of others; nor to despair of attaining what his predecessors had attempted in vain. He was one of the most distinguished Knight-errants of the age; and his actions in Florida sufficiently attest his courage, hardihood, and romantic turn of mind. He explored almost all parts of that Country with the speed of a courier; and the long time he remained in it was mostly employed in seeking new dangers, and in encountering them. He attacked the natives every where, and every where committed great slaughter; destroyed their towns, and subsisted his men on the provisions found in them. He even spent some winters among them, particularly one in the Chickasaw nation; the next spring crossed the Mississippi, explored the regions to the westward of it, and in 1542 ended his days on Red river.

This was the first dawn of the Spanish power in Florida. Most of the Indian nations were either extremely intimidated, or greatly reduced. They became convinced of their own weakness, and found themselves obliged to yield to the superior skill of their enemies. Notwithstanding this, they disdained to become slaves, or to survive the loss of their freedom; and therefore gradually retired from the coast, and planted themselves beyond the reach of the invaders.

After the death of Ferdinand de Soto, no more discoveries were undertaken in this quarter; the prospects of mineral wealth abated, and the poor Spanish settlers left to bewail their misfortunes. They found themselves obliged, much against their inclinations, to turn their attention to agriculture and the fisheries. They opened an intercourse with the few remaining Indians along the coast; but this proved unprofitable, and the only refuge they found from want was in manual labor.

The French about this period began to view, with jealous eyes, the discoveries and settlements of the Spaniards. France was among the last of the European nations to explore distant regions, and to plant Colonies in them. Her ambitious views were for a long time confined to the Milanese, and the two Sicilies, to which she had some ancient claims: Nor was she easily persuaded, that any permanent advantages were to be derived from the establishment of distant colonies, particularly at a time when the nation was agitated by religious disputes and commotions. Yet, notwithstanding she entertained these sentiments, she secretly envied the progress of her rival in the new world, determined to interrupt it, and to participate in the glories of enterprise.

The execution of this project was wholly confided to the discretion of the great Admiral de Coligny. He therefore fitted out a considerable fleet in 1562, and embarked a Colony of French Protestants. Ribaud conducted the expedition to Florida, and planted the settlers within about thirty miles of St. Augustine, where they erected a Fort for their protection, and named it Charles, in honor of Charles IX.

Astonishment seized the Spaniards at this unexpected intrusion. Menendez, however, after recovering from the first shock of perturbation, assembled the forces of the province, attacked Fort Charles, and carried it by storm. Those of the miserable French, who escaped the sword were doomed to the halter, with this label on their breasts, " *not as Frenchmen, but as heretics.*"

France was not then in a situation to punish this outrage; nor, perhaps, as she was evidently an aggressor, had she just cause to complain. But a private Gentlemen of rank, by the name of Dominique de Gourgues, resolved to become the avenger of his nation. In 1567, therefore, he fitted out a fleet at his own expense, arrived in Florida, attacked the Spanish settlements, and those who fell into his hands, were suspended by the neck, with this inscription, " *not as Spaniards, but as assassins.*"

This success was productive of no important benefit. The French were obliged, in the course of a few years, to retire from the Country; and the Spaniards in this quarter experienced no more trouble from them till after the discovery and settlement of Louisiana.

Even at this early period the French were not wholly unacquainted with the continent more to the northward: For Verazzani, in 1524, coasted it from Florida to Newfoundland, and gave to the territories he discovered the name of *New France*. The commercial importance of the fisheries was satisfactorily ascertained by him: But the hopes of more profitable discoveries, added to the peculiar situation of France, served to postpone the pursuit of them.

Ten years elapsed before the French determined to form settlements in the more northern regions. Cartier was employed in 1534 to explore the coast about Newfoundland, and to select some suitable place for a Colony. During this expedition he examined the shores of Acadia, entered the straits of Belleisle, and visited the harbors on the coast of Labrador. In the bay of Gaspé he performed the ceremony of taking possession of the Country in the name of the French King. This seems to have been understood by the Indians; for one of their Chiefs, clothed in a Bear-skin, gave the intruder to understand, that the Country belonged to him. Cartier sailed some distance up the river St. Lawrence: but the advanced state of the season obliged him to return to France.

The next year he was again despatched to the continent with three ships. He now sailed up the river St. Lawrence to the Isle of Orleans, secured his fleet in the mouth of the St. Croix, took formal possession of the Country, and spent the winter in it. He visited Hochelaga, the Indian Capital, and the hill in the vicinity of it he named MONTREAL. The scurvy made great havoc among his people; and this, together with the failure of his provisions, rendered it necessary for him to return to France as soon as the ice disappeared in the river.

The information obtained on this voyage served to awaken the curiosity of the French. The Indians gave Cartier to understand, that he might continue sailing up the river for three months, passing over two or three great lakes, beyond which there was a sea of fresh water, (probably lake Superior) of which they knew no bounds; and that on the other side of the mountains there was another great river, (no doubt the Mississippi) which flowed to the south-west, through a Country full of delicious fruits, and destitute of snow and ice. They at the same time led Cartier to believe, that the Country abounded in silver and gold; particularly as they described to him the colors, and in some measure the qualities of those metals.

He was sent out on his third voyage in 1540. He spent another winter at his old station in the mouth of the St. Croix. Roberval spent the succeeding winter at the same place. Both obtained some additional information relative to the interior. These voyages exposed both to imminent dangers.

The French made no other attempts on Canada till after the lapse of half a century; though they carried on the fisheries and peltry trade along the coast.

When France found herself in some measure recovered from a succession of religious and other wars, she resumed her projects of discovery, and was enabled to prosecute them with more system, and with better prospects of success. She readily perceived, that any attempts to dislodge the Spaniards from Florida, would be attended with more loss than gain; particularly as their jealousy was excited, and their ports strongly fortified. She was likewise well aware, that the fisheries were of consequence, and that the skins and furs obtained in northern regions were more valuable than those about Florida; and she was in hopes of finding a water communication to China by means of the great lakes in Canada. Another voyage was therefore undertaken in 1603, and the prosecution of it confided to Champlain. He arrived at Cartier's station in the river St. Lawrence, endeavored to investigate the geographical position of the lakes, and became acquainted with the Iroquois, or five nations, into whose Country he penetrated by the way of the lakes Champlain and George; after which he returned to France.

All the territory between the fortieth and forty-sixth degrees of North latitude was the same year granted by the French King to Du Monts, who formed a settlement in Acadia; which, in the course of five years, was partly destroyed by the English, and partly exchanged for Canada.

The Canadian coast was visited by the English and Spaniards prior to the discoveries of the French; but as neither of those nations attempted settlements in that quarter, a secure and lasting possession seemed to present itself to view. A sufficient number of Colonists was soon collected, a fleet fitted out, and the whole committed to the direction of Champlain. They sailed directly for Canada, where they arrived in 1608, and laid the foundation of the City of Quebec. This was the first permanent settlement made by the French in this part of the new world.

At the time of their arrival a destructive war raged between the several Indian nations of Canada and the Iroquois, situated at some distance from them. They conceived it good policy to assist their neighbours; particularly as such a step seemed likely to secure their friendship and trade. The Dutch settlers of New York espoused the cause of the Iroquois from similar motives. Both unfolded to the natives the use of the musket, and liberally supplied them with ammunition. The dreadful ravages committed by the hostile parties, served not only to increase the effusion of human blood, but likewise to retard and embarrass the French settlements in Canada.

Such indeed was the wretched condition of that Colony in 1628, owing in part to Indian wars, and in part to the religious dissensions among the settlers, that the crown was easily prevailed on to grant the province to a Company: But as the conditions of the transfer were not fulfilled, the grant was eventually rescinded. The next year an English squadron appeared in the river St. Lawrence, when Quebec and all Canada submitted without a struggle. In 1631 this conquest was abandoned; and the French four years afterwards extended their discoveries to Lakes Huron and Michigan.

The war with the Iroquois proved destructive and ruinous to the French. They at first engaged in it from choice, and were soon obliged to continue it from necessity. The French ministry witnessed the retrograde tendency of the province, and reflected with pain on its defenceless condition, liable to become an easy prey to the first foreign or domestic invader. Such indeed was the crisis of affairs about the year 1660, that the existence of Canada in a great measure depended on the extirpation of the Iroquois; and it was resolved to make one great effort to humble that people. In the course of the four subsequent years, two large reinforcements arrived from France, and the war was prosecuted with vigor*.

A new difficulty opposed itself to the French. In 1664 the English dispossessed the Dutch of New Belgia†, or New York, who immediately furnished the Iroquois with the means of carrying on the war to advantage. Even at that early day the progress of the settlements of the two nations afforded reciprocal uneasiness, and each endeavoured to circumscribe the other as much as possible. The English planted themselves among the Iroquois, partly for the purposes of trade, and partly to extend their claims by new discoveries. The French were actuated by similar motives; but the frequent and powerful incursions of their enemies, and the unfriendly disposition of the Indians about the lakes, kept them in a state of war, and rendered it unsafe for them to leave their settlements. During this time their rivals remained at peace, and pursued their trade without interruption.

Canada stood in need of large reinforcements to supply her losses. One arrived in 1667, when it was found on examination, that 3000 men were ready for the field. In this enumeration the settlers, as well as regular troops, were included.

About this period the French authorities in Canada, for the first time, viewed their situation in its true light. The destruction of the natives was of no use to them; on the contrary, the more they killed or drove away, the less remained to yield them commerce. A predatory contest with barbarians was prolific of blood, but not of glory; it

---

* A memorable event took place in 1663. Canada was terribly shaken by an earthquake; and, according to contemporary writers, it buried a lofty chain of mountains, 300 miles long, and changed this immense tract into a plain.

† This was confirmed to the English by the treaty of Breda, in 1667.

interrupted the prosperity of the settlements, and evidently pointed to their ultimate extinction. The Iroquois entertained the same sentiments. A war of sixty years' continuance, carried on with various success, operated to the injury of both, and both secretly sighed for some remission from the toils and waste of perpetual hostility. The French ventured to make proposals on the subject; and a peace was concluded in 1668.

Both parties were extremely pleased at this event; the Indians, because it removed their fears of total ruin; the French, because the navigation of the lakes was less precarious, and an extended trade and intercourse appeared practicable.

The first symptom of Canadian prosperity manifested itself at this period. As the days of adversity appeared to be past, the troops were disbanded, and a suitable quantity of land bestowed on them as a reward for their services. An unsuccessful attempt made by the English on Quebec in 1691, caused a temporary alarm: But the peace of Ryswick in 1697, put an end to the disputes about these regions; and Canada was no more menaced till it was forever wrested from the crown of France.

It was extremely unfortunate for the French, that they entertained erroneous conceptions of Canada, and of the means of wealth it afforded. The romantic tales published by some of the first adventurers, particularly by those who had a deep interest in colonizing the Country, led them into error. Many of the agriculturalists of France exchanged their fruitful fields and vineyards for the inhospitable wilds of the new world, not to pursue their former occupations, but to seize on opulent fortunes. The success of the Spaniards served to increase their expectations. Great indeed was their disappointment when they came to realise their condition. The Indian trade furnished the only means of subsistence. They took no pains to ascertain the quality of their lands, or the different grains suited to the climate. They seldom aimed at more than the cultivation of gardens. The consequence was, that poverty dwelt in almost every mansion. The labor of nine tenths of the population on the distant lakes and rivers, exposed to hunger, nakedness and death, served only to augment the wealth of a few traders and merchants. Hence the colony, poor at first, was never able to prosper. The physical strength of a people depends more on agriculture than any other pursuit; and the progeny of the ancient French, with the sad experience of more than two hundred years before their eyes, appear to be still ignorant of this truth. The inhabitants of the Spanish provinces are extremely poor, though planted in a fruitful soil, and in a world of precious metals. The French and Spanish colonists were ever engaged in the pursuit of phantoms; and this pursuit will probably be continued as long as there remains a vestige of peltry, or of mineral wealth.

During the long war with the Iroquois, the French traders were not allowed to pass beyond the bounds of the settlements; while the English extended their intercourse, much indeed to the injury of their rivals. The peace, however, released them from these restraints; and the French authorities, for the first time, permitted their traders to carry goods into the Indian nations, and at the same time granted them exclusive privileges as inducements to enterprise. Prompted by the thirst of gain, the Colony became much weakened by a wide dispersion of its members, many of whom exposed themselves to great dangers, and some to inevitable destruction. These exclusive privileges were found to be impolitic, and their dissolution was pronounced. Other measures were devised to supply the Indians, and to circumscribe the English.

The most important of these was the establishment of a chain of military posts from Quebec, along the lakes, to

Michillimakinak; and the respective commandants of them were alone authorised to carry on the Indian trade. This measure was likewise found to be pernicious. The commandants put too high a price on their commodities, by which means the English were enabled to undersell them. The French authorities, therefore, again took the trade into their own hands.

In establishing this chain of posts, the French were actuated by other motives than the acquisition of the Indian trade, and the interdiction of the English; they aimed to immortalize themselves by new discoveries. An inland passage to China was considered as practicable. They were apprised of the information received by Cartier about 150 years before, that there was a great river to the south west, where Silver and Gold abounded. These prospects were strengthened by subsequent enquiries, and they prepared to gratify their curiosity.

It must not be forgotten, that the French, as well as Spaniards, usually confided their inland voyages of discovery to one or more Catholic missionaries, at least none was undertaken without them. No doubt these pious Priests were actuated by a laudable zeal to propagate their religion, and at the same time to become acquainted with unknown Countries. Certain it is, that we are indebted to this order of men for most of the knowledge we have, correct or spurious, of the early history of the French and Spanish Colonies.

There is some dispute as to the time when, and by whom, the Mississippi was first discovered. No less than three nations contend for the honor of this discovery. The English allege that Wood discovered it in 1654, and Bolt in 1670; but without much foundation. The Spaniards are persuaded, that it was seen by Ferdinand de Soto, and even crossed by him as early as 1541 near the Chickasaw nation. This is questioned by the French on the ground that, when they entered the country, no vestige of his wars remained, nor had the Indians any tradition of him. But the journal of his expedition affords indubitable proofs, that he explored the interior of Florida, and that he discovered and crossed the Mississippi. The description it contains of that great river, and of the Country on each side of it, could not have been given by any other than an eye-witness. If no monuments remain of him, it is because his march was rapid ; as he was in pursuit of mines, which eluded his grasp, he had the strongest temptation to accelerate his movements.

There is some dispute among the French, by whom of their own nation the Mississippi was first discovered. But this honor is unquestionably due to two Missionaries of Canada by the names of Jolliet and Marquette*, who traversed the lakes, with five men only to assist them, and entered that river by way of the Ouisconsing. Jolliet says in his journal, that they entered the Mississippi June 15, 1674; but as he had lost all his papers, and wrote from memory only, he probably mistook the year, as Marquette, in the journal left by him, states this discovery to be June 15, 1673. They descended that river to the Arkansas, a distance of about 990 miles, and then returned to Canada by way of the Illinois. They have described the Country and Rivers so accurately as to render it certain, that they made the discoveries attributed to them.

This bold adventure opened a wide field of specula-

---

* Charlevoix relates, that Marquette was a native of Leon in Picardy, born of reputable parents, and an illustrious Missionary of New France. He travelled over all the parts of it then known, and made several important discoveries, the last of which was the Mississippi. On the 18th of May 1675, while on his way from Chickago to Michillimackinac, he entered a river bearing his own name, when he let drop some expressions, which plainly indicated, that he should end his days in that place. Soon after the boat landed, he erected his altar, and said mass; after which, he retired a short distance to return thanks, desiring the men with him to absent themselves for half an hour. They did so, and on their return, found him dead.

tion, which seemed to promise an ample reward for the greatest toils and dangers. M. de la Salle, the proprietor and commander of Fort Frontinac, situated at the lower end of lake Ontario, resolved to gratify his curiosity in exploring a Country, represented as the finest in the world. The reparation of an exhausted fortune furnished not the least of the motives, which stimulated him to undertake the arduous enterprise. The discovery and settlement of the Country about the mouth of the Mississippi evidently assured wealth and fame ; and happily his talents, courage, and activity, were admirably calculated to inspire the adventurers with the most flattering hopes of success.

It was not easy to make the necessary preparations for this voyage; an almost insuperable difficulty arose from the want of means, which caused considerable delay. M. de la Salle was at last enabled to build a small vessel, in which he sailed from the lower end of Lake Erie near the close of the summer of 1679. His party at first consisted of Father Louis Hennepin, a Franciscan Friar, and thirty four men; and on his voyage over the Lakes he was joined by several more. On their arrival in Lake Michigan, the vessel was loaded with peltries, and ordered to return; but her progress was soon arrested by the Indians, who doomed her to the flames, and the crew to the scalping-knife. M. de la Salle and his followers, now thirty two in all, descended the Illinois river, and in January 1680 halted at an Indian village on its banks, about 150 miles from the Mississippi. The Iroquois had extended their destructive ravages to this Country, where they obtained 800 prisoners at one time, and carried them into slavery; and this circumstance induced the Illinois Indians to treat their new visitors with great hospitality. Here the French, for their better security, built a Fort, and aptly named it *Crevecœur*, or broken heart. As soon as they were secure in winter quarters, M. de la Salle selected three men, and with them returned to Canada over land in pursuit of additional supplies and adventurers.

The original plan was, that M. de la Salle should proceed to the mouth of the Mississippi, while Father Hennepin penetrated that river to its source; and accordingly M. de la Salle, when he set out for Canada, directed him to prosecute the enterprise with all possible despatch. Father Hennepin therefore set out, with two men only with him, and entered the Mississippi March 8th, 1680. But he pretends, that he departed from his instructions, and, instead of the source, resolved to find the mouth of that river; at which, if he be believed, he arrived on the 25th of the same month. On the first of April, according to his account, he set out on his return, and ascended the Mississippi to the falls of St. Anthony, where he and his two men were made prisoners, robbed of their property, and taken to some Indian villages situated on one of the upper branches of that river. They were soon liberated, and returned to Canada by way of the Ouisconsing. Father Hennepin went immediately to France, where he published a splendid account of the vast Country he had discovered, which he named LOUISIANA, in honor of Louis XIV, and dedicated it to the great Colbert. No mention is made in this publication of his descending the Mississippi.

The writers of history and geography seem to have taken it for granted, that Father Hennepin was the first who discovered the Mississippi, and the first who traversed that river to its mouth. It has already appeared, that Jolliet and Marquette entered the Mississippi several years before him; and it will soon be found, that Father Hennepin never descended that river, as he has stated, and that the first discovery of the mouth of it must be attributed to M. de la Salle.

That Father Hennepin entered the Mississippi, and ascended it to the falls of St. Anthony, there can be no manner of doubt. But the truth of what he states, relative to his descent and discovery of the mouth of that river, may be safely questioned on several grounds.

I. He endeavors to create a belief, that he was the first, among the Europeans, who obtained a view of the Mississippi. If he was unacquainted with the discoveries of Ferdinand de Soto, he could not be ignorant of those made by Jolliet and Marquette; and when he alleges, that Jolliet, by his own confession, went no further than the Hurons and Outtaonats, it was to make himself considered as the first discoverer of a new Country, and to snatch the laurels from two contemporary travellers of integrity and virtue. The separate journals of Jolliet and Marquette were published, and they afford a pretty accurate description of the Country, its rivers, and productions. What they call *Painted Monsters* on the side of a high perpendicular rock, apparently inaccessible to man, between the Missouri and Illinois, and known to the moderns by the name of *Piesa*, still remain in a good degree of preservation. They mention the Missouri by the name of *Pekitanoni*, and accurately describe the peculiar color of its waters.

II. The various distances laid down by him are much too short; whereas it is usual for travellers in unknown regions to consider them much greater than they really are. The account of the upper Mississippi, as given by Hennepin himself, may be adduced as an instance of this.

III. If his statement be correct, he descended from the mouth of the Illinois river to the mouth of the Mississippi (a distance of more than 1350 miles) in seventeen days, though he devoted the nights to sleep on shore, spent some time among the Indians, and still more in procuring provisions from the woods. It is therefore difficult to conceive, that he performed the voyage in so short a period; particularly as it usually requires about the same number of days, at the same season of the year, for one of our trading boats to descend from St. Louis to New-Orleans.

IV. He has neglected to describe the mouth of the Mississippi, and the Country about the Delta. These are so singular in many respects, and of such importance to a maritime nation, that the omission was unpardonable, if he had it in his power to gratify curiosity, or to afford useful information to his Government. His silence, therefore, must be attributed to his total ignorance of what he pretends to have discovered.

V. How shall we account for his rapid ascent against the current of the Mississippi! If we believe him, he and the two men with him rowed a Canoe from the mouth of that river to the Illinois in twenty four days! Seventy and eighty days are usually allowed to our trading Row-Boats, assisted too by Sails, to ascend from New Orleans to St. Louis; a voyage about 140 miles shorter than the pretended one of Hennepin: And yet, according to his declaration, he performed it in one third of the time, and under circumstances calculated to retard his progress.

VI. The reasons assigned by him, in the English Edition of his book, for not including his discoveries on the Lower Mississippi in his first publication, dedicated to Colbert, are by no means satisfactory. To omit this, because he had departed from his instructions, and because he wished M. de la Salle to reap the honors of the discovery, manifests an extreme delicacy, which neither the importance of the subject, nor the character of Hennepin, will justify. He complains, that M. de la Salle had injured him in France on account of the Mississippi transactions, and that he was obliged to seek safety in England. Here he published, in 1698, a new Edition of his travels, in which he included his discovery of the mouth of the Mississippi, and dedicated it to King William. At this period M. de la Salle was dead; and it is asserted on good authority, that some of his papers fell into the hands of Hennepin. It is, therefore, reasonable to conclude, that, to revenge himself on the memory of M. de la Salle, and to arrogate to himself the honor of an important discovery, he appropriated the papers of his deceased rival to his own use. It is equally reasonable to conclude, that the notes of M. de la Salle were incomplete, designed only as hints to aid the memory in detailing occurrences more at large, and unintelligible, perhaps, to every body but the writer. The few accurate hints he has given of the Mississippi, and of the Country, between the Illinois and Arkansas, furnish no proof, that he visited or explored them. He either purloined them from the notes of M. de la Salle, or from the remarks of Jolliet, who frequently detailed to him and others the particulars of his discoveries. It is also worthy of notice, that it was eleven years after the death of M. de la Salle before Hennepin pretended to the discovery of the Lower Mississippi. During this time M. Tonti had descended from the Illinois to that place; and the information derived from him and his party, enabled Hennepin to impose on the world, a volume of surreptitious discoveries. Peter Kalm, the Swedish naturalist, in his account of Niagara fall, published in the Annual Register for 1759, speaks thus of his character: " Father " Hennepin calls the fall six hundred feet perpendicular: " But he has gained little credit in Canada; the name of " honor they give him there, is, *the great liar;* he writes " of what he saw in places *where he never was."* These circumstances seem to destroy the authority of Hennepin; his pretensions to the discovery of the mouth of the Mississippi, are founded in fraud and imposture.

M. de la Salle was extremely pleased with the Country about the Illinois river. On his return to Canada, as has been already stated, he endeavoured to persuade his Countrymen to accompany him to the Mississippi. A disposition for enterprise prevailed among them ; but they were poor, and the repeated losses of M. de la Salle had deprived him of all resources, except those of his fertile genius. M. Tonti, whom he left in command of Fort Crevecœur, followed him to Canada; by their united exertions supplies were eventually procured, as likewise a considerable number of adventurers, who were inclined to seek their fortunes in unknown regions. They set out with the design of forming new settlements, and in 1683 arrived on the Mississippi. They established themselves on the east side of that river; and Cahokia, Kaskaskia, and some other villages, were founded at this period. M. de la Salle, after he had regulated the affairs of his little Colony, left M. Tonti in command, and then proceeded with a number of men to the mouth of the Mississippi, where he made such observations as time and other circumstances permitted. He speedily returned to Quebec, and from thence passed over to France, and communicated the particulars of his discoveries to the French ministry.

The certainty of a great inland water communication from the gulf of St. Lawrence to that of Mexico, a distance of about 3,500 miles, awakened the surprise and curiosity of the French Cabinet. This discovery was the foundation of that policy, which was ultimately adopted to extend round the English settlements a strong cordon, calculated to draw them gradually into the embraces of France. This policy had less of hypothesis in it than was at first believed by the English. To carry it into effect, the French adopted the most artful and prudent precautions, and all their subsequent colonial measures tended to this point.

A strong settlement was already formed on the Upper Mississippi, and it was deemed of primary importance to form another at the mouth of that river. M. de la Salle was therefore supplied with four ships, their several crews, and 170 landsmen. After various difficulties and delays, occasioned by storms and other accidents among the West India Islands, he at length made the continent, and landed his Colony, February 18th, 1685. Deceived by the currents in the gulf, or by his former observations, he sailed about three hundred miles to the westward of his destination, and debarked his settlers at the mouth of the river Guadaloupe, on the west side of the bay of St. Bernard, in about N. Lat. 29 degrees. Here they were strongly opposed by the Indians, and a Fort was erected for their security. Here several other misfortunes awaited them, sufficient to check the ardor, and to break down the spirits of ordinary men. All their Vessels, and part of their provisions and stores, were soon destroyed either by the violence of the winds, or the negligence of the Officers and Pilots. The diseases contracted in St. Domingo assumed a fatal type on their arrival, and about one hundred of the adventurers miserably perished. A voyage over land to the Illinois Country, where M. Tonti commanded, seemed alone to promise the means of relief.

Such indeed was the painful situation of the Colony, that it required more than ordinary firmness and caution in M. de la Salle to remedy the evils of it. In April 1686 he selected twenty of his best men, and proceeded by land in a north-east direction about 450 miles; but was obliged to return on account of the desertion of four of his men, the sickness of himself and others, and the want of ammunition. In this excursion he visited many powerful nations of Indians, who in general treated him with kindness, and this created a spirit of desertion among his men.

This retrograde movement was a terrible misfortune, as it protracted the period of relief. M. de la Salle felt the full force of it. The effect was to stimulate his exertions, and to animate him with the hopes of arriving at the Illinois in season to save his people from famine and death. He set out again in January 1687, with the same number of men, and directed his course more to the eastward, perhaps to find the Mississippi. The rains had raised all the rivers, which impeded his progress, and imposed on him and his men the most incredible hardships. He likewise on this journey visited many nations of Indians, and some of them manifested hostile designs; but his penetration and vigilance enabled him more than once to preserve the lives of his men.

Some remission from about two months' incessant toil was rendered necessary, not only to recruit the strength and spirits of the men, but likewise to prepare a stock of provisions. M. de la Salle, therefore, halted for these purposes in a delightful part of the Country, where there appeared to be plenty of game. In this situation the men under his command had time to reflect on the fatigues they suffered, and secretly to deliberate on the means of escaping them. They readily fancied, that their companions, who deserted the year before, were happy among the Indians, and they felt a secret desire to participate with them the enjoyments of rural life. Under these extravagant impressions, they soon reconciled themselves to the commission of the blackest crimes. These " poor " fellows" had been accustomed " to beg their bread about " the streets of Rochelle," and honor and gratitude formed no part of their character. In fine, they resolved to murder such as were likely to obstruct their designs. M. de la Salle sent his nephew, servant, and hunter, in pursuit of game; and these fell the first victims. Their long absence rendered him uneasy, particularly as he had discovered treacherous symptoms in the conduct of his men; and he went in search of his lost companions with the most awful presages of their destruction, and of his own fate. He finally found their dead bodies. The two murderers fired from their obscure retreat, and gave him a mortal wound, of which he shortly expired.

Thus perished M. de la Salle on the 19th of March, 1687, illustrious for his courage as well as misfortunes, and one of the greatest adventurers of the age in which he lived. His discoveries were extensive, and of importance to his nation. He laid the foundation of the Colony of Louisiana. The difficulties and dangers he encountered, added to his private virtues, seem to entitle him to our esteem and admiration.

Immediately after this tragical event, a quarrel ensued about the command. The bosoms of all the men were not inaccessible to remorse ; and in this quarrel the two murderers were shot. The remainder of the party (among whom was Father Anastasius, who has left us an account of these transactions, and likewise a Priest by the name of Cavalier, brother to M. de la Salle) directed their course northward, and soon arrived among the Cenesians and Nassonians, where they were joined by the four men who deserted them the preceding year. The Cenesians prevailed on some to take up their abode among them, particularly those in any way concerned in the late mutiny. The remaining seven, with Father Anastasius and Cavalier at their head, set out for the Illinois. The Cenesians furnished them with horses and guides to conduct them to the Cahirmois. These likewise furnished them with horses and guides to conduct them to the Arkansas, where they all arrived (except one man, who was drowned by the way) in July 1687, and where, to their great joy and surprise, they found a Fort already erected, and a number of Canadian settlers planted about it.

At the time of the expected arrival of M. de la Salle, more than two years before, M. Tonti descended to the mouth of the Mississippi to meet him. After a fruitless stay of some weeks, he proceeded on his return to the Illinois. He entered the Arkansas river for the purposes of discovery, and soon found himself among the Indians of that name. He made a treaty with that people, opened a trade with them, built a Fort, and made preparations for a settlement. The Soldiers he left here were soon joined by adventurers from Canada; many of whom married Indian women.

Father Anastasius calculates, that the distance from the bay of St. Bernard to the Arkansas, following the route of the party, was about six hundred miles. Many of the Colonists left at the former place perished with hunger and sickness, and by the stratagems of the Indians. About two years after the death of M. de la Salle, the surviving few were seized by the crews of some Spanish Vessels, and conducted to New Leon.

The Spaniards about St. Augustine were not ignorant of the discoveries made by the French on various parts of the Mississippi, and they resolved to prevent, if possible, their settlement in the Country, or at least to confine them to the Delta, where it was believed they would perish. For this purpose they founded Pensacola in 1696, and strongly fortified it; well aware, that the French would soon appear again on the coast. They even endeavoured to excite the prejudices of the Indians against them, and to engage them to commence hostilities on their arrival.

Ibberville was the first royal French Governor, and he arrived with the first Colony in 1699; and from this period the Country was known by the name of Louisiana, which was given to it about nineteen years before by Father Hennepin. He entered the mouth of the Mississippi, and hovered on the coast for some time, in search of the settlement made by the unfortunate M. de la Salle. At length he landed his Colonists at old Baloxi, situated at the mouth of the *Rio Perdido*, and twelve miles west of Pensacola river or bay, where he erected a Fort with four bastions, on which he mounted twelve pieces of ordnance. He went several times to France in pursuit of settlers and necessaries for the province, and finally died in one of the Islands, while fitting out an expedition against the English of Carolina.

The success of colonization in a great measure depends on the reputation and resources of the first Colonists. Those of Canada were not famed for either; but they much surpassed those of Lower Louisiana in both. Two descriptions of Colonists came out under Ibberville. The first were unaccustomed to manual labor, but they possessed enterprise, and expected to gather fortunes from the mines and Indian trade. The second, and much the most numerous, were poor and idle, and expected to subsist on the bounty of Government rather than on the avails of their own industry. It may be readily conceived, that both were frustrated in their expectations.

Disappointment and apathy succeeded the allurements held out to the adventurers. They had no inclination to labor; nor were they supplied with the tools and implements necessary to their various professions: Their situation was rendered still more deplorable from the gradual additions made to their number; for, previously to the death of Ibberville, several hundred arrived, who were planted on Isle Dauphin, and along the Mobile and Perdido. An intercourse was opened with the Spaniards at Pensacola, from whom they obtained some supplies of provisions. They even extended their trade to the Havanna and Vera Cruz, and drew from them many of the necessaries of life, particularly vegetables! They appeared wholly ignorant, that their own grounds were calculated for the growth of the very articles they imported, or they were too indolent to try experiments in agriculture. The consequence was, that during the short administration of Ibberville, upwards of sixty persons perished with hunger; so that, at the close of the year 1705, the Colony was reduced to one hundred and fifty persons.

No doubt these distresses were multiplied from the want of power in the Colonial authorities to remedy abuses, and to guard against anticipated evils. The French Cabinet, from an ill-timed jealousy, reserved to itself the power of devising the necessary Colonial measures, even those of a local and sumptuary nature; and hence the evils it aimed to avert, generally arrived, and oppressed the settlers, before any steps were taken for their relief. This ruinous system was persisted in till Louisiana fell into the hands of Crozat.

One instance is sufficient to illustrate the bad policy of the French Cabinet. It was rumored in France, that fatal endemics prevailed on the Perdido. Peremptory orders were sent out to remove the Settlers to Isle Dauphin, and Mobile, places equally unfavorable to health, and these orders were partly carried into effect in January 1702; a small Garrison and a few settlers only, were suffered to remain. The seat of Government, hitherto established on the Perdido, was likewise transferred to Isle Dauphin, where it remained till New Orleans was founded. So eager were the authorities in France to ascribe to the climate what was the effect of their own inefficient measures! This removal operated to the great injury of the people. To abandon their dwellings, and be compelled to form new settlements in the wilderness, produced a train of misfortunes, not easily avoided by their slender means. It must be acknowledged, however, that they were partly the authors of their own distresses. They depended on the Government for those supplies, which the lands about them were calculated to yield in abundance, and with little labor. Notwithstanding the evidence of their senses, they persisted in the discovery of rich mines, and in the acquisition of fortunes in Indian Countries.

During this period the settlements in the Illinois were in a much more prosperous condition. The climate was favorable to health, and the soil prolific. The inhabitants pursued agriculture as a secondary object only; yet they were plentifully supplied with provisions. They were likewise exempt from Indian wars, which enabled them to prosecute their trade in safety. The same may be said of the lower Colony: For Ibberville made it his first care to establish peace among the Indian tribes, and between them and the French; which continued, with one or two unimportant interruptions only, for several years.

Notwithstanding the embarrassments of the French, projects of discovery were formed, and carried into effect; more, perhaps, to ascertain the existence of mineral wealth, than to gratify mere speculative curiosity. Shortly after the arrival of the Colony, M. de St. Dennis penetrated several hundred miles up Red River; and in 1700 M. Biainville ascended the same River to the Yattersee villages on Bayou Pierre, and at the same time explored the Washita. The next year both these Rivers were more fully explored by M. de St. Dennis, who spent six months on them; and in 1703 a settlement was made on the banks of the latter. Another settlement, with a mission, was established at the same period on the Yazous.

The French of Kaskaskia, as early as 1683, discovered some copper mines on the Mississippi, about six hundred miles above the mouth of the Illinois River, as likewise great quantities of different colored clays, which were considered as valuable. In 1695 they formed an establishment at these mines, which so much incensed the Indians, that they were soon obliged to abandon it.

Expectations of mineral wealth induced the Farmer-General to send out with Ibberville some experienced metallurgists. He had orders to attempt a settlement in the vicinity of the mines; and this enterprise was undertaken in 1702. The French in that year erected a Fort, named *L'Huiller*, at the mouth of Blue River, said by them to be in N. Lat. 44 deg. 13 min. This was considered by the Indians as a fresh encroachment; and the French, to avoid hostilities, retired in the course of a year to the mouth of a small River about twenty one miles above the *de bon secours*, or about one hundred miles above the Ouisconsing, where they built another Fort, and commenced a settlement. Here they procured two thousand quintals of fine clay, and opened some mines of Copper. At another place, about forty miles above the River St. Croix, they found considerable quantities of Virgin Copper, particularly one piece (they say of *native brass*) weighing sixty pounds. The Indians still cherished prejudices against them; and they finally became so troublesome, that the French found it prudent to abandon this part of the Country.

These repeated interruptions were the more severely felt, as they blasted the prospects of a settlement at the source of the Mississippi, which the ministry designed, and had much at heart. The French next turned their attention to the Missouri; which they ascended in 1705 to the mouth of the Kansas River, where they met with a welcome reception from the Indians. Their success in this quarter soon obliterated from their minds the reverses they had experienced on the Upper Mississippi, as likewise the very existence of the Copper mines.

About this period the English concerted a plan to seize on Louisiana, and to expel the French. Several armed Vessels of that nation arrived in the Mississippi under the mask of friendship. Their object was suspected by M. Biainville, who commanded in the absence of the Governor; but he was in no condition to oppose them. The English, however, did not believe themselves in the Mississippi, and conceived it to be more to the westward. This idea was encouraged by M. Biainville; but it served only to postpone the meditated blow. They soon after landed on Isle Dauphin, and plundered the French to the amount of fifty thousand livres.

On board of one of these Vessels was a French Protestant, who, with a number of others, had fled from religious persecution, and taken refuge in Carolina. He found means to present a petition to M. Biainville, stating, " that " if the King would allow them the free exercise of their " religion, upwards of four hundred Protestant families " would remove from among the English into Louisia-" na." This petition was laid before the King, who returned for answer, " that he had not expelled them from " his kingdom to form a republic of them."

Perhaps no Colony, for the first few years of its existence, ever suffered more than that of Louisiana. Between negligence and disappointment, connected with poverty and the endemics of the climate, the settlements gradually declined. The loss of Ibberville was severely felt, and the more so as, during the long vacancy occasioned by his death, jealousies were excited among the several Colonial authorities, and their contentious proceedings poisoned the minds of the people. The Governor, or rather his Representative, frequently exercised the power given him of suspension from office; but this, instead of healing the public disorders, served only to embitter them. This power of suspension was greatly abused; it was therefore withdrawn. The Governor was authorised to suspend the *exercise* of official functions, and suspension from *office* was reserved to the ministry.

To an improper management, and want of system, may be traced most of the misfortunes we have stated. The crown was liberal in both men and money. During the first thirteen years, about 2500 Settlers arrived, and few of them ever returned; and the money expended on the Colony, during the same period, amounted to the enormous sum of 689,000 livres : Yet such were the sufferings of the Colony, that, in 1712, it contained only four hundred Whites, twenty Negro Slaves, and three hundred head of Cattle.

At this time the wars in Europe demanded all the attention and resources of France. The King, though obliged to withhold from Louisiana the usual supplies of men and money, was determined to keep it out of the hands of his enemies; and for this purpose granted it to Crozat in 1712. The great wealth and credit of this Gentleman, and the important services he had rendered the crown, were sure pledges of his ability and exertions; and it was confidently expected, that he would prevent the extinction of the Colony. Another motive, perhaps still stronger, led to the concession. The provincial authorities were hostile to each other, and it required some steady and energetic hand to heal the disorders among them. M. de la Motte, who was the first Governor under the grant, arrived in 1713, and took possession of his Government.

The English were always jealous of the French Colonies, and took no small pains to obstruct their prosperity. They at length prevailed on the Spaniards to shut their ports against them, and to suspend the usual intercourse. This was the more injurious, as the French depended on Pensacola, and the other Spanish settlements, for most of their supplies. Perhaps their wants were as great at this as any former period, particularly as Crozat sent out a considerable number of Settlers. In fine, this suspension of intercourse produced an unpleasant state of things, which eventuated in actual war. If, indeed, peace had hitherto subsisted between the French and Spaniards, it resulted more from mutual fear than friendship.

About this time a rumor prevailed, that the Mexican Spaniards meditated an establishment on the east side of the Rio Bravo. To ascertain the fact, and to gain other intelligence, M. de St. Dennis was despatched in 1714 to Natchitoches with thirty men; part of whom he left at that place to form a settlement, and the remainder attended him in his inland voyage of discovery. No Spaniards were found to the eastward of the Rio Bravo, nor had any passed that river; but a number of them, under the command of a Captain Raymond, had just arrived on the west bank of it, where they erected a Fort, called St. John Baptist. M. de St. Dennis was received in a friendly manner, and while there, married the sister of that officer, and a near relation of the Viceroy of Mexico.

The main object of the Spaniards was to penetrate to Red River, and in this way to circumscribe or weaken the claims of the French; but they dreaded them too much to make the attempt, or to interrupt them in their voyages of discovery. They were content to create a province, without inhabitants, on the east side of the Rio Bravo, and to call it Texas.

The policy of this measure was understood; and to defeat it, the French the same year (1714) sent two detachments into that Country. One built a Fort, called the *Dout*, near the source of the Sabine, which was maintained till Louisiana changed masters. The other penetrated to a nation of Indians, called the Assinais, situated on a small River about twenty seven or thirty miles to the westward of the present Spanish village of Nacogdoches, or about 140 miles to the westward of Red River, where they built a Fort, the ruins of which still remain, and took every other precaution in their power to vindicate their rights. During the two or three succeeding years, they several times visited the Rio Bravo; both to watch the motions of the Spaniards, and to gain additional information of the Country.

No complaints of intrusion were made by the Spaniards. They meditated a deeper game, and artifice was the weapon with which they designed to accomplish their wishes; particularly as they knew the Indians to be friendly to the French, and felt themselves incompetent to contend with both. They conceived it practicable to seduce the French into an approbation of their measures, and even to render them subservient to their own views.

A Spanish Franciscan Friar, by the name of Ydaldo,* was the principal agent in this affair. He addressed a letter to M. de la Motte, and requested his assistance and concurrence in a mission to the Assinais. It was common in those times for the Missionaries of two rival nations, not to say belligerents, attended by the troops of both, to unite in spreading the light of the Gospel among the children of darkness. The conversion of the heathen was considered by them as a sacred duty, and paramount to all secular views and obligations. Still many frauds and impositions, and even crimes, were committed under the mask of religion, and ambition was as incident to the mitre as the crown. The Spaniards meditated the expulsion of the French from the Assinais, and they eventually effected it.

M. de la Motte penetrated the motives of this mission, and he saw the danger with which it was pregnant: But he was inclined to assent to it, though not without an ample equivalent; he entertained the belief that he should be able to frustrate the views of the Spaniards, and at the same time, from a temporising policy obtain provisions and other necessaries for the Colony. He anticipated many insuperable difficulties from a state of war, and therefore resolved to avoid it, particularly as he was not furnished with the means of carrying it on, and as the people were destitute of the necessaries of life.

Instead of entering into any discussion with Ydaldo, he conceived it most prudent to send an Agent to Mexico, properly authorised to conclude a Treaty, and to obtain a revival of the commercial intercourse, which was some-

* This man was an artful cunning priest, extremely bold and daring in his actions. He was at the head of the missions in Texas, and makes a conspicuous figure in the history of that Country. He published an account of the most material transactions of his life, which was long and active, and several families in Nacogdoches are in possession of the work. And finally, he was canonized for the services he had rendered to his religion and Government!

time before suspended at the instigation of the English. M. de St. Dennis was deemed the most suitable person to conduct the negociation, particularly as he was intimately acquainted with the concerns of the Colony. In addition to this qualification, he commanded at Natchitoches, and his courage and military talents had gained him universal respect. The Spaniards dreaded him as an enemy; many Indian nations so much esteemed him as to make him their Chief; and it was likewise conceived, that his marriage with a Spanish Lady of rank would ensure him a welcome reception at Mexico, and add much to his influence. He was accordingly invested with full powers to negociate a commercial Treaty, and to remove the obstacles in the way of a friendly intercourse between the French and Spaniards.

On his arrival at Mexico in June 1715 he was favorably received by the Viceroy, who pledged himself to conclude the Treaty in question, and to suffer the French of Louisiana to import provisions and other necessaries from the Spanish Provinces, as soon as the Mission was established among the Assinais. In making this verbal arrangement, the Viceroy was unquestionably sincere; and to exact of the French the fulfilment of a previous condition, was deemed by him as mere matter of precaution.

M. de St. Dennis, on reporting to M. de la Motte the conditions of the agreement, was directed to carry them into effect. He accordingly hastened to the fortress of St. John Baptist, where he formed a caravan, put himself at the head of it, and in the early part of the year 1717 conducted the Spaniards to the Assinais. He assembled the Chiefs and old men of that nation, and persuaded them, much against their inclination, to admit the strangers among them. This was the first time the Spaniards ever appeared on the east side of the Rio Bravo; except in one instance by way of the Gulf, when they took away the wretched remains of the Colony planted by M. de la Salle on the bay of St. Bernard.

In the month of May of that year, M. de St. Dennis arrived the second time at Mexico, expecting a punctual fulfilment of the stipulations already made, and taking with him a considerable quantity of merchandise to exchange for such articles as were indispensably necessary in Louisiana. But what was his chagrin and disappointment, when he found the old Viceroy on his death-bed, and his successor indifferent to his claims! Still greater was his disappointment when he found himself arrested, and confined in a dungeon, denounced as a Smuggler and Spy, and his merchandise seized and condemned as contraband. This act of injustice excited the murmurs of the Spanish populace, particularly as M. de St. Dennis was a public authorised Agent, and not only highly respected among them, but connected by marriage with some of the first families in the Spanish Provinces. Such indeed was the irritation of the public mind, that he was liberated from confinement, but restricted to the limits of the City. His situation was extremely disagreeable, if not dangerous, and he determined to seize the first favorable moment, and attempt the recovery of his liberty. Accordingly in September 1718 he escaped from Mexico in the night, soon procured a good Horse by dismounting the rider, and finally arrived in Louisiana in April 1719.

In the mean time, immediately after the death of the Viceroy, the Spaniards gradually added to their numbers at the Assinais, till the French at that place found themselves too weak to counteract their designs. The fate of M. de St. Dennis but too clearly pointed out what they had a right to expect for themselves, and concluded it best to retire in season from the snare evidently preparing for them.

Thus the Spaniards, by fraud and deception, and in violation of mutual agreements, established themselves within the territory previously discovered and occupied by the French; and hence they never acquired a legitimate right to that part of the Country.

During the existence of this fruitless negociation (in 1716) the French formed a settlement at the Natchez, and built Fort Rosalie for their protection. M. de la Motte likewise died, and was succeeded in the Government by M. Biainville, who had been concerned in most of the events subsequent to the arrival of the first Colony. This accession, though a mark of honorable distinction, proved to him a source of great vexation. As he was both a Statesman and a Soldier, he was much better qualified than his predecessor to stem the tide of adversity; but such was the reduced state of the province, that he almost despaired of preserving it. All the ports on the continent were closed against the French, and they found it difficult to obtain supplies from France.

Five years experience convinced Crozat, that he had nothing to expect from Louisiana. Notwithstanding he had furnished large supplies of men and money, no prospect of indemnity presented itself. The Settlers entertained a rooted aversion to agriculture, and immense sums were lavished in purchasing provisions for them. During these five years he expended 425,000 livres, while the whole trade of the province yielded him no more than 300,000 livres, leaving a balance against him of 125,000 livres. Under these circumstances, in 1717, he relinquished his patent to the Mississippi Company, projected by the celebrated John Law. At this period the province contained only seven hundred Persons, and four hundred head of Cattle.

From the ability and enterprise of this Company, great expectations were formed, and Louisiana began to attract the attention of the monied capitalists of Europe. An extensive and lively commerce, and the discovery of mines (which for more than two centuries had eluded the avidity of the Spaniards) were to fill the exhausted coffers of France, and to yield princely fortunes to the numerous adventurers. These prospects, however, were not to be realised without an increase of population. Exertions were made to obtain and send out settlers; but an inadequate provision was made for their support in the Colony.

In the course of the first six years, the Mother Country and the Islands furnished four thousand and forty four Settlers, likewise one hundred and fifty Galley Slaves, and several hundred females taken from the charity and correction houses. During the same period, one thousand four hundred and forty one Africans were landed in Louisiana. Such an accession of inhabitants contributed only to augment the general distress. The consequence was, that many hundreds of them perished with hunger and sickness. Perhaps the year 1721 may be selected as the period of the greatest calamity in Louisiana; every countenance was covered with a melancholy gloom; the sick were without medicine, as well as the other comforts adapted to their situation; and children perished from want in the arms of their mothers. Such indeed, in that year, was the want of provisions, that the troops, stationed on the Perdido, Isle Dauphin, and Mobile, were divided among, and obliged to seek support from, the Indian villages about the Country.

The interdiction of commerce, which took place in 1713, not only rendered it difficult for the French to obtain supplies, but was always considered by them as the precursor of war; and this broke out in 1719. The King of Spain refused to accede to the triple alliance; and this refusal drew from France a declaration of war in the month of March of that year. On the arrival of this intelligence in Louisiana, a council of war was immediately convened, and it was resolved to attack Pensacola before it could be reinforced from the Islands. Accordingly M. Biainville, with four hundred Indians and a party of Canadian French, hastened to invest that post by land, while three armed Vessels joined in the attack by Sea. The Spanish Commandant, to avoid an escalade, conceived it prudent to capitulate. The French agreed to save the Fort from pillage, and to send the prisoners to the Havanna. On the arrival in that port of the two Vessels employed to transport them, they were seized and condemned by the Spaniards, and their crews secured in dungeons, contrary to the laws of war. In the mean time a number of Spanish Vessels, unapprised of the capitulation, entered the harbor of Pensacola, and were captured.

The Spaniards were not backward in attempting to repossess themselves of that place. In the month of August their Flotilla appeared before it. They found means to excite a mutiny among the French Soldiery, which obliged the town to surrender at discretion. The prisoners were sent to the Havanna.

This partial success led the Spaniards to believe, that they were able to drive the French out of Louisiana. During the same month, their Flotilla arrived before Isle Dauphin*. The Spanish Commander peremptorily demanded of M. Biainville an unconditional surrender, and declared that, in case of a refusal, he should treat him " *as an incendiary ;*" that he would give no quarter, and that the prisoners taken at Pensacola should experience the same fate. To this angry rodomontade an answer was returned, and it was such as became a brave man. The Flotilla then invested and bombarded the Island during thirteen successive days, sometimes attempting to land troops, and at others keeping up a regular and constant

---

* This island is situated near the mouth of the Mobile River, in about N. Lat. 30 degrees, 10 minutes. At the time of which we speak, it was eighteen miles long.

fire on the Garrison, and on a small Vessel of war in the harbor. But the unexpected appearance of a French squadron on the coast induced the Spaniards to make a precipitate retreat.

This squadron arrived at Isle Dauphin on the first of September, laden with goods and provisions, troops and settlers. These supplies revived the hopes of the French, and they again resolved to attempt the reduction of Pensacola, particularly as a Spanish fleet was hourly expected from Vera Cruz. M. Biainville rendezvoused on the Perdido a considerable body of French and Indians. He immediately put himself at their head, and marched and laid siege to the principal Fort, while the fleet entered the harbor, where it met with a warm reception from a small battery. But the Spanish Ordnance was speedily silenced, and the pallisades, with which the town was enclosed, levelled with the ground. The French then entered without opposition. The lives of the inhabitants were spared, but their dwellings were given up to the pillage of the Indian auxiliaries. The number killed was not considerable on either side. The French obtained eighteen hundred prisoners. From these were selected three hundred and sixty, who were transported to the Havanna, accompanied with a request, that the Spaniards would return the French prisoners at that place. This was the more readily granted, as the staff and principal officers were retained as hostages at Isle Dauphin.

In this, as in the former case, several Spanish Vessels entered the harbor of Pensacola soon after its reduction, and were captured by the French; by which means they obtained some prisoners, and no small quantity of provisions and stores.

As they were apprised, that a strong fleet was fitting out at Vera Cruz, which was probably destined for Florida, they destroyed the fortifications, and reduced the town to ashes; and then repaired to the Mobile, leaving behind an Officer, and a few men, to watch the motions of the enemy. Things remained in this state till 1722, when the truce put the Spaniards again in possession of Pensacola. From this period the Perdido was considered as the boundary line between the two Colonies; the Spanish laws operated on one side, and those of the French on the other.

The Mississippi Company, even in the midst of the troubles already stated, aimed to form new barrier settlements, partly to maintain the territorial claims of France, and partly to arrest the progress of the Spaniards. For this purpose, immediately after the reduction of Pensacola in 1719, a considerable detachment was ordered to the bay of St. Joseph, where a Fort was erected. This was intended, in conjunction with the other establishments on the coast, to exclude the Spaniards wholly from this part of Florida. The troops, however, suffered great hardships from the want of provisions, and desertions were finally so prevalent, that the French abandoned the position.

Bernard de la Harp*, the same year, with a body of troops, ascended Red River to the villages of the Caddoques in N. Lat. 33 deg. 55 min. where he built a Fort, called *St. Louis de Carlorette*, on the right bank of that river. He wrote to the Spanish Commandant at the Assinais, informing him, that he was directed by his Government to assume a station on Red River, and charged to cultivate a good understanding with the subjects of Spain. He at the same time forwarded to him a letter

* The author has had access to the manuscript journal of this Gentleman, which has been transmitted to this time. It in a great measure comprehends the history of Louisiana from its first discovery to 1722. As his authority is of weight, the author is bound to acknowledge, that he is indebted to him for many important facts recorded in the first part of this chapter, as also in that respecting the extent and boundaries of Louisiana.

from M. Biainville. M. de la Harp likewise wrote to the superior of the missions in Texas, and expressed a desire to open a trade with the Spaniards, assured him of his friendship, and professed to have much at heart the conversion of the Infidels. He proposed to him to receive the merchandize, and to be the Agent in this traffic.

The Spanish Commandant returned for answer, that while he was disposed to maintain peace with the French, it was his duty to inform him, that the post he occupied was within the territory of his master, and that if he did not abandon it, he should be obliged to attack him.

The answer of the Priest exhibited a more conciliatory aspect. He wished for a mutual correspondence, and for an opportunity of serving M. de la Harp; but as it did not become a Clergyman to be concerned in mercantile enterprises, their intercourse ought to be kept a secret, more particularly as his commandant was unfriendly to him. Yet he at the same time observed that, as his commandant had treated the Indians improperly, and disobeyed the orders of the Viceroy, such charges had been forwarded against him as would probably cause his removal from office.

The contents of this letter afforded M. de la Harp some idea of the character of his adversary, which the better enabled him to reply to his threat and pretensions.

He therefore told him, that his dispositions to maintain peace did not agree with his proceedings; that Biainville was well informed of the limits of his Government; that the post he then occupied was not within the dominions of Spain; that the Spaniards well knew the province, which they called Texas, to be part of Louisiana; that M. de la Salle took possession of it in 1685, and that this possession had been renewed at various times since that period; that the Spanish adventurer, *Don Antonio du Miroir*, who discovered the northern provinces in 1683, never penetrated east of New Mexico, or the Rio Bravo;

that the French were the first to make alliances with the Indian nations; that the rivers flowing into the Mississippi, consequently the lands between them, belonged to France; and that if he would do him the pleasure of a visit, he would find, that he occupied a post, which he knew how to defend.

Here ended the contest about this post, which was maintained by the French till Louisiana fell into the hands of Spain, and during this time the Spaniards never gave them any trouble. They formed a small settlement, and built a mill at this place. They cultivated wheat, corn, and tobacco, and carried on a trade with the Indians. They discovered a saline in this quarter, which yielded plenty of salt; and M. Dutisne of Kaskaskia, about the same time discovered another " of mineral rock salt" near the Kansas river.

M. de la Harp pursued his discoveries to the Arkansas. On that river he visited an Indian village of three miles in extent, containing upwards of four thousand persons. It was situated about one hundred and twenty miles south west of the Osages. The excursions of the Spaniards were at that time limited to the sources of Red River and the Arkansas in the Mexican mountains, " where they found plenty of rock salt," and where " they worked some silver mines."

At this period an attempt was likewise made to form a settlement in the bay of St. Bernard. The conduct of the expedition was confided to M. Beranger, who sailed three hundred and ninety miles to the westward of the Mississippi, and landed in N. Lat. 27 degrees, 45 minutes. Here he built a small Fort, and leaving five of his men to defend it, returned with the remainder to the Mobile for a reinforcement. During his absence the Indians took one of his men, and killed the other four. The Company always had it in contemplation to form a strong settlement in this quarter, and considerable blame was attached to the Colonial Officers for their negligence. But the Indians were opposed to the admission of the whites among them; and the fate of M. de la Salle and Colony, cooled the ardor of subsequent adventurers.

The population had become so numerous in 1720, that the French authorities were constrained to devise some efficacious measures to relieve the wants of the Colony. They therefore resolved to strengthen their barrier posts, and to disperse the people on plantations. A large number went to Natchitoches, and on their arrival attacked the Spaniards at the Adaize, deprived them of their property, and drove them from that place. Another party repaired to their plantations about Natchez, and the St. Catharine's; others fixed themselves in the Delta, particularly at New-Orleans, which was founded at this time, and soon after became the seat of Government. The French likewise erected Fort Chartres in the neighbourhood of Kaskaskia, and took every other precaution in their power to guard themselves against their enemies, and to raise a sufficient quantity of provisions for the consumption of the Colony.

The French were at last apparently convinced of their destructive policy, and now for the first time attempted an innovation. If this had not been carried to extremes, the benefits resulting from it would have been more perceptible and permanent. Sensible of the sterility of the lands about the Old Baloxi, or Perdido, the settlers were removed in the first instance from that place to Isle Dauphin and Mobile, and subsequently to New Baloxi, situated about forty miles to the westward of that river. This proved extremely injurious to them, and expensive to the Government; especially as such frequent removals deprived them of the opportunity of raising their crops, and as the last position was not less sickly and barren than those they had previously occupied. This fatal step was soon discovered, but not easily retraced, and the several branches of the Government were eager to throw the blame on each other. Hence those animosities and suspensions from office already noticed. The dispersion of the people on plantations was likewise productive of a serious evil, though of a temporary nature. They found it difficult to subsist during the growth of their first crops; and hence those calamities and distresses, particularly in 1721, to which the attention of the reader has already been drawn. These and other embarrassments extorted from the company vast sums of money; so that the expenditure for the year 1722 only, amounted to no less than 1,163,256 livres.

The dispersion of the settlers rendered a new system of jurisprudence indispensible. Before this period all suits were decided at the seat of Government. Lower Louisiana was now divided into Districts, to each of which was assigned a Commandant and a Judge, though in most instances both offices were united in the same person. The jurisdiction of the District Judge extended to all civil and criminal suits, except capital offences; and appeals lay in every instance to the provincial council. The same system, with some slight modifications, was maintained till the country fell into the hands of the United States.

Notwithstanding the French had been more than once frustrated in their attempts to form a settlement on the Bay of St. Bernard, yet the Company determined to make another effort. For this purpose M. de la Harp, in 1721, embarked at New Orleans under a royal order, with a detachment of troops, engineers, and draftsmen, and was directed to take a more accurate view of the Country than his predecessors had done. He found eleven and an half feet of water on the bar, and at the entrance of the bay, four large rivers falling into it, probably the Trinity, Brassos, Guadaloupe, and Colorado. He also found the soil along the coast extremely fertile, the Country beautiful and variegated with woods, prairies and streams of pure water. On the coast of this bay he planted the arms of France, and took formal possession of the territory in the name of his Sovereign. The right of France to it was said in his instructions to be derived from the actual possession of M. de la Salle in 1685, as well as from subsequent discoveries; and he was particularly directed, that if the Spaniards opposed his establishment, to defend himself to the last extremity. The Spaniards were unpopular in this quarter, and therefore had not visited it over land, and only once by sea. But the Indians still retained their former enmity to the French; they still remembered the slaughter made among them by M. de la Salle, and the more recent trespass of M. Beranger. Such indeed were their threats and hostile preparations, that M. de la Harp did not deem it prudent to attempt an establishment; he therefore seized several of them, put them on board his Vessel, and then returned to New Orleans. The object he had in view by this seizure was to excite in the minds of the Indians a favorable opinion of the French by means of the captives, whom he intended to return to their nation, after inspiring them with confidence, treating them with kindness, and loading them with presents; but, thinking themselves doomed to destruction, they found means of escaping in the night, and some of them, on their way home, perished with hunger in the wilderness. Hence this stratagem, instead of promoting the interest of the French, destroyed all hopes of a friendly intercourse with the Indians about the bay of St. Bernard.

Neither the French nor Spanish Colonists were inclined to carry on a systematic war; but as they were competitors in the Indian trade, and the rights of territory frequently came in question, they maintained a kind of predatory warfare for several years. The perfidy practised on M. de St. Dennis kept alive the resentment of the French: and the reduction of Pensacola, and the unfriendly disposition manifested by some of the Indian tribes in Louisiana, wounded the pride of the Spaniards. Hitherto the French had been remarkably successful in their attempts to maintain peace with the Indians in their neighbourhood. The Chickasaws alone gave them trouble; the English often instigated them to hostilities. The depredations made by the French and Spaniards on each other, even while their mother Countries were at peace, may be traced in the first instance to mutual jealousies, and in the second to the mutual infliction of real or imaginary injuries.

The Spaniards exulted in the treacherous expulsion of the French from the Assinais; and as they were so successful in forming an establishment at that place, they resolved to repeat the experiment in a distant quarter, particularly as their rivals began to appear formidable on Red River. They well knew the importance of the Missouri, and were anxious to secure a strong position on its banks. They readily perceived, that such a measure, if prosecuted with success, would effectually hold in check the Illinois French, confine their territorial claims to the borders of the Mississippi, and turn the current of the Indian trade. Their first object was to attack and destroy the nation of Missouris,* situated on the Missouri, at no great distance from the Kansas river, within whose jurisdiction they meditated a settlement. These Indians were the firm friends of the French, and this rendered their destruction the more necessary. At this time they were at war with the Pawnes, and the Spaniards designed to engage these as auxiliaries in the enterprise. A considerable Colony, therefore, started from Santa Fè in 1720, and marched in pursuit of the Pawne Villages; but they lost their way, and unluckily arrived among the Missouris, whose ruin they meditated. Ignorant of their mistake, (the Missouris speaking the Pawne language) they communicated their sentiments without reserve, and re-

* This nation is now nearly extinct.

quested their co-operation. The Indians manifested no surprise at this unexpected visit, and only requested time to assemble their warriors. At the end of forty eight hours about two thousand of them appeared in arms. They attacked the Spaniards in the night, while reposing themselves in fatal security, and killed all of them, except the Priest who escaped the slaughter by means of his horse. Various writers assert, that these colonists aimed to find the Osage villages; but the records of Santa Fé authorize the statement we have given.

This boldness of the Spaniards in penetrating into a Country with which they had no previous acquaintance, at least six hundred miles from their own, apprised the French of their danger, and warned them to provide against a repetition of encroachment. M. de Burgmont, therefore, was despatched with a considerable force, who took possession of an Island in the Missouri, some distance above the Osage river, on which he built Fort Orleans.

On his arrival at that place, he found the various nations about him engaged in a sanguinary war, which diminished the trade, and rendered all intercourse extremely hazardous. Hence it became an object of importance to bring about a general peace. This was attempted with the desired success in 1724. Soon after this event, however, Fort Orleans was attacked and totally destroyed, when all the French were massacred, but it was never known by whom this bloody work was performed. About this period the French began to experience troubles of a serious nature from the Indians, which were not entirely surmounted till after a lapse of sixteen years.

Of all the Indians known to the French, the Natchez were the most serviceable, and at the same time the most terrible to them. Ibberville visited them soon after his arrival in the country. Settlers at various times planted themselves among them, particularly a large body of them, when the Government dispersed them on plantations. Some indeed, penetrated to the Yazous, where they built a Fort, which was destroyed in 1722 by the Chickasaws. The French adventurers were favourably received by the Natchez, who supplied them with provisions, assisted them in their tillage, and in building their houses: In fine, their friendly exertions saved the strangers from famine and death.

It happened in this as in most other connexions of the kind, that the Whites encroached on the rights of the Indians, and excited their jealousy. The Natchez possessed the strongest disposition to oblige, and would have continued eminently useful to the French, if the commandant of Fort Rosalie had not treated them with indignity and injustice. The first dispute between them occurred in 1723. An old Natchez warrior had obtained credit of a soldier, and agreed to deliver some corn in payment. About the time the debt became due, the latter demanded his pay; he was answered, that the corn was too green to be gathered, but that it should be delivered as soon as possible. Not satisfied with this excuse, the soldier threatened to beat the old man, which so much incensed him, that he retired from the Fort, and challenged his opponent to single combat. This induced the soldier to cry murder! when the old man departed for his village. The Guard was pressed to fire, and one of them was so imprudent as to do it, when the old man received a mortal wound. No punishment was inflicted on the perpetrators of this deed; they received a slight reprimand only from the commandant, who, in other respects, had rendered himself extremely obnoxious to the Natchez.

As revenge is the predominant passion of the Indians, no wonder the murder of a warrior prompted the Natchez to take up arms. They attacked the French in all quarters, and killed many of them. At last the Stung Serpent, an influential chief, was prevailed on to interpose his authority, and the slaughter ceased. This generous interposition probably prevented the utter extermination of the French in this quarter. A treaty of peace was the result; mutual confidence was restored ; and all former enmities appeared to be buried in oblivion.

This peace had no other effect than to lull the Natchez in security, and to precipitate the French into the blackest treachery. It was duly ratified by M. Biainville ; yet he took advantage of it to inflict a sudden and dreadful blow on these innocent people ! He found means to elude their cautious vigilance, and soon after the peace, arrived at Fort Rosalie with seven hundred men, when he attacked the defenceless natives, slaughtered them in their huts, and demanded the head of one, whom he styled a mutinous Chief, as the price of peace, with which they were obliged to comply. This war, or rather wanton slaughter lasted four days.

From this moment the Natchez despaired of ever living in peace with the French, who, although loaded with benefits, daily usurped their lands, and inflicted personal injuries, and whose insolence and rapaciousness increased with their numbers. They reflected on the ingratitude of the French, who studiously rewarded their kindness with injustice ; they even anticipated the assumption of a still more dreadful power over them, calculated at no remote period to destroy their existence as a nation. Hence they perceived no medium between their own ruin, and the total annihilation of their enemies. This painful alternative rendered them thoughtful, distrustful, and pensive, and extremely timid in devising the means of future security.

Shortly after the slaughter just mentioned, a French Officer accidentally met the Stung Serpent, who appeared disposed to avoid him. " Why do you wish to shun me ? " we were once friends ; are we no longer so ?" said the Officer. The indignant Chief replied in a long speech,

HISTORICAL SKETCHES OF LOUISIANA. 49

and among other things observed ; " Why did the French
" come into our country ? we did not go to seek them.
" They asked us for land, and we told them to take it
" were they pleased ; there was enough for them and for
" us; the same Sun ought to enlighten us both, and we
" ought to walk together as friends in the same path;
" we promised to give them food, assist them to build,
" and to labour in the fields. We have done so." The
Natchez were well convinced, that they could not openly
contend with the French. This made them the more patient of injuries, and they resolved to bear them as long
as they were tolerable.

Affairs remained in this situation till 1729, when a circumstance occurred, which justified the highest resentment of the Natchez, but which ultimately plunged them
into ruin.

M. de Chopart, the Commandant of Fort Rosalie, had
been guilty of such repeated acts of injustice, as to render an investigation of his conduct indispensable ; and for
this purpose he was ordered to New Orleans. This event
excited much joy among the Indians, but it was of short
duration. That Officer appeared before M. Perier, who
at that time administered the Government, and found
means to justify his proceedings in such a manner as to
be re-instated in his command. On his return to his
post he conceived himself at liberty to indulge his
malice against the Indians; partly on account of the trouble they had given him, but much more on account of the
satisfaction manifested by them at the prospects of his
disgrace. As some gratification to his spite, he suddenly
resolved to build a town on the site of the village of the
White Apple,* " which covered a square of about three

* This village was situated about twelve miles below the present city
of Natchez, and nearly three miles to the eastward of the Mississippi ;
on the site of which is the seat of the late Col. Anthony Hutchings.
Not a vestige of Indian industry now remains, except a few mounts.

miles in extent." Accordingly he sent for the Sun, or, Chief, of that village, and directed him to clear the huts, and to plant themselves in some other place. The Chief replied, perhaps rather hastily, " that their ancestors had " lived there for many ages, and that it was good for " their descendants to occupy the same ground." This noble and dignified language served only to exasperate the haughty Commandant, and to extort from him the declaration, " that unless the village was abandoned in a few " days, the inhabitants of it should repent of their obsti- " nacy." The Chief then retired to consult the old men, and to hold a council. As a bloody conflict was inevitable, the Indians resorted to such expedients as were calculated to gain time. They wished to create an indissoluble union among themselves, and to devise means adequate to the end: one of these was the assistance of their allies, which they deemed of infinite importance. They therefore represented to M. de Chopart, " that their " corn had just come out of the ground, that their hens " were laying their eggs, and that to abandon their village " at that time would prove as injurious to the French as to " themselves." M. de Chopart treated these reasons with disdain, and menaced immediate destruction, unless his desires were gratified. The Indians in general are fruitful of expedients; and the Natchez, who were well acquainted with the avaricious disposition of their adversary, at last resorted to one, which for a while suspended his wrath. They obtained permission to remain in their own houses till after harvest, on condition, that each hut should pay him a fowl and a basket of corn.

During this short interval the Natchez frequently and privately assembled in council, and a plan of operations was carefully concerted. They unanimously resolved to make one great effort to preserve their independence, and to defend the tombs of their fathers. They proceeded with caution, and omitted nothing to ensure success.

They invited the Chickasaws to share in the arduous enterprize; but by a strange fatality, occasioned by the treachery of one of their own women, the latter were deceived as to the time of the intended blow, and therefore did not arrive in season to participate in the struggle. The massacre of all the French was what they had in view, and it was concluded to commence the work at the time of presenting the tribute of corn and fowls. Notwithstanding all their precaution, and the inducement each one had to observe inviolable secrecy, yet one of their chief women suspected the plot; and either offended at the seclusion of her sex, at least of one of her rank, from a knowledge of it, or influenced by private attachment, communicated her suspicions to some soldiers and others. Even just before the fatal catastrophe, M. de Chopart was cautioned to be on his guard; but his evil genius led him to disregard the admonitions given him, to punish those who prognosticated danger, and to repose himself in criminal security.

At length the fatal period arrived, when the vengeance of the injured and vindictive Savages was to burst on the devoted heads of the French. Near the close of the last day of November 1729, the grand Sun, with some warriors, repaired to the Fort with the tribute of corn and fowls agreed on. They seized the gate and other passages, and the Soldiers were instantly deprived of the means of defence. Such was their number, and so well distributed, that opposition was vain. Other parties repaired to their appointed rendezvous, and the houses of the French about the country were filled with them. The massacre was general among the men; the slaves, and some of the women and children were spared. The chiefs and warriors, disdaining to stain their hands with the blood of M. de Chopart, he fell by one of the meanest of the Indians. This settlement contained about seven hundred French, and very few of them escaped to carry the dreadful tidings to the Capital. The Forts and Settlements at the Yazous and Washita shared the same fate. Thus these extensive possessions of the French, which were gradually progressing to maturity, and the most wealthy of any in the Colony, presented a melancholy picture. They were first plundered, and then exposed to the flames.

The news of this disaster created much confusion in the Capital, and all seemed to imagine, that the merciless Savages were at their doors. M. Perier was very active in contriving measures to punish his enemies. The Chickasaws were offended with the Natchez Indians for commencing the attack without them, and therefore readily accepted the invitation of the French. In February 1730, about fifteen hundred of them arrived in the neighbourhood of the Natchez, where they were joined the next month by a detachment of troops from New Orleans, under the command of M. de Loubois.

The Natchez Indians, anticipating the storm, endeavoured to provide against it. They strongly fortified themselves in the Fort; but on the appearance of the French, supported by their numerous auxiliaries, and some pieces of heavy ordnance, they were induced to sue for peace. They offered to release the prisoners in their custody, on condition that friendship and amity should be restored, and permission given them to live on their own ground, and their future repose secured. The French were not disposed to grant these favors, nor did they return an explicit answer. Deception was practised on both sides, and for once the French were completely duped. The Natchez wished for an opportunity of leaving their country; the French aimed at the possession of the prisoners, after which they intended to indulge themselves in the indiscriminate slaughter of their enemies. M. de Loubois finally proposed to suspend the attack, provided the Natchez would agree to release the prisoners the next day. This proposition was accepted.

The Natchez were highly pleased with this arrangement, as it seemed to afford them the means of escape. During the following night they silently deserted the Fort, loaded with their plunder and baggage, and crossed the Mississippi! This dextrous manœuvre filled the French with astonishment; but they were in no condition to pursue the fugitives. Their first care was to build a terrace Fort, to supply it with cannon and ammunition, and one hundred and twenty effective men. The auxiliaries were then dismissed, and the remainder of the French returned to New Orleans.

In the mean time the Natchez retired to the mouth of Silver Creek,* about one hundred and eighty miles up Red River, where they erected a fortification for their defence. The arrival of one hundred and fifty soldiers from France, enabled M. Perier to march at the head of a respectable force in pursuit of them; he was soon before them, opened a battery of mortars on their Fort, and put them into great confusion. They made several desperate sallies, and were repulsed with great slaughter. They endeavoured to escape, but this was impracticable. In vain they attempted to negociate; they struggled in vain to avoid the leaden messengers of death, and at last surrendered at discretion. The women and children were immediately reduced to slavery, and dispersed among the plantations. The remains of this wretched people were eventually sent in the same condition to St. Domingo. On the first arrival of the French among them, their villages contained about twelve hundred souls.

Thus the Natchez Indians, once so useful to the French, became almost extinct. The fugitives, who es-

---

* At no great distance below Natchitoches. No creek in that quarter is known by that name at the present day.

caped the carnage and the chains of bondage, united themselves to the Chickasaws and Creeks, and their ancient language is still preserved among them.

Of all the Indians in this quarter known to the Whites, the Natchez were the most polished and civilized. They had an established religion amongst them, in many particulars rational and consistent, as likewise regular orders of Priesthood. They had a temple dedicated to the Great Spirit, in which they preserved the eternal fire. If their religion was occasionally stained with human sacrifices, particularly on the death of their Suns, or Chiefs, we ought to be the less surprised, as many other nations on the globe admit of the same practice. To them were denied the advantages of literature, and above all, the blessings of our revealed religion. They were guided alone by the dictates of nature; and hence their aberrations were less criminal. Perhaps their religious rites and ceremonies were originally derived from a pure source; for who will pretend to say that their ancestors six or eight centuries ago were unacquainted with the Scriptures? No doubt these tokens of religion were greatly obscured and perverted by tradition; but this is rather the misfortune than the crime of the Indians. This remark is applicable to all the aborigines of America.

The civil polity of the Natchez partook of the refinements of a people, apparently in some degree learned and scientific; it exhibited penetration and wisdom, and was calculated to render them happy. They had Kings, or Chiefs, whom they denominated Suns, invested with absolute power, as likewise a kind of subordinate nobility; and the usual distinctions created by rank were well understood and preserved among them. They were just, generous, and humane, and never failed to extend relief to the objects of distress and misery. They were well acquainted with the properties of medicinal plants; and the cures they performed, particularly among the French, appear almost incredible. What is much more to their praise, they never deemed it glorious to destroy the human species, and for this reason seldom waged any other than defensive war.

History is seldom seen to smile; and perhaps no one presents a more frightful picture than that of the conquests in the new world. The work of death carried on by ancient conquerors, was in some instances more magnificent, but in none so prolific of human blood. Besides, the ancient nations had nearly the same knowledge of the art of war, at least they made use of the same weapons; and hence their contests were in some measure equal. But the Europeans on this continent, furnished with superior weapons of destruction, often vanquished numerous armies of the natives, with little or no loss on their side; many of whom, terrified at their mode of warfare, suffered themselves to be enslaved, and even empaled, at discretion. The Spanish history, in particular, for more than two centuries, affords nothing but a series of complicated crimes, the black catalogue of which will continue to excite in every breast, the mingled emotions of pity and indignation. They made war on defenceless nations without provocation, spilt oceans of blood, and involved millions of their fellow creatures in misery. They trampled on all those laws deemed sacred by the civilized world, and their misdeeds find no other excuse than what is derived from the gratification of their avarice.

The ways of Providence are inscrutable. Good appears frequently, to our limited conceptions, to be the result of evil. Perhaps the United States owe their existence as a nation, to the religious persecutions of the Mother Country. The victorious progress of the Romans diffused the arts and sciences among the States of Europe, and to this cause may be attributed, in a great measure, their present perfection. Still more are they indebted to the conquests in the new world for the wide extension of their commerce, and even for the intercourse, which they have established with the other great continents. The desolations occasioned by the Spaniards have, more than any other, produced a wonderful change in the political and moral character of nations; if they have multiplied their wants, they have at the same time elicited the means of gratification. Yet we must ever deplore the primary causes of these events, and regret the hard conditions imposed on the original proprietors of the soil in this quarter of the globe.

The Spaniards wholly abjured the pacific character of Christians, and followed the example of those nations whom they pronounced barbarous. They not only enslaved the prisoners taken in battle, but likewise those peaceable and effeminate people, who submitted themselves at discretion. They compelled them to labour in the mines of Hispaniola and Cuba, where vast numbers perished.

The first contained more than a million of inhabitants, and at the end of fifteen years from the first discovery of that place, they were reduced to less than sixty thousand! On the second upwards of half a million perished. A similar destruction took place on the continent.

Those who ought first to know the evils of the State, are generally the last to be made acquainted with them. Thus it happened in the reductions of the Indians to slavery. Their fate was unknown to the Spanish Monarch for many years. The eloquent Father de las Casas, who witnessed their miseries, was the first to carry their complaints to the throne; and in him the unhappy Indians found an able advocate and friend. On this occasion the avaritious colonists became his inveterate opposers, and devised a thousand expedients to defeat his measures. Even the pious ministers of the Christian Church, who were sent out to propagate the glad tidings of salvation among the heathen; those heralds of meekness, mercy,

and peace, condescended to advocate the bondage of the
Indians; for, in one of their synodical assemblies held a-
bout this period, they pronounced the Indians incapable of
receiving the Eucharist, because they manifested a defect
of understanding, and accordingly decreed their exclu-
sion from that privilege. The Roman Pontiff was of a
different opinion; he not only abrogated the decree, but
likewise declared, that the Indians were entitled to the
rights of human nature; and therefore authorized their
admission into holy orders, and to the participation of the
sacraments. The Spanish monarch was disposed to accede to these sentiments; but when it was represented to
him, that the Europeans were unable to labor in the
warm climates of the precious metals, and that, unless
the Indians were employed, the acquisition of silver and
gold must cease, he began to doubt, to deliberate and to
waver. The danger did not escape the penetration of de
las Casas; and, apprehensive of the consequences, he
seized the critical moment, and proposed the slavery of
the Africans as a substitute for that of the Indians. Hence
this good man has been stigmatised as the first advocate
of negro slavery. But the truth is, that of the two evils
he wished to adopt the least; for he concluded, that the
distance of Africa from America, and the difficulty and
expense of procuring slaves in that part of the globe,
would serve to render the system less pernicious. If he
was mistaken in his opinion, the motive by which he
was actuated, must ever be deemed pure. The king of
Spain remained no longer undecided. He sanctioned negro slavery in 1517, and at the same time decreed, that
the Indians should be liberated from their imperious masters and overseers; no longer be obliged to till the lands,
or to labor in the mines, except at certain fixed periods in
rotation, and at fixed wages. This regulation still exists
in the Spanish provinces; so that, while the Indians are

exempted from the badges of servitude, they cannot be pronounced absolutely free.

This kind of middle character attached itself to those of the conquered provinces only. The Spaniards for a long time carried havoc and desolation among those nations, who were disposed to maintain their liberty, and many of them remain unconquered to this day. The noble stand made by the Araucanians, a people of Chili, casts a shade over the deeds of valor displayed by the Greeks and Romans in the brightest periods of their history. These proud sons of liberty, by no means numerous, with the imperfect weapons in use among them, vanquished, and even annihilated, several veteran armies, who had gathered a harvest of renown in the wars of Europe under their military monarch. They even had the courage to besiege fortified cities, and the address to make themselves masters of them, after which they reduced them to ashes. They soon obtained the European art of war, (though not the weapons) as practised in those days, and their hopes of success never deserted them amid their greatest dangers. To mitigate the terrible effects of the Spanish musketry and cannon, they precipitated themselves into the thickest ranks of their enemies, and contended hand to hand. The war commenced in 1550, and continued without intermission for ninety years, when a short peace only ensued, the precursor to a still more bloody conflict; and be it recorded to their immortal honor, that they have maintained their independence to this day.

The Spaniards found their country divided into provinces, and these again into counties or districts. Their system of government, both general and local, resembled in theory, some of those deemed the most perfect in Europe, and indeed it was not much unlike that of the United States in most of its essential features. They cultivated eloquence, poetry, and music. They had some knowledge of the arts and sciences, particularly of astronomy; for they divided the year (of three hundred and sixty five days) into seasons, months, days, and hours. The names of their several months indicated some remarkable quality or thing common to each period, like those of the ancient Egyptians and Persians, and of the modern French. Their language was copious and flexible, and their eloquence of no ordinary kind. Are these people the proper objects of slavery? Say rather, they are entitled to the respect of the present age, and to the homage of posterity.

Men are imitative creatures, and examples are contagious. This is particularly verified in the conduct of the French. In imitation of the first conquerors of America, they reduced the Natchez to slavery, because they dared to contend for their rights. Near the close of their government in Louisiana, the people on Red River purchased several Indian prisoners brought from the bay of St. Bernard; but their successors, the Spaniards, liberated them. At a subsequent period the Spaniards themselves connived at the slavery of several Indians of both sexes in another quarter of the province. Their parents were free; and yet the highest court of the United States in that country has lately sanctioned their cruel fate by a solemn decision. The Spanish authorities had no such legal power. Where shall we look for that exercised by their successors?

It is of no use to enter into a disquisition on the right of conquests, or to ascertain the obligations due from the conquerors to the countries and inhabitants subdued by them. All these were prostrated by the Spaniards; in a much less degree by the French; and even our pious English ancestors stand charged with violating their own principles on these points.

It is evident from what we have seen, that the Mississippi Company acquired Louisiana at a moment unfavourable to its interests. The expectation of a profitable revenue, and an anxiety to rival in power the English and Spaniards of the new world, induced it to be liberal in the advances of money. But as Mr. Law was a foreigner, he was of course unpopular. He had many powerful enemies, about the French court, who finally completed his ruin, and destroyed the credit of the Company; so that in 1731, the charter was resigned to the crown.

The Mississippi scheme was no less bold in its conception, than disasterous in its consequences. It seized within its grasp the bank, the mint, all the trading companies, and all the revenues of the kingdom. The object was to employ this vast capital in opening the rich mines of Louisiana, and in cultivating its fertile soil; in carrying on the whole commerce of the nation, and in managing the royal revenues. The company created three hundred thousand shares, at five hundred livres each; fifty thousand shares at five hundred and fifty livres each; three hundred thousand shares at five thousand livres each; all of which were sold in market, and before the completion of the sale, they rose to an enormous height. The amount of the stock thus created, without taking the rise into calculation, amounted to sixteen hundred seventy seven millions, five hundred thousand livres, or three hundred and ten million, six hundred forty eight thousand, one hundred forty eight dollars! Such indeed was the phrensy of speculation, that the whole nation, clergy and laity, peers and plebeians, princes and statesmen, mechanics, and even ladies, employed their wealth in purchasing these shares. The scheme was calculated to enrich the nation as well as the holders of the scrip; but a perfidious breach of royal faith destroyed the credit of the paper, and multitudes were involved in ruin, though the public treasury gained by it the annual sum of twenty three millions of livres. The enemies of the financier, (and these were the dignified clergy, who were ambitious of getting him superceded in office by one of their own order) prevailed on the Regent to reduce by an arret the value of the paper, so as to bring it on a level with the coin, and other commodities of the kingdom. This reduction destroyed all public confidence; it proved fatal to the minister, and to the splendid paper fabric, which vanished like a dream, and left the multitude to bewail their credulity, and to execrate the authors of their ruin.

Whoever takes a correct view of the transactions of the Mississippi Company, must be convinced that it was of infinite utility to Louisiana, perhaps the preservation of it; particularly as it possessed energy and resources. The great misfortune was, that its exertions were not sufficiently seconded by the colonial authorities. We have already witnessed the extreme liberality of the company, and this liberality enabled the French to survive the pressure of war, and the still more dreadful scourge of famine. The dissolution of it replenished the public treasury, and furnished the crown with the means to be generous. Hence, on the conclusion of the Natchez r, the colony began to flourish, though it had lost much of its credit. The security of the people was less precarious, and the timely and liberal aids of the mother country, contributed to their prosperity. From this period may be dated the gradual progress of the colony to a more eligible condition, though it was occasionally interrupted by the Indians and Spaniards.

The earliest settlements, as has been stated, were formed on the Perdido, and about the Mobile; but after the erection of New Orleans, and the dispersion of the people on plantations, they considerably declined. At those places, however, regular garrisons were maintained; and another was eventually established on the Tombigbee, designed to keep in check the Chickasaws, and to interrupt the communication between them and the English. About these posts a number of settlers remained; some to till the lands, but most of them to carry on the Indian and lumber trade. Other posts were established on some of the rivers, which were intended as annoyances to the English and Spaniards, and to monopolize the internal commerce. A trade was likewise opened with the Islands, and the advantages it afforded, gave a spur to agriculture, which enabled the planters, for the first time, to send to foreign markets the valuable products of their own industry. The war with the Chitimaches, and the conspiracy of the negroes to murder all the whites, inflicted no material injury on the colony. These evils were temporary, and soon repaired by the prompt measures and activity of the French.

The Chickasaws, from their attachment to the English, were never disposed to have much intercourse with the French; and as they were powerful within themselves, and powerfully supported, they stood in no great fear of their neighbors. The French anxiously waited for an opportunity of measuring their strength with them, and in this they were influenced by two motives; they wished in the first place, to drive the English from among them, and secure the trade to themselves; in the second place, they deemed it of importance to destroy their influence among the other tribes, and by this means render their frontiers, and trading parties, less exposed to depredation. A plausible pretext for a quarrel occurred in 1736, and the French seized it with avidity. Part of the Natchez Indians, who escaped the general slaughter, claimed the protection of the Chickasaws, and were incorporated into their nation. M. Biainville demanded them; and as this demand was treated with contempt, he resolved to carry the war into the Chickasaw country. He therefore marched a considerable army up the Mobile, attacked their fortification without success, and was obliged to make a digraceful retreat. The troops from the Illinois, who attacked them on the opposite quarter, where also obliged to seek safety in flight. These, when they marched up to the attack, had wool-sacks suspended from their necks in front of their bodies, as a security against the shot of the Indians. This kind of armor was first discovered by the English traders, who directed the Chickasaws to aim their shot at the heads and legs of the French.

These repulses served only to stimulate M. Biainville to another exertion, particularly as the people began to doubt his talents and skill as a general. He wrote to France for succors, and obtained them. In 1739, he ascended the Mississippi, with much the largest army, including the Indian auxiliaries, ever witnessed in Louisiana, and landed at the mouth of Margot river, where he built fort Assumption. Here he incurred as much disgrace by a peace he made in 1740, as he had experienced by his defeat four years before. Had he attacked the Chickasaws on his arrival, he might have obtained an easy victory. But, instead of pursuing prompt and vigorous measures, he kept his army encamped in a state of inactivity, till his provisions were mostly expended, till his auxiliaries were uneasy, and ready to abandon him; and he suffered the important moment to escape, when the terror, occasioned by the extent of his preparations, was little short of a defeat. In this situation he was compelled to offer peace to the Chickasaws; and happily for him, unacquainted with his weakness, they negociated with him.

Some years previously to these events, the European French began to entertain a more favorable opinion of Louisiana. They perceived, that the soil was prolific, and capable of yielding, with moderate industry, not only the necessaries, but also the luxuries of life. The peltry trade too, in their estimation, was nearly of equal importance; and a commercial intercourse between the colony and Europe, particularly the Islands, seemed to promise an opulent harvest. Full of these expectations, they embarked considerable wealth in the trade of Louisiana; and although they met with disappointment, (owing to the indolence of the settlers, and the great reduction of their number) the colony derived no small benefit from their enterprise. The pursuit of internal commerce was by no means profitable to those who engaged in it; nor were the products of agriculture sufficiently numerous and valuable to reward the hopes of the European capitalists. Yet the first served to conciliate the minds of the Indians, and to excite a violent competition between the French, Spaniards, and English; not more indeed from motives of wealth, than a mutual disposition to inflict mutual injuries. A regular intercourse with the Islands was of primary importance to the poor planters, as they obtained from them, in exchange for the scanty avails of their labor, many indispensable supplies. The Chickasaws, and sometimes the Chocktaws, were in the interest of the English. Some chiefs of the latter went to England in 1730, and were presented to the king. They laid their regalia at his feet, and acknowledged themselves and nation as subjects of his dominion. Most of the other Indians on the Mississippi, and indeed along its numerous waters, were the friends of the French.

That the early history of most of the American colonies should describe little else than Indian affairs, is, perhaps, not to be wondered at. The resistance of the aboriginals in some instances wholly obstructed colonization, and it proved in nearly all, a source of lasting troubles. Like other nations, jealous of their territorial and other rights, they repelled encroachments, and endeavoured to punish aggressors. Some writers have represented them as treacherous and faithless. This character is inapplicable to much the greatest proportion of them. They are in general extremely scrupulous in regard to the fulfilment of national compacts; though, in their individual capacities, they are less honest, and more inclined to evade their engagements. Their want of faith in most instances, where it has been manifested, may be traced either to the hard conditions imposed on them, or to the advantages taken of their ignorance. Whoever attentively examines into the merits of the numerous quarrels between them and the whites, will be apt to find, that the latter were almost uniformly the aggressors. The French and Spaniards, in particular, never deemed their engagements any longer obligatory than while they contributed to their interests. The least infraction of natural or stipulated rights, excited the jealousy of the Indians; and if justice was denied them, as it almost uniformly was, they knew of no other mode of redress than a resort to war. If their mode of warfare appears cruel and barbarous, let it be remembered, that this mode is universal among them; that it is adapted to their situation; and that it seems, according to their apprehension, to be absolutely necessary. "Strike, but conceal the hand," is no less a maxim among them, than with some of their more civilized contemporaries. This maxim, indeed, as applicable to war, is a dictate of nature and self preservation.

From the year 1740, to the commencement of the war between England and France, in 1754, few events of importance occurred in Louisiana. The colonists were exempted from disastrous wars, which enabled them to extend their settlements, to cultivate their fields, and to prosecute their trade with the islands. They surmounted their poverty, the usual attendant on all infant colonial establishments, and began to export some cotton, as also considerable quantities of indigo, peltry, hides, tallow, pitch, tar, ship timber, and various other raw materials. These exports continued, and gradually increased, till the country was ceded to Spain; though they were never sufficient to procure the necessary supplies in return.

K

One of the first symptoms of an approaching war between France and England, was a dispute about boundaries as early as 1747. The English extended their claims to the river St. Lawrence, while the French on their part contended for all the country to the westward of the Apalachean mountains. It was not believed at that time, that either intended to insist on the extent of its claims; but it will appear in the sequel, that France was extravagant in her pretensions. Perhaps the proximity of settlement, and the reciprocal attempts to corrupt the Indians, and to precipitate them into hostilities with the whites, served to inflame the gathering storm, and to hasten its approach.

After the peace of Aix-la-Chapelle, in 1748, the French ministry more attentively examined the strength and resources of Canada and Louisiana. The position of these colonies, stretching from the mouth of the St. Lawrence to that of the Mississippi, with an almost uninterrupted inland water communication between the extremities of both, seemed to unfold the means of subduing the English power in America. This scheme was the more readily adopted by the French, as they were anxious to rival the Spaniards in the splendor of their conquests, and to share with them the wealth, and other resources, of the new world. A sudden and unexpected blow was deemed impolitic. Exertions were therefore made to postpone hostilities, and to appease the fears and suspicions of the English. They gradually strengthened their posts on the lakes, and along the Mississippi, and endeavoured to render the communication between them as safe and expeditious as possible.

The French in 1740, explored the Ohio, and ascertained the geography of the country about it, and its proximity to the English settlements. They even flattered themselves with the hope, that the Apalachean mountains would prove an insuperable barrier to the incursions of th r rival neighbors. They took measures to extend their trade among the Indians; well aware that, in case of a rupture, they would prove useful friends, or dangerous enemies. Their supplies, however, were scanty, and inadequate to the wants of the Indians, who were obliged to resort to the English traders. These carefully watched the policy of the French, and endeavoured to counteract their influence. They formed what was called the Ohio Company, intended as a counterpoise to the numerous French traders on our frontier; and to facilitate their schemes, a considerable tract of land was granted them on that river, as also an exclusive trade. But the exertions of this company failed of the desired success. The Indians were displeased with the grant, especially as they had not been consulted. The French took advantage of the irritation it excited, and thereby secured the affections of the Indians. They therefore seized on the English traders, confiscated their property, and then loudly complained of the encroachments made on their territory.

This, and some other checks experienced by the English, so much emboldened the French that, in 1753, they began to erect new forts, and to form new establishments, more in the neighbourhood of their rivals, particularly at Crown point, Niagara, Riviere au Beuf, and at the junction of the Monongahela and Alleghany rivers. These advances, attended too with hostile appearances, were not viewed with indifference. Complaints were made to the French court, which extorted reiterated promises of redress, without the least intention of performing them; and, to gain as much time as possible, the English were amused with the most specious reasons for the delay of retribution. This evasive conduct was considered as tantamount to a direct denial of justice; particularly when it was known, that the French were fortifying themselves along the lakes, and on the Ohio and Mississippi.

The English cabinet resolved to be no longer amused by the artifices of the French. Orders were despatched in 1754, to the governors of provinces, directing them to resort to force in defence of their rights, and to drive the French from their station on the Ohio. The New England provinces formed a political confederacy for mutual defence. Measures were taken to detach the Indians from the French, but with little or no effect. The illustrious Washington now commenced his military career. He was appointed to the rank of colonel, and detached from Virginia with four hundred men to erect some works of defence on the banks of the Ohio. Here he was attacked by a superior force, and obliged to capitulate; after which he was severely handled by the Indians on his return from the expedition.

Complaints were again made to the French king on the repeated aggressions of his subjects: But as it was evident, that he considered the Ohio, and all the recent establishments made in that quarter, as within his territories, a rupture was deemed inevitable, and both nations prepared for it. French troops were sent out to Canada, and all the posts in that province, as well as in Louisiana, put in the best possible state of defence. A temporary disunion among the English colonies, rendered it difficult to collect a sufficient force to oppose them in season.

In 1755, general Braddock arrived with a considerable body of troops from England, and marched over the mountains to attack fort *du Quesne*, the ruins of which are still to be seen at Pittsburgh. He suffered himself to be drawn into an ambuscade a few miles from the fort, in in which he lost his life, and seven hundred of his men perished with him. His ignorance of savage warfare was probably the cause of this disaster. He rejected the advice of Washington, to whose lot it fell to collect the fugitives, and to lead them back to fort Cumberland. This loss was in some measure compensated the same year, by the defeat of the French at fort Edward under Baron Dieskau, who was wounded and taken prisoner.

The clamors raised in England against the tardiness of the ministry, for a while disconcerted the military operations of the English. In 1757, the celebrated William Pitt, afterwards Lord Chatham, came into office, when the war was prosecuted with vigor, though at first with various success. The French laid siege to fort William Henry, and obliged the garrison to capitulate. The troops were permitted to march out with the honors of war, when they were attacked by the savages, and many of them inhumanly butchered.

The year 1758, is memorable from the conquest of Cape Breton, the reduction of *Cadaraqui*, and fort *du Quesne*. The English and provincial troops, however, were shamefully defeated near Tyconderoga, where Lord Howe was slain.

From this period the exertions of the English were attended with uninterrupted success. Crown point and Tyconderoga were considered as the keys of Canada, yet the French were obliged to abandon them in 1759, especially after their defeat near Niagara, and repair to the defence of the capital. The contest on the plains of Abraham decided the fate of the French possessions in North America. The intrepid Wolfe was wounded, and expired in the arms of victory. The no less brave Montcalme was likewise wounded, and lived only to witness the disasters of the day, and to lament the misfortunes of his country. Quebec was invested, and it soon fell into the hands of the victorious English; and its fall drew after it the cession of Louisiana.

Thus on the heights of Abraham two illustrious generals expired on the bed of honor. Their respective nations have done justice to their memories. Westminster Abbey contains a magnificent monument of Wolfe, descriptive of his dying moments. The French minister requested, and obtained permission to erect a monument at

Quebec, to perpetuate the memory of Montcalme. Such national honors paid to the manes of military men, serve to animate those in arms to deeds of enterprise and glory.

Notwithstanding the success of the English, the Indians continued their depredations on our frontiers. In the year 1760, the Cherokees were instigated by the French of Louisiana to fall on the English traders and settlers among them, whom they pillaged and slaughtered without mercy. About twelve hundred men from South Carolina marched against them, attacked and defeated them, laid waste their towns, and destroyed their provisions. The Indians soon assembled again, and in their turn laid siege to fort Loudon, and obliged the garrison to capitulate. These brave troops, while retiring homewards, on the faith of stipulated agreements, were ambuscaded, and many of them put to death.

Yet these inroads of the Indians had no effect on the great contest between the two nations. As the power of France in America rapidly approached its dissolution, she resolved to retrieve all her misfortunes by the invasion of England. No sooner was this resolution made known to the English ministers, than they despatched two formidable fleets to sea. Admiral Boscawen attacked and defeated the Toulon squadron near the straits of Gibraltar; and within three months afterwards, Sir Edward Hawke obtained a signal victory over another French fleet in the bay of Biscay. These misfortunes effectually checked the spirit of invasion.

Never was France more humbled in her pride and glory than during this war. Her subjects were oppressed with taxes, her fleets destroyed, and her islands captured. Her armies were likewise hard pressed on the continent of Europe, and the terrible defeat before Minden in 1759, seemed to be the precursor of still greater calamities. With infinite regret she found herself obliged to solicit peace, and to accept it on such terms as England was pleased to prescribe. The treaty was finally concluded between them February 10th. 1763; by which France ceded Canada to Great Britain, as also all her possessions on the east side of the Mississippi. On the third day of the preceding November, France ceded to Spain all her territories on the west side of that river, including the island and city of New Orleans, which cession was accepted by the latter power on the thirteenth of the same month.

Prior to this period the whole territory on both sides of the Mississippi, situated between the lakes and the gulf of Mexico, and between the Mexican and Alleghany mountains, went under the general name of Louisiana. That part of it ceded to the English lost the name; but the new acquisitions of Spain retained it.

The fate of the Louisianians was made known to them by a letter signed by the French king, dated April 21st, 1764, addressed to M. D'Abbadie, whom he calls the Director General and Commandant of Louisiana, informing him of the treaty of cession, and directing him to give up to the officers of Spain the country and colony of Louisiana, together with the city of New Orleans, and all the military posts. He expressed a desire for the prosperity and peace of the inhabitants of the colony, and his confidence in the friendship and affection of the king of Spain. He at the same time declared his expectation, that the ecclesiastics and religious houses, which had the care of the parishes and missions, would continue to exercise their functions; that the superior council and ordinary judges would continue to administer justice according to the laws, forms, and usages of the colony; that the inhabitants would be preserved and maintained in their estates, which had been granted to them by the governors and directors of the colony; and that, finally, all these grants, though not confirmed by the French authorities, would be confirmed by his catholic majesty.

The treaty of cession, dated the third of November 1762, was never published, and the terms of it remain a secret to this day; but there is good reason to believe, that the sentiments expressed by the French king corresponded with the stipulations it contained. His letter was published in New Orleans in October 1764, and it created a great ferment in the colony. Don Ulloa, in 1766, arrived with a detachment of Spanish troops, and demanded possession of M. Aubry, who at that time exercised the functions of governor.* This gentleman united with the people in opposing the designs of Spain. They complained that a transfer without their consent, was unjust, and in a moment of irritation resorted to their arms, and obliged the Spaniards to measure back their steps to the Havanna.

Things remained in this situation till the 17th of August 1769, when O'Reilly arrived, and took peaceable possession of the colony. He immediately selected twelve of the most distinguished leaders of the opposition, as the victims of resentment. Six of them were devoted to the halter, to gratify the malice of arbitrary power, and to strike terror into the other malecontents. The other six deemed less guilty, and surely they were much less fortunate, were doomed to the dungeons of Cuba. This scene of blood and outrage made a deep impression of horror on the minds of the people, and will never be forgotten. In 1770, the Spanish authorities were established in Upper Louisiana, where some small settlements were made four years before, under the direction of their French predecessors.

O'Reilly was the first governor and intendant general, who exercised the Spanish power in Louisiana. As governor-general he was vested with the supreme power of the province, both civil and military; and as intendant-

* M. D'Abbadie died just before this period.

general he granted lands, prescribed the conditions, and confirmed the concessions made by his subordinates ; superintended the fiscal department, and the affairs of the Indians. This arrangement, with some slight modifications, continued till 1799, when a department of finance was created.

The English in 1764, took possession of Florida under the treaty of the preceding year. A regiment on its way up the Mississippi to Natchez, was attacked by the Tonnicas at the clifts, where fort Adams now stands, and entirely defeated. In this rencounter Major Loftus lost his life, and ever since that period the clifts have borne his name. The bones of those killed in the action have been uncovered by the ebrasion of the rains, and a considerable slaughter appears to have taken place.

After the Spanish authorities had gained possession of Louisiana, it was not long before the people became in some measure, reconciled to the change. The severity exercised on the leaders of the opposition excited horrible sensations in their minds ; though, when their hopes were blasted, and their fate inevitably fixed, they endeavored to bear their misfortunes with becoming fortitude. Perhaps the similarity of their religious principles, and modes of worship, urged them the more readily to a speedy acquiescence; especially when they found themselves abandoned by their mother country, and menaced by the whole power of Spain.

The new Spanish governor was active in organizing the government, and in establishing such military posts as tended to promote the welfare of the colony. The French code was in part abolished, and the Spanish colonial system introduced. The subordinate offices were mostly filled by Frenchmen, because the province was destitute of a Spanish population. This compulsive generosity, however, was of great advantage ; it served to secure the fidelity of the officers, and to meliorate the irritated feelings of the inhabitants.

During the eight or nine succeeding years, few events occurred in Louisiana worthy of record. Population and improvement gradually increased. Agriculturists from the English settlements began to turn their attention to the country about Natchez, and their enterprise imparted animation to industry, and the culture of cotton became an object of importance. The example of the English excited the ambition of the Spanish colonial government, and the encouragement it afforded to foreign and domestic commerce, created a great demand for surplus produce. Among the items of export, that of sugar was found to yield the greatest profit. Hence the planters in the Delta procured an additional number of slaves, and engaged in the culture of that article. Much knowledge of the interior was at the same time obtained, but industriously concealed. The Indians in a great measure ceased to trouble the frontiers, and the peltry trade was prosecuted with some degree of success.

The era of the American revolution was not viewed by Spain with indifference, and she found it no easy matter to decide on the policy which it became her to pursue. England was justly alarmed at the dangerous situation of Florida, (now divided into two provinces, and called east and west Florida) especially as they were exposed to the attacks of the revolutionists on one side, and to those of the Spaniards on the other. In a pecuniary point of view, these isolated colonies were of no real value to England; yet it was for her interest to maintain them, and for this purpose a considerable number of troops was sent out to Mobile, Pensacola, St. Augustine, Baton Rouge, Natchez, and some other places of inferior note. If ultimately, by events of an unpropitious nature, she should find it necessary to yield them, the conclusion of the war presented the most advantageous period for such a measure. In deciding on the number of troops requisite to defend the Floridas, she undervalued the skill and bravery of those the most likely to attack them.

Nothing disturbed Spain more than the contemplated establishment of an independent empire in America. She was apprehensive, that the spirit of innovation would make its way into her provinces, and eventually dismember them from the parent country. But she could not resist the lures held out by France; and when she engaged in the war, it was merely as an auxiliary, and with a determination to promote her own interest, and to remain quiescent as regarded the independence of the United States. The acquisition of Gibraltar, Jamaica, Minorca, and the Floridas were splendid objects in her view. She readily perceived that, in case the United States succeeded in breaking their connexion with England, the Floridas would change masters, and she deemed it prudent to add them to her own dominions before we had a legitimate claim to them.

Louisiana at this period was governed by general Galvez, a man of daring ambition, and not destitute of genius and talents. He perceived the advantages which would accrue to his country from the conquest of the Floridas, and resolved to make an attempt on them. His measures were dictated with more than ordinary caution, as he was obliged mostly to depend on an undisciplined militia; and he was so fortunate as to carry them into effect with address and success. He suddenly appeared before Baton Rouge with about two thousand three hundred men, supported by several pieces of heavy ordnance. The fortification at that place, defended by about five hundred British troops under the command of lieutenant colonel Dickson, was immediately invested, and the Spanish batteries constructed with ardor. But as the works of the English were too defective to resist a siege, and the soldiery too much afflicted with sickness to repair them, lieutenant colonel Dickson, with the loss of a few killed and wounded, was obliged to surrender by capitulation on the twenty first day of September 1779. His troops were allowed to march out with the honors of war, when they submitted as prisoners. In this capitulation the fortress at Natchez was included, though the troops at that post were permitted to pass to Pensacola.

The fall of Baton Rouge, and with it the country between that post and the Yazous, infused into the Spaniards a confidence of their own strength, and inspired them with the hopes of new successes. Another attempt was resolved on; and in 1780, general Galvez sailed from New Orleans with a considerable force of militia and regulars, though almost destitute of naval support, to attack the English at Mobile. The fleet was overtaken by a storm in the gulf; one of the armed vessels stranded; the troops were exposed to great dangers; the water found its way to the provisions and ammunition, and these were either ruined, or rendered useless for some time. In this wretched condition, general Galvez finally succeeded in landing his army, together with the ordnance, military stores and provisions, near Mobile bay, and took immediate measures to repair the damage they had sustained.

If the English had attacked the Spaniards at this critical juncture, an easy victory would have rewarded their exertions; and so sensible was general Galvez of this, that he made preparations to abandon his artillery and baggage, and to attempt a retrograde movement over land to New Orleans. Surprised, however, at the seeming ignorance, or weakness of the English, he began to assume courage, and to raise the dejected spirits of his men. As soon as his provisions and stores were put in order, he boldly marched to invest the town and fort, which were defended by militia and regulars. He erected six batteries against them. A practicable breach was soon made in the fort, when the garrison surrendered by capitulation. This was an important acquisition to the Spaniards, and it led to the eventual reduction of Pensacola.

The English troops in this quarter suffered extremely from their inactivity and indecision. General Campbell had an army at Pensacola, sixty miles only to the eastward of Mobile, of sufficient force to have driven the Spaniards out of Florida; yet he suffered an important fortress and harbor to fall into the hands of his enemy! His attempts at relief were so long delayed, that, when his army arrived, the town and fort were in possession of the Spaniards.

Great Britain was never, perhaps, less triumphant on the ocean than at this period. The combined fleets of France and Spain manifested a confidence seldom before witnessed, and the pride of the British commerce and navy appeared on the decline. Spain was particularly anxious to recover her ancient dominions in Florida, and resolved to employ a considerable force under the fortunate general Galvez for that purpose. The capture of Mobile induced her to send to the Havanna nearly twelve thousand men, together with a formidable fleet, under admiral Solano. At that place, and on the voyage from Spain, vast numbers died of sickness, and several large ships, filled with men, went to the bottom in a subsequent gale.

Just before the arrival of this fleet and army, general Galvez made two unsuccessful attempts on Pensacola, and then repaired to the Havanna in pursuit of competent supplies, and a force equal to the object in view.

From the fleet of admiral Solano he obtained all the requisite means, and early in February 1781, set sail with a strong naval and military force. But a violent storm in the gulf sunk some of his heavy ships, as already mentioned, dispersed the remainder, and obliged him to make the best of his way back to the Havanna.

The fortunate arrival of some store ships from Spain, enabled him to repair his losses, and speedily to be at sea again. On the ninth of March the Spanish fleet entered the bay of Pensacola, and general Galvez proceeded to land the troops, ordnance, and military stores. The next day the ships of war made an attempt to enter the harbor; but they met with such a warm reception as obliged them to retire. On the nineteenth they succeeded under a tremendous cannonade from the English land batteries, and cast anchor before the town. Some Spanish troops from Mobile arrived the following day, and were very roughly handled as they entered the harbor.

The Spaniards lost no time in opening a land communication between the bay and town, and in preparing to attack the fortifications. They were provided with a good train of artillery; and such was the nature of the country, and the materials with which it abounded, that their works were soon consructed.

From the Spanish fleet on one side, and the land batteries on the other, the English soldiery were exposed to such a dreadful fire as frequently to be driven from their guns. Yet amid this scene of dangerous hostility they never despaired of the issue, till an unlucky accident occurred, which obliged them to propose terms of capitulation. The magazine in one of the advance redoubts of the English was blown up by means of a shell; the work was completely destroyed by the explosion, and a free passage opened into the town.

The Spanish commander was not disinclined to accede to favorable terms, particularly as his troops smarted severely under the effects of the English ordnance. On the ninth of May, generals Galvez and Campbell signed articles of capitulation. The whole of the territory, then denominated West Florida, was resigned to Spain. The English were allowed to retain their baggage and private property, and to retire where they pleased, stipulating only not to serve against Spain till an exchange took place. General Campbell was charged, at least in the publications of the day, with a premature surrender of this important fortress and colony. Success is too often considered as the only criterion of merit, and the want of it seldom meets with a favorable interpretation from the public.

The number of killed and wounded among the Spaniards was never precisely known; but it was considerable. About one hundred of the English were killed, and a great number wounded. The capitulation included about one thousand prisoners.

An occurrence took place during the siege, which involved some of the English settlers in difficulty. A considerable fleet made its appearance in the offing, and it was on both sides conjectured to belong to the English. General Galvez was so apprehensive of it, that he prepared to abandon the advantages he had gained, and to lead his army over land to Mobile. The hopes of the besieged experienced a momentary elevation; but it was soon ascertained that the fleet in question belonged to the French. The tidings of relief, however, soon spread over the country; and so confident were the people of the total expulsion of the Spaniards from Florida, that those in the neighborhood of Natchez rose in arms, and seized on the Spanish garrison at that place. The news of the fall of Pensacola, which arrived soon after, convinced them of their error. The garrison was immediately restored; but some of the most active leaders deemed it prudent to seek safety in flight, and a reward was offered for their scalps. It does not appear, however, that any blood was spilt on the occasion.

While the Spaniards were aiming at the possession of West Florida, the English endeavoured to divert their attention to another quarter. The commandant of Michillimakinak in 1780, assembled about fifteen hundred Indians, and one hundred and forty English, and attempted the reduction of St. Louis, the capital of Upper Louisiana. During the short time they were before that town, sixty of the inhabitants were killed, and thirty taken prisoners. Fortunately for them, general Clark was on the the opposite side of the Mississippi with a considerable force. On his appearance at St. Louis with a strong detachment, the Indians were amazed. They had no disposition to quarrel with any other than the Louisianians, and charged the English with deception. In fine, as the jealousy of the Indians was excited, the English trembled for their safety, and therefore secretly abandoned their auxiliaries, and made the best of their way into Canada. The Indians then retired to their homes in peace. This expedition, as appears, was not sanctioned by the English court, and the private property of the commandant wat seized to pay the expenses of it; most likely because it proved unfortunate.

Thus terminated the dispute between the English and Spaniards in this quarter of the globe. At the peace of 1783, Great Britain ceded East Florida, and guaranteed West Florida to the crown of Spain.

The terms of this peace opened a wide field of dispute between the United States and Spain, which continued to agitate the two nations for about twelve years. Great Britain by treaty relinquished the Floridas to Spain, without any specific boundaries, and by another treaty of a simultaneous date, ceded to the United States all the country to the north of the thirty first degree. Soon after the treaty of 1763, she divided Florida into two provinces. The northern boundary of what she denominated West Florida, was at first limited to the thirty first degree, but was eventually extended to the Yazous in north latitude thirty two degrees, twenty eight minutes, where it actually existed at the time of the guarantee in 1783. This boundary had no existence under the French government; what was afterwards called West Florida, was ut that time included in Louisiana. Besides, at the time of the guarantee already mentioned, the Spaniards were in possession of West Florida, as antecedently occupied by the English, in virtue of the right of conquest. Hence the pretensions of Spain to all the territory south of the Yazous, were, perhaps, as well founded as those of the United States.

Another point of still greater magnitude was involved in the dispute; the United States claimed the right of navigating the Mississippi, and Spain contested it. The treaty of 1763, allowed both Great Britain and Spain an equal participation of this right. The latter contended that the reduction of West Florida by force of arms, vested in her an exclusive right to that river below the upper boundary of her dominions on the east side of it, and even denied to the United States the least shadow of claim to participate it with her.

But Spain had other and more powerful reasons for obstructing the navigation of the Mississippi. She was apprehensive that New Orleans would be glutted with the produce of the country about the Ohio, and of course exclude her own subjects from a profitable market. It was likewise her policy to have as little intercourse as possible with a people, whose rapid population and enterprise, added to the nature of their political principles, excited serious apprehensions for the safety of her colonies. To open the navigation of the Mississippi appeared to her the same as to invite an attack, particularly as it would draw to the capital, an army of boatmen, equal to the conquest of Louisiana. Besides, she contemplated the annexation of some of our western territories to her dominions, and conceived, that an interdiction of commercial pursuits was the most likely means of facilitating that desirable event.

At the close of the American revolution, the country about the Ohio and its waters was rapidly populated; and so early as 1785. Kentucky alone contained about twelve thousand souls. The propriety of forming a new state on the western waters was now for the first time suggested, and Virginia was disposed to accelerate the measure. A convention met at Danville to deliberate on the subject; but a majority of the members declared against it.

The political relations of these people were much embarrassed. Their legislature convened six hundred miles from them, and the confederation was so defective as to leave them almost unprotected by the United States. Their distance too from the Atlantic markets, (rendered difficult of access from an almost impenetrable wilderness, and a chain of stupendous mountains) exposed them to many serious inconveniences. Vain were their attempts to obtain a market at New Orleans for their produce. The navigation of the Mississippi was strictly prohibited by the Spaniards, and even the United States seemed disposed to acquiesce in this prohibition for at least a term of years! The courts of justice established among them by the legislature of Virginia, served to remedy some of their local evils; but those of a more universal nature, and of the greatest magnitude, still remained to be removed.

The climate and soil of Kentucky proved extremely favorable to agricultural pursuits. The planters soon found themselves in possession of large quantities of surplus produce, and a rapid accumulation was rendered certain from their industry. This made them the more impatient of the restraints under which they labored, and incited them to utter their complaints to the legislature of the union.

For this purpose another convention was formed in Kentucky in 1788. A petition to congress was agreed on, and a redress of grievances demanded, particularly the renovation of the Mississippi commerce. Not much was expected from this measure, and the convention resorted to it more from a sense of duty than any prospect of success. Our confederated government at that time was extremely weak at home, and not much respected abroad. The warm remonstrance of congress, however, produced a temporary relaxation of the usual restrictions; yet as the impediments were not fully removed, and the duration of the indulgence uncertain, the ferment continued to rage among the western people.

Abandoned in a manner by their own government, and denied admittance to the ocean by the Spaniards, they felt some alarm for their interest, and much more for their safety. The exertions of congress in their favor had proved ineffectual, and the hardy lessons of experience persuaded all, that their future fate almost wholly depended on themselves. Many expedients to obtain redress were suggested, though the majority acceded to none of them. A diversity of mere opinion only, at first prevailed among the Kentuckians; but this served in the end to excite their jealousy, and to mould them into no less than five parties of opposite sentiments and views. The design of the first was to become independent of the United States, to frame a government for the western settlements, and to enter into a commercial treaty with Spain. The second aimed to annex Kentucky to Louisiana, and to admit the Spanish laws among them: This scheme was strenuously supported by the government of Spain, which endeavored by means of its partizans to corrupt the minds of the people. The third was anxious to wage war with the Spaniards, and to seize on New Orleans. The fourth exerted itself to maintain the connexion between the western settlements and the Atlantic states; and at the same time to intimidate the Spanish authorities with threats of invasion, and thereby to extort from them what they were inclined to refuse. The object of the fifth was to induce France to obtain the retrocession of Louisiana, and then to receive the western people under her protection. Each party had its views in the plans proposed, and some of them had a favorable effect.

The fears of an invasion, much more than the execution of any other project, alarmed the Spaniards, and occasionally induced them to soften the rigor of their commercial restrictions. The settlements on the Ohio appeared formidable, and the character of the people was not much liked among them. They still kept in view the plan of disunion, and conceived it good policy to vary their mode of operations; particularly as, with all their exertions, they had not been able to raise a party sufficiently strong and respectable to justify a public manifestation of their designs. In fine, they determined to try the effect of lenient measures. They conceived it practicable, by moderate concessions, and the distribution of money and other largesses among the leading characters, to bring about a gradual revolution in the public sentiment.

Exclusive privileges in trade were never deemed anomalous under the Spanish government; and the authorities at New Orleans conceived it good policy to extend them to Kentucky, especially as they were sure to find a friend in every privileged trader. These grants were restricted to a few influential individuals: But as these soon discovered their inability to transport all the surplus produce of the country, permission was given them to sign passports for such of their friends as wished to try the market; and New Orleans in the end swarmed with people from the Ohio. Pensions were likewise granted to a number of individuals in Kentucky; not more, perhaps, to detach them from the interest of their own country, than to induce them to resist any preparations to attack the territories of Spain. The Spaniards expected that these commercial privileges and pensions would perform wonders, and operate like a charm on the stubborn and refractory sons of Kentucky.

Our present federal government, soon after its establishment, began to extort the respect of the powers of Europe. Perhaps the character of Washington not a little contributed to the lustre it shed. It was among his first cares to attempt the settlement of the difficulties between us and Spain. The free navigation of the Mississippi, and the designation of the territorial limits, were claimed in a tone not to be rejected; and after a variety of discussions, the points in dispute between us and that power were happily adjusted.

Pending this negociation, which was of several years continuance, the English and French were not inattentive to the distresses of the western people, nor unacquainted with the attempts of Spain to extend its jurisdiction over them. Both of these powers aimed at the possession of Louisiana and the Floridas, and were equally desirous of detaching Kentucky, and the other settlements on the Ohio, from the United States. The Spaniards redoubled their efforts to procure a division of the union, and by this measure to frustrate the policy of their enemies.

Emissaries from Canada tampered with some of the defectious citizens of Kentucky. The Spanish possessions on the Mississippi, according to them, were soon to be in the hands of England, when the money and rich fabrics of that nation would amply reward the industry of the planters. New Orleans was to be opened for the reception of their provisions and raw materials of every kind, and commercial privileges of an advantageous nature were to be enjoyed by all the inhabitants on the west side of the mountains. The delta, indeed, was to be the grand emporium of the western world, from which floods of wealth were to roll into the wilds and recesses of the regions on the Ohio.

The people, however, were not much moved by these flattering prospects. They still entertained antipathies against the English, and were not disposed to come again under their dominion. Besides, the hopes of escaping from their difficulties had not entirely forsaken them, and they were unwilling to incur the stigma of an ignominious desertion of their country.

Lures of the same nature were held out by the French, and with more effect. We had received benefits from that nation, and were disposed to consider her revolution as a struggle between tyranny and liberty. An imprudent diplomatic character took advantage of this generous partiality, concerted a plan to attack Louisiana, and to carry it into effect by means of the citizens of the United States. This was one of the boldest steps ever taken by a public minister. Had he succeeded in his endeavors, a war between us and Spain would have been inevitable. Nothing but the wisdom and firmness of our government saved us from the impending calamity; and at the same time procured the recall of the minister, who, by repeated acts of aggression, had forfeited all claim to inviolability.

These measures of the English and French, extorted loud complaints from Spain: Those of the former were the most dreaded by her. The Spanish minister alleged to our government, that an expedition from Canada, by way of the lakes, was in agitation against Louisiana; peremptorily demanded the arrestation of it, and the vindication of our sovereignty. The government was not fully convinced of the truth of this allegation; yet, to appease the fears of Spain, and to remove the impediments in the way of the pending negociation with that power, it strengthened our frontier posts, and issued strict orders to interdict the passage of any British troops across our territory. The English never attempted to carry such a plan into effect; but a knowledge or suspicion of their views, served to keep Louisiana in a state of alarm, to induce the Spaniards to strengthen their barrier posts, to keep the United States out of the possession of the territory to the north of the thirty first degree, and to exclude them from the commercial advantages of the Mississippi. These two objects were finally adjusted by the treaty of October 1795.

This treaty, which had occupied the attention of the United States for many years, and was so ardently desired, enfeebled the seductive practices of contending rivals, and resuscitated the physical energies of the western people. Measures were immediately taken by our government to carry the stipulations into effect. Andrew Ellicott, Esquire, who was appointed commissioner on the part of the United States, arrived at Natchez in February 1797, accompanied by a small guard of soldiers under the command of lieutenant John M'Clary. But, from a variety of causes, the demarcation of the boundary was delayed for more than a year.

It was stipulated between the parties, that one commissioner from each, should meet at Natchez within six months after the ratification of the treaty, attended by guards drawn from the troops of their respective nations; at which time the Spanish posts to the north of the thirty first degree were to be evacuated.

For the purpose of receiving possession of these posts, a detachment of troops under the command of lieutenant P. S. Pope, soon followed Mr. Ellicott. The orders given to this officer render it sufficiently probable, that the government apprehended some difficulties in the way of the execution of the treaty. He was directed to proceed in the first instance, to fort Massac on the Ohio, and there to wait the return of an officer previously despatched to New Madrid, in pursuit of official information relative to the delivery of the posts; and on the certainty or probability of such an event, he was authorized to descend the Mississippi to Natchez. He was particularly charged, on his arrival at that place, " to establish the most perfect " discipline among the troops, to prevent every kind of " disorder, and to promote harmony, and a friendly inter-

" change of good offices with the *subjects of his catholic*
" *majesty*, and to treat the *Spanish flag* with due respect
" on all occasions."

It may be safely doubted, whether Spain ever seriously intended to carry the treaty into effect, unless compelled to it by a concurrence of unfavorable events. The clamors of the western people, and the occasional disposition manifested by them to invade Louisiana, in some measure extorted it from her, and therefore the fulfilment or non-execution of it, depended on future contingencies. To detach those people from the union was what she had most at heart, and of course was slow to despair of success. She was not ignorant, that they expressed much dissatisfaction at the tardy measures of government relative to the navigation of the Mississippi, and that their isolated situation had often suggested the necessity of a separation from the Atlantic states. She was well aware, that the publication of the arrangement between the two nations, would bring her projects of disunion to a crisis, and in a manner compel the western people to make a decided election, either to adhere to the Atlantic states, or to embrace the splendid advantages held out to them on the Mississippi. It was deemed highly probable, indeed, that, by the distribution of money, and the promises of an unimbarrassed trade, the Kentuckians would eventually accede to the propositions made them by the Spanish authorities. At any rate, as the fulfilment of the treaty would render abortive all future measures of disunion, she determined to make another effort to accomplish her purposes.

Considerable time was necessary for this experiment, and it was obtained under various pretexts. The Spanish minister intrigued at the seat of government, and the authorities in Louisiana ably seconded his views. The first object was to prevent our commissioner, and the guard attached to him, from descending the Mississippi. The commissioner on the part of Spain, don Manuel Gayoso,* governor of the district of Natchez, under pretence, that he was not ready to evacuate the posts, and dreading, as he pretended, the approximation of the troops of the two nations, forwarded an express to Mr. Ellicott, and requested him to leave his guard at Bayou Pierre till the preparatory arrangements were made. This request, however, was disregarded, and they landed and encamped at Natchez. Lieutenant Pope soon followed with another detachment, and as it seems, contrary to his instructions, and was detained at the Walnut Hills by the orders of Gayoso. Mr. Ellicott secretly invited him to descend to Natchez in opposition to the Spanish authorities; though Gayoso, before his arrival, was prevailed on to sanction the descent.

The arrival of Mr. Ellicott and the troops of the United States at Natchez, was contrary to the wishes and expectations of the Spanish authorities: Yet they resolved to delay the execution of the treaty; and the treaty itself, as well as the peculiar circumstances of the times, furnished several plausible pretexts for the measure. They alleged, that, as the treaty had not stipulated for the security of the landed property of the inhabitants, nor was explicit as to the delivery or demolition of the public buildings and fortifications, it was necessary to postpone the evacuation till these unexpected difficulties were settled by the two governments. They likewise alleged that the Canadian English contemplated the invasion of Louisiana by way of the lakes; and hence the posts at the Walnut Hills and Natchez were necessary to cover New Orleans. The noted conspiracy of Blount was calculated to excite their fears.

These allegations, however plausible and well founded, were urged by the Spanish authorities more to procure

* He acted however, under the orders of the baron Carondelet.

delay, than from any other motive. Their final evacuation or retention of the posts wholly depended on the defeat or success of the measures, which were taken to detach the western country from the union.

For, when the conclusion of the treaty was first known in Louisiana, an emissary was despatched to Tennessee and Kentucky, authorized to enter into engagements, to encourage the leading characters to seduce the minds of the people, to stipulate for the delivery of large sums of money, and to promise independence and a free trade. This was the last effort at disunion, and had it resulted in success, the treaty would have been totally disregarded.

But it was found, that the people were less disposed for a change than ten years before. Some of the most prominent characters, who formerly advocated a separation, and were probably stimulated in their exertions by pecuniary rewards, now discovered an aversion to the hazardous experiment, especially as they were likely to acquire by amicable arrangement, the free enjoyment of the Mississippi navigation, which had been the great object of all their efforts. Hence they were not inclined to incur the danger of defeat, when even the most ample success would not place them in a more prosperous situation than that contemplated by the treaty.

Mr. Ellicott, during this period, was not an idle spectator of events, nor ignorant of the designs of the Spanish authorities, and he took measures to defeat them. Whether these measures were prudent and wise, or injudicious and reprehensible, perhaps may admit of dispute. Some will unquestionably be inclined to think, that in one instance he tergiversated, and in several openly violated the sovereignty of Spain; while others will find in his peculiar situation and motives, a complete justification of his conduct. To his irregular proceedings, indeed, has been imputed the detention of the posts, at least six months longer than was actually contemplated by the Spanish authorities.

On his arrival at Natchez he insultingly displayed the flag of the United States in full view of the Spanish garrison. Lieutenant M'Clary, who acted as he directed, proceeded to augment the number of his guard by the enlistment of Spanish subjects, and by the apprehension of deserters from the army of the United States, who had taken refuge in the territories of Spain. Governor Gayoso loudly complained of this conduct; he even directed the flag to be taken down, and demanded the liberation of the deserters. Mr. Ellicott was not disposed to yield the points in issue; and the Spanish governor conceived it best not to press the subject a second time. No one will maintain, that he had a right to infract the laws of nations, or to attack the sovereignty of Spain. From the nature of the instructions given to lieutenant Pope, may be pretty clearly inferred the pacific tenor of his own.

A considerable proportion of the people in the district of Natchez had removed from the United States, and no wonder they were solicitous for the meditated change. They fully comprehended the motives, which induced the Spanish authorities to postpone the execution of the treaty, and therefore became impatient. A confidence of impunity led them to associate for the purpose of accelerating the desired change, and they were in a great measure guided by the hints and insinuations of Mr. Ellicott. In the end they unguardedly proceeded to such acts of opposition to the established authorities, as rendered them highly culpable in the eye of the law, and therefore, to avoid its penalties, found it necessary to acquire by violent means, what they had a right to expect from solemn stipulations. From these Mr. Ellicott selected what he called his " Little Council," and the members of it were not disposed to pacify the tumult among the people.

The disorders in the district did not escape the notice of Gayoso, who, by a proclamation dated March the twenty ninth 1797, and another of a subsequent date, endeavored to appease the impatient disposition of the people, and adverted to the reasons or pretexts, already stated, for the inexecution of the treaty. He approbated private meetings for the purposes of devotion, and interdicted all processes for debt till after the planters had prepared their ensuing crops.

These acts of condescension failed of their intended effect, particularly as they were believed to result from a sense of danger. The people were extremely jealous, and seemed to discover in the sudden augmentation of the military force at Natchez and the Walnut Hills (though for the avowed purpose of obstructing the descent of the English) a deliberate design to seize the malecontents; and an apparent conviction of this truth precipitated them into measures of a hostile nature. Such indeed, were the commotions in the district, that Gayoso and his family, on the tenth of June, repaired to the fort for safety.

About this period the people were indirectly invited by Mr. Ellicott, to assemble and deliberate on their grievances. Such a measure accorded with their most ardent wishes; but as it would be in opposition to legal authority, they were apprehensive of an attempt by the Spanish troops to disperse the meeting, and to arrest those who should attend it. To dissipate their fears on this head, lieutenant Pope, on the twelfth of June, addressed them a letter, wherein, among other things, he declared, " that " he would at all hazards protect them." He called on them " in the most solemn manner to come forward and " assert their rights," and at the same time offered his " sincere co-operation to accomplish that desirable ob- " ject." He requested their assistance in return " to re- " pel any troops or hostile parties that might make an at- " tempt to land for the purpose of reinforcing the garri-

" son, or other purposes detrimental to the interest of the
" country." At the bottom of this address, Mr. Ellicott
added a note in these words: " From the present alarm-
" ing situation of the country, I fully approve of lieute-
" nant Pope's letter of this date to his fellow citizens as-
" sembled at Mr. Belts."*

Some time prior to this event, the baron Carondelet had
publicly charged Mr. Ellicott with menacing the Spanish
government. Gayoso on the thirteenth of June, the day
after the date of the above mentioned letter, and while
confined to the walls of his garrison, repeated the same
charge in a communication to Mr. Ellicott, and demanded of him a statement of the part he took in the rebelli-
ous proceedings of the people. Mr. Ellicott on the same
day answered, " since you demand a positive reply to the
" general question, whether I am concerned in measures
" destructive of his catholic majesty's interest, or in an
" attempt to attack the fort, I give you my word of honor,
" that I am not !"

It by no means accorded with the temper and feelings
of Gayoso to be immured within the walls of the fort,
and to be deprived of his power. The laws authorized
coercive measures; but of what avail were the laws without the means of carrying them into execution ! Gayoso
felt himself humbled; and on the fourteenth of June,
while under a strong perturbation of mind, addressed an
elaborate proclamation to the people, requesting those in
bodies to disperse, and to resume their usual occupations ;
the consequences of which he declared to be, an amnesty
for the past, and security for the future. This proclamation conceded every thing desired by the people ; it exhibited more the features of a humble remonstrance, than
the dignified language of magisterial reprehension : Yet
Mr. Ellicott says, that " it contained some expressions

* About eight miles in the rear of Natchez

"very offensive to the people." Why then has he omitted to record it in his journal? It does not appear, after an attentive perusal, to contain any such expressions.

Certain it is, however, that incredible pains were taken to find in this official document some secret reservation, some occult quality, artfully designed by Gayoso as a pretext for future punishment, should it ever be in his power to inflict it. Many of the people resorted to their arms, formed themselves into military bands, and elected their officers. Occasions were dexterously seized to insult the Spanish authorities, and to wound their pride. Lieutenant Pope repeatedly put himself at the head of his men, sounded the charge, and menaced the garrison with an escalade. One of his men, by his contrivance, eluded the vigilance of the Spanish sentinels in the night, cut a small piece of wood from the door of the magazine, and made his escape; and lieutenant Pope, to tantalize Gayoso, immediately sent him the fruit of this successful enterprise.

The extent and progress of the opposition at last began to alarm Mr. Ellicott, and he resolved to check it; more indeed from a wish to escape the odium of it, than to prevent the expulsion of the Spanish authorities. He was not disposed to ride in the whirlwind, but he had an inclination to direct the storm, and to gratify his purpose prevailed on the people to delegate their power to a committee, a body deemed more manageable, and less liable to be exacerbated by the fluctuating occurrences of the times.

The people assembled on the twentieth of June, to deliberate on their affairs. The pacific declarations of Gayoso, contained in his proclamation, excited their jealousy, and they trembled, lest they were designed as a snare. They felt an inclination to prescribe the conditions of their own security, not only to avoid all ambiguity of expression, but seemingly to extort what they knew was ready to be granted them. They therefore acceded to the proposition of Mr. Ellicott, and appointed a committee of safety, invested it with extensive powers, and that gentleman and lieutenant Pope were chosen members of it. This committee proposed to Gayoso, that he should recognize its existence as a body; that the people should not be prosecuted nor injured on account of the part taken by them against the government; that they should be exempted from serving in the militia under the Spanish authorities, except to repel the invasion of the Indians, or to suppress riots; that they should be considered as in a state of neutrality, though governed by the Spanish laws, and not be sent out of the country on any pretext whatever. Gayoso readily yielded his assent to these propositions; and they were soon after ratified by the baron Carondelet, with an exception of no great moment, when the Spanish authorities resumed their functions, and the storm in a great measure subsided.

Thus the people gained a complete victory over the constituted authorities. These became pledged to obliviate all transactions of a treasonable nature; to sanction and to legalize the existence of a dangerous power within their jurisdiction, able at any moment to subvert the government; to exempt the militia from obedience, except in two specified instances, and tacitly to authorize it to obey the mandates of a rival nation, or its agents. These conditions are not destitute of point, and manifest a considerable degree of policy and skill.

Some of the members of the committee were not fully in the confidence of Mr. Ellicott. He suspected colonel Anthony Hutchings, in particular, of entertaining views detrimental to the United States; and the more so, as he had been a British officer, and was then a known pensioner of Great Britain. He therefore prevailed on Gayoso to dissolve the committee of safety by proclamation, and to authorize the election of another, which was to be considered as permanent. This new committee was organized about the first of July, and the electors did not think proper to bestow their suffrages on colonel Hutchings. Hence a permanent committee was now formed, much more dangerous to the Spanish authorities than the other, because it was elected and organized by virtue of their own mandate. It is strictly true as Mr. Ellicott boasts, " that this measure, as was really intended, put " a finishing stroke to the Spanish authority and jurisdic- " tion in the district."

About this period a considerable change took place in the Spanish colonial government. The baron Carondelet was transferred to the province of Quito, and Gayoso succeeded him as governor general of Louisiana, and repaired to New Orleans. Colonel Grandpree was appointed governor of the district of Natchez; but the permanent committee resolved, that he should not be received as such, and he never made his appearance. In the mean time, and until the evacuation of the posts, the Spanish government in the district devolved on major Minor, a gentleman originally from Pennsylvania, and at this time one of the most wealthy planters in the Mississippi territory.

Colonel Hutchings was not a little chagrined and disappointed at the defeat he experienced in the late election; and the doubts entertained of his patriotism served to wound his pride, and to excite his resentment. No wonder, then, that he became inimical to the permanent committee, and meditated its destruction. After the departure of Gayoso he attempted the dissolution of it, and the organization of another. He failed in his first object, and succeeded in the second. Hence the district was violently agitated by the bitter contests of the two rival committees. The Spanish authorities were too feeble to resist the views of opposition, or to impart energy to a rival power.

One of the first steps taken by the new committee was to prepare a petition and memorial to congress, in which the measures of Mr. Ellicott and lieutenant Pope were severely reprehended. The other committee endeavoured to shield these gentlemen from the resentment of the executive of the United States; and resolved, that the neutral position of the district resulted from the friendly and salutary advice of the first, and that the second " deserved " well of his country."

Captain Guion arrived at Natchez in December with a considerable detachment, and assumed the command of all the troops of the United States in the district. From the tenor of his instructions, it is evident, that they were dictated with a view to the prevalent disturbances. At any rate, he conceived it his duty to discountenance the hostile attitude of the people, and to disconcert the efforts of the permanent committee: He even threatened to disperse the members of that body, and to put Mr. Ellicott in confinement, whose conduct he reprobated in the strongest terms.

This decisive tone, added to measures of a corresponding nature, at once arrested the progress of the disorders; the ferment gradually subsided, and tranquility was restored; the Spanish authorities resumed their former consequence, and no longer hesitated to prepare for an evacuation of the posts. No doubt this event was accelerated in part, by the restoration of order in society, and in part, by the complete failure of all attempts at disunion.

The evacuation of all the posts to the north of the thirty first degree, took place in the early part of the summer of 1798. The demarcation of the boundary line commenced near the same period, and was completed in March 1799, except a small portion of it along the borders of East Florida, which was suspended on account of the hostile appearance of the Indians. William Dunbar, esquire, distinguished in the republic of letters, and major Minor, were successively the commissioners on the part of Spain.

It has already been hinted, that the acquisition of our independence excited the jealousy of Spain. That memorable event led the politicians and statesmen of that power to speculate on our future views. They dreaded the example we had afforded to the world, and trembled at the probable introduction of the spirit of liberty into the Mexican dominions. In 1787, the intendant of Louisiana prepared an elaborate memoir on this subject by order of the Spanish court, in which he represented the people of the United States as extremely ambitious, as animated by the spirit of conquest, and as anxious to extend their empire to the shores of the Pacific. He then suggested a line of policy, which, in his opinion, it was incumbent on Spain to adopt. The dismemberment of the western country, by means of pensions and commercial benefits, was considered by him as not difficult. The attempt was therefore strongly urged, particularly as it would, if successful, greatly augment the power of Spain in this quarter, and forever arrest our progress westward. These suggestions were favorably received, and formed the ground work of that policy, which Spain afterwards pursued. If she interdicted our commerce, it was from an apprehension that our government under the confederation was too weak to assert with effect the rights of the nation; that this weakness would eventually alienate the affections of the western people, cool their patriotism, and induce them to become Spanish subjects: At any rate, the measure seemed well calculated to remove to a distant day, the dangers of mutual intercourse, which it was feared would disturb the tranquility of the provinces. On this ground the proposition of some of our revolutionary officers to form an extensive settlement in the heart of Louisiana, was rejected both by Guardoqui, and the authorities at New Orleans.

That Spain actually resolved on the non execution of the treaty, is fully explained in a letter written by governor Gayoso in June 1796, to a confidential friend, which has lately come to light. He was persuaded from many and powerful reasons, that it would never be carried into effect. He alleged that, at the time the treaty was signed, the affairs of Europe rendered the neutrality of the United States of the greatest importance to Spain, particularly as it had a tendency to destroy a plan in agitation to renew a destructive war. According to him, the object of Great Britain, in her treaty with the United States, about this period, was to attach them to her interests, and even to render them dependent on her, and therefore, the Spanish treaty of limits was made to counterbalance it; but as Great Britain had totally failed in her object, it was not the policy of Spain to regard her stipulations. Besides, it was expected, that several states would separate from the union, which would absolve Spain from her engagements; because, as her contract was made with the union, it would be no longer obligatory than while that union lasted: That Spain, contrary to her expectations, was not likely to derive any advantages from the treaty, and that her views and policy would be changed, particularly if an alteration took place in the political existence of the United States. He therefore concluded, that, all things considered, nothing more would result from the treaty than the free navigation of the Mississippi. These are some of the reasons urged by governor Gayoso against the fulfilment of mutual stipulations. They fully account for the obstacles thrown in the way of the demarcation of the boundary line, and likewise explain the objects of the several secret missions of a Spanish emissary to the territories of the United States on the western waters.

During the period of these local transactions, the conflicts in Europe began to trouble the repose of the United States. The belligerents paid little or no regard to the rights of neutrals, and prostrated them on the ocean. The privateers and armed ships of Spain, regardless of treaties, committed numerous and destructive spoliations on our commerce. That power most likely again contemplated the separation of the western people from the union; and there is but too much reason to believe, that its friends and agents in that quarter represented such a revolution as among probable events.

The Spaniards did not limit their outrages to our property on the ocean; they even denied us the right of deposit at New Orleans, and manifested a disposition to revive their former occlusions in their utmost extent. This produced a strong ferment in the public mind. The government remonstrated, but without any advantageous effect. This conduct was deemed the more culpable on the part of Spain, as she had just before agreed to allow us the free navigation of the Mississippi, and stipulated for the admission and deposit of our produce at New Orleans. A convincing proof was now exhibited, that no faith was to be reposed in the engagements of that power, and that something more substantial than treaty stipulations was necessary to ensure the enjoyment of our rights. The injury inflicted by these last restrictions was the more severely felt by the western states and territories, as their population and industry had greatly accumulated within a short period.

President Adams had been no stranger to the pernicious intrigues of foreign nations on our interior waters; and he readily perceived that, if justice was suffered to sleep, the same intrigues would be revived, and perhaps with more effect. As the arts of negociation had been exhausted to no purpose, he concerted a plan of redress, not less bold in conception, than difficult, and even delicate, in execution. Nothing less than the acquisition of New Orleans appeared to him in the least calculated to indemnify the United States for the losses they had sustained, and to appease the fears and inquietudes of the western people.*

The success of this enterprize almost wholly depended on conducting it in such a way, as not to awaken the suspicions of Spain; and happily our dispute with France served as a cover to the real design. The depredations committed on our commerce by that power, and the rejection of our ministers, excited a spirit of resentment in the public mind, and incredible efforts were made to inflame it. Hence twelve regiments were added to the army in 1799, which engaged to serve during the existing differences between the United States and the French republic.

When this additional army was nearly ready for the field, three of the old regiments, then stationed on the western waters, were ordered to assume a position near the mouth of the Ohio, and to keep their boats in constant repair for service. The intention was that, with the approbation of congress, these regiments should descend the Mississippi, and seize on New Orleans. The new levies were to march from the Atlantic states about the same time; and it was conceived probable, that they would be able to join their companions before the arrival of any Spanish troops in the country. It was expected that a successful expedition of this nature would induce Spain to accede to such terms as the United States were disposed to prescribe.

---

* As this portion of history may probably be new to most readers, it seems necessary to state, that the Author derived it from the late General Knox. This Gentleman was appointed a major-general on the new establishment; but considerations of a personal nature induced him to decline the service. It was understood, however, that he was well acquainted with the military views of our government at that period.

This plan of operations was well concerted, and must have succeeded if attempts had been made to carry it into effect. But the certainty of a change in the presidency, which took place soon after, induced Mr. Adams to recommend the dissolution of the twelve regiments and they were accordingly disbanded in the summer of 1800.

Mr. Jefferson, on his accession to the presidency in 1801, reiterated to Spain the infractions of the treaty, and demanded redress. She restored to us the right of deposit, but no longer claimed Louisiana as her own. On the first of October 1800, she entered into a conditional agreement to retrocede that colony to the French republic; and this retrocession actually took place by treaty on the twenty first of March 1801. The French made preparations to take possession of Louisiana, and an army of twenty five thousand men was designed for that country; but the fleet and army were suddenly blockaded in one of the ports of Holland by an English squadron.

This unexpected occurrence, joined to the gloomy aspect of affairs in Europe, and the want of funds to carry on a complicated war, induced the French republic to cede Louisiana to the United States, by treaty bearing date the thirtieth of April 1803. The Spanish authorities early in December of the same year, delivered possession of Lower Louisiana to M. Laussat, the French commissioner, and it was by him duly transferred on the twentieth of the same month, to the commissioners of the United States, governor Claiborne, and general Wilkinson. The author of these sketches was the constituted agent of the French republic in Upper Louisiana, and in her name received possession of that province on the ninth day of March 1804, and the next day transferred it to the United States.

Congress took an early opportunity to provide for the temporary administration of justice in Louisiana. An act was passed, vesting all the military, civil, and judicial powers, exercised by the Spanish authorities, in such person or persons, and to be exercised in such manner, as the president of the United States should direct. His excellency William C. C. Claiborne was appointed governor and intendant general of Louisiana; and the author of these sketches was appointed first civil commandant of Upper Louisiana, and legally commissioned to exercise the powers and prerogatives of the Spanish lieutenant governor of that province. On taking possession, he deemed it adviseable to publish the following circular address to the inhabitants:—

" The period has now arrived, when, in consequence of amicable negociations, Louisiana is in the possession of the United States. The plan of a permanent territorial government for you, is already under the consideration of congress, and will doubtless be completed as soon as the importance of the measure will admit. But, in the mean time, to secure your rights, and to prevent a delay of justice, his excellency William C. C. Claiborne, governor of the Mississippi territory, is invested with those authorities and powers (derived from an act of congress) usually exercised by the governor and intendant general under his catholic majesty; and permit me to add that, by virtue of the authority and power vested in him by the president of the United States, he has been pleased to commission me as first civil commandant of Upper Louisiana.

" Directed to cultivate friendship and harmony among you, and to make known the sentiments of the United States relative to the security and preservation of all your rights, both civil and religious, I know of no mode better calculated to begin the salutary work, than a circular address.

"It will not be necessary to advert to the various preliminary arrangements, which have conspired to place you in your present political situation; with these it is presumed you are already acquainted. Suffice it to observe, that Spain in 1800, and in 1801, retroceded the colony and province of Louisiana to France; and that France in 1803, conveyed the same territory to the United States, who are now in the peaceable and legal possession of it. These transfers were made with honorable views, and under such forms and sanctions as are usually practised among civilized nations.

"Thus you will perceive, that you are divested of the the character of subjects, and clothed with that of citizens. You now form an integral part of a great community, the powers of whose government are circumscribed and defined by charter, and the liberty of the citizen extended and secured. Between this government and its citizens, many reciprocal duties exist, and the prompt and regular performance of them is necessary to the safety and welfare of the whole. No one can plead exemption from these duties; they are equally obligatory on the rich and the poor; on men in power, as well as on those not intrusted with it: They are not prescribed as whim and caprice may dictate; on the contrary, they result from the actual or implied compact between society and its members, and are founded not only on the sober lessons of experience, but in the immutable nature of things. If therefore the government be bound to protect its citizens in the enjoyment of their liberty, property, and religion, the citizens are no less bound to obey the laws, and to aid the magistrate in the execution of them; to repel invasion, and in periods of public danger, to yield a portion of their time and exertions in defence of public liberty. In governments differently constituted, where popular elections are unknown, and where the exercise of power is confided to those of high birth, and great wealth, the public defence is committed to men who make the science of war an exclusive trade and profession ; but in all free republics, where the citizens are capacitated to elect, and to be elected, into offices of emolument and dignity, permanent armies of any considerable extent are justly deemed hostile to liberty ; and therefore the militia is considered as the palladium of their safety. Hence the origin of this maxim, that every soldier is a citizen, and every citizen a soldier.

" With these general principles before you, it is confidently expected, that you will not be less faithful to the United States, than you have been to his catholic majesty.

" Your local situation, the varieties in your language and education, have contributed to render your manners, laws, and customs, and even your prejudices, somewhat different from those of your neighbors, but not less favorable to virtue, and to good order in society. These deserve something more than mere indulgence; they shall be respected.

" If, in the course of former time, the people on different sides of the Mississippi, fostered national prejudices and antipathies against each other, suffer not these cankers of human happiness any longer to disturb your repose, or to awaken your resentment; draw the veil of oblivion over the past, and unite in pleasing anticipations of the future; embrace each other as brethren of the same mighty family, and think not, that any member of it can derive happiness from the misery or degradation of another.

"Little will the authority and example of the best magistrates avail, when the public mind becomes tainted with perverse sentiments, or languishes under an indifference to its true interests. Suffer not the pride of virtue, nor the holy fire of religion to become extinct. If these be different in their nature, they are necessary supports to each other. Cherish the sentiments of order and tranquillity, and frown on the disturbers of the public peace. Avoid as much as possible all legal contests; banish village vexation, and unite in the cultivation of the social and moral affections.

"Admitted as you are into the embraces of a wise and magnanimous nation, patriotism will gradually warm your breasts, and stamp its features on your future actions. To be useful, it must be enlightened; not the effect of passion, local prejudice, or blind impulse. Happy the people, who possess invaluable rights, and know how to exercise them to the best advantage; wretched are those, who do not think and act freely. It is a sure test of wisdom to honor and support the government under which you live, and to acquiesce in the decisions of the public will, when they be constitutionally expressed. Confide therefore in the justice and integrity of our federal president; he is the faithful guardian of the laws; he entertains the most beneficent views relative to the glory and happiness of this territory; and the merit derived from the acquisition of Louisiana, without any other, will perpetuate his fame to posterity. Place equal confidence in all the other constituted authorities of the union. They will protect your rights, and indeed your feelings, and all the tender felicities and sympathies, so dear to rational and intelligent creatures. A very short experience of their equitable and pacific policy, will enable you to view them in their proper light. I flatter myself that you will give their measures a fair trial, and not precipitate yourselves into conclusions, which you may afterwards see cause to retract. The first official acts of my present station, authorized by high authority, will confirm these remarks.

" The United States, in the acquisition of Louisiana, were actuated by just and liberal views. Hence the admission of an article in the treaty of cession, the substance of which is, that the inhabitants of the ceded territory shall be incorporated into the union, and admitted as soon as possible to the enjoyment of all the rights, advantages and immunities of citizens of the United States; and, in the mean time, be maintained and protected in the free enjoyment of their liberty, property, and religion.

" From these cursory hints you will be enabled to comprehend your present political situation, and to anti_cipate the future destinies of your country. You may soon expect the establishment of a territorial government, administered by men of wisdom and integrity, whose salaries will be paid out of the treasury of the United States. From your present population, and the rapidity of its increase, this territorial establishment must soon be succeeded by your admission as a state into the Federal Union. At that period, you will be at liberty to try an experiment in legislation, and to frame such a government as may best comport with your local interests, manners, and customs; popular suffrage will be its basis. The enaction of laws, and the appointment of judges to expound them, and to carry them into effect, are among the first privileg of organized society. Equal to these, indeed, and connected with them, is the inestimable right of trial by jury. The forms of judicial processes, and the rules for the admission of testimony in courts of justice, when firmly established, are of great and obvious advantage to the people. It is also of importance, that a distinction be made between trials of a capital nature, and those of an inferior degree, as likewise between all criminal and civil contestations. In fine, Upper Louisiana, from its climate, population, soil, and productions, and from other natural advantages attached to it, will, in all human probability, soon become a star of no inconsiderable magnitude in the American constellation.

"Be assured that the United States feel all the ardor for your interests, which a warm attachment can inspire. I have reason to believe that it will be among some of their first objects, to ascertain and confirm your land titles. They well know the deranged state of these titles, and of the existence of a multitude of equitable claims under legal surveys, where no grants or concessions have been procured. What ultimate measures will be taken on this subject, does not become me to conjecture; but thus much I will venture to affirm, that the most ample justice will be done; and that, in the final adjustment of claims, no settler or landholder will have any just cause to complain. Claimants of this description have hitherto invariably experienced the liberality of government; and surely it will not be less liberal to the citizens of Upper Louisiana, who form a strong cordon across an exposed frontier of a vast empire, and are entitled by solemn stipulations to all the rights and immunities of freemen.

"My duty, not more indeed than my inclination, urges me to cultivate friendship and harmony among you, and and between you and the United States. I suspect my talents to be unequal to the duties which devolve on me in the organization and temporary administration of the government; the want of a proper knowledge of your laws and language, is among the difficulties I have to encounter. But my ambition and exertions bear some proportion to

the honor conferred on me ; and the heavy responsibility
attached to my office, admonishes me to be prudent and
circumspect. Inflexible justice and impartiality shall guide
me in all my determinations. If, however, in the discharge of a variety of complicated duties, almost wholly
prescribed by the civil law and the code of the Indies, I be
led into error, consider it as involuntary, and not as the effect
of inattention, or of any exclusive favors or affections. Destined to be the temporary guardian of the rights and liberties of at least ten thousand people, I may not be able
to gratify the just expectations of all; but your prosperity
and happiness will claim all my time and talents ; and no
earthly enjoyment could be more complete, than that derived from your public and individual security, and from
the increase of your opulence and power."

SKETCHES OF LOUISIANA.

CHAPTER II.

OF THE FLORIDAS.

THE proximity of the Floridas to the United States, and our claim to no inconsiderable portion of them, render some account of them of the greatest importance at this time. It must be confessed, however, that the subject is barren of materials. That extensive country, nearly destitute of roads, and most parts of it equally destitute of inhabitants, offers no allurements to men of enterprise; it is not calculated to reward the trouble and expense of itinerant excursions, nor to gratify the curiosity of the speculative philosopher. Its isolated position, and want of commerce, have likewise contributed to conceal it from the eye of observation, and to render it almost as little known at the present day, as it was two hundred years ago.

While the French were in possession of Louisiana, all that part of Florida, between the Perdido and Mississippi, was included in that province. The remainder was in the possession of the Spaniards, and extended along the gulf and Atlantic coast from the Perdido to the claims of the English on the north of them. West Florida owes its name to the English government; and when this province was created, the name of Louisiana became extinct in that quarter.

Antecedent to 1763, while the Spaniards were in possession of what is now called East Florida, a dispute was long maintained relative to the boundaries between them, and the then British colonies. As early as 1604, attempts were made, without effect, to adjust the pretensions of the two powers in America. These attempts were revived in 1670; and as neither party was disposed to yield its pretensions, it was finally stipulated, that the English should continue to occupy *what they then possessed*. This by no means served to compose the differences; for the southern limits of Carolina according to the second charter of Charles the second, extended to the twenty ninth degree of north latitude, which included the whole of the Spanish settlements in Florida, and even part of the peninsula. Besides, the immense tract of uninhabited territory between the settlements of the two nations, was claimed by both, and perhaps with equal pretensions. The charter of Georgia was granted in 1732, which bounded that colony to the southward on the most southern stream of the Altamaha. With this boundary the Spaniards appear to have been satisfied; but they strongly contended for the tract between that river and the St. Mary's, included in the Carolina charter, of which general Oglethorpe was directed to take and keep possession. It was, however, the policy of Great Britain to avoid a rupture on account of this boundary; and so late as 1756, she directed some settlers, who had clandestinely planted themselves on the St. Mary's, to be removed by force. At the peace of 1763, when Florida passed under the dominion of Great Britain, the river St. Mary's was established as the boundary line between that province and Georgia.

One of the first acts of the English, after Florida passed into their hands, was to fix its boundaries and to divide it into two colonies, denominated east and west Florida. The north boundary of East Florida, was the river St. Mary's from the sea to its source, and thence westward to that part of the Apalachicola, where it is joined by Flint river. The north line of West Florida was fixed on the Mississippi, at the thirty first degree, and thence due east to the Apalachicola, and thence down that river to the sea. But in 1764, under an apprehension suggested by the board of trade, that this line would not include the Mobile, the northern boundary of that colony was extended to the mouth of the Yazous, in about thirty two degrees twenty eight minutes north latitude, and thence due east to the Apalachicola. Each of these colonies had a governor, appointed by the crown, and a legislature chosen by the people; their laws approached as near as circumstances would permit, to the laws of England. These arrangements continued till the conquest of West Florida by the Spaniards in the time of our revolution. At the peace of 1783, Great Britain relinquished to the crown of Spain, both the Floridas without any specific boundaries, and on the same day ceded to the United States all the territory to the north of the thirty first degree; so that Spain had at least a plausible claim to all the territory below the Yazous river; and hence a foundation was laid for a dispute between us and that power, which was ultimately adjusted by treaty.

That the reader may become the better acquainted with the country we have undertaken to notice, a rapid geographical sketch of the two Floridas will be given; after which the several kinds of land, and the nature of the climate, will come under consideration.

The Floridas are bounded north, partly on the thirty first degree, and partly on the southern boundary of Georgia; east on the Atlantic; south on the gulf; and west on the Mississippi. We have no accurate data for their length or breadth: The former, exclusive of the peninsula, and following the sinuosities of the coast, may be estimated at about eight hundred miles; the latter will probably average from seventy to eighty miles. The peninsula is narrow, and stretches in a southern direction about four hundred miles into the gulf; the extremity of which is within one hundred miles of Cuba.

West Florida, as designated by Great Britain, is situated between the Apalachicola and the Mississippi, and contains about four hundred miles of sea coast. To accommodate the different settlements, formed mostly on the opposite extremities of this tract, the Spanish government divided it into two districts. Pearl river forms the boundary between them. That on the east retains the name of Florida; that on the west, extending to the Mississippi, is called New Feliciana. This district is mostly populated from the United States. It contains a few French, mostly planted at Baton Rouge; as likewise some English and Scotch, who came out under the British government. The number of souls may be estimated at about twelve thousand. The inhabitants are mostly situated on, or in the neighbourhood of the Mississippi. They formerly cultivated indigo, and pursued the lumber trade; but these articles are now nearly abandoned, and the planters have turned their attention to the culture of cotton.

The lands in this district are unquestionably the most valuable, in an agricultural point of view, of any in the two Floridas. They are generally elevated, except near the coast, and yield large crops of cotton. In fine, all the productions common to the Mississippi territory and lower

Louisiana, except sugar, are cultivated here with success. The district is watered by the river Amit, which falls into the Ibberville, and by Thompson's creek, and Bayou Sara, which join the Mississippi, and are navigable some distance into the country. A variety of creeks and bayous of less note are formed along the coast, which will serve to facilitate the exportation of produce as soon as the lands about them become settled.

The capital of New Feliciana is Baton Rouge, situated on the east bank of the Mississippi, and about fifteen miles above the Ibberville. On ascending from New Orleans, the first high grounds commence at this place. The general elevation of them is from twenty five to thirty feet above the highest floods; and they alternately recede from the Mississippi, and approach that river, forming occasional indentations of swamp, till intersected by the thirty first degree. The inhabitants of Baton Rouge are mostly French. They formed a settlement here as early as 1722. The fort is in a ruinous condition. The officer who commands it, has the title of governor, and administers the Spanish laws in the district.

Pearl river annually inundates large tracts of land, particularly near its confluence with the gulf. It heads in the high grounds near the Chickasaw country, and may be made navigable for at least one hundred and fifty miles. The country on the west side of it along the coast, is generally low, and covered with swamps, or pine barrens, except were it is watered by creeks and bayous. On each side of these are found some oak bottoms, which are dry part of the year, and considered as fertile. A few indigent settlers are scattered here and there along the coast. They raise some corn and cattle, and manufacture lime from a species of clam shell, found in such immense banks as to justify the expectation, that this article will not be exhausted for many years to come. They likewise manufacture considerable quantities of pitch and tar,

These articles are transported about thirty miles across lake Pontchartraine to New Orleans, and from thence no small part of them find their way to the Havanna and La Vera Cruz. The growth on the more elevated grounds near the lake, is pine; and this kind of wood more or less covers the ridges for some distance into the interior.

From Pearl river to the Apalachicola the lands on the coast are similar to those just noticed, except that they are of a more spungy nature, and a greater proportion of them covered with water. The high grounds are sandy, and covered with pine. The low grounds, which embrace much the largest district of country, are either occasionally covered with water, or composed of swamps and marshes, and most of the year impassible by man or beast. These extend along the coast, and up the rivers and other water courses some distance into the interior. The scattered tracts of high ground, capable of cultivation, are so isolated among the swamps as to be rendered inaccessible, except by water. This immense coast, if we except Mobile and Pensacola, contains not much more than one hundred families. They are mostly planted along the bays of St. Louis and New Baloxi, at the mouth of the Pascagola, and some other water courses. The whole of that tract to the eastward of Pensacola, may be considered as an uninhabited wilderness.

The tract under consideration is watered by a number of rivers; such as the Pascagola, the Mobile and its numerous branches, the Escambia, and other streams falling into the bay of Pensacola, the Apalachicola and its several branches, and a variety of smaller streams, which intersect the low country in almost every direction. Some of these rivers head in the back part of Georgia, and others in Tennessee. They are of infinite importance to our settlers above the line of demarcation, and this importance daily increases with the increase of population. The duties exacted by the Spaniards on our imports and exports, are severely felt. They serve to check the prosperity of the interior country, to irritate the minds of the settlers, and to paralyze the hand of industry.

The free navigation of the Mobile river is of great consequence. Some of the branches of this river rise in Tennessee, and one of them interlocks with the waters of the Tennessee river. Indeed, the navigable waters of these two rivers approach within nine miles of each other. The Mobile affords a boat navigation of three hundred and fifty miles; and coasting vessels may ascend above the line of demarcation, to fort Stoddert, about which we have some extensive and wealthy settlements. Just below this line, the river is separated into two or three channels, forming in its progress several large islands, one of which is about thirty miles long, and eight miles broad, yielding large crops of cotton, and calculated for the culture of rice. The city of Mobile, as it is called by way of eminence, stands on the western channel, about thirty miles from the gulf, and in thirty degrees forty minutes north latitude. It was founded by the French in 1702; at which time Isle Dauphin, situated near the mouth of the harbor, became the seat of government for Louisiana, where it remained till it was removed to New Orleans in 1722. The city now contains about seventy or eighty houses only; some of them exhibit the appearance of wealth. The inhabitants are a mixture of French, Scotch, and Irish. Near the lower end of the city stands a regular fortress of brick, erected, or rather repaired, by the British government; the area of which is of considerable extent, containing a spacious square of barracks for the accommodation of troops. The trade has much declined, and the little that remains is almost wholly engrossed by an English firm. The city is surrounded by swamps, and intermittents are prevalent during the last of summer, and the beginning of autumn.

The town of Pensacola, at present the capital of the Floridas, was founded by the Spaniards in 1696, and intended by them to frustrate the settlement of the French in Louisiana. It is situated on the gulf of Mexico, at the head of a delightful bay or bason, formed by the Escambia and some other rivers, about sixty miles to the eastward of the city of Mobile, and in thirty degrees twenty five minutes, north latitude. It stands at the foot of gale hills, extending about one mile along the beach of the bay, in the form of a crescent and nearly surrounded by two rivulets of fresh water. In 1772, the town contained about one hundred and eighty habitations; but since the Spaniards conquered it from the English in 1781, it has gradually declined. In 1794, the population did not exceed four hundred, exclusive of the military, and retainers of the government. Many of the houses and public structures were formerly spacious and elegant; but some of them already exhibit the appearance of decay. This place is plentifully supplied with shell and other fish, and the climate about it is deemed healthful. The bar at the entrance of the harbor has no more than four fathoms of water over it. A fortification placed on Rose's island, and another on the main opposite to it, would effectually prevent the entrance of armed vessels into the bay, and of course defend the town from maritime attacks.

The country about Pensacola is barren, mostly composed of sand hills; it will not even admit the growth of garden vegetables, except where vegetable mould is collected, and mixed with the sand. The same may be said of the lands about the mouth of the Mobile and the Perdido. The lands, however in the rear of these places, and at some distance from them, yield all the necessaries, and some of the conveniences and luxuries of life. The country is particularly adapted to the raising of cattle, and vast droves of them are scattered over it.

St. Augustine is situated on the Atlantic coast in about thirty degrees, or, as some make it, twenty nine degrees forty minutes north latitude, and almost surrounded by water. It is of an oblong figure, intersected by four streets, which cut each other at right angles. It is enclosed with a ditch, and strongly fortified. In addition to a formidable bastion, it is defended by a castle, called fort St. John, and all the works are well supplied with ordnance. It has a church and monastery of the order of its name.

This town anciently contained nine hundred houses, and nearly four thousand inhabitants. In 1772, it was reduced to three hundred houses, and one thousand inhabitants: But the apparent stability of the Spanish government since 1783, has been of great advantage to it; symptoms of its ancient opulence and splendor begin to be manifested. The English, while it was in their possession, erected a government house with materials procured in New York, as likewise spacious barracks for the use of the military, calculated to accommodate five regiments of men.

The site of St. Augustine is extremely pleasant and healthful, and the inhabitants are abundantly supplied with fresh water. They generally live to a good old age, and are seldom attacked by dangerous diseases. Multitudes of invalids from the islands rendezvous here, and no doubt St. Augustine will soon attract the notice of our gouty valetudinarians in the north. There is some good land about the town, which is highly cultivated. The swamps and lagoons are too remote from the population to prove injurious. Fish of all kinds are found here in plenty. The harbor is penetrated by two channels, occasioned by breakers, and the bars of each afford no more than eight feet of water.

At what time the country about St. Augustine was first settled, is not certainly known; but it has experienced many vicissitudes from war, and often changed masters. It was attacked and destroyed by the French protestants as early as 1562; who, in their turn, experienced a similar fate three years afterwards. The French obtained possession of it again in 1567, when they annihilated the Spanish settlements, and then hastily retired never more to return. The Spaniards first planted themselves at the mouth of St. Nicholas' creek; but they soon discovered a more eligible position, to which they removed, and founded St. Augustine. From some inscriptions remaining on the houses, it appears that they were built in 1571. This town was attacked by the English in 1586, under sir Francis Drake, when the Spaniards fled, leaving fourteen cannon behind them, as also their military chest, containing two thousand pounds in specie. In 1665, it was plundered by captain Davis at the head of the buckaneers. At this period the town was defended by a regular octagonal fort, with a tower bastion at each angle. It was again attacked in 1702, by the English and Indians under governor Moore of Carolina, who destroyed some farms and small villages; but after a siege of three months he was obliged to make the best of his way over land to the English settlements. In 1740, general Oglethorpe, with a small fleet, together with the militia of Carolina and Georgia, and a body of Cherokee Indians, attacked and bombarded the town and castle; but his exertions to reduce the place proved ineffectual. Another attempt was made on it during the American revolution; but without success. If this place be well defended, it will be no easy matter to gain possession of it.

As the Floridas have often changed masters, some variety in the population may be expected. The Spaniards were the first to make permanent settlements in them. The peace of 1763, put them in possession of Great Britain, when a number of English, Scotch, and Irish, were incorporated with the ancient inhabitants. They also received an accession during the American revolution, when many of those disaffected to our cause, obtained refuge in the Floridas; and the proximity of our settlements has prompted many of our citizens since that period to become Spanish subjects.

One remarkable fact relative to the population of the Floridas must not escape notice. While these were in possession of the English, a plan was concerted to entice a colony of Greeks into the country. Sir William Duncan and doctor Turnbull were at the bottom of this transaction. The country was represented to the Greeks in the most favorable light; they were promised fertile fields and lands in abundance, and also transportation and subsistence. Hence fifteen hundred souls were deluded from the islands in Greece and Italy, and landed in East Florida. They were planted at a place called New Smyrna, situated about seventy miles to the southward of St. Augustine. But what was their surprise when, instead of cultivated fields, they were ushered into a desolate wilderness, without the means of support! What mortified them still more was, that some of them were tantalized with the use of rented lands for ten years, at the expiration of which they reverted again to the original proprietors, when the poor settlers were once more reduced to poverty and misery. Some of them indeed could not obtain land on any terms. Hence they were obliged to labor for the planters in the character of slaves, and to experience hunger and nakedness. Overseers were placed over them, and whenever the usual task was not completed, they were goaded with the lash. Families were not allowed to live separate from each other; but a number of them were crouded together in one mess, and condemned to promiscuous repose. The poor wretches were not even allowed to procure fish for themselves, although the sea at their feet was full of them. People were forbidden to furnish them with victuals; severe punishments were decreed against those who gave, and those who received the charitable boon. Under this treatment many of them died, especially the old people. At length in 1769, seized with despair and sensible of no other alternative than escape or death, they rose on their cruel tyrants, and made themselves masters of some small vessels. But their designs were frustrated by the prompt exertions of the military; and this revolt closed with the deaths of five of the unhappy ringleaders.

This transaction is so contrary to the reputed humanity of the English nation, that it requires some credulity to believe the solemn report of a British officer, who was an eye witness to what we have related.

Various other settlements are formed along the gulf and Atlantic coast, and on their numerous rivers, particularly to the north of the twenty eighth degree. The inhabitants have either fixed themselves contiguous to navigation, or resorted to the rich bottoms, which bound some of the water courses.

East Florida has but few large rivers. The St. Mary's and Apalachicola wash the northern and southern extremities of it. The St John's, which falls into the bay of Apalache, is nearly two hundred miles long, and presents an easy communication with St. Augustine. Indian river stretches along the peninsula in a longitudinal direction, and may prove useful at some future period. Numerous streams of less note penetrate the shores of the coast, affording a boat navigation from twenty to thirty miles, and will one day bear to the ocean the opulence of the back country.

In the two Floridas are to be found a variety of soils; some equal to any in the world; others indifferent; and immense tracts exist which are of no value. Those the best acquainted with the lands, usually enumerate seven different kinds.

The first is denominated pine barrens, which extend over almost the whole of the peninsula, and are frequently found in other parts of the country. These lands mostly

consist of a grey or white sand, or of a red or yellow
gravel. They produce vast quantities of yellow and pitch
pine, which are suitable for boards, timber, and various
other articles. They also produce a variety of shrubs,
and a kind of wire grass, which yield sustenance to an
immense number of cattle. Intermixed with the pines
on the more elevated grounds, are the horse chesnut, and
several kinds of oak. In wet seasons, these sandy and
gravelly soils are not altogether useless in another point
of view; orchards of peach and mulberry flourish remarkably well on them. From three to five feet beneath the
surface is a stiff clay. Some of these lands are extremely
rocky, especially near the extremity of the peninsula.
In West Florida this kind of land affords many symptoms
of iron ore.

The second is called hummock land, because it rises in
tufts or small mounts among the pines. Most of the upland in the northern parts, remote from the sea, is of this
kind. The soil of it is various; in some places composed
of white sand; in others of a mixture of clay and black
sand; also a kind of ochre, and a stratum of black mould.
Lands of the latter description are very fruitful, particularly in cotton, indigo, potatoes, and pulse.

The third is called prairie, because it is destitute of
timber; and this is of two kinds. The first is to be
found in the pine barrens; and as it is covered with sand,
it is unfit for tillage. The second is found on the high
grounds, and are similar to those scattered over many
parts of the western country, particularly Louisiana.
Some of them are of considerable extent; their soil is
luxuriant, mixed with shells, flint, chalk, and marl.
They produce a wild grass, of which cattle and other
animals are extremely fond.

The swamps, as distinguished from marshes, compose
the fourth kind. These are divided into river and inland
swamps. The latter are the most valuable, because they

produce large crops of rice, and in some instances the best cotton, corn, and indigo in the country. The grounds in them are composed of either clay or sand, and generally of both. The soil is prolific, and produces trees, particularly cypress of the largest kind. In wet seasons they are filled with water. Were they properly drained, perhaps hemp might be cultivated on them to advantage. The natural growth of the river swamps consists of several species of cypress, canes, reeds, withes, vines, briars; and these are so numerous, and so matted together, as to be impenetrable to man or beast.

The fifth is composed of marshes; and these are of four kinds: Two of them are occasionally covered with salt water, and two with fresh water. Some of the former are soft, and consist of a very moist clay or mud, and have never been converted to any useful purposes. Others again consist of a marly clay, and in dry seasons are very hard. These afford pasture for graminivorous animals, though the milk and flesh of them imbibe a bad taste, and at some seasons cannot be eaten. The fresh water marshes are similar to those already described, except that they are not impregnated with saline particles. The hard ones, with very little labor, may be rendered fit for culture. The soft ones require much more labor, but they would be the most productive. They produce plenty of wild oats *(zizania aquatica)* of which the Indians frequently make bread.

The sixth is denominated galls; and these are of two kinds. The first are called bay galls, and are properly water courses, covered with a spungy earth, and mixed and bound with vegetable fibres. They tremble like a jelly for a considerable distance about the spot impressed; like quicksands they gradually absorb whatever be placed on them. Cattle, horses, and other animals, are often swallowed, and it is frequently dangerous to attempt a passage over them. They produce a stately tree, called the loblolly bay, and a variety of vines, briars, thorny withes, and on their margins a species of summer cane. When drained they produce rice, and are sometimes used for pasture grounds. The second are called cypress galls, the soil of which is mostly composed of sand. They produce a kind of swamp cypress, as also plenty of wild grass. All these galls contain a species of very white clay, which is manufactured into utensils of various kinds: They also contain great quantities of nitrous and bituminous earths, fossils, marls, boles, magnetic and other iron ore; as likewise lead, coal, chalk, freestone, chrystals, and white topazes. Ambergris, and natural pitch, or *asphaltos*, are found among these galls.

The seventh is composed of the more elevated grounds, commonly called uplands, which extend along the heads of some of the water courses, near the line of demarcation. They are generally covered with large trees of different species, similiar to those in Georgia and the Mississippi territory.

Part of the natural growth of the country has already been noticed. It produces no less than eight kinds of oak, one of which is the live oak; plenty of white and black walnut, hickory, chesnut; three kinds of mulberry; four kinds of the magnolia; orange and fig trees, peccon, persimmon, and sycamore; as also a vast variety of plums, and other indigenous fruit, several kinds of which are delicious.

No part of the world can boast of finer esculent plants. Flora and Pomona are liberal in their gifts. The products of the torrid and temperate zones are cultivated with success, particularly in the peninsula.

West Florida, as already hinted, exhibits the greatest fertility. Wheat grows here, as also barley, oats, corn, peas, buckwheat, rye, and rice; these flourish best along the water courses. All the different soils are adapted to some kinds of grass. Apple trees are common; but the peach and pear trees yield the most abundantly. The country produces plenty of indigo, flax and tobacco; but cotton is now the staple commodity. Oranges and olives are cultivated with success. St. John's river, and some of the lakes, are festooned with orange groves. The annona, lime, and mahoe, are indigenous, as also many medicinal plants. Various articles, usually denominated naval stores, are produced here; such as hemp, pitch, tar, turpentine, and shipping timber. The lumber trade has flourished in this quarter for nearly a century. Vast quantities of fish are cured on the coast, suitable for the West India markets; such as the drum, carp, pampanos, soles, sea trout, the roes of the mullet and black drum. Bees are plentious in the western and southern parts of the United States, the Floridas, and Louisiana, and they usually precede the whites in their progress into the interior.

The water, as to taste and quality, is various. Salt, brackish, nitrous, and sulphureous springs, are scattered about the country; as also salt and fresh lakes, lagoons, and rivers. Springs of a fresh and pure quality abound in the more elevated parts of the country, and contribute to the convenience and health of the inhabitants.

The climate in the Floridas is more changeable than that in the eastern and middle states, but much less on the extremes. The heavy winds, charged with moisture, from the coast of Labrador and Nova Scotia, which rage with violence in New England, are rendered less troublesome as they approach the borders of East Florida; and the thick forests over which they pass in their way to West Florida, in a great measure deprive them of their humidity and cold.

In the peninsula the climate is deemed remarkably pleasant; it is more temperate on the west than on the east side of it. On the east side the trade winds prevail, and cool the air in summer; but on the west side the air is refrigerated by the breezes from the Apalachean mountains, which are still more agreeably temperate. The most serene weather is to the south of the twenty seventh degree, where frosts seldom make their appearance. Here the products of the more northern climates mix with those of the tropics. During the summer, heavy gales of wind beat against the east side of the peninsula. The west side is subject to dreadful squalls, and hardly a day passes without one or more of them, especially if the wind be from between the south east and south-south west; but they are generally of short duration. Thunder and lightning are less frequent and violent here than in Georgia and the Carolinas.

The climate in West Florida, with one or two exceptions, is similar to that just mentioned. Frosts are frequent, and of such severity as to kill fruit and vegetables. At the close of winter in this quarter, the winds are mostly at west, and north west. In the spring, and the early part of autumn, they are usually at east. Just before and after the autumnal equinox, storms and hurricanes are common along the gulf; they sometimes extend a considerable distance up the Mississippi, though their violence abates as they recede from the coast. These tempests swell the rivers, and cover the low lands with water. Here the south, and south west winds occasion damp weather, perhaps because they traverse the gulf. The south east and north east winds are cool and dry, perhaps because they sweep over extensive forests and sandy plains. The winds between north and west are still more salubrious. The mercury in Farenheit seldom falls below thirty degrees, and seldom rises higher than ninety four degrees in the shade.

The extremes of the climate are somewhat greater in the Mississippi territory. It has been observed that, of late years in this quarter, the summers have been warmer, and the winters colder, than formerly. Orange trees, and other tender exotics were once cultivated here to some advantage; but, for some years past, they have suffered from the frosts. In former years the mercury never fell below twenty six degrees; latterly it has sunk to seventeen, and in December 1800, to twelve degrees. In winter the north west winds are cold and dry. East winds, for the most part, either produce rain, or create considerable humidity in the air. The north east and south east winds are also charged with vapors. The north winds usually produce sleet and snow. The southerly winds begin to prevail in February, when the spring commences. During the summer they are generally from the south east and south west; yet they are frequently known to follow the course of the sun, blowing from the north east in the morning, and dying away at south west in the evening. About eight or nine o'clock at night the cool zephyrs from the west and north west begin to rise, and brace the human system, rather too much relaxed by the heats of the day. These heats begin to be oppressive in May, and continue till about the last of August; and during this time the mercury vibrates between ninety and ninety six degrees in the shade. From about the middle of September to about the twentieth of November, the weather is excellent, the mercury varying between sixty five and seventy degrees, and the winds blowing from every point of the compass, attended with frequent showers of rain. The winter commences the last of November, when the mornings and evenings begin to be cold, and sometimes frosty. The frost first appears in the valleys along the rivers and streams, and a difference of ten degrees is frequently known to exist between the atmosphere of these and that on the high grounds, at the distance of three miles only. At this season of the year the weather is changeable, and perhaps in no part of the world is the human frame more susceptible of it. It is apt to produce pluretic and other inflammatory diseases. Bilious fevers sometimes make their appearance, and intermittents are endemical. No great quantity of snow falls in this country, though seldom a winter passes without some.

Hence we perceive that the climate in the Mississippi territory is materially different from that of West Florida, though about a degree only to the north of it; and that some of the winds in the two places, blowing from the same points, produce opposite and contrary effects. This problem is well worthy of investigation.

The prevalent winds in East Florida are nearly similar to those in West Florida, though their effects are rather different. The gales from the east and north east are more severely felt, while those from the opposite points make much less impression. The air is clear and pure; heavy dews fall at night; fogs are seldom seen, except on St. John's river. The spring and autumn are dry, though the temperature of the latter is variable. The winter commences about the last of November, with wet and windy weather. From October to June the climate is generally excellent. The months of July, August, and September, are extremely hot and uncomfortable; but the temperature is less variable here than in Georgia, and frosts are much more rare. After storms, attended with thunder and lightning, the wind generally veers to the the west, and is very welcome to all; particularly to those whose bodies are exhausted by the heats.

From the first of July to the middle of October, fevers are prevalent in both the Floridas. They are usually preceded by heavy rains, and sultry weather. Those of plethoric habits, and sanguine constitutions, are the most liable to be attacked. Inflammatory fevers of domestic origin are rarely experienced. The yellow fever occasionally makes its appearance; but it has always been traced to the islands, particularly to the Havanna. Intermittents are endemical, and often prove tedious; but they commonly yield to the prescriptions of skilful physicians.

It has already been hinted, that the transitions in the temperature of the weather were much less on the extremes in the Floridas than in the eastern states. This circumstance is particularly favorable to health along the the gulf, where the heat is considerable, and where sudden transitions in the temperature of the atmosphere would generate dangerous diseases. If men in this quarter avoid intemperate excesses, fatigues, and the violence of the heats, no great danger is to be apprehended.

Before we conclude, it seems necessary to observe, that the English, when they took possession of the Floridas, endeavoured to infuse an agricultural spirit into the minds of the people. They were forward to set the example, and commenced improvements in the culture of such articles as were of commercial importance, particularly rice and cotton. In a very few years the face of the Floridas was changed; and had they remained much longer in the country, agriculture and population would have arrived at their maximum. They found the Spaniards without agriculture, and without energy of character sufficient to stimulate them to it. They awakened them from the slumbers of more than two centuries, and surprised them with the advantages of manual industry, properly directed; yet these renovated beings, on the departure of the English, resumed their ancient habits, and sunk again into inaction; in which they still remain in all the pride of poverty, and overwhelmed in the pleasures of a negative existence!

SKETCHES OF LOUISIANA.

CHAPTER III.

EXTENT AND BOUNDARIES OF LOUISIANA.*

THE discovery of the Mississippi by Ferdinand de Soto in 1541, was never considered by Spain as authorizing a claim to any part of the country about it. The subsequent discoveries and settlements of the French were ultimately acquiesced in by that power.

Among civilized nations the right derived from discovery is as conclusive and indisputable at that derived from purchase, particularly if it be succeeded by possession. We shall soon discover the extent of the claims of France in Louisiana, and distinguish those of a legitimate from those of a doubtful nature.

---

* A paper on this subject was published by the author in the Aurora in October 1806, which is introduced in this chapter, though with many additions and alterations, made in 1809.

By the treaty of St. Idelfonso, dated the first of October 1800, Spain " promises and engages on her part, to " retrocede to the French republic, six months after the " full and entire execution of the conditions and stipula- " tions therein contained relative to the duke of Parma, " the colony or province of Louisiana, with the same " extent *that it actually has in the hands of Spain, that it* " *had when France possessed it*, and such as it should be " after the treaties subsequently entered into between " Spain and other states." This clause was confirmed and enforced by a subsequent treaty, between the same powers, made at Madrid, March the twenty first 1801; it also makes a part of the treaty of cession of April the thirtieth, 1803, between the French republic and the United States, and is particularly referred to as descriptive of the boundaries of Louisiana. These boundaries underwent no alteration in the hands of Spain, except what resulted from the provisions of the treaty of 1795, between that power and the United States.

The words " that it actually has in the hands of Spain," and " that it had when France possessed it," seem to bear on the face of them a considerable degree of diplomatic uncertainty: A cause of dispute appears to be the object of both parties; and each was aware that the strongest would prevail. But the meaning undoubtedly was, and this corresponds with the known rules of construction, that the French republic should possess Louisiana in its *fullest extent*. All the territory between the Mississippi and the Perdido was included in Louisiana at the time Spain acquired it by the treaty of 1762, and though the transfer extinguished the name, it did not obliterate *what France possessed* prior to that period.

If indeed the boundaries of Louisiana were limitted to the territory in the *actual possession* of France in 1762, the question about them would hardly admit of dispute, But the terms of the treaty of retrocession in 1800, which are incorporated in the treaty of cession of 1803, and make a part of it, place the dispute on a very different ground, and much more in favor of the United States. The real question now is, *What was the extent of Louisiana when France possessed it ?* The import of the words in the retrocession fairly includes, *what she had a right to possess*, not simply what she actually did possess at that period.

The boundaries of Louisiana may be partly ascertained by a reference to the grant made of the commerce of that country to Crozat in 1712. This document is the more important, as it probably contains the first formal and official recognition of some of these boundaries; and such parts of it as serve to illustrate them, will now be quoted.

" LOUIS (the fourteenth) by the grace of
" God, king of France and Navarre : To all who shall
" see these presents, greeting. The care we have always
" had to procure the welfare and advantage of our subjects,
" having induced us, notwithstanding the almost continual
" wars which we have been engaged to support from the
" beginning of our reign, to seek all possible opportuni-
" ties of enlarging and extending the trade of our Ame-
" rican colonies, we did in the year 1683, give our orders
" to undertake a discovery of the countries and lands,
" which are situated in the northern parts of America be-
" tween New France (Canada) and New Mexico. And
" the Sieur de la Salle, to whom we committed that
" enterprise, having had success enough to confirm the
" belief, that a communication might be settled from
" New France to the gulf of Mexico by means of large
" rivers ; this obliged us immediately after the peace of
" Ryswic (in 1697) to give orders for the establishing a
" colony there, (under Ibberville in 1699) and maintaining
" a garrison, *which has kept and preserved the possession*

"*we had taken in the year* 1683, *of the lands, coasts and islands* which are situated in the gulf of Mexico, between *Carolina on the east, and old and new Mexico on the west.* But a new war breaking out in Europe shortly after, there was no possibility till now of reaping from that new colony the advantages that might have been expected from thence, because the private men who are concerned in the sea trade, were all under engagements with the other colonies, which they have been obliged to follow : And whereas upon the information we have received concerning the disposition and situation of the said countries *known, at present by the name of the province of Louisiana,* we are of opinion, that there may be established therein a considerable commerce, so much the more advantageous to our kingdom in that there has been hitherto a necessity of fetching from foreigners the greatest part of the commodities which may be brought from thence, and because in exchange thereof we need carry thither nothing but the commodities of the growth and manufacture of our own kingdom; we have resolved to grant the commerce of the country of Louisiana, to the Sieur Anthony Crozat, our counsellor, secretary of the household, crown and revenue, to whom we entrust the execution of this project. We are the more readily inclined thereto, because his zeal, and the singular knowledge he has acquired in maritime commerce, encourage us to hope for as good success as he has hitherto had in the divers and sundry enterprises he has gone upon, and which has procured to our kingdom great quantities of gold and silver in such conjunctures as have rendered them very welcome to us. For these reasons, being desirous to shew our favor to him, and to regulate the conditions upon which we mean to grant him the said commerce, after having deliberated the affair in our council, of our own certain knowledge, full power, and

" royal authority, we by these presents, signed by our
" hand, have appointed, and do appoint, the said Sieur
" Crozat to carry on a trade in all the lands possessed by
" us, and bounded by *New Mexico*, and by the English
" of Carolina, all the establishments, ports, havens, rivers,
" *and particularly the port and haven of Isle Dauphin*,
" heretofore called Massacre; the river St. Louis, here-
" tofore called Mississippi, from the edge of the sea *as
" far as the Illinois*, together with the river St. Philip,
" heretofore called the Missouris, and St. Gerome, here-
" tofore called Ovabache, (the Ohio) with all the coun-
" tries, territories, lakes within land, *and the rivers which
" fall directly or indirectly into that part of the river St.
" Louis*. Our pleasure is, that all the aforesaid lands,
" countries, streams, rivers, *and islands*, be and remain
" comprized under the name of the government of Lou-
" isiana."

Now this is the solemn declaration of Lewis the fourteenth, as to the extent of some of his claims in Louisiana; and we shall soon find how far they derive support
from discovery, possession, and settlement.

The commerce of Crozat extended *as far as the Illinois*. This expression had no reference to the river of
that name, but to the country in general, on both sides of
the Mississippi, above the mouth of the Ohio; which,
under the French and Spanish governments, was denominated *the country of the Illinois*, and this denomination
appeared in all their records and other official acts. Thus
letters, deeds, and other instruments, bore date at Kaskaskia of the Illinois, St. Louis of the Illinois, St. Charles
of the Illinois; not simply to signify the villages where
such documents were respectively executed, but more
particularly to denote the country in which those villages
are situated. Hence the commerce of Crozat, by the
terms of the patent, extended to the utmost limit of Lou-

isiana in that quarter; which, by the treaty of Utretcht in 1713, was fixed at the forty ninth degree. At this period the French had no competitors on the upper Mississippi; and therefore the Illinois river could not be intended as the northern boundary of Louisiana.

No doubt the commerce of Crozat was extended *to the lands of the English of Carolina* in consequence of the settlements made by the French about St. Augustine in 1562; and this is the more likely, as they always watched for an opportunity of reviving and prosecuting their ancient claims. These settlements, at the end of five years from their commencement, fell into the hands of the Spaniards, and no serious attempts were ever made by the French to recover them.

On the east side of the Mississippi, the *Rio Perdido* formed the boundary line between the French and Spaniards; and that the French had a *legitimate claim* to all the country between these two rivers, and actually *possessed it*, the following facts will afford sufficient proof.

They explored the country about the mouth of the Mississippi in 1683, at which time the Spaniards had no settlements nearer to that place than St. Augustine. In 1699, Ibberville, the first royal governor of Louisiana, planted a colony at the mouth of the Rio Perdido, where he built a fort, and mounted twelve pieces of cannon. In the year 1702, part of the colonists, together with the seat of government, were removed to Isle Dauphin, situated at the entrance of the Mobile. About the same period, settlements were formed up that river, and along the gulf to the westward; from none of which were the French ever expelled. Isle Dauphin was the seat of government for about twenty years; and when it was removed to New Orleans, a garrison remained to protect the settlers on the coast and rivers, who were governed by the French authorities till the treaty of 1763 was carried into effect.

EXTENT AND BOUNDARIES.

The first discoveries of the French about the mouth of the Mississippi, excited the fears of the Spaniards, and they conceived it good policy to erect some barriers against those whom they considered as intruders. For this purpose they founded Pensacola in 1696, three years before the arrival of Ibberville. The entrance of the harbor to this place, is about twelve miles to the eastward of the Perdido, and Pensacola is about sixty miles nearly in the same direction from Mobile. An appearance of harmony existed between the French and Spaniards for some years: Yet their proximity gradually created mutual jealousies and fears; and during the war of 1719, Pensacola changed masters three times, and was at last reduced to a heap of ruins by the French. The truce of 1722, restored it to the Spaniards; and from this period the Perdido was considered by both of them as the boundary line; it was acquiesced in by both; the laws of Spain operated on one side, and those of France on the other.

It is a circumstance of no small weight, that the Spaniards were never in possession of any part of the territory between the Mississippi and Perdido till they conquered it from England during the time of the American revolution. The actual possession of this tract by the French for about seventy years, seems to fix the national boundary, just mentioned, on such a solid basis as not now to be called in question. These facts may be adduced as unanswerable arguments against any modern pretensions of Spain to a more extended claim. Several treaties were made subsequent to Crozat's grant in 1712, and the peace of 1722, and in none of them are the rights of France impaired.

It is therefore difficult to comprehend the ground of the assertion, that no part of West Florida is included in the cession. If the original discovery and settlement of it by the French, the name of Louisiana given to it by them the recognition of it by the French monarchs, the establishment of a colonial government, and the administration of laws, the possession of it for about seventy years, and the acquiescence of Spain during the last half of that period, are not sufficient to vest an indisputable title in France, the territorial rights of nations are extremely precarious. The claims of Spain to West Florida, are without a precedent to sanction them; and they bid defiance to all those principles, which usually govern the conduct of civilized nations. She retroceded the country with the same extent it had when France possessed it. This stipulation effectually precludes every argument against the rights of France, drawn from the conquest of West Florida during the American revolution; because these rights, though extinguished for a time, existed antecedently to the conquest; the conquest enabled Spain to restore them; and she actually did restore them under the solemn sanction of a treaty.

It will be proper in this place to notice, in a cursory manner, the several treaties, which apparently have a bearing on the question of title, particularly on that now under consideration. Our claims in other quarters must be decided on different principles; no treaties appear to confirm or to oppose them.

England, France, and Spain, were parties to the treaty of 1763, and all signed it. France by that treaty ceded and guaranteed to England, in full right, the river and port of Mobile, and every thing she possessed, or ought to possess, on the east side of the Mississippi, except the island of Orleans. And Spain by the same treaty, ceded and guaranteed Florida, with St. Augustine and the bay of Pensacola, in full right to England. The island of Orleans, and the remainder of Louisiana, was ceded by France to Spain the year before.

Spain therefore admitted the right of France to the Mobile, and to all the country between that river and the

EXTENT AND BOUNDARIES. 139

Mississippi. And France admitted the right of Spain to Pensacola, and to that part of Florida to the eastward of it.

No part of the country between Mobile and Pensacola appears to be included in this treaty. If those two powers at that period disagreed as to the boundary line between their respective possessions, it ought now to be adjusted on known and acknowledged principles. Who first discovered and settled it? This question has been already sufficiently discussed.

Spain seizes with avidity on the apparently doubtful phraseology of the stipulation contained in the treaty of St. Idelfonso of 1800. She contends that the word " retrocede" obliges her to restore no more of Louisiana than she actually received from France under the secret treaty of 1762; and she likewise maintains, that this was the true intent and meaning of the parties. This construction would be admissible, were it not opposed by other words and expressions in the same treaty, and it is a good rule to interpret an ambiguous instrument, by a strict comparison of its several members or clauses, though in such a manner as to operate the most strongly against the party making the grant. That treaty retrocedes Louisiana with the same extent " *it actually has in the hands of Spain*," and " that it had when France *possessed it.*" What was the extent of it in 1800? Spain was at that time the rightful proprietor of West Florida, which was antecedently part of Louisiana, and ceded to England by the treaty of 1763; and although this cession extinguished the name, there was no subduction of the territory; it still remains identically and substantially the same, and is at this time possessed by Spain. What was the extent of Louisiana when France possessed it? This question as it respects West Florida has been already answered. If there be any ambiguity in the retrocession, it will doubtless be amply investigated by the constituted authorities of the union.

The boundaries of Louisiana to the westward of Red river are much less defined, and enveloped in more obscurity; yet we are not wholly destitute of lights on the subject, and an attempt will be made to place them in a proper point of view.

It is a fundamental maxim of Spain, "that the national "domain lands are those, not only in the actual enjoyment "of the nation, *but also those on which the nation has a* "*right to re-enter;*" or, in other words, a nation is never ousted of its rights by lapse of time, and a claim once good is never extinguished, except by regular transfer, or the imperious results of war. On this principle the question of title, between France and Spain, to the country on the west side of Red river, must be decided. To form a correct decision, priority of discovery and settlement must be stated and considered; and to illustrate these facts, it will be necessary to recur to such traits in the early history of Louisiana, as appear to bear on the points under discussion.

The right of discovery, to be perfect, must be followed by acts of sovereignty; and settlement is one of those acts. Perhaps, according to the latter part of this definition, the rights of France and Spain to the country on the west side of Red river, were imperfect for many years, and nearly of equal validity; therefore the imperfect right of discovery, must necessarily decide the question.

The French under M. de la Salle, landed, built a fort, and formed a settlement in 1685, on the west side of the bay of St. Bernard, and at the same time took possession of the country with the usual formalities: They explored it to the westward, and more particularly to the northward, of that place; What they did was sufficient to vest a complete title in France, unless Spain had acquired a prior one.* The eventual destruction of the French by the Indians did not weaken the claim of Louis the fourteenth; and accordingly, we find that, in his patent to Crozat, he expressly extends the boundaries of Louisiana to *old and new Mexico* on the west. The fact is, that old and new Mexico never included any part of the country to the eastward of the *rio Bravo;* and certain it is, that the Spaniards in the days of Crozat had not approached that river; their nearest settlement to it was about one hundred and fifty miles to the westward of it. This was undoubtedly known to the French monarch: His object was to embrace the discoveries made by M. de la Salle; and the boundaries he prescribed were grounded on the rights usually admitted as valid among civilized nations, particularly where there is no prior discovery.

The first time the Spaniards appeared on the west bank of the rio Bravo was in 1714, where they built a fortress called St. John Baptist; and so anxious were they to obliterate the title of the French, that they created a province without inhabitants on the east side of that river, and called it Texas.

The news of this proceeding soon reached the capital at Isle Dauphin. M. de la Motte, the governor of Louisiana, to prevent any encroachments of the Spaniards, directed M. de St. Dennis, with thirty men, to repair to Nachitoches on Red river. On his arrival at that place, not finding or hearing of any Spaniards, he advanced overland with part of his detachment to the rio Bravo, on the

---

* Baron Humboldt asserts, on what authority is not known, that M. de la Salle, on disembarking in the bay of St. Bernard, found Spaniards at that time among the Indians, whom he endeavored to combat. But Father Anastasius, who accompanied M. de la Salle from France to the bay of St. Bernard, where he resided more than two years, makes no mention of this fact in his journal; and his silence on a subject of this nature, may be adduced as almost conclusive evidence of the error, into which the learned baron has been led.

west bank of which he found a mission of Franciscans, and the Spanish *presidio*, or out post already mentioned.

To maintain possession of the country, and to secure the friendship of the Indians, the French immediately erected a garrison on the Sabine, about one hundred and fifty miles north west of Nachitoches, which was never troubled by the Spaniards. They likewise at the same time planted themselves among a nation of Indians, called the Assinais, situated about thirty miles to the westward of the present village of Nacogdoches, or about one hundred and forty miles to the westward of Red river, where they erected a fort. The perfidious deceit practised by the Spaniards in 1717, to expel the French from this place, and to secure it for themselves, has been detailed in the historical part of this work; from which no just title can be deduced by Spain. The French never acquiesced in this wrong; and their weakness at that and subsequent periods, alone prevented a successful reclamation of their rights. A fraudulent possession, obtained in time of peace, and in violation of mutual agreements, can never be converted into a just one, and be legitimated among sovereign states.

It is particularly worthy of remark, that the Spaniards never appeared on the east side of the rio Bravo, till they were conducted to the Assinais by M. de St. Dennis, as has been related in another place. This event enabled them to disperse small missions (generally attended by two or more soldiers) among the Indian tribes, situated between that river and Nacogdoches. In the year 1720, they formed an establishment at the Adaize, about fifteen miles to the westward of Nachitoches, from which they were more than once driven by the French.

The numerous difficulties experienced by the French, did not discourage them. In 1719, M. de la Harp ascended Red river with a body of troops, and built a garrison among the Caddoques, in about thirty three degrees fifty five minutes north latitude, and about four hundred miles above Nachitoches. This establishment was maintained, even without interruption, till Louisiana passed into the hands of the Spaniards. M. Beranger at the same time attempted to form a settlement in the bay of St. Bernard, where he erected a small garrison in twenty seven degrees forty five minutes north latitude, and three hundred and ninety miles to the westward of the mouth of the Mississippi, which was eventually destroyed by the Indians. M. de la Harp made a similar attempt in 1721, and with no better success.

These are some of the most material facts, on which rests the question of title to the country on the west side of Red river. It appears, that the French, more than thirty years before the arrival of the Spaniards in this quarter, formed a settlement, and built a garrison, on the sea coast; that, antecedently to such arrival, they explored the inland country, and took possession of it with the usual formalities, and made three establishments in the very heart of it; one at Nachitoches, a second near the source of the Sabine, a third at the Assanais; and soon afterwards, another high up on Red river. These facts must be admitted by the Spaniards; and all they have to oppose to them is, the continued possession of the country (acquired in the manner already stated) between the rio Bravo and Nachitoches, subsequently to the year 1717; during which time the French maintained their garrisons and settlements on the Sabine and Red river. If priority of discovery, followed by partial settlement, and other acts of sovereignty, such as making treaties with the Indian tribes, furnish a legitimate claim, the title of the French is not susceptible of much dispute : They were not deprived of their rights by the results of war, but by premeditated fraud; and they can with justice appeal to the Spanish maxim, *that the national domain lands are those on which the nation has a right to re-enter.*

It will be necessary to notice two other points, though of minor importance, because they have excited some dispute. The Spaniards contend that the rio Hondo is the utmost western limit of Louisiana; and that the Bayou Pierre was never within the jurisdiction of the French.

It is highly probable that the Spanish and French commandants at the Adaize and Nachitoches, agreed on the rio Hondo as the temporary boundary between them, and that the troops of both were restrained from passing it. This was merely intended to prevent those accidents, which often occur when the troops of different nations (between whom no permanent friendship exists) are suffered to visit the garrisons of each other. The rio Hondo is nothing more than a deep gully or ravine, over which passes the road leading to the Sabine, about five miles to the westward of Nachitoches. For some distance both above and below the road, it is generally dry, except in wet seasons, when it receives the water from the circumjacent hills, and conveys it into a small lake, which communicates with Red river, about two miles below Nachitoches. This gully or ravine heads in the hills near the road; and the whole distance from its source to where it joins Red river, does not exceed eight miles. It would be preposterous to suppose, that this diminutive object forms the boundary line between two extensive provinces or empires. Besides, the temporary stipulation of two subalterns was incapable of binding either nation; and even during the existence of this stipulation, the French maintained their garrisons on Red river and the Sabine.

The Spaniards are still more unfortunate in their claims to Bayou Pierre. The geographical position of this place deserves particular notice, because it is little understood. Just below the great raft, a portion of the water of Red river breaks over its right bank, forming a considerable branch, which meanders through the country till it joins that river again about ten miles above Nachitoches. The Bayou Pierre flows into this branch about sixty miles above the junction just mentioned. The Yattassee Indians formerly lived in this quarter, and they were visited by Biainville in 1700. The French formed settlements here as early as the year 1730; and they owed their origin to M. Verge, who established a trading house on Yattasee point, under an exclusive privilege granted him by the governor of Louisiana, and who for many years monopolized the trade of the neighbouring Indians. The inhabitants are not numerous, but they are wholly of French descent. All their land titles of a date prior to the accession of the Spanish authorities in 1769, were derived from the successive governors of Louisiana.

It is a fact now well known, that a warm dispute took place at New Orleans between the French and Spanish commissioners relative to the boundaries of Louisiana. The former contended that the rio Bravo was the western limit; while the latter declared himself bound by his instructions, which restricted him to the delivery of the country on the east side of the Sabine. During this dispute it was ascertained that Louisiana was ceded to the United States, when all arrangements between them ceased of course. It is worthy of remark, that the Sabine is known in geography by two other names, Mexicana, and Adaize; and that it is universally said to be a river of Louisiana.

Considerable light is thrown on the subject of boundaries by the Spanish and French maps.

In the year 1799, the gulf of Mexico was accurately surveyed, and a chart made of it, by the order of the king of Spain. This chart embraces the whole sea coast between the eighteenth degree of north latitude, and the river St. Mary's in Georgia, as also twelve degrees of longitude; together with all the soundings and islands. It is applicable to our present purpose in one particular only; it seems to represent the Sabine as the western limit of Louisiana.

Du Pratz resided in Louisiana from 1718 to 1734, during which time he held an office under the crown. In 1758, he published a large work, embracing the civil and natural history of that country, and accompanied it with a map. An epitome of it was soon afterwards translated from the French, and published in England. This map includes the whole of what we call West Florida, and likewise the whole of the gulf westward to the mouth of the rio Bravo, which is laid down by the Spaniards in twenty five degrees fifty three minutes north latitude, and by the English in twenty six degrees eight minutes north latitude; the line then extends up the easterly or left bank of that river, to a remarkable bend in it, in about twenty nine degrees twenty five minutes north latitude, near to which is the southern extremity of the Mexican mountains; it here leaves the river, diverges a little to the right, and runs along to the north west, on the summit of these mountains, till it terminates in the forty sixth degree of north latitude. It must not be forgotten that the Colorado, Trinity, Red river, Arkansas, Kansas, Platte, and some other large rivers, have their sources in these mountains.

All the French, and even some of the Spanish geographers, delineate the same boundaries to the west. In the atlas published in 1753, by the Prussian royal academy of sciences, the same boundaries are represented.

Part of the claim of the French, as mentioned in the patent to Crozat, extended to " all the countries, territo-" ries, lakes within land, and the rivers, which fall *direct-*" *ly*, or *indirectly*". into the Mississippi. Little need be said on this point, as the Spaniards seem not much disposed to extend their claims to the eastward of any part of Red river, or the Mexican mountains; nor indeed do they appear very anxious to possess any part of the country to the eastward of the Sabine. The French for more than eighty years almost exclusively possessed the navigation of all the western branches of the Mississippi and Missouri, and ascended many of them to their sources; made permanent establishments and granted lands on some, and exercised a civil and military jurisdiction on all. The Spaniards never even attempted to molest them on any of these rivers, except in one instance in 1720, when they perished by the hands of the savages. Hence the probality is strong, that they considered the Mexican mountains, or the sources of the rivers in them, as the western limit of Louisiana; and one fact, among a multitude of others, may be adduced in support of this idea.

While Louisiana was in the hands of France, some of the French traders from the upper Mississippi, transported a quantity of merchandise, by way of the Arkansas, to the Mexican mountains, where they erected a temporary store, and opened a trade with the Indians, and likewise with the Spaniards of north Mexico. The Spanish traders at or near Santa Fè, deeming this an infringement of their privileged rights, procured the imprisonment of the Mississippi adventurers, and the seizure of their effects; and demanded punishment and confiscation. The cause was ultimately decided at the Havanna. The prisoners were liberated, and their property restored, on the ground, that the store in question (situated on the east side of the summit of the mountains, and below the source of the Arkansas) was within the boundaries of Louisiana. One of the persons concerned in this transaction is now living, from whom were obtained the several circumstances attending it.

No doubt there are other facts, known to some, explanatory of the western limits of Louisiana. Those of the most importance, which the industry of the author has enabled him to obtain, are now detailed, and the deduction they afford will be left to the sagacity of the reader.

It may be proper, however, to repeat here, what has been before suggested, that the imperfect right of discovery, is, in all cases, paramount to that of a fraudulent possession. If such discovery be followed by settlement, or other act of sovereignty, the right becomes absolute, and cannot be extinguished, except by conquest, a regular transfer, or voluntary abandonment.

If the claims of France are sufficiently supported, Louisiana bounds thus: South on the gulf of Mexico; west, partly on the rio Bravo, and partly on the Mexican mountains; north and north west, partly on the shining mountains, and partly on Canada; east on the Mississippi from its source to the thirty first degree; thence extending east on the line of demarcation to the rio Perdido; thence down that river to the gulf of Mexico.

The boundaries of Louisiana to the north and north west, are not defined. To what point they will ultimately be sustained from the source of the Mississippi, seems to admit of doubt. If the treaty of Utrecht in 1713, or the more recent one of 1763, or even both, be assumed as the basis of decision, numerous difficulties will present themselves. The discoveries and settlements of a more recent date can have no bearing on the question. Till the conclusion of the latter treaty, the French were in possession of both Canada and Louisiana; and these provinces were wrested from them at the same time. As their discoveries and trade at that day were limited to the great lakes, and to the source of the Mississippi, on the one hand; and on the other to the Mandans on the Missouri, there seems to be an extensive territory calculated to excite conflicting claims. At any rate, it is presumed, that no part of the country washed by either of those rivers, or by their tributary streams, will ever be relinquished by the United States.

As these boundaries are undefined, it will be difficult to estimate the quantity of land in Louisiana with any degree of accuracy. If however, we assume as a datum, a line drawn from the source of the Mississippi in forty seven degrees, forty two minutes and forty seconds, north latitude, to where the Missouri leaves the shining mountains in nearly the same latitude, we may form some reasonable conjectures on the subject. From this extreme point, to the mouth of the Mississippi, on a straight line, is two thousand and five miles. The breadth is less certain. The abbe Raynal calculates it at six hundred miles. But the distance from St. Louis on the Mississippi to the summit of the Mexican mountains, has been determined by pretty accurate observation, to be about six hundred and fifty two miles, and this is believed to be nearly the average breadth of Louisiana. If these data be correct, the boundaries we have described, embrace one million, three hundred and seven thousand, two hundred and sixty square miles; or eight hundred thirty six millions, six hundred forty six thousand, four hundred acres! This estimate may stagger the belief of some; but if they will take the trouble to examine the geographical features of Louisiana, and to reflect on the great length of its numerous rivers, their doubts on the subject will vanish.

Before we conclude, it may be of use to remark, that the shining mountains, and Mexican mountains, though often confounded, are in a great measure distinct. The former are the Andes of South America. The latter commence some distance to the northward of the gulf, and near to the left bank of the rio Bravo, and extend in a north westerly direction, a little to the eastward of Santa Fè, till they intersect the former. They are probably branches or spurs of the shining mountains; and indeed, most of the mountains in new Mexico appear to be connected with that great chain or spine of the western part of our continent.

SKETCHES OF LOUISIANA.

CHAPTER IV.

NEW ORLEANS............THE DELTA.

THE French began to build New Orleans in 1720, and two years afterwards it became the seat of government.

This city, the great mart of all the wealth of the western world, is situated on the east bank of the Mississippi, about one hundred and nine miles (following the meanders of the river) from the sea, and in twenty nine degrees, fifty seven minutes, twenty seven seconds, north latitude, and ninety degrees, seventeen minutes, thirty seven seconds, west longitude. At the time it fell into our hands, it contained about one thousand houses, and eight thousand inhabitants, including blacks and people of color.

Six complete squares are embraced by the city. The fronts of these are three hundred and nineteen English feet in length, and extend north, thirty two degrees east, and south, thirty two degrees west, and are intersected by twelve streets at right angles. Each square is divided into twelve lots. Five of them measure sixty by one hundred and twenty feet. On the opposite side are two key lots, which measure sixty by one hundred and fifty feet. The streets are thirty seven feet and a half in width. On the back part of the city are two narrow rows of buildings, converging to a point.

The ground plot of the city may be considered as a plain, inclining north west two points west. It has a descent of about six feet from the bank of the river to the palisades in the rear of the buildings, and about three feet more to St. John's creek at its medium height. The lands in all the low country, gradually descend from the river, and soon terminate in lakes or swamps.

Nearly the whole of the old houses are of wood, one story high, and make an ordinary appearance. The suburbs on the upper or north end of the city, have been built since the fire in 1794, and contain about two hundred and fifteen houses, mostly composed of cypress wood, and generally covered with shingles or clapboards. Among them is one elegant brick house covered with tile. Several of them are two stories high, and two in the same quarter three stories high. One of them cost eighty thousand dollars, and the rest from fifteen to twenty thousand dollars. They are plastered on the outside with white or colored mortar; this, as frosts are seldom severe in the climate, lasts many years; it beautifies the buildings, and preserves the bricks, which, from the negligence or parsimony of the manufacturers, are usually too soft to resist the weather.

In New Orleans, as in all other parts of the low country, the houses have no cellars under ground; water is generally found within two or three feet of the surface, especially in wet seasons. The wells rarely exceed fifteen feet in depth. The water in them is clear, free from salt, but unpleasant to the taste.

The following are the public buildings; the cathedral, the town house, the prison, the barracks, the hospital, the convent and church, the charity hospital and church, the government house and stores, and some others of inferior note, which will be cursorily mentioned.

The cathedral stands at the head of a spacious open square, about four hundred feet from the river. This building is of brick, extending about ninety feet on the street, and one hundred and twenty back of it. The roof is covered with flat and hollow tile, supported by ten large brick columns, which are plastered, and afford an agreeable appearance. Each front corner has a tower considerably elevated, and the southerly one contains two small bells. This church has likewise a small organ, but on the whole is much less decorated than other catholic places of worship. It was governed by a bishop, two canons, one grand vicar, one parish priest, and four subordinate priests. Considerable funds in houses appertain to it. The bishop received an annual salary of four thousand dollars, charged on the revenues of some southern bishopric; the canons about seven hundred and twenty dollars, and the other priests about three hundred and sixty dollars each, exclusive of casual benefits arising from marriages, burials, and the like. There were likewise a few capouchins, and friars of the order of carmelites, who were paid by the crown.

The town house is rather an elegant building, two stories high, and about ninety feet long, with an arched portico, both above and below, along its whole front. The upper arches are glazed, which adds much to the beauty of the structure. The Spaniards occupied one part of the ground story as a guard house, and permitted a notary to occupy the the other as an office. The upper story was appropriated to the use of the cabildo.

In the rear of the town house, and adjoining to it, is the prison. Under the Spanish government it was a wretched receptacle of vice and misery; like the grave it received many tenents, who were soon forgotten by the world: Some of them perished with age and disease, and others by the hands of assassins. Criminals, under sentence of death, were often kept immured within its walls for years; owing either to the tardiness or lenity of the tribunal at the Havanna, without whose approval no sentence of death could be carried into execution.

The public barracks are situated at the lower end of the front street. They are accommodated with a spacious area, surrounded by a brick wall, as also an extensive parade ground between them and the river. The buildings are of brick, and one story high, covered with shingles, and calculated to receive about fifteen hundred men. They were built by the French, and have a spacious arcade in front and rear.

The building denominated the king's hospital, is on the same line, but higher up. It was originally intended as a receptacle for the sick and diseased belonging to the army and navy. It will accommodate about one hundred and fifty patients, and affords to the miserable a tolerable asylum.

The convent of the Ursuline nuns is situated on the upper side of the barracks, and beyond the hospital, which stands nearer the line of the street. This was likewise built by the French: It is of brick, and spacious; covered with shingles, and two stories high. An extensive garden is attached to it, extremely productive of fruit and vegetables. It will accommodate about fifty nuns, and from seventy to eighty young females, who resort to it for their education. Attached to the convent is a small house containing three rooms, divided longitudinally from each other by double gratings about six inches asunder, with apertures about two inches square, where strangers may see and converse with the nuns and boarders on particular business. Near to the main building, and on the street, stands an old school house, where the female children of the citizens appear at certain fixed hours to be gratuitously instructed in writing, reading, and arithmetic. This religious institution is possessed of considerable funds. Each nun on taking the final vow, or black veil, deposits fifteen hundred dollars, if she be able, which becomes part of the common stock, and cannot be alienated. The church belonging to the convent is small, and was the gift of a gentleman who died a few years ago at New Orleans. He was in early life a notary, and by various speculations amassed an immense property, and failed at last to leave an unspotted name behind him. He likewise built the cathedral church and charity hospital, and endeavoured by acts of beneficence near the end of his days, to atone for the errors of his youth.

The charity hospital stands on the westerly or back part of the city. Poor Spanish subjects, and sometimes strangers, (provided they paid half a dollar per day) were admitted into this asylum. Those entirely destitute were admitted gratis. They had medicine, sustenance, and other aid, afforded them.

The government house stands on the front street, and on the fifth square, reckoning from the upper side, and one hundred feet from the river. It is an ancient building, erected by the French, and two stories high, with galleries or arcades round the whole of it. The lower front was formerly occupied by the governmental secretary, and the clerks of offices. This structure is indifferent, both as to architecture and convenience.

On the southwesterly part of the same square were the lodges and stables of the regular dragoons; which, with the garden belonging to the government house, occupy about four fifths of the square.

On the corners of the second and third squares, lower down, are the public stores, built of brick, extending about thirty five feet on front street, and about two hundred feet on a cross street. They are one story high, and were built by the French.

On the opposite, or southerly side of the stores, is the artillery yard, or ordnance depot.

Opposite to this, on the very bank of the river, is the market house, which is usually furnished with beef, pork, some mullard and veal; fish of several sorts in abundance, and cheap; wild ducks and other game in season; tame turkies, fowls, ducks, and geese; and vegetables of all kinds during the whole year.

The Spaniards had the advantage of a free school, in which boys were instructed in the rudiments of their language. The two teachers attached to it were paid by the crown.

The grand powder magazine of the French and Spaniards, is situated over against the government house, on the opposite side of the river, where a guard was always stationed, and generally relieved weekly.

During the administration of the baron Carondelet, between 1791, and 1796, a ditch was extended round the city, of about eighteen feet in width, with ramparts of earth, and palisades nearly six feet high along the interior or inner side of them. Five large bastions were erected at proper distances, and likewise five intervening redoubts. The bastions were regularly constructed. Each of them was furnished with a banquette, rampart, parapet, ditch, covered way, and glacis. The curtains were wholly formed of palisades, planted at a small distance from each other, and therefore not capable of much defence even against musket balls; they had a banquette within, and a ditch and glacis without. A small redoubt or ravelin was placed in the center of each bastion; and all the latter were of sufficient size to admit of sixteen embrasures, four in each face, three in each flank, and two in the gorge facing the city.

These works of defence were badly supplied with ordnance. Few of the bastions were furnished with more than four or five pieces of cannon. That on the east or lower end of the city, had its full complement; and the covered way was likewise pretty well supplied. This arrangement or distribution of the ordnance was rather singular; it seemed to be mounted on those places the most invulnerable, and the least liable to be attacked. An assault by way of the sea was hardly to be expected, especially as the river was well defended eighteen miles below, and as a fleet wholly unobstructed by land batteries, would find it extremely difficult to ascend against the rapidity of the current. The south west bastion, with a counterguard and traverses, and a small redoubt on the back of the river, constituted the whole defence on the upper side of the city. The first was usually supplied with ten or twelve, and the second with five pieces of cannon. Not more than ten pieces, however, could be brought to bear on any body of men descending the river. As soon as an enemy landed on the open banks, which was by no means difficult, the bastions became totally useless. A skilful officer at the head of disciplined troops, in any degree acquainted with the country, would have experienced no great trouble from these works, especially as they were mostly defended by raw militia, among whom regular duty was irksome, and considered as a grievance.

The inhabitants and others passed in and out of the city by means of four gates. The two next the river were the most considerable, and they were situated sixteen hundred and twenty yards from each other. The two in the rear, or on the back part of the city, were of much less note; one of them was placed on the road leading to lake Pontchartraine: They were defended by a breast work of no great strength or utility. All the gates were of wood, formed of palisades ten or twelve feet long. They were shut every night at nine o'clock, and after that hour no one was permitted to walk the streets without leave from the governor; those who transgressed this regulation were seized by the guards, and detained till morning. House servants, by particular indulgence, were sometimes allowed to pass the streets on business for their masters or mistresses till eleven o'clock.

Exclusive of the fire in 1794, already mentioned, New Orleans suffered by a prior one in 1788, when about nine hundred wooden buildings of all descriptions, mostly old, were reduced to ashes. Those built on their ruins have contributed to the beauty of the city.

Such in some degree were the features of New Orleans at the time it fell into the hands of the United States. Since that period it has been greatly improved; population has increased; new springs are given to commerce, property immensely augmented in value; the works repaired and strengthened, and much additional security afforded to the capital of Louisiana.

The Delta comprehends all the low country between the sea and the elevated grounds. It extends on the east side of the Mississippi, from the Balize to the neighbourhood of Baton Rouge, and on the west side of that river from the gulf to the Chafalia, which is an outlet of the Mississippi just below the thirty first degree, and supposed to be the old bed of Red river.

Nothing is more certain than that the Delta has gradually risen out of the sea, or rather that it has been formed by alluvious substances, precipitated by the waters from the upper regions. It is calculated that, from 1720, to 1800, a period of eighty years, the land has advanced fifteen miles into the sea; and there are those who assert, that it has advanced three miles within the memory of middle aged men. The eastern part of New Spain along the gulf, exhibits abundant proofs of similar advances;

owing, perhaps, to the constant accumulation of sand by the trade winds, which is driven to the shore by the perpetual motion of the waves in that direction.

It is remarkable, that the banks of the river are much more elevated than the circumjacent country. This is occasioned by a more copious deposition along the margins, than at a distance from them. These are thickly covered with grass, and a vast variety of ligneous plants, which serve to filtrate the waters in their progress to the low grounds and swamps, and to retain the greatest proportion of the alluvious substances. Hence the lands along the the banks to a certain depth, generally from four hundred to seven hundred yards are excellent for tillage; while the whole surface in the rear of them, extending to the sea, is alternately covered by lakes and impassable swamps.

The waters precipitated over the banks never return into the same channel. Those from the west bank of the Mississippi find innumerable passages to the gulf; while those from the opposite bank fall into the lakes, which may be considered as arms of the sea, and bid fair to be reclaimed in time from the ocean.

That the Delta has been thus reclaimed may be inferred from a variety of circumstances, particularly from the existence of a vast number of logs and trees at unequal depths under ground, multitudes of which are found below the level of the ocean. These are buried in a substratum of black earth, and already begin to be decomposed, and converted into fossil fuel.

The Mississippi, near its confluence with the sea, is divided into five branches, and of course has its *embouchure* in the gulf by means of five mouths. These are denominated the north east, the east, the south east, the south, and south west passes. They are from three to nine miles in length, and furnish a sufficient depth of water for the largest ships, except on their bars. The east pass called the Balize, has about seventeen feet of water on the bar, and is the one usually navigated. The south pass was formerly of equal depth, but is now gradually filling up. The south west pass has from eleven to twelve feet of water. The north east and south east passes are traversed only by small craft. On the south side of the east pass, about three miles from the bar, is the pilot house, and a framed look-out house, about sixty feet high, where several men reside. They make use of row boats, and seldom venture out to sea, except in good weather. All vessels, of whatever tonnage or size, paid a pilotage under the Spanish government of twenty dollars.

About thirty miles above the Balize, bounded on each side by a strip of low marsh, covered with a species of reed of considerable height and strength, is the fort of Plaquemine, so called from a persimmon grove, which formerly covered the ground where the fort now stands. Under the Spanish government it was furnished with eighteen cannon, some of them of a large calibre, and garrisoned by fifty men. A redoubt was erected on the opposite side of the river, where ten men were stationed. Each of these works had a galley attached to it.

For some distance from the sea, the country is a low marsh, and without trees. These begin to make their appearance some distance below the fort; but no plantations of any consequence exists, till within twenty seven miles of New Orleans. Even at that distance below the capital, none of the land, except a strip of about four hundred yards in breadth on the river, is fit for cultivation. The plantations are usually about one mile and a half in length, and laid out at right angles with the course of the river; so that at least five sixth parts of each plantation, extend into the cypress swamps. These swamps are about six miles in depth, and bounded in the rear by inundated salt marshes, extending to the lakes.

Forty two miles above Plaquemine, is the first saw mill. Thirty six of these mills were formerly in operation between this place, and sixty miles above New Orleans. They were put and kept in motion by the waters of the Mississippi, which served them from the first of February till about the last of July. They were mostly engaged in sawing boards for sugar cases, which were sent to the Havanna. Twelve of these mills ceased to work in 1798, when the manufacture of indigo in the Delta was almost wholly exchanged for that of sugar. The other mills continued to saw boards for home consumption, as likewise building timber of various dimensions. No other wood than white and yellow cypress, was sawed, and the last was deemed the best for most purposes.

About fifty one miles from Plaquemine begins the English turn, or *detour des Anglois*. Here the course of the river varies from north to west, then to east, then to north again, and then to west by south, in a distance of little more than seven miles. This place is about eighteen miles below New Orleans.

On the east side of the Mississippi, and about twelve miles below New Orleans, a dry strip of land extends from the river in a direction towards the lakes, where it terminates at the distance of about twenty miles. This tongue of land, called the *Terre au Bœuf*, is about a mile in width, and divided in the center by a creek or bayou; and, like the Mississippi, is bounded on each side by cypress swamps. This tract is mostly settled by Spaniards from the Canaries, who are poor, and generally cultivate the land themselves. They plant the sugar cane, which they sell, or grind on shares at the sugar mills of their more opulent neighbours; and at the same time raise a variety of articles for the market at New Orleans. The soil of this tract is excellent; it affords plenty of timber, and contained at the time of the cession about eight hundred souls.

Between this place and New Orleans, there are several fine sugar estates. The Delta in 1803, contained eighty one of them. The houses of the planters are comfortable but not elegant. Their plantations front on the river, and are from three fourths of a mile to a mile and an half in depth. The lands situated on the projections formed by the incurvations or inflections of the river, are deemed much the most valuable. Some of these planters are affluent, and possess from thirty to sixty slaves.

But the most wealthy of this class are to be found above the city, some of whom before the cession, made crops valued from ten to sixteen thousand dollars. Since that period the number of slaves has increased; sugar estates are cultivated on a more extensive scale, and the number of them greatly multiplied; so that the annual crops of some are now worth from twenty five to thirty thousand dollars. As population and industry advance, this article of luxury, wealth, and commerce, will be still more abundantly cultivated. The sugar cane is not raised above the island of Orleans, nor is it believed that the climate will admit of it. No sugar estates are found more than one hundred miles above the city; but cotton is cultivated in all parts of the country.

South west of the city is another elevated dry strip of land, which is deemed highly valuable.

The road leading from the back part of the city, forks two miles from the Mississippi. The one on the right runs north east on a tongue of land, about half a mile in width, generally known by the name of Chantilly, and terminates in marshes and swamps at the distance of about twenty miles. The one on the left extends about west, crosses St. John's creek over a drawbridge, and intersects the river road about fifteen miles above the city.

This creek or bayou, heads in a cypress swamp south west of New Orleans; and, after meandering about six miles, in a north by east direction, falls into lake Pontchartraine. The depth of the water in it varies from three to nine feet, as it happens to be affected by the winds, and the rise and fall of the lake. From the bar to the canal of Carondelet, there is usually from nine to ten feet of water.

This canal rises in a basin directly behind the charity hospital, which is sufficiently capacious to accommodate several small vessels. It extends in a direct line about two miles to St. John's creek, and is about twenty feet wide. This is of great advantage to the city, particularly as the products of the lake and back country, such as fish, lime, tar, pitch, and various other articles, find an easy water access to the inhabitants; whereby a difficult and expensive cartage of three miles from the bridge is avoided. This canal was partly excavated by condemned criminals, and partly by laborers hired for the purpose, and paid out of a fund raised by subscription among the inhabitants.

The lakes and fresh water streams supply the market with fine sea and other fish. Oysters and crabs are plenty. The Mississippi is not remarkable for good fish. This part of it, however, furnishes plenty of excellent eels, shrimps, and a species of small sturgeon, seldom more than three feet long, with a soft shell resembling the sea turtle. It produces a kind of fresh water sheep-head, and likewise the carp or buffaloe fish, both of which are indifferent. The *poisson armé*, a kind of gargraws, is an inhabitant of this part of the river; it is usually eight or nine feet long, and has tremendous teeth and scales; the latter of which resist the sharpest hatchet, and have the appearance of a concretion of flinty substances. Cat fish abound in all parts of the Mississippi. Some of them weigh one hundred and seventy pounds; though their weight generally varies from sixty to one hundred and twenty pounds. The old wife, or hickory shad, as they are called, appear in the river about the Delta. Alligators of various sizes are numerous in all the waters of the low country, particularly in the bayous and lakes. They are amphibious, and considered as harmless, except when attacked or wounded, though they sometimes destroy hogs and other small animals, found along the water courses. These, according to Buffon and other naturalists, are the crocodiles of Egypt, so terrible to the ancients, which animated the pens of historians and poets. Some of those in the Mississippi are fifteen feet long. They frequently ascend that river to the Arkansas. Great numbers of them are found on the lower part of Red river.

The people who live on the banks of the Mississippi, prefer its water to any other. When filtrated, it is transparent, light, soft, pleasant, and wholesome. This great river not only fertilizes the country, but contributes to the health of the inhabitants in the warm regions. The salubrious quality of its water is attributed in part to the nitre and sulphur it contains, and in part to its deep and rapid current; and, as it is precipitated from the cold regions, it tempers the fervid atmosphere on the lower Mississippi, and renders it more healthful.

Such indeed is the depth of that river, and so bold its shores, that ships may discharge their cargoes on the banks at New Orleans, by means of a stage or bridge, supported by two forty feet spars. The depth of the water in the channel, at various places, is noticed in our account of that river. The tides have little effect on the water at New Orleans; they sometimes cause it to swell, but never to slacken its current. Heavy winds roll in the water from the gulf, and cause sudden rises of the river, in some instances equal to a spring freshet. The difference between the highest and lowest stages of water in the Balize, is about three feet; at the city about twelve feet; and this difference increases rapidly above the island of Orleans.

In ascending from New Orleans, the country rises gradually along the banks of the river, especially on the east side of it, though subject to inundation when not banked out. What is called the Levee, is a broad bank of earth thrown up to confine the water of the Mississippi within its bed, and every man is obliged by law to make and keep that part of it in repair, which crosses the front of his lands. These banks extend on both sides of the river from the lowest settlements to point Coupeé on one side, and to the neighborhood of Baton Rouge on the other, except where the country remains unoccupied. Along these banks in high freshes the surface of the river is elevated many feet above that of the adjacent lands, and exhibits a curious spectacle to the eye of the traveller. The great road, extending from the Mississippi territory to New Orleans, usually runs on the top of the Levee.

On the east side of the Mississippi, about one hundred and twenty miles above New Orleans, is the Ibberville, which is one of the outlets of that river during the freshes, and its waters flow into the lake Maurapas. In the season of low water its bed is always dry near the Mississippi; but at some distance from that river, it has considerable water at all times. The river Amit, which heads in the Mississippi territory, joins the Ibberville, and near its junction stands the village of Galvez, containing thirty or forty houses.

On the west side of the Mississippi, from the sea to the mouth of Red river, a distance of about three hundred and fifty miles, the face of the country is similar to that just described on the opposite shore, though much more thinly inhabited. Not a gentle rise of ground, not even a hilloc, is presented to the eye, except a small ridge or clift, about one mile long, just below the wealthy settlement of Point Coupeé. All the land of a cultivable nature is contained in a narrow strip along the margins of the river, and its outlets; while the vast territory between this strip and the gulf to the south west, and west, about ninety miles in breadth, abounds in lakes and marshes, and is impassable by man, except along the water communications. That no more than one twenty seventh part of the Delta is susceptible of cultivation, may be deduced from pretty accurate data.

This part of the Mississippi has three outlets from its right or west bank, which afford passages for part of its superabundant waters, and two of them present a good boat navigation.

On ascending the river the first is called the *La Fourche*, about eighty one miles above New Orleans. The bed of this outlet is about ninety feet in width, and usually dry in the summer season for a few miles, when the water makes its appearance, probably collected from the swamps, and gradually deepens as it rolls towards the gulf.

The second is the *Plaquemines*, about thirty one miles still higher up the river. It so much resembles the *La Fourche* as to render a particular description of it in this place unnecessary. It unites with the *Chafalia* at some distance from the Mississippi, and contributes to improve the navigation from that union to the sea.

The third is the *Chafalia*, about one hundred and twenty eight miles above the *Plaquemines*, and three miles below the mouth of Red river. The upper end of this outlet is in a bend or curve of the Mississippi, and in the season of freshes the water rushes into it with great force, and is apt to carry boats and other craft along with it. This is supposed to be the old bed of Red river, particularly as the materials composing its banks exhibit the same color and features, which are entirely different from those exhibited by the banks of any other river in this quarter. No doubt the Mississippi once flowed more to the eastward. The remains or traces of an old bed on the east side of that river just below fort Adams, and the sudden change in the direction of the current from south to west, and even to north west, seem to favor the idea, that a junction was formed at some former period. The Mississippi is known to seek new channels; and there is good reason to believe, that it has from time to time varied its course from one extreme of its valley to the other. The channel of the *Chafalia*, a few miles only from the head of it, is completely obstructed by logs and other materials. Were it not for these obstructions, the probability is, that the Mississippi would soon find a much nearer way to the gulf than at present; particularly as it manifests a constant inclination to vary its course.

The distances of these outlets from each other, are estimated by the course of the river, which is remarkably crooked. The *Plaquemines* and *Chafalia* gradually converge to each other, and finally unite about one hundred and fifty miles (following the course of the stream) from the upper end of the latter. This united stream finally empties itself, by a narrow mouth, into the gulf, about ninety miles to the westward of the Balize, and about the same distance on a straight line, from the upper end of the *Chafalia*, but about one hundred and eighty miles, following the serpentine progress of this outlet. It must be remembered, that we have no correct map of the country, and that the Spanish government was entirely unacquainted with its geography.

As the *Chafalia* is considered of some importance in several points of view, we propose to give some further account of it in the next chapter.

The usual water communications between New Orleans, and the *Atacapas*, and *Apalousas*, are by means of the *La Fourche* and *Plaquemines*. The cultivable lands on each side of all the outlets, at least for some distance below their heads, are similar to those on the Mississippi, much limited by low grounds and cypress swamps. The settlements on the *La Fourche* extend downwards about forty five miles, and comprehend upwards of two hundred families, mostly Spaniards, who are by no means in affluent circumstances. They cultivate rice, corn, cotton, and flax, and also afford to the New Orleans market considerable quantities of provisions. The borders of all the outlets furnish good ranges for cattle, and swine, and multitudes of them are raised without much expense to the owners.

The Delta produces various kinds of excellent fruit; such as sweet and sour oranges, figs in great plenty, some lemons, limes, citrons, and shaddock; garden grapes of several kinds; fox and wild black grapes; peaches, quinces, plums, and some good pears; the apples are fit only for tarts; pomegranates and strawberries; excellent water and musk mellons of all kinds in abundance; wild cherries, mulberries, blackberries, and dewberries. The country to the north of lake Pontchartraine furnishes plenty of whortleberries.

Vegetables of most kinds are likewise common to the country; particularly sweet and Irish potatoes, though the latter are indifferent; and fresh seed is required every year from the northward; every kind of peas and beans, carrots and parsnips; the best of lettuce and various other salads; cabbage, spinage, artichokes, the egg fruit, red peppers, tomatoes, pepper grass, cucumbers, pumpkins of an excellent quality, asparagus, turnips, mushrooms, pastaches, and many other valuable articles.

In the swamps are found plenty of cypress trees. They are tall and majestic, and some of them grow to a large size. These swamps produce olive trees, so called, because they bear a fruit similar in appearance to the real olive. The wood of them is white and beautiful, and serves to adorn many articles of cabinet work. On the dry or more elevated lands appear the great magnolia; but this tree does not answer the extravagant description given of it by Bartram. On the same kind of ground appear the ash, three kinds of live oak, the cotton wood, which is a species of the poplar, the button wood, or sycamore, and a tree called *unknown wood*, because it has no name, nor is it known to what tribe it belongs; it is of considerable size, and bears a small berry, with a stone, something like the cherry; grafts of peaches and plums take on it. Here likewise grow red and shrub oaks, hiccory, sassafras, and the peccon tree, the nut of which is fine, and deemed by some superior to the shell bark and walnut. The elm is found on many plantations, but it is not indigenous. The wet grounds are generally covered with willows. The persimmon trees are numerous. They grow to a great size, and their fruit is much larger, and deemed better, than that found in any part of the Atlantic states. The cucumber tree bears an elongated green fruit, which much resembles the garden cucumber in appearance. The pawpaw is produced in great perfection. Most of the low lands are covered with underwood, vines, supple jacks, and cane; so that it is extremely difficult, and in most instances impossible, to penetrate them. On some of the highest grounds, along the water courses, the cane frequently grows to the height of thirty five or forty feet. Bears formerly inhabited these impervious recesses; but population and agriculture have rendered them less numerous.

The climate on the lower Mississippi has never been fairly represented. It may be said with truth to be uniformly the same along the banks of that river from New Madrid to the sea. The inhabitants, who live at and near the latter place, as well as below it, situated within the vicinity of the swamps, are as sickly as those in the Delta, and the same diseases prevail among them. It is true, that the atmosphere at New Orleans, and below it, is more abundantly charged with vapours and miasmata, than that six degrees more to the north; but it is equally true, that the Delta is always more or less refrigerated by the sea breezes, which serve to correct the poisonous exhalations, and thereby to produce an equality of climate, as it respects health, for nearly one thousand miles along the Mississippi. This equality is wholly confined to the low grounds and swamps; it is by no means sustained on the long chains of elevated grounds in their rear, and beyond their influence.

The Delta is much more sickly than the native inhabitants are disposed to allow, and by no means so insalubrious as is believed in the Atlantic states. The constitutions of those born and educated in that country, are adapted to the climate; and the creoles can hardly conceive of a portion of the globe more healthful than their own, or less pregnant with dangerous diseases. Several persons more than seventy, and some over eighty years of age, are now living in that quarter. Just before the cession, three died in New Orleans, neither of whom was less than one hundred years old.

Diseases of the intermittent kind, prevail in all parts of the Delta; and in New Orleans, a highly inflammatory bilious fever, occasionally makes its appearance. Strangers, much more than natives, are apt to fall victims to the endemics of the country, particularly the boatmen from the Ohio. Those unaccustomed to the climate, and of intemperate habits, exposing themselves to the heats and dews, are sure to experience dangerous maladies. But strangers of contrary habits, who avoid fatigues and the excessive heats of summer, seldom complain of any thing more than a troublesome lassitude and debility. It is well known that the best livers enjoy the best health; and that those who subsist on unwholesome or unsuitable provisions, and are not sufficiently sheltered from the extremes of the climate, are candidates for a sick bed, if not for the grave. It is a truth confirmed by long experience, that more perish from the want of medical aid, proper nourishment, and attendance, than from the virulent nature of prevalent diseases.

Strangers who reside in New Orleans, and sometimes the native inhabitants of that city, are occasionally attacked with an inflammatory bilious fever, which has gradually obtained the name of yellow fever. There is no proof of its contagious effects: On the contrary it has never been communicated to nurses and attendants. Many have died in the highest state of inflammation, and before their deaths vomited a substance like coffee grounds; their families and friends were in the same room with them, and no injury was experienced.

Perhaps the soldiery of the United States have suffered more from the climate on the lower Mississippi than any other class, and several reasons may be assigned for this excess. The first is, that our garrisons in that quarter are situated amid the vapors of the swamps. The second is, that their profession is unavoidably productive of many evils. They are obliged, in the performance of indispensable duties, to experience the extremes of heat and cold, and the other vicissitudes of the weather; liable to constant privations of comfortable shelter, and often furnished with provisions, either bad in quality, or not adapted to the climate. The third is, that our soldiery are unfortunately too much addicted to intemperance, and the sick among them not always furnished with the shelter, and never with the nourishment and other comforts, which their situations in a warm and humid climate require. Recruits, particularly from the middle and eastern states, on their arrival in that country, are usually seized with moderate intermittents; which, from want of the aids already mentioned, gradually assume a dangerous type, and in too many instances terminate in death.

There is a vast difference between the atmosphere along the Mississippi, and that a few miles only from the swamps. The soldiery who have been stationed in the Apalousas, and at Nachitoches, enjoyed excellent health; while those quartered at the Chickasaw bluffs, fort Adams, and other places on the banks of the lower Mississippi, were severely afflicted with sickness. The fatal diseases experienced by the troops on the elevated grounds at Columbian spring in the summer of 1807, were not contracted at that place. These troops were quartered the preceeding rainy winter at New Orleans; they ascended the river in the early part of summer to fort Adams, where they encamped on a low bottom in the neighbourhood of the swamps, and necessarily remained in tents for several weeks. Hence their systems were gorged with a complication of animal, vegetable, and other noxious effluvia, which predisposed them to the attacks of violent disorders. This state of things was unavoidable; but it is adduced here as a proof, that men exposed for any considerable time to the pestilent regions of the swamps, will be subsequently attacked by dangerous diseases. Another proof is this; men detached from healthful positions in the summer season, and employed in boats for two or three weeks on the Mississippi, are afterwards generally seized with the intermittents of the country. In fine, the high grounds on the lower Mississippi, if not within the influence of the swamps, are productive of nearly as much health among the soldiery and others, as is usually enjoyed, under like circumstances, in any of the Atlantic states.

If the people in the Delta are annually exposed to fevers, they are mostly exempted from some other painful maladies, which prevail in more salubrious climates. Consumptions, rheumatisms, and cutaneous complaints, are almost unknown among them; the gravel and stone in the bladder are equally rare. From 1799 to 1803, two cases only of the latter occurred in New Orleans. The people in this quarter retain their sight longer than those in more northern regions; and this is attributed to the scarcity of snow among them.

The creoles or natives of the country, are sprightly, active in a remarkable degree, and gentle in their manners. The females of New Orleans are handsome both in their shapes and features, and possess ease and grace in their movements and conversation. The men are deficient in literature, but display a good share of genius and penetration. In the early part of life they attend to dancing, riding, and music.

An alluvial soil cannot be supposed to abound in rock. Neither on the island of Orleans, nor along the immense flat country on the west side of the Mississippi, below the mouth of the Ohio, is even a single pebble to be found.

SKETCHES OF LOUISIANA.

CHAPTER V.

OF THE COUNTRY BETWEEN THE MOUTH OF THE CHAFALIA AND THE ARKANSAS; BETWEEN RED RIVER AND THE RIO BRAVO.

THE distance from the mouth of the Chafalia, on the gulf to its outlet near Red river, following its meanders, is about one hundred and eighty miles; and the distance from the latter river to the Arkansas is estimated at rather more than four hundred miles, according to the course of the Mississippi. In this chapter will be included some sketches of the country to the westward of Red River and the Chafalia, and to the northward of the gulf.

It must not be supposed that what is called the Delta includes all the lands formed by alluvion: On the contrary, these lands extend along almost all the great rivers nearly to their sources; and those occasionally deluged by the freshes on the Mississippi, continue to some distance above the mouth of the Ohio. But the higher the Mississippi is ascended from its mouth, the more elevated are the lands on its banks. Perhaps the only reason why the Delta is usually limited to the Chafalia on the north and west, is, because the country below it is more generally flooded than that above it.

The territory now to be noticed is of great extent, and is as little known as any other part of Louisiana. A small portion of it only has been explored. The Spaniards have formed some settlements on its borders, and they exercise a jurisdiction over a considerable extent of country, which we conceive to be embraced by the treaty of cession. These circumstances, added to their extreme jealousy and caution, and a variety of other obstacles to discovery, serve to keep us in a great measure ignorant of the south western part of the territory within our claims.

As the Chafalia divides the Delta from what is called the elevated country, a more particular description of it, than we have hitherto given, will be necessary in this place.

This outlet, on leaving the Mississippi about three miles below Red river, is nearly two hundred yards wide; in low water it is about eighteen feet, and in high water about thirty three feet in depth. Thirty miles from the Mississippi, it is obstructed by a raft of wood, bound together by a heterogeneous mixture of ligneous and other matter. In the course of twenty miles the navigation is choaked by ten or twelve similar rafts; and it is calculated that the aggregate obstruction occasioned by them is not less than nine miles. Some of them form good bridges, and are passable at all seasons. Many of them are covered with willow trees, and a considerable proportion of them are ten inches diameter. These rafts rise and fall with the water, and are therefore justly termed floating bridges.

Below these rafts the Chafalia affords a beautiful sheet of water, at least as far down as Cow island, from seventy five, to one hundred and fifty yards wide, and from twenty five to thirty feet deep in the dry seasons. At Cow island the stream is divided; one part spreads into a large lake; the other part continues its course, and seems to maintain its usual breadth and depth. The current of the Chafalia is gentle till it is joined by the Plaquamines about one hundred and fifty miles from the outlet on the Mississippi, where its velocity is considerably increased. It communicates with lake Natchez by means of several bayous, the largest of which is bayou Long. This bayou is connected with lake Flat, Grand river, and Grand lake, by means of several bayous, most of which are navigable in the season of high water. Grand lake is about forty miles long, and from three to ten miles wide, into which the Chafalia is emptied by a channel of about two hundred and fifty yards wide; and a depth of nearly forty feet. It then passes through Berwick bay, which is from half a mile to two miles wide, and from sixty to eighty feet deep; and after a course of about twelve miles, it falls into Vermillion bay, which is an arm of the gulf. The navigation of the Chafalia is obstructed by a bank of oysters, which stretches across it in Vermillion bay, over which there is seldom more than eight or nine feet of water. The bayou *Tersh*, which affords a navigable communication with the settlements in the Atakapas, joins the Chafalia near Grand lake. In the season of low water the tide flows to Cow island.

There is an island of about three miles in circumference, situated in the gulf, a few miles to the westward of the mouth of the Chafalia, elevated more than two hundred feet above the level of the sea, and connected with the main land by a low marsh. Most of the islands along the shores of the Mexican gulf, exhibit this proud pre-eminence, while the country for a great depth is most of the time covered with water. Some of them are impregnated with sulphur, and one of them has been known to be on fire for at least three months.

The Atakapas and Apalousas are situated on the right bank of the Chafalia. The first bounds on the gulf, and the second joins it on the north, and spreads between it and Red river. These include the oldest and most opulent settlements in this quarter. Those in the Atakapas are generally formed along the Bayou *Tersh*, and some other bayous of inferior note. The lands near the Chafalia are low and swampy, though some of them abound in excellent timber. Most of those along the sea coast are also covered with swamps and marshes; yet small tracts are occasionally found sufficiently elevated for cultivation, and extremely fertile. The interior of the district is diversified by prairies and bayous; and along the latter, to the depth of two or three hundred yards, plenty of wood is to be found. The lands suitable for cultivation extend in narrow borders along on each side of the bayous; the rest is low and boggy, and fit only for the pasturage of cattle. Such, however, is the number of bayous, that the elevated lands are nearly equal in quantity to those of a low and spungy nature. The soil is of a luxuriant quality, calculated for the growth of the sugar cane, tobacco, cotton, indigo, corn, and rice. Perhaps the lands along these bayous are not exceeded in fertility by any tracts of the same extent in Louisiana. The country is pleasant, and the inhabitants are furnished with plenty of fish, oysters, crabs, and wild fowl; as also with the orange, and all the other fruits, vegetables, and plants, incident to the Delta. The climate in this district is nearly similar to that of the Delta; with this advantage, however, that it is refreshed by breezes from the sea. In fine, this district is intersected by small navigable streams, and the inhabitants communicate with the sea and New Orleans with the greatest facility. Vessels of sixty or eighty tons burthen may enter the Chafalia by way of the sea, and pass some distance up the *Tersh*. But the most convenient navigation to New Orleans is by means of the lower part of the *Chafalia, Plaquamines, La Fourche*, and the Mississippi.

The Apalousas is situated to the north of the Atakapas, and the best settlements in it are about fifty miles to the southwest of the outlet of the Chafalia on the Mississippi. The intermediate lands are low and swampy, and covered with water during the wet seasons. The lands in this district are much more elevated than those of the Atakapas; but they are less fertile, and the orange tree, and sugar cane appear in less perfection, though they are cultivated to advantage. The country is beautiful and pleasant, and covered with a variety of extensive prairies. It is intersected by a number of navigable streams. These are bordered with woods, which yield fuel and timber, and afford a pleasing variety to the view. This district is level, but not flat; and in the spring of the year, the face of the country appears like a boundless meadow, covered with immense herds of cattle, flocks of sheep, and gangs of horses. This scene is diversified by the houses and plantations scattered along the edges of the woods. Cotton and cattle are at present the staple commodities of the district; but the inhabitants are about to direct their attention to the culture of the sugar-cane, which is much more profitable. This has hitherto been delayed from the want of capitals to carry it on. The profits arising from crops of sugar, in successful years, are very considerable; each good slave will annually earn his master from four hundred, to four hundred and fifty dollars. But the culture of this article is frequently attended by accidents, against which no human prudence can provide. Sometimes the fields of sugar-cane are levelled by tornadoes, or sudden gusts of wind; at others they are blighted by early frosts. These accidents are less frequent in the Atakapas, where the country is much lower, and where early frosts are not common. It has been observed, that sugar-cane does not grow in Egypt, and in some other eastern countries, to the north of the twenty-ninth degree. In Louisiana it flourishes pretty well one degree and a half further north. When this district was first settled, indigo was the staple commodity; but the planters gradually turned their attention to cotton. In the culture of this article, each slave will earn his master from two hundred and fifty to three hundred dollars *per annum*; it requires no other capital than land and labourers, and it is liable to no other accidents than what result from the common vicissitudes of the weather. In cultivating sugar and cotton, large fortunes have been made. Soon after the American revolution, a great number of enterprising adventurers from the United States removed into the Mississippi territory and lower Louisiana. At that period most of them were poor; but their industry soon made them opulent, and a considerable number of them can at this time boast of an annual income of from fifteen to twenty five thousand dollars.

The lands to the westward of the Chafalia are so situated as to enable the planters to pursue several objects to advantage. In addition to their cotton and sugar-cane, they raise vast numbers of cattle. This is attended with very little expense, as the prairies are covered with grass during the whole of the year. Some persons own several thousand head of cattle. It is common for them to milk from eighty to one hundred and twenty cows, and to mark more than one thousand calves each year. This may seem incredible to some, but nothing is more true. An advantageous market for beef, hides, butter, cheese, and tallow, always exists in New-Orleans; and these articles are transported to that city with facility, and without much expense. It is estimated among the planters, that the stock of a vaccary doubles every four years, and that of a cotton plantation every three years.

At the proper season there are plenty of deer and wild turkies in the two districts we have described. They are frequently run down by the hunters on horseback, and noosed by a cord, which is thrown with astonishing dexterity, even at full speed.

The natural growth in these districts is similar to what we find in the Delta, intermixed with several species of trees incident to the elevated country. Near the mouth of the Chafalia, numerous clusters of live oak are found.

The population of these two districts may be estimated at about three thousand one hundred whites, and three thousand slaves. About one thousand two hundred and fifty of the former are enrolled in the militia.

The climate in this quarter is deemed much more healthful than in any other part of the low country. Agues and fevers sometimes prevail; but they seldom assume a dangerous type: They are usually of short duration, and readily yield to medicine, if seasonably administered. Few countries produce more old people in proportion to the population, or larger families of children. These two districts are constantly fanned by the breezes from the sea: and to these must be attributed the prevalence of so much health. They temper the heat of the sun, and deprive the vapors, and perhaps the miasmata, occasioned by the bayous and swamps, of their pernicious qualities. The air is remarkably soft, and pleasant to the feelings.

All the country about the gulf is evidently alluvial. At what time it was redeemed from the sea, no one can conjecture; but as some of the oldest inhabitants can remember when the lands were less dry, much oftener flooded, and to a much greater extent and height, than at present, perhaps its redemption is much nearer to our time than many are willing to allow. At the mouth of the Mississippi the land constantly advances into the gulf; and there is every reason to believe, that its advances are equally rapid at the mouth of the Chafalia, and along the shores of the gulf. No doubt the elevated islands, scattered along the coast, and already in most instances connected with the main land by marshes, were not long ago situated at some distance in the sea. These projections are caused by the deposition of the sediment from the rivers, particularly from the Mississippi. The gulf of Mexico, though of great extent, is filled with shoals and sand banks, especially near the land, which render the navigation dangerous; and the materials of which they are composed, have been rolled from the sources of the great rivers.

Red river joins the Mississippi just below the thirty-first degree. It is about five hundred yards broad at its mouth; but it gradually contracts to about three hundred or two hundred and fifty yards as it is ascended. The lower part of this river, for about fifty miles, rolls through the Mississippi swamps. A short distance below where it receives Black river, about twenty seven miles from its mouth, it approaches within three miles of the Mississippi, and then flows in nearly a parallel direction to it, till they unite their waters. The country for this distance exhibits a gloomy prospect; it presents to the eye a world of waters. The author of these sketches ascended Red river in February 1809, at which time, owing to the swell of the Mississippi, the whole country was buried about ten feet under water; and it was then about six feet below its usual rise. Only two or three elevated spots of ground appeared, where boats were able to land, and these were but a few yards in circumference. The first appearance of any lands not occasionally flooded is in the neighborhood of the Avoyelles; and even between this place and the rapids, at a distance of more than one hundred miles from the Mississippi, most of the country adjacent to one side or the other of Red river, is deluged in the wet seasons. All that vast tract below the Avoyelles can never be of any use, except for the hickory, ash, and oak, it produces. It is intersected by innumerable bayous, and checquered by a vast number of lakes, which receive the surplus waters of Red river and the Mississippi. Some of the former, after meandering through the swamps, unite with the main channel again: Others fall into the Chafalia and Mississippi; so that in the season of high water usually from February till June, boats may pass over a great extent of country in every direction, except where obstructed by the trees.

The first settlement in ascending Red river, is at the Avoyelles, about sixty miles from the Mississippi. This settlement is formed about an extensive prairie, and the inhabitants have a ready communication with Red river by means of some navigable bayous, which penetrate its right bank. The settlers are partly French, and partly emigrants from the United States. They seldom cultivate wheat, because they have no mills to grind it. Corn and cotton are almost the only articles cultivated by them, except garden vegetables. They raise large stocks of cattle and swine; the first range the prairie, and the latter the woods, which are filled with oak, hickory, ash, and grape vines. They prepare considerable quantities of beef and pork for market, which are deemed of a good quality. The population of this place may be estimated at about four hundred and fifty whites, and one hundred and fifty slaves. Above the Avoyelles the lands gradually rise, and few of them, except near the river, are subject to inundation. Some considerable tracts exhibit large prairies, with very few trees, and even these few are mostly pine. The lands less elevated furnish a variety of excellent timber. Above the Avoyelles, and back of the river, the country is of a rolling nature, and not destitute of good springs.

The next settlement of consequence is at the rapids, about sixty miles still higher up the river. The village of Alexandria is situated just below them, and on the right bank of Red river, in north latitude, thirty one degrees, twenty minutes. Most of the settlers have planted themselves some miles back; and the whole population may be computed at about six hundred and forty whites, and two hundred slaves. The greatest proportion of this part of the country is cultivated by emigrants from the United States. The land is of a good quality, and produces abundantly. A saw mill has been erected on a bayou or stream near the settlements, which has proved of great utility to the inhabitants. The lands on the left bank of the river are rather broken; the soil mostly of a stiff clay: the timber is of large oak, and hickory, intermixed with a few pine, thinly scattered over the country, which is well watered. This kind of land extends along to the north east to the Ocatahola, a distance of about forty miles. The plantations about the rapids exhibit the appearance of wealth. The wood lands and prairies are so happily intermixed as to be of the greatest utility to the planters, who raise many cattle and swine, and cultivate such articles as are common to the country.

The rapids in Red river are formed by two ledges of hard indurated clay, or soft rock, which extend across the channel at about three-fourths of a mile from each other. In low water each of them has a fall, and during this season it is dangerous for loaded boats to attempt the passage of them. When the waters are high they are not perceptible, and the Mississippi frequently flows back to them. A good boat channel may be cut over each at a small expense. If the legislative authority were to grant a suitable toll, no doubt a safe navigation would be made.

From the rapids to Nachitoches, a distance of about one hundred and ten miles, the settlements are thinly scattered along the river, and mostly on the right bank of it. Nearly the whole of this tract, especially along the water courses, is composed of bottom land of the richest kind, and well covered with wood, though in some instances for the space of fifteen or twenty miles no settlements have been made. These, however, begin to be numerous and wealthy about thirty miles below Nachitoches, and they multiply as that place is approached. One great inconvenience is, that the bottom lands suitable for cultivation extend only in narrow borders along the river, generally from three hundred to four hundred yards in depth, and are bounded in the rear by cypress swamps and lakes. These swamps and lakes almost invariably extend parallel to the river, and are seldom more than one or two miles wide. They are bounded on the opposite side by the high lands, which are of a rolling nature, interspersed with extensive rich prairies, and small ridges of pine and other timber; and the lands of this mixed quality extend westward to the Sabine. Many elevated situations occur along the river, and back of it, which afford delightful views. From some of them the eye may glance over vast natural meadows, thickly studded with copses of trees, and adorned with variegated herbage.

Nachitoches, situated in north latitude, thirty one degrees, forty six minutes, was settled by the French as early as 1714, and was once much more considerable than at present. It now contains between forty and fifty families, mostly French. The village was originally built on a hill or elevation at some distance from the river; but it was abandoned by the Spaniards after they came into possession of Louisiana, who caused another to be erected on the bottom a short distance higher up on the right bank of the river. The inhabitants formerly subsisted almost wholly by the Indian trade, and this induced them to live contiguous to each other; but as this resource became less profitable and more precarious, they gradually turned their attention to agriculture, and resorted to their plantations. This place experiences some inconvenience from the want of good water. The river is impregnated with salt and alum, and the water taken from the wells is equally unpleasant. The high grounds about a mile from the river afford some good springs;— but the inhabitants mostly use rain water collected and preserved in cisterns. The bottom lands in this quarter are composed of a rich sandy texture, and produce a thick growth of wood. The soil on the high grounds is generally of a stiff clay; and though it produces considerable pine, it yields good crops of cotton, corn, and tobacco. Perhaps cotton and tobacco are raised on Red river in greater perfection than in any other quarter of the union; certain it is, that they command the highest prices in the market. It must be confessed, however, that agriculture is but little understood among the old settlers of the country, and it will probably be some time before they will become acquainted with the practical duties of agriculturalists.

The village of Nachitoches will always preserve some importance, particularly as it is the usual thoroughfare over land from the settlements east of the Mississippi to the Mexican dominions. A garrison was always kept here by the French and Spaniards, and the United States still maintain one at the same place.

In the neighbourhood of Nachitoches are several considerable lakes. The country, indeed, about the lower half part of Red river, is full of them; some of which are from thirty to fifty miles in circumference. They produce an abundance of several sorts of good fish. At some seasons of the year prodigious numbers of wild fowl resort to them, particularly several kinds of ducks, geese, brant, and swan. They invariably communicate with the river, and in the season of high freshes receive the surplus water precipitated from the upper country, and by these means prevent the inundation of vast tracts of low land. These lakes uniformly rise and fall with the river.

From Nachitoches in a north east direction to the Washita or Black river, the country swells into gentle hills and ridges; it contains a mixture of prairie and wood lands, and the natural growth of many considerable tracts is pine. The soil is of a good quality, especially on the broad bottoms, which extend along the numerous streams.

The upper settlement on Red river is at a place called Compti, about thirty miles above Nachitoches. The lands about this settlement are very irregular and broken, and much injured by numerous bayous and lagoons.

About eighty miles above this settlement, part of the waters of Red river break through its right bank, and finally unite with the main stream again just above Nachitoches. Nearly sixty miles above this union or junction, the outlet of Red river just mentioned receives the bayou Pierre, on which the French formed some settlements about the year 1730. The inhabitants at this place make considerable quantities of butter, cheese, and bacon hams, which they usually sell to the people below them on Red river. The lands about bayou Pierre are a mixture of prairie and wood, and the soil in general is deemed of a good quality. The inhabitants cultivate wheat, corn, cotton, and tobacco. They are furnished with many excellent mill seats, and plenty of good building stone, an article seldom found in the country below them.

Perhaps the number of inhabitants between the rapids and the bayou Pierre may amount to about twelve hundred whites, and to nearly as many slaves.

At the distance of about one hundred and thirty miles above Nachitoches commences what is called the great raft. The distance from the lower to the upper end of it is estimated at forty-five or fifty miles. This obstruction is similar to the one in the Chafalia; and is broken and unconnected in many places; so that in a variety of instances, for several miles in extent, a good navigation exists: Yet, as the channel is frequently and wholly obstructed by vast collections of logs, and the branches of trees, firmly bound together by the alluvial substances precipitated from above by the current, no boat can possibly ascend the river. A passage, however, is found round this raft by means of a chain of lakes and bayous, connected with each other; though in some places it is difficult to navigate, and the distance is upwards of ninety miles. It is said, that there is no better land on Red river than along this raft.

Red river has never been explored more than about two hundred miles above this raft, except by Indian traders and hunters. Some of these have explored it to its source in the Mexican mountains at no great distance from Santa Fé. This source appears from the best accounts to be about one thousand four hundred and fifty miles north west of its confluence with the Mississippi. It is a remarkable fact, that the nearer the Mexican mountains are approached, from whatever point, the less wood is to be found. This is verified on Red river; for no trees are to be seen, except along the water courses, above Boggy creek, which is estimated at six hundred miles above Nachitoches. All that immense tract beyond this creek, of about six hundred and fifty miles on the river, and extending in an opposite direction from near the Spanish settlements about St. Antonio to some of the head waters of the Missouri, is one immense prairie or natural meadow, except on the bottoms along the numerous rivers and streams, which are generally covered with a thick growth of timber. The Mexican mountains, in which nearly all of the great westerly branches of the lower Mississippi and Missouri have their sources, are also mostly destitute of wood; but they produce a short grass, which attracts to them in summer vast herds of wild horses, buffaloe, bears, wolves, elk, deer, foxes, wild hogs, antelopes, and a variety of other animals. In winter these are driven by the cold, and the want of food, to the plains or prairies below; and the number of these animals, as described by hunters, almost exceed the bounds of credibility. The soil in these mountains is represented as sandy and steril, and the face of the country as extremely broken, covered by abrupt hills and rocky clifts, and by deep gullies or ravines formed by the rains. Here rock or mineral salt is found, as also mines of silver; but of what value is unknown.

Between the mountains and the great raft, the lands are of various qualities. On Red river, and on some of its branches, many of the bottoms are from ten to fifteen miles broad, and generally covered with the growth peculiar to such lands in other parts of Louisiana. The soil is considered as luxuriant; and the grass, particularly in the prairies, is of an uncommon height. The higher the river is ascended, the more it is confined within its banks; and above the great raft, instances of inundation are not common, though the soil on all the bottoms is evidently alluvial. The high grounds produce good wheat; and this was fully ascertained by the French, who formerly settled themselves among the Caddoques.

The climate on Red river, though not refrigerated by the sea breezes, is deemed as healthful as that along the gulf. This is the more remakable, as the surface of nearly six tenths of the country about the settlements is constantly covered with water, and the atmosphere loaded with vapors, which in other places produce troublesome and fatal endemics. Perhaps this general exemption from diseases may be traced in part to the dry and sandy soil of the high grounds, many of which are covered with pine, and in part, more especially to the numerous salines about the country; to the brackish nature of the water, both in the rivers and lakes, and in the wells and springs, and to the saline qualities of the ground. Whatever the cause may be, certain it is, that the inhabitants on Red river enjoy as much health as is usual in any part of the United States; and the climate, though warm and humid in summer, is not productive of diseases even among strangers unaccustomed to it.

Little is known of the vast country, situated between Red river on the east, the rio Bravo on the west, and the gulf of Mexico on the south, except along the road extending from Nachitoches to St. Antonio. The whole of this tract fronts, or has a regular and gradual descent to the south, and its rivers and other streams flow through it in an oblique south east direction, and fall into the gulf. The road from Nachitoches to Nacogdoches runs nearly west, and from the latter place to St. Antonio it extends about west south west. The north shore of the gulf from the mouth of the Mississippi to the head of the bay of St. Bernard extends in a west north west direction; so that the tract between the road and the sea is of unequal breadths; much wider at the Sabine than at St. Antonio. The road at the former place is about one hundred and fifty miles from the gulf, while at the latter it is not more than eighty or ninety miles. The average width of this tract, situated between the sources of the rivers and the gulf, may be estimated at about four hundred miles; though some of the rivers from their oblique direction as just mentioned, flow more than seven hundred miles before they fall into the sea, and afford a boat navigation for about three fourths of that distance.

The Sabine (called in some maps the Mexicano, and in others the Adaize) is about fifty miles to the westward of Nachitoches. Most of the lands between these two places, particularly along the road, are considerably broken, and of an inferior quality. This tract is rather deficient in good water, and contains more pine than any other wood. This river has its source in the extensive plains to the north west of Nachitoches.

From the Sabine to Nacogdoches, a Spanish village, is about sixty miles. The lands are thinly timbered, except along the water courses, covered with vast bodies of flint stones, and afford many symptoms of rich iron ore. This village is situated in an elevated country, in about thirty one degrees twenty five minutes north latitude, and continually washed on three sides by a beautiful stream of pure water: It is badly built, and contains no more than thirty or forty indifferent houses, with a chapel; and as it is at a distance from any navigable water, it never can arrive to much importance.

The river Trinity, or Trinidad, is about ninety six miles to the westward of Nacogdoches, and between them are two or three considerable streams, probably branches only of some of the rivers. Perhaps the country about the Trinity is better calculated for settlements than any other in this quarter. It is pretty well wooded, and abounds in excellent water. The soil is fertile and the climate healthful. This river estimated at three hundred and fifty miles in length, is navigable for large boats in the season of high water, and vessels of considerable size can enter the mouth of it. Here commence the high grounds on the gulf, which continue to bound the shore to the head of the bay of St. Bernard. On the contrary, between the mouth of the Trinity and that of the Mississippi, the country along the gulf for a considerable depth is covered with marshes, in which some of the rivers are in a manner lost, and their channels obstructed. The Spaniards begin to estimate the importance of the Trinity; for they have planned a town on its banks near the road, and called it *Salsedo*, in honor of the governor-general of the internal provinces, whose capital is the city of Chihuahua, laid down in north latitude, twenty eight degrees fifty minutes, and longitude, one hundred and six degrees, fifty minutes, west from Paris. To encourage the growth of this place, which now (1809) contains twenty five or thirty miserable mud cabins only, liberal grants of lands are made to settlers, in some instances two and three leagues square. It may be safely doubted, however, whether the town of *Salsedo* will even arrive to much importance under the Spanish government, and the reason is obvious. Agriculture, commerce, and manufactures, are hardly known in the province of Texas; and without them no country can expect to flourish.

From the Trinity to the river Brassos is about eighty miles. Between these two rivers are several small creeks, probably branches of larger streams, on the borders of which are some extensive tracts of valuable land, well wooded and watered, and furnished with a pure and wholesome air. The bottoms along the Brassos are also extensive and fertile, though portions of them are usually deluged in the spring. This river is about seven hundred miles long, and affords a good navigation for some distance above its mouth.

The next river of any consequence is the Colorado, about eighty five miles to the westward of the Brassos. The land between these two rivers is of a good quality; but the want of wood and water will probably obstruct the settlement of it. The Colorado is a beautiful river, navigable nearly to its source in the season of high water, a distance of about four hundred and fifty miles. On its borders are large bodies of excellent well timbered land; and perhaps the period is not far distant when populous settlements will be formed on them, especially if industry and enterprise be sufficiently encouraged. This river falls into the head of the bay of St. Bernard.

From the Colorado to the river St. Marks, (one of the branches of the Guadaloupe) is about fifty miles. This river is about one hundred yards wide where the road crosses it, and the lands on its borders are extremely rich and productive, but they are mostly destitute of wood.

About twenty five miles to the westward of the St. Marks, is the river Guadaloupe, which is about the size of the former. The lands on this river are good, well watered, and contain a fine growth of timber. This river is about two hundred miles long, and falls into the bay of St. Bernard, at the mouth of which was planted the colony under M. de la Salle in 1685.

From the Guadaloupe to St. Antonio, the capital of Texas, is about sixty miles. This capital is situated in about north latitude, twenty nine degrees, on one of the head branches of the Guadaloupe, and is said to contain about two thousand five hundred inhabitants; but these are probably overrated. The country about it is elevated, and fanned by a pure air. It has been remarked by travellers, that more old people are found in this quarter than are known to exist in any other territory of the same extent. The houses in St. Antonio are very indifferent; generally one story high, with flat roofs, supported by uprights sunk in the ground, and built of combustible materials. There are, however, one or two public squares, round which the houses make a better appearance. The chapel or church is an ordinary structure, though it is considered by the inhabitants as a splendid edifice. At no great distance from the town, a spring of an uncommon size, yielding pure lime stone water, breaks out of the side of a hill, and soon becomes a river. A dam is erected across it in such a position as to precipitate the water in almost every direction among the houses by means of canals or sluices, which are so constructed as to convey it over the cultivated fields below. This irrigation is the more necessary, as it seldom rains in the neighborhood of St. Antonio during the summer season.

If the preceding calculations are correct, St. Antonio is about five hundred and five miles to the west-south-west of Nachitoches. The several distances we have mentioned were computed in 1806 by a gentleman of intelligence and observation, who traversed the country in that year between Red river and the capital of Texas. From him also were derived in part the few descriptive hints we have given of that country.

In addition to what has been said of the country to the westward of Red river, it may be observed, that it possesses many advantages denied to other portions of Louisiana under the same latitudes. It is elevated; and the air is untainted by noxious exhalations, which in other places are more or less prejudicial to health. The springs afford excellent water; and even the water in most of the rivers is free from impurities, and impregnated with the qualities of the lime stone. It is believed also, that this part of the country contains plenty of salt, as the hunters have discovered several salt springs. Another great advantage attached to it is, that it has a variety of easy and short communications with the sea, by means of the rivers already named, and no doubt some good ports. Hence the facilities to the exportation of cotton, tobacco, and provisions, (perhaps even sugar) which these extensive regions are calculated to yield, and which will be considered as the staple commodities of them.

The country in general is of a rolling nature, destitute of any considerable mountains, and may be considered as an inclined plane from the great Mexican ridge; it is almost wholly free from swamps and marshy grounds, except along the gulf between the mouths of the Sabine and the Trinity. The greatest obstacle to the settlement of some parts of it, is the scarcity of wood; yet the prairies, which are always covered with luxuriant grass, will afford fine ranges for cattle, and therefore cannot be deemed useless in an agricultural point of view. The portion of the country covered with wood, were it even limited to the borders of the rivers, is sufficient for a considerable population; and it is said that, in the neighborhood of the gulf, especially to the westward of the Trinity, a good growth of timber is to be found. We may therefore safely pronounce, that these regions are destined to yield, at no distant period, great quantities of surplus produce, and to open new and important sources of wealth to the agricultural and commercial world.

The road we have traced out is the great thoroughfare between Red river and the city of Mexico, as well as the internal provinces. The Spaniards at all the villages, and at nearly all the rivers on this route, have established small military posts, composed of eight or ten men each; not merely as guards of security, but to facilitate the passage of public letters and despatches, which are carried with as much expedition between the Sabine and the most distant provinces, as in any part of the United States. All these posts are provided with mules. As soon as the mail arrives at one post, it is hastened by a fresh mule and rider to the next, and so on; it travels night and day, and is seldom obstructed, or even retarded, by the weather. Carriages have passed the road from Nachitoches to Mexico; a distance of little more than one thousand miles; some say twelve hundred miles.

Of the country about the sources of the rivers we have named, very little is known. These rivers, at least most of them, head in the extensive plains to the north west of the gulf. The Trinity and Brassos flow from near the upper part of Red river; a small ridge, indeed, only divides them.

The rio Bravo is about one hundred and fifty miles to the westward of St. Antonio, following the course of the road. The lands are generally the same as those already noticed, though the produce of them is probably more valuable. They yield several rare and useful kinds of wood, as also considerable quantities of cochineal.

It is taken for granted, that the Spaniards will never seriously contend for any part of the country to the eastward of the Sabine; and it is also presumed, that the United States will extend and maintain their claims to the rio Bravo. This tract, then, may be computed at about six hundred and five miles in length, and four hundred miles in breadth; containing two hundred and forty two thousand square miles, or one hundred and fifty four million, eight hundred and eighty thousand acres.

There is is some confusion in the maps relative to the latitudes of the rivers, and other remarkable objects, along the gulf of Mexico. The Spanish maps, in particular, lay down nineteen rivers, or large water courses, between the Sabine and the rio Bravo. The mouth of the Sabine is placed in north latitude, thirty degrees, nearly; that of the Trinity in twenty nine degrees; that of the Brassos in twenty nine degrees twenty minutes; the entrance into the bay of St. Bernard in twenty eight degrees thirty minutes; the mouths of the Colorado and Guadaloupe, in the vicinity of each other, in about twenty eight degrees fifty minutes; and the mouth of the rio Bravo in twenty six degrees eight minutes. These calculations of the latitudes, though probably incorrect, will afford the reader a general idea of the relative positions of the several objects, to which they refer. The bay of St. Bernard is said to exhibit one of the most beautiful sheets of water in the world; it contains many islands, and is well stored with various kinds of fish; nearly twelve feet of water is found on the bar at its entrance; its shores are pregnant with delightful scenery.

The paucity of materials forbid a more copious account of this part of Louisiana. The attention, therefore, is necessarily diverted to another quarter.

Black river penetrates the left bank of Red river about thirty miles from the Mississippi, and it has been explored to the hot springs in north latitude, thirty four degrees twenty seven minutes, a distance of five hundred and nine miles. Black river, however, loses its name at the junction of the Ocatahola, Washita, and Tenza, about sixty nine miles from Red river. The Washita is the principal branch, and near it are the hot springs already mentioned. This river, as it is ascended, inclines for some distance to the north west; so that fort Miro, built by the Spaniards, as likewise the settlements in that quarter, situated two hundred and seventy miles from the mouth of Red river, are at no great distance from the Walnut Hills on the Mississippi.

The lands on Black river, below the junction just mentioned, are of an alluvial nature. The banks in general are pretty elevated, and some portions of them seldom buried under water; but the lands gradually slope from the river, and are bounded in the rear by cypress swamps, which are annually inundated. These elevations along the banks are generally one plantation deep, and the soil is composed of black marle, mixed with sand, which have been rolled from the upper country. The trees are not so high and large as those on the Mississippi; they are red and black oaks, ash, peccon, hickory, some elms, cotton wood, and willow: But they gradually increase in height and size as the river is ascended.

An opinion prevails, that these and other alluvial lands in the low country are at this time much more elevated than formerly; and that they are gradually rising above the freshes by the annual depositions made on their surface. This opinion is fully supported by three known facts; the advances of the land into the sea; the existence of trees and other woody substances at a considerable depth under ground, apparently deposited there by the waters; and the annual formation of an alluvious stratum by means of the expansion of the Mississippi and other rivers.

The same kind of land continues to fort Miro on the Washita, though somewhat more elevated, and studded with a few primitive ridges. On the left bank of that river are extensive prairies, the soil of which is luxuriant and productive, bearing a high coarse grass. On the opposite side, between the Washita and Red river, the lands have frequently an elevation of three hundred feet; part of which is prairie, and the remainder mostly covered with pine, and extremely poor and barren.

The fort and settlement on the Washita are situated in north latitude, thirty two degrees thirty minutes, nearly. The first settlement made here was by the French, which was destroyed by the Natchez Indians in 1729, and never revived till the country passed into the hands of Spain; it now extends about thirty miles above fort Miro, and comprehends between five and six hundred souls. Many fine creeks and bayous intersect this part of the country, bounded by rich and extensive bottoms. Just above the fort commences the grant of baron Bastrop, which embraces a square of thirty six miles on each side of the river. Here the banks are elevated about thirty feet; the bottoms are at least half a mile wide, and the high grounds in the rear of them covered with pine.

The uplands, properly so called, make their first appearance about one hundred and thirty miles above the fort, covered with cane breaks, birch, maple, holly, persimmon, and black grape vines. The margins of the river are fringed with a variety of vines and plants, among which is several species of convolvulus. The banks at this place and above it, in some instances suffer from the ebrasion of the waters, though mostly skirted with rocky clifts from eighty to an hundred feet in height, and covered with pine. Hills of freestone are common in this quarter. The lands, among other trees, produce the elm, sycamore, dog and iron wood.

About three hundred and forty five miles above the fort, the country suddenly assumes a more rugged aspect. Hills frequently rise out of the level plains, and exhibit an abundance of rocks, free stone, and blue slate, among whose fissures are found plenty of sparry and chrystaline matter.

This kind of land continues to the hot springs; its surface is covered with a stratum of vegetable earth, from six to twelve inches in thickness, of a dark brown colour, mixed with loam and sand, and well calculated for tillage. The navigation is good in the season of high water, and the climate one of the finest in the world. The distance from the hot springs to the source of the river, is unknown. It is probable, that the country about it is broken, and much less inviting than that lower down.

These springs are numerous, and situated in the neighborhood of the river. Four of them only, are worthy of much notice. The first raises the mercury in Fahrenheit to one hundred and fifty degrees; the second to one hundred and forty five degrees; the third to one hundred and thirty six degrees; and the fourth to one hundred and thirty two degrees. The temperature of the water increases or diminishes in proportion to the size of the spring. The water in none of them, when suffered to cool, is unpleasant to the taste. It is supposed to contain some medicinal virtues, and on this account the springs begin to be visited by valetudinaries.

The sketches now given of the country about the Washita are derived from several sources, particularly from the observations of Mr. Dunbar and Dr. Hunter. It is unfortunate, that all the other great rivers of Louisiana have not been equally well explored and surveyed.

It has been recently found, that the bayou Tenza is of much more consequence than was apprehended. It is an outlet or branch of the Mississippi, which leaves that river near the Arkansas, and meanders along the swamps till it joins Black river. In some places it makes near approaches to the Mississippi; in others it diverges from fifteen to twenty five miles from it, and in its progress passes through several long and narrow lakes, probably formed by occasional dilatations of the stream. This bayou, with very little labor and expense, would afford a good boat navigation for about four hundred miles; and as the current is comparatively weak, it is calculated to facilitate the ascent of boats to the upper country. The lands along the Tenza are as elevated, and as well covered with cane, as those on the Mississippi, and of equal breadth. Many people, under an expectation of acquiring pre-emtive titles, have surveyed and taken possession of large tracts of these lands, admirably adapted to the culture of cotton, and such other articles as are common to the country.

The west bank of the Mississippi, from the mouth of Red river to that of the Arkansas, presents an almost perfect level, and the land is much more elevated on the river than in the rear of it. This vast tract affords a thick growth of large and tall trees, mostly cotton wood and cypress, with extensive cane breaks. This kind of cane near the Arkansas is from fifteen to twenty feet in height; opposite to Natchez and fort Adams, from thirty five to forty feet. All these lands are of an alluvial nature, and extremely fertile. Most of those within half a mile of the Mississippi are sufficiently redeemed from the floods. The swamps extend westward to the high grounds, generally from twenty to thirty five miles breadth, and in the spring season are buried from twelve to twenty five feet under water. During the latter part of summer, the whole of autumn, and the beginning of winter, they are usually dry, and afford excellent pasturage for cattle and wild animals. The water they receive in time of freshes, is mostly precipitated from the Mississippi by means of the creeks and bayous; and as the floods subside, part of it returns to the river by the same channels or drains; but much the greatest part is left to be exhausted by evaporation and absorption.

It must not be supposed, however, that these extensive swamps, situated between the mouth of Red river and that of the Arkansas, and embracing near eight thousand square miles, will always remain entirely useless. They afford plenty of large and excellent cypress, and some other valuable trees, especially along the banks of the water courses. As soon as settlements are formed on the high grounds in the rear of them, or on the borders of the Tenza, they will be occupied as ranges for cattle. Besides, the water communications afforded by them at certain seasons, will be of great use to the opulent planter.

Of the immense country between these low grounds and the rivers to the westward of them, and between the Washita and the Arkansas, no correct information was ever obtained. It was partly explored by the French in the early part of the last century; but no record of their discoveries, at least of any merit, has been handed down to us. Some hunters, however, have occasionally penetrated it. They represent it as mostly destitute of wood, except along the water courses, and somewhat mountainous.

Few settlements are formed on the west bank of the Mississippi, within the tract just noticed. They are thinly scattered along from Red river to the mouth of the Yazous. Planters, however, begin to turn their attention to this quarter, which, at this time receives nearly its proportion of new settlers from the States. The lands cultivated by them are of the first quality for cotton, and yield an abundance of corn and other provisions.

Every part of the country we have noticed produces several sorts of wild fruit, particularly pawpaws, grapes of different kinds, mulberries, figs, persimmons, and a variety of nuts and plums. Perhaps no part of the world yields finer peaches and mellons. Apple and pear trees flourish extremely well on the high grounds; but their fruit is indifferent.

SKETCHES OF LOUISIANA.

CHAPTER VI.

UPPER LOUISIANA.

UNDER the Spanish government the south boundary of Upper Louisiana was a place called *Hope Encampment*, nearly opposite to the Chickasaw Bluffs. In this chapter a general description will be given of all the known parts of Louisiana, situated above the Arkansas; the mouth of which is in about north latitude, thirty three degrees forty minutes: Some attention will be paid to the natural divisions of the country, as well as to the divisional lines of districts.

The country about the mouth of the Arkansas is rather low, and most of it overflowed in seasons of high water.

The village on that river is situated about forty five miles from the Mississippi. The French visited this place as early as 1685, where they opened a trade with the natives, built a fort, and formed some settlements about it. At that period the Arkansas nation of Indians was deemed one of the most powerful in the country, and the French to preserve peace with them, and to secure their trade, intermarried with them. Most of the inhabitants of that village, are of mixed blood, and the same mixture is observable among the Indians, who are now reduced to a very few in number, and live in two small villages above that of the whites. They formerly contended with the Chickasaws for superiority; and their wars with that people, and the use of ardent spirits, have nearly extinguished them as a nation. The village of the whites at present contains thirty or forty houses only, and a garrison, in which a few troops are quartered. In the neighborhood of it are a few plantations, and the country about it is well adapted to tillage. But the Indian trade, at present very inconsiderable, occupies the attention of the inhabitants, who are altogether of French extraction, and in a great measure unacquainted with agricultural pursuits.

It is certain, that the French nearly a century ago penetrated the Arkansas to its source: But they have left us no accounts of the country in that quarter; and for the few traits we have of it, and of the regions between the Arkansas and the Missouri, we are indebted to the enterprise of English Americans. A few prominent features, therefore, must suffice.

From the Arkansas village to Verdigris river, a distance of at least five hundred miles, the shores are generally lined with reeds or cane, and furnish many rich and extensive bottoms. The country below the upper extent of the Osage hunting grounds, is well supplied with wood. Craggy clifts frequently make their appearance along the

Arkansas, at least as far up as a branch of that river called Negrocka. All that vast country, which lies between Verdigris river and the Mexican mountains, and between the Arkansas and the Kansas and Platte rivers, may be considered as one immense prairie, with very little else to attract attention. Between the Osage villages and the head waters of those rivers, the country is sandy, and almost destitute of herbage; the surface of it is irregular and broken, interspersed with a variety of small streams, some fresh and some salt, with barren sand hills, and some level tracts covered with grass, and others with flint and lime-stones. The nearer the Arkansas is approached from this quarter, the more regular and the less stony is the surface of the country; though even here it has the appearance of a barren waste, and exhibits to the eye an arid and steril soil. Few trees are to be discovered, except along the water courses, and these are generally the cotton wood, a species of the poplar. Many of the small branches of the Arkankas are strongly impregnated with salt, and the shores of that river, in many places, are frosted with nitre. The water of many of the springs or salines are too salt for soups, and it even renders corn, when boiled in it, unfit for use. Immense herds of buffaloe, elk, deer, and a species of the goat, range about this open country, which produces a short grass, of which they are fond; and a gentleman of veracity has asserted, that he has seen a drove of them, containing at least nine thousand.

These regions, however, although they are at the distance of several hundred miles from our present settlements, are not wholly useless. They produce vast quantities of peltry, and the lands along the numerous rivers and streams are suitable for cultivation. A series of years must elapse before the country between them and the Mississippi is settled; and at whatever time our settlers approach the vast prairies already noticed, they will experience one advantage not common in other new and interior countries, a fruitful supply of salt.

The flat country on the Mississippi extends from the mouth of the Arkansas to the head of what is called Tiwappaty bottom, a distance of nearly four hundred and fifty miles. The river St. Francis runs nearly parallel to the Mississippi, and from thirty to forty miles, (in some places less) to the westward of it, for the distance of about four hundred and sixty miles, and mostly through the flat country already mentioned. Nearly half of the lands between these two rivers are covered with swamps and ponds, and periodically inundated. These swamps, filled with cypress, are mostly dry in summer; though, unless they be drained at great expense, or banks constructed to keep the water from them, they will never be of any service to agriculturalists, other than as ranges for cattle. Many creeks or bayous take their rise in them, and they flow into both rivers; and it is calculated, that there are as many of them as one to every fifteen miles. These swamps are generally in a central position between the two rivers; they mostly communicate with both by forming creeks or bayous, which are navigable in the time of freshes. The lands along the banks of the rivers and other streams are much more elevated than the intermediate tracts; they are seldom overflowed, and present a thrifty growth of large trees. Prairies abound in the interior, as also some tracts of upland, calculated for rich and extensive plantations.

This tract contains no varieties of soil. The lands are mostly what are called bottoms or intervals, and are composed of a deep rich mould, calculated for most kinds of grain, cotton, tobacco, flax, and hemp. The more elevated grounds yield thirty bushels of wheat, and eighty bushels of corn, by the acre. Tiwappaty bottom, which is situated above the mouth of the Ohio, is equal in fertility to any part of the western country. It produces a thick growth of timber, and many of the trees are of an extraordinary size. Part of this bottom, which is about twenty miles long, and from three to six miles broad, produces an immense quantity of rushes. These grow to the height of about eight feet; they are large, and stand so thick, that it is difficult for a man to make his way among them. Large droves of cattle resort to them in winter, and fatten on them.

Most of the settlements are formed along the Mississippi, not only because the lands near the banks are less exposed to inundation, but because that navigable stream affords the desired facilities to commerce. The settlement at Little Prairie, thirty miles below New Madrid, was formed by Canadian traders about the year 1795; and in 1803 it contained about one hundred and fifty souls.

New Madrid also situated in north latitude, thirty six degrees thirty minutes, (seventy miles by the course of the Mississippi below the mouth of the Ohio, and forty-five miles over land) was first settled by hunters and traders. In 1787 it assumed the form of a regular built town under the direction of general Morgan, then of New Jersey, but now of Pennsylvania. In consequence of some obstacles to his designs, created by the Spanish government, he finally abandoned his pursuits, and retired from the country. The town is situated on the west bank of the Mississippi, bounded on the north by the bayou St. John, which always affords plenty of water, and on the south by a creek, which heads in a cypress swamp in the rear of the town, and is generally destitute of water in the dry seasons. The river never rises so high as to inundate the town: But the banks of it are very unstable; portions of them annually cave in; the houses were originally erected over the present channel, and the inhabitants are annually obliged to remove some of them, otherwise they would be destroyed; and the probability is, that the encroachments of the river will eventually scatter the population of this place.

This town was originally so laid out as to extend as the French express it, forty acres in length along the river; the back part was contracted to twenty acres on account of some swamps, and the depth was sixteen acres. It contained ten streets running parallel with the river, and eighteen others crossing them at right angles. The former were sixty feet, and the latter forty five feet in breadth. Six squares were also laid out, and reserved for the use of the town, each of which contained two acres. A street of one hundred and twenty feet in breadth was likewise reserved on the bank of the river.

The tract of country already mentioned, between the Arkansas and Tiwappaty bottom, is more insalubrious than any other part of Upper Louisiana; and from the situation of it a stranger would be inclined to believe, that it was more subject to dangerous diseases than it really is. Complaints of an epidemic nature, are unknown. Deaths are more frequent among children than adults; and this is imputed to the green fruit, which the former indulge themselves in eating during the most sickly season of the year. The mephitic exhalations from the swamps and low grounds must necessarily poison the air; they produce intermittents, and some bilious fevers, though they have never been considered as very malignant. Indeed, the sick have suffered more from the want of medicine than from the obstinate nature of the endemics; and more mortality has occurred from old age and accidents than from prevalent diseases.

A considerable number of Delawares, Shawanese, and Cherokees, have built some villages on the waters of the St. Francis and White rivers. Their removal into these quarters was authorised by the Spanish government, and they have generally conducted themselves to the satisfaction of the whites. Some stragglers from the Creeks, Chocktaws, and Chickasaws, who are considered as outlaws by their respective nations, have also established themselves on the same waters; and their disorders and depredations among the white settlers are not unfrequent.

The population of this tract in 1804 was estimated at one thousand three hundred and fifty, including one hundred and fifty slaves; of which about four hundred, according to the best accounts, were capable of bearing arms. One company of militia at Arkansas, another at Little Prairie, and three in New Madrid and its vicinity, were regularly organised. The more distant and scattered settlers were not included in the organised militia; they were excused from the ordinary duties of this corps on account of the inconvenience of attending to them. About two thirds of the population is composed of English Americans; the other third of French. It is believed, that the population of this tract has not much increased in several years. For three years, commencing in 1800, the increase was only six persons. About New Madrid, and below it, the population evidently diminishes; while it increases more to the north, particularly above the mouth of the Ohio.

The natural growth of this portion of the country is somewhat different from that among the upper settlements; and it partly consists of mulberry, locust, sassafras, walnut, peccon, cotton wood, cypress, willows, and dogwood. On the highest grounds some persimmons, hickory, oak, and ash, are to be found. This enumeration is not complete; but it is sufficient to afford a general idea of the natural growth of this tract.

It has been the misfortune of most of the first settlers in Louisiana, particularly the French, to neglect agriculture, and to turn their attention almost wholly to the Indian trade, which at best only afforded a precarious subsistence; and none but a few of the principal traders ever derived any profits from it. The first settlers at New Madrid, and those of most of the other places already named, were of this description. Not till about the year 1794, when the game was nearly exhausted, did they begin to cultivate the lands, except for gardens and the raising of scanty supplies of corn; and since that period the people have gradually turned their attention to agriculture. In 1803 the several settlements, exclusive of that at Arkansas, produced thirty three thousand eight hundred and eighty bushels of corn, three hundred and ten bushels of wheat, fourteen thousand eight hundred pounds of flax, four thousand five hundred and sixty pounds of tobacco, and one hundred and sixty two thousand nine hundred pounds of cotton. They also during the same time manufactured seven hundred and forty gallons of whiskey, tanned four hundred hides, and procured of the Indians six hundred and sixty five packs of different kinds of peltries. Agriculture and the manufacture of various articles, are at this time in a progressive state; and the prospects of success in these branches will eventually supercede the desire of an Indian traffic.

At the head of Tiwappaty bottom, and about twelve miles below cape Gerardeau, the high grounds commence on the Mississippi. At this place is a high rocky bluff, which stretches at about right angles with the river across the country to the St. Francis. This may be said to divide the low from the high country. The settlements to the north of it are the most populous; and, in whatever light we consider them, they are of much the most consequence.

In the territory now to be noticed are several districts or counties, and the face of them exhibits a happy medium between a mountainous and level country. No part of this extensive tract is subject to inundation, except now and then, and small portions of it only are unfit for tillage. It is much less mountainous and broken than the eastern and middle states, and not so low and flat as the southern states on the Atlantic side of the mountains.

All the bottoms, and many of the prairies, are level; but the lands back of the first, and generally those in the neighborhood of the latter, are formed into gentle swells and vales, and exhibit to the eye what is commonly called a rolling country. It must not, however, be understood, that there are no high mountains, or any abrupt high grounds; on the contrary, there are many of both; but they are too few in number, and too limited in extent, to injure the character of the country, or to lessen the value generally conceived of it.

Both the bottoms and the high grounds are alternately divided into wood lands and prairies. Some of the bottoms are covered with trees of a large size. Those on the high grounds are more scattered, and generally of a different species. The prairies are covered with grass. These were probably occasioned by the ravages of fire; because, wherever copses of trees are found on them, the ground about them is low, and too moist to admit the fire to pass over it; and because it is a common practice among the Indians and other hunters to set the woods and prairies on fire, by which means they are able to kill an abundance of game. They take secure stations to the leeward, and the fire drives the game to them. These prairies are numerous; but very few of them within our settlements, or in the neighborhood of them, are of any considerable extent. Some of them, indeed, are many miles long; but they are narrow, and are so situated as to be of great utility to agriculturists. When practicable, prairie lands have been included in plantation surveys. They afford an early grass for cattle, and produce an abundance of hay of no very inferior quality. The soil of them is generally stronger than that of the circumjacent grounds; and almost the only labor required to convert them into tillage fields, is making the necessary fences round them.

The district of cape Gerardeau extends from Tiwappaty bottom to Apple creek, a distance on the Mississippi of about thirty miles, and without any definite boundaries to the westward. The first house built in this district was in 1794 at the cape, and by a Frenchman. Since that period settlements have been rapidly formed by emigrants from the United States; and it is generally believed, that the lands in this quarter are inferior to none in Upper Louisiana: Certain it is, that the richest and most industrious farmers in this part of the world are the proprietors of them. In 1803 the population of this district was one thousand two hundred and six. During the three preceding years its increase was four hundred and sixty six; so that in 1804 it contained about one thousand four hundred and seventy whites, as also a few slaves; and the increase has been equally rapid since the country passed under our jurisdiction. Not more than three or four Frenchmen live in this district; the rest are English Americans, who were organized into three large companies of militia soon after we assumed the government.

The people, among many other articles, raise wheat, corn, tobacco, flax, hemp, and cotton, and manufacture large quantities of maple sugar. They annually export considerable quantities of beef, pork, lard, smoked hams, and some peltry. They also cultivate various kinds of fruit, small grains, and garden vegetables. The lands in this district are elevated, and well supplied with springs; free from stagnated waters and low marshy grounds, and the climate is deemed healthful. It contains only one swamp, which is just below the cape, and extends across the country to the St. Francis; this swamp is filled with cypress trees of no great value.

Not many of the settlers in this district have planted themselves on the Mississippi; they preferred the country about twelve miles back of that river. Several considerable settlements are formed on the waters of the St. Francis, about sixty miles in the rear of the cape, where the lands are of the first quality. All the lands in this district are of a rolling nature; they possess a luxuriant soil, are well covered with timber, and are intersected with a variety of excellent streams and springs.

Apple creek enters the Mississippi from the west about eighteen miles above the cape, and affords an inland navigation at some seasons of the year. About twenty miles up this creek, and near to it, are three villages of Indians, one of Delawares, and two of Shawnees, which were erected about the year 1794. The settlement of the Indians in this quarter was favored by the Spanish government, to whom a considerable tract of land was promised. They had several hundred warriors among them; who were considered as a safe-guard to the whites, and at the devotion of the Spanish authorities. One of these villages contains about eighty houses. The houses of all the villages are built of logs, some of them squared, and well interlocked at the ends, and covered with shingles. Many of them are two stories high; and attached to them are small houses for the preservation of corn, and barns for the shelter of cattle and horses, with which they are well supplied. Their houses are well furnished with decent and useful furniture. These Indians are said to be the most wealthy of any in the country; but they are greatly debauched and debilitated by the use of ardent spirits. The country about them is too much settled to afford plenty of game. They mostly hunt on the waters of the St. Francis, and White river; and sometimes they penetrate into the territories of the Osages, between whom a predatory war has been maintained for many years.

The district of St. Genevieve is bounded on the south by Apple creek, and by the Merimak on the north; and the breadth of it on the Mississippi is upwards of an hundred miles. The boundaries to the west have never been designated. This district, perhaps, is more hilly and uneven than any other settled part of the same extent in Upper Louisiana. It contains two regularly built villages, St. Genevieve and New Bourbon, which were founded soon after the peace of 1763; and these were the first settlements made in the district, except some scattering ones, occasioned by the appearance of mineral riches. The former contains about one hundred and eighty, and the latter thirty five houses, exclusive of some other buildings. On the Mississippi are some extensive bottoms, the soil of which is prolific. Some of them are nearly three miles in breadth. The extensive one between the Mississippi, and St. Genevieve and New Bourbon, and claimed as the property of these villages, which are erected on the margin of the high grounds, is under good cultivation; it is, however, flooded once in about ten or twelve years. The high grounds for fifty miles back, are more or less cultivated; but they are in some instances broken, steril, and less productive than the lands of the other districts. These defects, however, are more than counterbalanced by the great quantities of lead, which are found in various quarters, and by the salines, which yield a sufficient quantity of salt for the consumption of the inhabitants, and some for exportation. The settlements are extended to some of the waters of the St. Francis, which take their rise among them. Several streams, navigable for fifteen or twenty miles, intersect this district. On the Merimak, navigable for a hundred miles, is a silver mine, which was formerly worked by the French; and on its banks considerable quantities of lead and salt are manufactured. The settlements extend about fifty miles up this river.

Between St. Genevieve and the Merimak, the banks of the Mississippi are in many places extremely high and rocky; some of them have an elevation of at least three hundred and sixty feet, and are so disposed as, on a distant view, to exhibit the appearance of artificial towers. They are solid masses of lime stone, deposited in horizontal strata.

The agricultural productions of this district are similar to those of the district of cape Gerardeau. Hemp is indigenous; it grows to the height of eleven feet, and is said to be equal in goodness and texture to that of the north of Europe; it covers the fields of the farmers in spite of their efforts to destroy it. About fifteen hundred weight may be obtained from the acre. Rope and duck manufactories are much wanted in this country; and the avails of them might always be disposed of to advantage at New Orleans and the Havanna. Such manufactures would probably enrich the proprietors, and at the same time prove useful to our numerous river navigators, who are now obliged to supply their wants from Kentucky. Perhaps, however, a business of this nature might be carried on with more profit higher up the Mississippi, where the hemp is undoubtedly better.

This district produces some articles of natural growth not common among the other settlements in Upper Louisiana. These are several kinds of pine, which are mostly found at some distance up the Merimak, and from which the inhabitants manufacture considerable quantities of pitch and tar, nearly sufficient for the consumption of the country. The banks of the Merimak also produce some excellent cypress; and this species of wood is not common to the country to the northward of the district of New Madrid. From this and the pine, boards of a good quality are manufactured; but the price of them are so exorbitant, that few only can afford to purchase them. Cedar is also found in plenty on the banks of the Mississippi, and some other rivers, above the mouth of the Illinois; and this is converted to a variety of useful purposes.

The population of this district in 1804, cannot be precisely ascertained; but from the census of 1800, and the probable increase in four years, it must have amounted to about two thousand three hundred and fifty whites, and five hundred and twenty slaves. Since we have been in possession of the country, the population has been much more rapid than before. Only three companies of militia existed in this district under the Spanish government, but on the change six of them were organized.

In addition to the several articles usually sent out of the country to market, those of lead and salt form a considerable branch of commerce in this district. They are exported to the states of Ohio, Kentucky, Tennessee, to part of Pennsylvania and Virginia, and to New Orleans. Lead, indeed, is frequently sent from this quarter to the Atlantic markets; sometimes by way of the sea, and sometimes by way of the Ohio.

The district of St. Louis has the Mississippi on the east, the Missouri on the west, and the Merimak on the south. It contains several good settlements, as also three compact villages, St. Louis, Carondelet, and St. Ferdinand.

St. Louis, the capital of Upper Louisiana, is situated on the west bank of the Mississippi, eighteen miles below the mouth of the Missouri, and fourteen miles above that of the Merimak, and, according to Hutchins, in latitude thirty eight degrees twenty four minutes north. It was founded in 1764 by " Pierre Laclade, Maxan, and company," who associated for the purposes of trade. They conceived it a position where the trade of the Missouri, Mississippi, and the other rivers, was most likely to center; and since that period, St. Louis has been the emporium of trade in Upper Louisiana. In 1766 this village received a large accession of inhabitants from the opposite side of the river, who preferred the government of Spain to that of England. The situation of the town is elevated; the shore is rocky, which effectually prevents the encroachments of the river. It has two long streets running parallel with the Mississippi, with a variety of others intersecting them at right angles. It contains about one hundred and eighty houses, and the best of them are built of stone. Some of them, including the large gardens, and even squares, attached to them, are enclosed with high stone walls; and these, together with the rock scattered along the shore and about the streets, render the air uncomfortably warm in summer. A small sloping hill extends along in the rear of the town, on the summit of which is a garrison, and behind it an extensive prairie, which affords plenty of hay, as also pasture for the cattle and horses of the inhabitants.

After the attack made on St. Louis in 1780 by the governor of Michillimakinak, the Spanish government found it necessary to fortify the town. It was immediately stockaded, and the stone bastion and the demilune at the upper end of it, were constructed. The succeeding peace of 1783 lessened the danger, and the works were suspended. In 1794 the garrison on the hill in the rear of the town and government house, was completed. In 1797, when an unfriendly visit was expected from Canada, four stone towers were erected at nearly equal distances in a circular direction round the town, as also a wooden blockhouse near the lower end of it. It was contemplated to enclose the town by a regular chain of works, and the towers were intended to answer the purposes of bastions: But as the times grew more auspicious, the design was abandoned, and the works left in an unfinished state.

The village of Carondelet is situated on the Mississippi about five miles below St. Louis. It contains forty or fifty houses, inhabited by Creoles and Canadians.

About fourteen miles to the north west of St. Louis, is the small village of St. Ferdinand. It contains about sixty houses; most of them are situated on a rising ground, at the foot of which is a considerable stream of pure water, and on the opposite side is one of the most fertile and valuable prairies in the country. The inhabitants of this village are also Creoles and Canadians. The inhabitants of all the compact villages are of this description: But the extensive settlements about the country have been made by English Americans; these form about three fifths of the population, and perhaps more.

The lands in this district are more fertile, and much less broken, than those in the district of St. Genevieve. Between the Merimak and St. Louis, the banks of the river are mostly high and rocky. Just above St. Louis a bottom commences, and continues to the mouth of the Missouri. On this river the bottoms are extensive, generally from one to one-and a half miles in width, mostly covered with a thick growth of large timber. Settlements are formed as high up as the *Du Bois*, about sixty miles from the Mississippi. Back of St. Louis is an extensive elevated prairie, the soil of which is good, but which from the want of timber to fence it, will probably remain uncultivated. The people of St. Louis, however, derive from it a plentiful supply of hay and pasturage. The prairie in the vicinity of St. Ferdinand is about twelve miles long, and two miles broad, and is so situated as to be of great utility to the inhabitants. It extends nearly parallel to the Missouri, and from one to two miles from it. The plantations on each side of this prairie are so laid out as to embrace suitable portions of it, as also the necessary woodlands. Considerable settlements are formed along the borders of it. Those extensive ones on the long point, formed by the junction of the Mississippi and Missouri, are near the lower end of it, and those at *Maries des Liards*, are at the opposite extremity. These settlements are wealthy; the people industrious; and the lands cultivated by them of the first quality. On the right bank of the Missouri, and not many miles above its mouth, is a bluff or mountain of pit-coal; but this article is so much intermixed with sulphur, that it is too apt to consume iron, and therefore the smiths pretty generally decline the use of it.

The largest and best settlement in this district is that called St. Andrews, situated on a small river, which joins the Missouri a few miles above St. Charles. This settlement is about twenty four miles to the south west of St. Louis, and is composed of excellent farmers, who have introduced a more correct agriculture than is commonly practised, and who have cultivated with success some of the most useful grasses in the Atlantic States. The lands in this quarter contain a happy mixture of prairie and wood, of bottom and high grounds, and the soils of all of them are productive.

Considerable settlements are also formed along the Merimak. From the large bodies of good land along the borders of this river, the salt works on it, the lead and iron mines in the vicinity of it, and the facilities it affords to navigation, we have a right to conclude, that the settlements in this quarter will soon acquire more importance than other interior ones.

The population of this district, like most of the others, can only be conjectured by reference to the census of 1800, adding to it the probable increase between that period and 1804, when the United States took possession of Upper Louisiana. This district then contained about two thousand two hundred and eighty whites, and five hundred blacks. Its productions are similar to those of the district of St. Genevieve, except the article of lead; and except cypress and pine, the natural growth is also the same. The exports principally consist of various kinds of furs and peltries, salted pork, beef, and lead. The latter article is obtained from the other districts. The militia of this district was only partially organised under the Spanish government; but it soon assumed a more regular form under our own.

The district of St. Charles is situated between the left bank of the Missouri and the right bank of the Mississippi, and contains immense bodies of valuable land: Its boundaries up these rivers are undefined. Perhaps the climate, the lands, and the navigable streams in this district, combined with other natural advantages, point it out as the most eligible part of the country for farmers. Exclusive of the two great rivers already mentioned, it is intersected by a variety of smaller ones; some of them afford among the present settlements an inland navigation of fifteen or twenty miles, and most of them are calculated for mills and other water works: But when our settlements in this district have a little more than doubled their present extent, they will embrace a variety of others, some of which furnish an inland navigation of several hundred miles. The country is rolling, but not mountainous; the soil is deep and strong; there is no want of timber, or sweet and wholesome water, except on some of the extensive prairie bottoms, particularly those along the Mississippi.

Extensive bottoms are to be found along all the great rivers. Those on the Missouri are generally covered with wood, and are seldom inundated, except when the water is unusually high. A prairie bottom stretches from the mouth of the Missouri along the west bank of the Mississippi to sandy creek or bay, about sixty five miles, where our settlements in that quarter terminate; and the width of it is from four to six miles, and in some places it exceeds ten miles. The soil is of a luxuriant nature, and yields in abundance; but the want of wood and spring water, of which this prairie bottom is almost destitute, obliges the settlers to plant themselves on the margin of the high grounds. The small village of *Portage des Sciouxr* stands on this bottom. Few other settlements have been formed on it, though some part of it is culti-

vated by the farmers, who have established themselves a-
long the interior borders of it.

This district presents us with only two compact villages, St. Charles, and *Portage des Sioux*; and these are
almost wholly peopled with Creoles and Canadians. The
other settlements have been formed by emigrants from the
United States, who compose nearly four fifths of the population.

St. Charles was founded in 1780, and is situated on the
left bank of the Missouri, about twenty four miles above
its mouth. It contains only one street, which extends
upwards of a mile on the river, and is lined by about one
hundred houses. The banks of the river along the town
are not of a firm texture, and encroachments are apprehended. Owing to a hill, which extends along in the rear
of the town, and nearly the whole length of it, the streets
cannot be multiplied, nor any buildings erected, except on
the borders of the present street. This village is remarkable for the health enjoyed by the inhabitants of it.
Health, indeed, is more generally experienced on the
Missouri than on any other of the rivers; and perhaps
this results from the rapidity of its current, and from the
cold and lively nature of its water, added to the nitrous
and sulphureous qualities it contains.

The village of *Portage des Sioux* is situated on the
right bank of the Mississippi, about six miles above the
mouth of the Missouri, and on the extensive prairie bottom already noticed. The origin of this village is of recent date, and contains only about twenty or twenty five
houses; but the fertility of the lands about it will probably
cause an increase of population, and eventually render it
of some importance.

Small rivers and creeks are numerous in this district,
and many settlements are formed on their borders. One
of the principal of these is on the river *Femme Osage*, some
distance above St. Charles on the Missouri. Perhaps

the only mills of any consequence in Upper Louisiana, except one at St. Louis, are to be found in this district; and a spirit of industry prevails among the settlers.

In 1804 the population of this district was estimated, partly by official documents, at about one thousand four hundred whites, and one hundred and fifty blacks; and perhaps its increase is greater than that of any other district, except cape Gerardeau. Only two organised companies of militia existed under the Spanish government; but five large ones were formed soon after the country fell under our jurisdiction. The agricultural productions in this quarter are similar to those of the adjoining districts, though some articles yield more abundantly, particularly wheat, hemp, and most kinds of esculent roots and vegetables. Salt is manufactured on or near the Missouri, and on one or two small rivers at some distance up the Mississippi; these manufactories may be rendered productive. Here are also plenty of iron ore, and some of the richest lead mines in the country; as likewise various kinds of clay and stone of peculiar qualities, out of which household and other utensils may probably be manufactured.

The population of Upper Louisiana, if we take into view the commencement of it, may be considered as rapidly formed. The first settlers from Canada planted themselves on the east side of the Mississippi. Before the treaty of 1763, few grants of lands only were made on the opposite side of that river. These were mostly designed to embrace mineral riches; and as the surface of the country about the mines appeared steril and broken, the old inhabitants were not disposed to change their situations. We have already seen, that St. Louis was founded in 1764, and that in 1766, in consequence of the inability of France to maintain her possessions in North America, much of the population was transferred to the west side of the Mississippi; and from this circumstance the settlements in Upper Louisiana derived their origin. Two subsequent causes served to increase this population, and to diminish it on the opposite side of the Mississippi. The first was the ordinance of 1787, which prohibited slavery and involuntary servitude in what was then denominated the north western territory. The slave holders were disposed to preserve this species of property; and to do it effectually they abandoned their ancient habitations, and joined their friends in the new dominions of Spain. The second was the rupture in 1797, when an attack from Canada was projected on the Spanish possessions along the Mississippi. At this period, Spain was bound to evacuate all her military posts on the east side of that river to the north of the thirty first degree; and Upper Louisiana was the only barrier she had to oppose the descent of the English. The distance of this province from the capital, added to a wilderness of nearly a thousand miles in extent between them, seemed to point out the necessity of strengthening it;—and she conceived it good policy to populate it by the citizens of the United States, especially as they appeared disposed to act with vigor against the English. Additional prospects, therefore, were held out to settlers, and pains were taken to disseminate them in every direction. Large quantities of land were granted them, attended with no other expenses than those of office fees, and surveys, which were not exorbitant; and they were totally exempted from taxation. This sufficiently accounts for the rapid population of Upper Louisiana; which, in 1804, consisted of more than three fifths of English Americans.

It was customary under the Spanish government for each district to furnish an annual census of the inhabitants, with the number of births and deaths, the number of swine, cattle, and horses on hand, the various articles produced by agriculture, and industry, as also those exported. The persons employed to furnish the census never took the pains to be accurate; and in consequence of this inattention the population was probably underrated, particularly as its annual increase in many of the districts exceeded what mere superficial observers had reason to apprehend. This is not the only difficulty in the way of accurately estimating the population. No census was taken of some of the districts subsequent to 1800; others furnished them as late as 1803; so that we have no precise data for the population in 1804. It was, however, the general opinion at the latter period, that it exceeded eleven thousand. This calculation is probably too high, as those who made it did not allow for deaths, and for the occasional removals out of the country. If therefore we estimate the population of Upper Louisiana at the time we took possession of it at nine thousand and twenty whites, and one thousand three hundred and twenty blacks, we shall not be very wide from the truth. The same defects exist in the census of New Orleans, and in those of the several districts in Lower Louisiana. They enable us, however, to calculate with some degree of certainty the annual increase of population from 1799 to 1804, when, by the best accounts, it consisted of about forty one thousand seven hundred whites, and thirty eight thousand eight hundred blacks, besides several hundred people of mixed color. Hence the province of Louisiana, at the time we acquired it, contained about fifty thousand seven hundred and twenty whites, and forty thousand one hundred and twenty slaves; total ninety thousand, eight hundred and forty, exclusive of the free people of mixed color, who mostly resided in New Orleans, and were estimated at about two thousand five hundred.

In a country so young and so lately settled as that of Upper Louisiana, it cannot be expected, that agricultural experiments have been numerous or extensive. The first care of a settler is to raise the necessaries of life;

and beyond this his views do not extend for some years, because he is either destitute of slaves, or the markets are too distant to authorise the hopes of success. Until greater industry and enterprise be excited, we shall hardly know what the soil is calculated to produce. We have reason to believe, that cotton, tobacco, hemp, and rice, exclusive of the various kinds of grains, may be cultivated to advantage in the district of New Madrid. Indeed, hemp and tobacco flourish extremely well in the more northern districts. Cotton produces very well in the neighborhood of St. Louis, where some of the farmers raise a sufficient quantity of that article to clothe their families. One of them, who emigrated from the state of Georgia, is of opinion, that the cotton raised in that state is longer, but not so fine as that cultivated on the high grounds by himself. He declines the cultivation of it on a large scale, as he is apprehensive that the summers are too short to authorise the hope of good crops, though, during the three years he had raised this article, it never experienced any injury from the frosts. May not cotton by repeated cultivation, like many other articles, become in some measure naturalized to the climate? Tobacco is an indigenous plant on the lower part of the Mississippi; and in no part of the United States does it grow larger than in Upper Louisiana, where it is cured and made into carrots for the Indian trade, and in this way it becomes an article of commerce. The people, however, seldom use it when they can obtain any other; perhaps because they are unacquainted with the manufacture of it.

Exclusive of the articles just mentioned, those more common to all the districts, and more generally cultivated, are the following: Indian corn, wheat, rye, oats, barley, buckwheat, and flax. The soil also produces all kinds of esculent roots, and culinary vegetables; a multitude of different berries and plums of a delicious flavor, all of which are indigenous; cucumbers and all sorts of mellons grow in the greatest perfection. Sweet and Irish potatoes are common to the country. Apple, pear, and peach trees have a rapid growth, and the latter are generally so loaded with fruit as to break down. The peaches are manufactured into brandy, and some of the farmers annually distil four hundred gallons of this spirit; an excellent substitute for foreign distilled spirits, the expense of which in a great measure prevents the use of them. Whiskey is also distilled from rye and Indian corn, which is mostly disposed of to the Indians, like the tobacco, in exchange for furs and peltries. The country is filled with wild grape vines of a large size; some of them are seven inches in diameter, six feet above the ground, and they run to the tops of the tallest trees. They bear grapes of a tolerable flavor, especially when fully exposed to the sun; and it is said that, in 1769, the settlers in the Illinois country made a hundred hogsheads of good wine from them. The grape vines imported from France and the south of Germany, and cultivated at St. Louis, flourish extremely well.

It has been found on experiment, that the bottoms are too rich for the culture of wheat, oats, and some other grains. These articles grow to an extraordinary height and size; but they contract a rust about the time they are in blossom, which prevents the formation of the edible substance. They are raised on the high grounds; and the farmer is able to obtain thirty five and sometimes forty bushels of wheat from the acre, each of which will weigh from sixty five to seventy pounds. The bottoms are suitable for roots and vegetables of all kinds, grass, corn, hemp, flax, fruit trees, and many other articles. When properly cultivated, an acre will yield a hundred bushels of corn, and this is common. But from some cause or other, probably the heats and the want of slaves, tillage is much neglected; most of the farmers only pass the plough occasionally between the rows of corn, and seldom make use of the hoe; and in this way they obtain from fifty to sixty bushels from the acre. All these bottoms are formed by the alluvious substances rolled down by the rivers, and will never require the aid of manure. Some of them on the east side of the Mississippi about Cahokia and Kaskaskia, have been under cultivation for more than one hundred and twenty years, and are at this time as fertile and productive as those of recent culture.

The country produces all the substantial provisions of life in abundance; particularly mutton, fowls, beef, pork, butter, and cheese. It is common for a farmer to own from a hundred to a hundred and fifty head of cattle, and as many swine; nor ought this to be deemed extraordinary, when it is considered, that the rearing of them is productive of very little expense and trouble. The former in summer subsist on the grass, with which the country is covered; and in the winter they retire to the bottoms, where they find plenty of cane and rushes. The latter subsist on the mast found in the woods: and hence both the cattle and swine keep fat most of the year. No hay is necessary, except for such cows and horses as are stabled, and plenty of this is always to be obtained in the proper season from the prairies. The high grounds are seldom so thickly covered with wood as to prevent the growth of grass. They exhibit more the appearance of extensive meadows than of rude and gloomy forests. In 1803 large quantities of beef were sold for three dollars per hundred, and some for fifty cents less; but since that period the price has gradually risen. When a farmer has an inclination to export a quantity of beef and pork, he carries his barrels and salt into the woods, and with his rifle he kills his cattle and swine, and packs away the meat ready for market. The same practice is followed in most other parts of the western country. Considerable quantities of butter and cheese are also made for exportation, though the latter is of an inferior quality. In a country so fertile, and so well adapted to the raising of cattle and swine, the inhabitants have it in their power to live as they please, and to become opulent with little labor. The greatest inconvenience they suffer is from the want of ready markets in their neighborhood. The custom of exporting the surplus produce to New Orleans is not general. The raw materials and surplus produce of an interior country most usually pass into the hands of traders and merchants, and are by them exported. This practice has not obtained in Upper Louisiana, where men of this description mostly receive peltries, lead, and salt, in exchange for their goods. Hence the beef and pork, and other surplus items of provisions, as well as raw materials, are mostly conveyed to New Orleans by the original owners.

Part of the natural growth of the country has been cursorily mentioned; but it is necessary to be more particular. Some species of trees are common both to the high and low grounds, and we shall endeavor to distinguish them.

The low grounds produce the cotton wood, swamp maple, peccon, sycamore, aspin, pawpaw, *annona*, and willow. On the high grounds are found the persimmon, mulberry, chesnut, seven or eight kinds of oak, iron wood, and the crab apple. Common to both the high and low grounds are sugar trees in abundance, several kinds of walnut, several kinds of hickory, cherry, buck-eye, black and honey locust, three kinds of elm, gumtree, lyn, sassafras, nine bark, spice and leather wood, two kinds of ash, several kinds of poplar, beech, two kinds of birch, dogwood, and the coffee tree. Near a hundred different kinds of trees are enumerated by some; but the selection we have made will sufficiently explain the nature of the country, and the qualities of its soil. The country also produces the several species of wild nuts and berries commonly found in the United States; likewise some of an indigenous nature, and a variety of medicinal plants, which are of importance to the people of those regions, and some farinaceous vegetables in use among the natives.

The forests are filled with about fifty species of indigenous animals; among which are the buffaloe, two kinds of elk, two kinds of deer, the roe, the bear, the beaver, the otter, two species of the fox, a species of the goat, the mink, the raccoon, the opossom, the rabbit, and seven kinds of squirrels. These forests also, according to the best accounts, contain about a hundred and thirty species of birds. The most useful of them are several kinds of ducks, three kinds of teal, the wood-cock, the plover, the pheasant, the partridge, the quail, the pigeon, the prairie hen, or grouse, the wild goose and turkey. Here the lovers of sport may be gratified at all seasons of the year; and epicures can be at no loss for variety and delicacy of food.

The rivers and lakes produce but few fish, and some of them are of an indifferent quality. The carp and catfish are found in the large streams, and some of them are of a very large size. The perch, trout, and sunfish, inhabit some of the small streams and lakes; but they are too scarce to be of any material use to the settlers. These are considered as a great delicacy; and the price of them when purchased, is exorbitant.

From the mouth of the Arkansas to the head of Tiwappaty bottom, a distance of about four hundred and fifty miles very few, if any stones, are to be found. This immense tract of country is wholly composed of alluvion, and this accounts for the scarcity of rock. The rocks make their appearance just below cape Gerardeau; and in all the districts to the northward of that place more or less of them are to be found: sometimes on the margins of the rivers where they rise to a prodigious height, and sometimes on the more elevated grounds about the country. The village of St. Louis is almost wholly built on a rock, and the other villages generally have a supply of it in their neighborhood. As the country becomes settled, the want of this material will be felt, particularly as it is not scattered about in equal portions, but is rather confined to ridges, and to the banks of some of the rivers and streams. The rocks in this country are almost universally of the calcareous kind, and as universally deposited in horizontal strata. Petrified testaceous shells, and coralline substances are found in various places on the Mississippi, particularly in the neighborhoods of Kaskaskia and St. Genevieve. These animal exuviæ are always connected by a calcareous cement. Petrified nuts and vegetables of various kinds, as also the excrement of the buffaloe and other animals are scattered about Upper Louisiana, and on some parts of the Ohio.

Perhaps it may not be deemed impertinent to give a sketch of the settlements on the east bank of the Mississippi, especially as these once belonged to the French, and were within the boundaries of Louisiana. The first settlements made by them in the country were at Cahokia, St. Philips, La Prairie du Rocher, and Kaskaskia. The first is situated nearly opposite to St. Louis, and contains about one hundred and twenty houses; the second has become extinct; the third is about twelve miles above Kaskaskia, and contains thirty two houses. Kaskaskia is situated about seven miles up a river of the same name, though not more than three miles from the Mississippi, nearly opposite to St. Genevieve, and about fifty five miles below Cahokia. This village was once considered as the capital of the country, and was rich and populous; even so late as 1772 it contained five hundred whites, and as many blacks: but it is now reduced to about forty five families. The causes of this declension have already been detailed. In the time of father Charlevoix, 1721, this village contained a Jesuit's college. The ruins only of this fabric now remain. All these villages were founded about the year 1683 by the unfortunate M. de la Salle, or by his followers.

These villages, as also the intermediate settlements, are situated on a fertile bottom, which commences at the mouth of Kaskaskia river, and extends nearly to the Illinois, a distance of about eighty miles, and is from four to six miles in depth. That part of it along the Mississippi, about a mile in breadth, is covered with a thick growth of heavy timber; the rest is mostly prairie. It is bounded in the rear by a lofty ridge of lime rocks, the front of which is in many places perpendicular, and elevated to the height of one hundred and fifty to two hundred feet. This ridge commences below Baton Rouge, and approaches the east bank of the Mississippi in a variety of places; it crosses the Ohio at what is called the grand chain, about twelve miles above the mouth of that river, and extends along back of Kaskaskia to some distance up the Illinois. This extensive bottom furnishes excellent land, and a considerable portion of it is under good cultivation. The French mostly inhabit the villages, and the rest of the country is settled by English Americans. The lands back of the ridge are by no means indifferent; many good settlements are formed on them; and, in addition to the other articles usual to the country they produce cotton of a good quality.

While the French were in possession of the country, they built several forts. The one at Kaskaskia is almost wholly destroyed. They also had one on the Ohio, about thirty six miles from the Mississippi; the Indians laid a curious stratagem to take it, and it answered their purpose. A number of them appeared in the day time on the opposite side of the river, each of whom was covered with a bear skin, and walked on all fours. The French supposed them to be bears, and a party crossed the river in pursuit of them. The remainder of the troops left their quarters, and resorted to the bank of the river in front of the garrison to observe the sport. In the mean time a large body of warriors, who were concealed in the woods near by, came silently up behind the fort, and entered it without opposition, and very few of the French escaped the carnage. They afterwards built another fort on the same ground, and called it *Massac* in memory of this disastrous event; and it retains this name to the present time.

Fort Chartres was built in the year 1720, and much repaired in 1750. It is situated in the neighborhood of La Prairie du Rocher, and was originally about one mile and a half from the Mississippi. Its figure is quadrilateral, with four bastions, the whole of which is composed of lime stone well cemented. Each side measures about 340 feet. The walls are fifteen feet high, about three feet thick, and still entire. The stone walls of a spacious square of barracks, are also in good preservation, as likewise a capacious magazine, and two deep wells very little injured by time. Each port or loop hole is formed by four solid clefts or blocks of what is here called free stone, worked smooth, and into proper shapes. All the cornices and casements about the gates and building are of the same material, and appear to great advantage. The area of this fort is now covered with trees, which are from seven to twelve inches in diameter. In fine, this work exhibits a splendid ruin. It was originally intended as a place of refuge for the inhabitants of the adjacent country in time of war. Some years after it was built, the Mississippi broke over its banks, and formed a channel so near the fort, that one side of it, and two of its bastions were thrown down. This circumstance induced the English to abandon it in 1772; and since that period the inhabitants have taken away great quantities of materials from it to adorn their own buildings.

In summer the winds in Upper Louisiana are variable, though those from the south and south west are the most prevalent. Those from the north east and east are productive of considerable humidity in the air; and if they blow with violence they are usually attended with rain, probably because they pass over the great reservoirs of fresh water on the borders of Canada. Westerly winds are common; they cool the air, and render it less humid, and more easy of respiration; they are sometimes attended with thunder, and heavy showers of rain. These brace the system; while those from the southern and other quarters create lassitude and sluggishness.

It is observed in the notes on Virginia, that, as we proceed westward from the Atlantic, the heats gradually abate till we arrive at the summit of the Allegheny mountains; and that from thence to the Mississippi they gradually increase. As these mountains are much nearer to the Atlantic ocean than to the Mississippi, it seems to follow that the heats are greater at the latter than at the former place in the same latitude; and this indeed is the fact. It is estimated, that these mountains are on an average, about two hundred miles from the Atlantic Ocean. They stretch along through the back part of Georgia, and terminate in a cluster of sand hills near the line of demarcation; But more to the northward they gradually diverge from the Mississippi, so that in latitude forty degrees north, they are about seven hundred and fifty miles from it. The Mexican mountains in the same latitude are rather more than six hundred miles to the westward of it; and from the known declivity of the country each way to it, determined partly by observation, and partly by the rapidity of all the currents, we may readily presume that the Mississippi rolls its waters through an immense valley, and nearly at equal distances from two lofty and distant mountains on each side of it. It must be remarked also, that the atmosphere in Upper Louisiana is never refrigerated by the breezes from the ocean.

The settlements in that country are between the thirty third and fortieth degrees of north latitude. The winters among them are much more severe than in the corresponding latitudes on the sea coast. They generally set in about the twentieth of November, and continue till near the last of February; though hard frosts, and even snow, are common in October and March. For three successive winters, commencing in 1802, the Mississippi at St. Louis was passable on the ice before the twentieth of December each year; and it was clear of all obstruction, with only one exception, by the last of February. In January 1805, the ice in that river rather exceeded twenty two inches in thickness. There is seldom more than six inches of snow on the ground at the same time; but the severity of the weather at St. Louis, in latitude thirty eight degrees twenty four minutes north, is generally about the same as in the back parts of the state of New Jersey. The mercury frequently falls below 0; and the cold keeps it depressed as low as ten or fifteen degrees for several weeks during each winter.

If the cold in these regions in winter is greater than that in the same parallels of latitude on the sea coast, the heat in summer bears a proportionate increase. We cannot estimate the degrees of heat by any regular thermometrical observations, for any number of years: But in the summer of 1805 a thermometer was suspended in a large drawing room at St. Louis against a stone partition wall, and constantly in a current of air; and from about the last of June to sometime in August, the mercury frequently rose to ninety six degrees, and remained at that point for several hours in the day. The heats in this quarter while they continue are supposed to be more oppressive than those in the Mississippi territory; Owing, perhaps, to the greater concentration of the rays of the sun in the deep and spacious valley of the Mississippi. They continue, however, only about two months in each year in Upper Louisiana; whereas they rage with violence for at least four months at Natchez.

Hence a stranger might be apt to conclude, that the climate among the upper settlements on the Mississippi is unfavourable to health. Experience, however, enables us to draw a different conclusion. For reasons mentioned in another place, the country between the Arkansas and the neighborhood of cape Gerardeau is deemed less salubrious than the more northern districts. But even here the native inhabitants, particularly the French, enjoy as much health as the people of any other country, and many instances of longevity occur among them. The endemics in Upper Louisiana are almost exclusively confined to English Americans, who were born and educated in more northern climates; and even these after a residence of one or two years in the country, generally enjoy a good degree of health. The heats produce lassitude and languor, and exercise becomes irksome. In this state of the bodily system, people who live on the borders of great water courses are seized with diseases, generally of the intermittent kind. Those from the eastern and middle states are subject to these diseases, especially the first summer after their arrival. Those from the southern states generally enjoy good health. The settlers of all descriptions, who plant themselves in the interior at a distance from any large body of fresh water, are seldom attacked by endemics. It is evident, therefore, that the diseases already mentioned are usually superinduced by the pestilential vapors, which arise from the rivers, and from the decayed vegetable substances, produced in great abundance on the bottoms along the borders of them. These diseases, however, are easily conquered by a few simples, and the patients soon restored to health. The general salubrity of the climate is ascertained from this circumstance, that fewer people die in it according to their number than in most other countries. Pleuritic disorders are prevalent in the spring in all parts of Louisiana, and these sometimes prove fatal, especially among the old people. Flannel worn next the skin, both summer and winter, has been found to be an almost certain antidote to the endemics of the climate.

When we consider the intense heats in Upper Louisiana, the vast bodies of fresh water in it, the flat and inundated grounds in some parts of it, and the extensive diffusion of vegetable putrefaction, so fruitful of fatal diseases in other parts of the world, we are naturally led to enquire, what is the cause of the uncommon salubrity of the climate? A number of causes may probably unite to produce the prevalent health; but perhaps the most prominent one may be traced to the vast ledges and precipices of calcareous rock found in various places on both sides of the Mississippi above the lower line of cape Gerardeau. St. Louis and several other villages are either built on, or contiguous to, vast strata of this rock, which fortunately appear in those places where vegetable putrefaction and the noxious vapors are the most common. No other rock, indeed, abounds in the country. Where this appears in plenty the people are not often troubled with dangerous diseases; and it is well known to physicians and chemists, that the properties it contains are either calculated to neutralize and to destroy the deleterious qualities of putrid exhalations, or to prevent the existence of them. The city of Lisbon, situated in about thirty-eight degrees, north latitude, nearly in the same parallel with St. Genevieve, is deemed one of the most healthy spots on the globe, and it is resorted to in summer by valetudinarians from almost all the nations of Europe. What can be the cause of such a great degree of health in the city of Lisbon? It is the calcareous rock on which it stands, and of which its houses are built. The very streets of that city are excavated from this rock, and the clouds of dust raised in them by the winds are of a calcareous nature. The villages at a small distance from this city, are furnished with silicious stones; and though more elevated, and more fully ventilated by the air, are sometimes almost desolated by endemics; while the capital, populated by at least one hundred and twenty thousand souls, has invariably escaped them. The country in most places about the gulf of Mexico is extremely low, and the air is so much impregnated by a deadly effluvia as either to obstruct settlements, or to thin them of their inhabitants; yet there are some very populous villages, even in the latitude of *La vera Cruz*, founded on beds of lime stone, and are surrounded by lofty mountains of calcareous rock, in which very little sickness is known, and the physicians cannot live by their professions. Calcareous earths not only act on the air, but they neutralize the water, and render it wholesome.

All circumstances considered, the climate in Upper Louisiana is favorable to health. If the heats debilitate the system, the extreme luxuriancy of the soil admits of a partial exemption from labor; and during the heat of the day the laborers usually retire to the shade, and indulge a temporary indolence.

Perhaps it may be proper in this place to notice a remark found in the American travels of Mr. Volney. He is of opinion, that the country to the eastward of the mountains arose in former times from the bed of the ocean, because all the vast masses of rock, with which it abounds, are jumbled together, and bear evident marks of disruption. He is also of opinion, that the country to the westward of the mountains has never been shaken by earthquakes, because all the masses of rock are deposited in horizontal strata.

The confused disposition of the rocks in the low country in the neighborhood of the sea coast, particularly those in New England, may perhaps with more propriety be imputed to earthquakes than to a recession of the ocean; for in the history of that part of the union is enumerated forty five earthquakes between 1628 and 1782, a period of one hundred and fifty four years; and some of them not only created alarm, but their progress was marked with considerable ruin and disruption. These dreadful visitations of nature might have occasionally shaken the borders of the Atlantic for ages before they were discovered by civilized man, and no doubt some of them disfigured the face of the country. If the shells and other marine substances, found in various places be sufficient to prove, that the low country contiguous to the sea arose from the bed of the ocean, they will also prove, that the Andes and other high mountains on our continent emerged from the same abyss, and perhaps too the whole of this quarter of the globe. Mr. Volney is correct with respect to the horizontal strata of rocks in the western country. The first appearance of them is near the top of the Alleghany mountains, and they uniformly abound on the Ohio and Mississippi.

But how shall we account for Mr. Volney's ignorance of the earthquakes, which have been so frequently experienced in Upper Louisiana? He spent some time at Vincennes, where he might have obtained correct information on the subject. The fact is, that earthquakes are common in that country, and may be traced to the first settlement of it. A severe shock was experienced in 1795; and the author of these sketches witnessed two others at Kaskaskia in the nights of the twentieth and twenty first of February 1804. Their oscillations were nearly from west to east; they produced an undulating motion in the earth like the swell of a sea; the buildings were considerably raised, and much shaken and disjointed; the soldiery were awakened from their sleep, and so much alarmed as hastily to abandon their quarters. Not a breath of air seemed to move; the sky was serene and clear, and the moon shone with unclouded lustre. Another shock was experienced on the nineteenth of the succeeding April; but it was not very perceptible.

Pumice stone of considerable size have repeatedly been found floating down the Missouri; and the existence of a volcano on some of its waters is now fully ascertained by some late discoveries.

SKETCHES OF LOUISIANA.

CHAPTER VII.

OF LAND TITLES.

THE settlers in Louisiana held their lands, both under the French and Spanish governments, by *allodial tenures*. This country was originally discovered and settled from Canada, where *feudal tenures* and a *noblesse* existed; and the liberality of Louis XIV., in whose reign Louisiana was first settled, must be ascribed to the peculiar situation of his affairs; the wars in which he was engaged left him no resources to assist the colonists, and he therefore resorted to favorable conditions as the best means of preserving his acquisitions in the new world. In the two successive grants he made of the colony, first to Crozat in 1712, and then to the west India company in 1717, the principles of *allodium* are plainly recognized, reserving nothing to himself but *liege homage and fidelity*, which every subject owes to his sovereign. The same principles were recognized by the Spanish government in all its concessions, though in many other respects it invaded the privileges of the people as derived from their former sovereigns.

The first settlements formed by the French on the Mississippi were at Kahokia and Kaskaskia in 1683. These villages are on the east side of that river. During the early part of the last century they conceded some scattering tracts of land in the neighborhood of St. Genevieve, which were supposed to be impregnated with valuable minerals; but the most ancient archieves of the French authorities in this quarter are either lost or were removed to New Orleans, and therefore no satisfactory information can be obtained of these old concessions.

The oldest French grant on the records at St. Louis bears date April the twenty seventh, 1766; and the French authorities continued to concede lands till May 1770, when Spain took possession of Upper Louisiana under the treaty of 1762. These concessions were made by St. Ange, the commandant, and by Lafebvre, succeeded by La Bussiere, both of whom are styled judges. It is probable that some of their concessions were never registered; and it is also as probable, that others were forfeited or disannulled, and the lands comprehended in them reconceded. In the years 1770, 1771, and 1772, sixty four concessions, mostly French, comprising four thousand eight hundred arpents, were surveyed by order of the first Spanish commandant. Even so late as 1788 no more than six thousand four hundred arpents had been surveyed in the district of St. Louis.

Particular care was taken in 1804, soon after the United States took possession of Upper Louisiana, to have all the land titles properly registered. Probably some few were omitted; but it is presumed, that these omissions will have no sensible effect on the general result. The quantity of land actually surveyed was accurately ascertained from the office of the surveyor general, where all surveys are recorded, and it amounted to eight hundred and sixty eight thousand seven hundred and seventy one arpents. The conceded lands not surveyed, though duly registered, amounted to eight hundred and fifty two thousand seven hundred and twenty two arpents; so that the quantity of land claimed in Upper Louisiana under French and Spanish titles was one million seven hundred and twenty one thousand four hundred and ninety three arpents; a quantity by no means exorbitant when compared with the population of that country.

The lands claimed at the Arkansas are not included in this estimate, as an accurate account of them could not be obtained.

Titles derived immediately from the crown, or those sanctioned by the superior authority at New Orleans, were deemed *complete*. But these formed a very small proportion of the whole. *Incomplete titles* were those derived from the naked concessions of the lieutenant governor, or of the commandants, and unsanctioned by the highest representative of the crown at the capital of the province. These formed more than nineteen twentieths of the whole; the people felt secure under their concessions, and most of them were too poor to defray the expenses of their ratification.

No lands were conceded, except on applications by way of petition, in which the quantity solicited was designated; and these concessions were either *general* or *special*. They were *general* when they authorised concessionaries to levy them where they pleased on the vacant lands of the public domain; and hence the name of floating or running titles. They were *special* when they designated certain metes and bounds. The former mode was the most common, as it put it in the power of the proprietors to select such tracts as suited their convenience, and in many instances to secure valuable mines. A proviso was usually inserted in the concessions, prohibiting their extent on lawful and anterior claims. If this was done through mistake, as sometimes happened, they were extended on other lands. In many instances after the concessions were extended, and the surveys made and recorded, the lands included in them were annexed to the domain, and others conceded more beneficial to the settlers on their application;—and this exchange became a matter of record.

The terms of petitions and concessions were drawn with great exactness; and those of the latter corresponded with those of the former; if the first were general, so were the second, and so on. The same exactness was observed in the transfers of lands from one individual to another. In both cases they were drawn by notaries or other public officers, and attested by them; and they were bound to insert no conditions in them contrary to law, to religion, to morality, or to the interest of the crown.

All grants and concessions of lands included a number of conditions, either expressed or implied. In Upper Louisiana the proprietor was obliged to clear some land, and to build a house within a year and a day, or his claim was forfeited, and liable to revert to the domain; or if he at any time abandoned the country without permission to dispose of his property, the same consequence ensued. In addition to these conditions, the grants and concessions in Lower Louisiana made it necessary for each proprietor, whose land bounded on water courses, to construct dykes or levees to secure the country along his own possessions from inundation, to open a public road on the top of them, to build the necessary bridges, and to keep the whole in suitable repair at his own expense. Lands, however, were seldom annexed to the domain for the non-fulfilment of the latter conditions. The roads, levees, and bridges, were usually made and repaired by the public when the proprietors proved delinquent; and they were compelled to defray the expense.

The same formality and solemnity were observed in the annexation of lands to the domain as when they were granted or conceded. All annexations were declared by an ordinance of Louis XV. in 1743 to be null and void, and of no effect, unless they were *judicially decreed*. The same principle obtained under the Spanish authorities, and they deemed it obligatory.

It will be perceived by the preceding statement, that nearly one half of the lands claimed in Upper Louisiana, were unsurveyed at the time the United States took possession of that country. Many of the inhabitants, however, had made a selection of their lands agreeably to the terms of their concessions, and were cultivating them, and their negligence in securing titles arose in most instances from their poverty. Others again had designated their lands in an informal manner, but had not taken actual possession of them. The holders of naked concessions, who had taken no subsequent steps to secure their titles, formed the most numerous class; and they were able to assign reasons for the non-extention of their claims. Some wished to secure valuable mineral lands; but could find none to please them. Others were solicitous to extend them about the heads of some of the rivers; but these were either too distant from the settlements, or danger was apprehended from the Indians. Others again resolved to fix themselves among the settlements; it required some time to explore the country, and to become acquainted with the various tracts of vacant lands dispersed over it. Many of these floating concessions were of an old date, and had regularly passed from one to another by permission of the Spanish authorities.

Before the year 1795 very few surveys were made. Those made under the French government were not accompanied with plots, and it does not appear, that they were sanctioned by public authority. Indeed, this business for more than twenty years was not sufficiently attended to by the Spaniards. Surveys were only occasionally ordered, and frequently not till many years after the concessions were made, and the claimants in possession of their lands. Hence it was that the surveys ordered by the lieutenant governors were generally of those lands conceded by their predecessors. But in 1795, a surveyor general for Upper Louisiana was appointed. This was the first appointment of the kind in that country. Under him the business soon assumed a systematic form. He appointed one or more deputies in each of the districts; the fees of survey were established; an office was opened for the registration of land titles; and as the country then begun to be populated, their attention was gradually drawn to the duties of their profession.

The right to concede lands in Upper Louisiana was vested in the lieutenant governor. It was usual for the commandants and syndecs to recommend settlers, and to certify, that the lands solicited by them were vacant. Concessionary titles were *incomplete* till confirmed by the supreme authority at New Orleans. The right of confirmation was formerly vested in the governor general: But on the seventeenth of July 1799, it was transferred to the tribunal of finance, as appears by a letter of office of that date, and received in St. Louis sometime in October of that year. Soon after this period, however, the assessor of his tribunal died, and confirmations were suspended. The crown neglected to fill the vacancy, probably in consequence of the retrocession of the colony; and to relieve the settlers from the embarrassment and expense of sending their claims to New Orleans, the intendant general wrote to the lieutenant governor under date of

December first 1802, not to permit any more concessions to be forwarded till his majesty was pleased to organize the tribunal of finance by the appointment of a new assessor. The settlers, indeed, were too poor at first to pay the fees of confirmation, and the subsequent derangement of the tribunal of finance put it out of their power to complete their titles.

About the year 1796, Spain found it necessary to populate Upper Louisiana as a barrier to the English in Canada, and she gave great encouragment to settlers; she preferred those from the United States, as their prejudices against the English were a sure guarantee of their attachment to the Spanish interest. Lands were gratuitously given them, and they were exempted from taxes. The fees of office, and the survey of eight hundred acres, cost forty one dollars only exclusive of the hire of chainmen. To these expenses must be added the fees of confirmation at New Orleans. These liberal encouragements, the fertility of the lands, and the prospect of mineral riches, in Upper Louisiana, extended the stream of population (hitherto limited to regions on the Ohio) to that country.

It is by no means difficult to ascertain the precise extent of the powers of the lieutenant governor in the concession of lands. True it is, that the land laws of the first Spanish governor, general O'Reilly, bearing date February the seventeenth 1770, and those subsequently made by Morales, the intendant general, dated July the seventeenth 1799, impose restrictions on the subordinate authorities, and allow only eight hundred arpents to be conceded to each head of a family. But these laws were never considered in any other light than as *general rules*, liable to exceptions when cases occurred to justify them. The settlers were usually poor, and eight hundred arpents to each were deemed sufficient. Some of the commandants were stationed from three hundred to one thousand miles from the capital, and could not speedily communicate with the great officers of the crown; nor could all of them be intrusted with discretionary powers. These land laws were partly intended to prevent improper speculations among the subordinate authorities, and partly to allure settlers to the country.

Besides, O'Reilly frequently departed from the tenor of his own laws, and his successors followed the example: Nor will it be pretended, that they were absolutely bound by them. The governor general was authorised by the crown to regulate the grants and concessions of lands, and he had an unquestionable right to abrogate them wholly, or to alter or modify them as he pleased. The laws of O'Reilly did not bind his successors any more than the laws of one legislature bind a succeeding one: Each necessarily possessed a discretionary power over the general regulations of his predecessors, and was at liberty to increase or to diminish the privileges bestowed on settlers, provided no infringement was made of the rights secured by anterior grants and concessions. This discretionary power was exercised by several successive *governors general*. Between the years 1790 and 1798 they confirmed a variety of concessions, each of which embraced a square league, and some of them a still greater quantity. One of them comprehended the most productive lead mine in the country. Another called for eight thousand two hundred and fifty arpents of valuable land in the neighborhood of St. Louis. All these confimations or ratifications were in consequence of the concessions previously made by the lieutenant governors of Upper Louisiana.

This is sufficient to prove the existence of a discretionary power in the *governors general*; and it also authorizes the inferrence, that the same power was vested in the respective lieutenant governors of Upper Louisiana. In the first place it may be observed, that they always exercised it, and it is difficult to presume, that they would contravene the known laws of their superiors without instructions to that effect. In all their concessions they were regulated by the wealth and importance of the settlers. To the ordinary poor they seldom conceded more in the first instance than three or four hundred arpents, though they were always ready to make additions as the ability to cultivate increased. To those of wealth and influence they conceded several thousand arpents; for, as their great object was to populate the country, they adopted such measures as were the most likely to produce the effect. As an instance of this we need only refer to the settlement of New Madrid in 1787. The governor general at first imposed considerable restrictions on the commandant relative to the concession of lands; but he afterwards found it necessary to be more liberal than even the land laws of O'Reilly. In July 1789 he wrote to the commandant as follows: " Notwithstanding the instructions here" tofore sent you, more or less front or depth may be giv" en according to the exigency of the ground, *as likewise* " *a greater or less quantity of land, agreeably to the wealth* " *of the grantee.*" This post was at that time immediately dependant on the superior authority at New-Orleans. It was annexed to the government of Upper Louisiana in August 1799.

Besides, it may be doubted whether the land laws of O'Reilly ever operated in Upper Louisiana. They bear date nearly three months before the Spaniards took possession of that part of the country, at which time there existed only a few miserable huts in it: The first settlement commenced only four years before. These land laws contain twelve articles. The operation of the first seven was evidently restricted to the island of Orleans, and that of the other five extended in part to the same place, but more particularly to the Apalousas, Atakapas, and Nachitoches. They regulated the grants and concessions of lands at these several posts, and in no particular did they refer to Upper Louisiana. Indeed, the regulations contained in them were totally inapplicable to that part of the country, and the Spanish authorities there always conceded lands on principles not derived from them.

The land laws of Morales contain thirty eight articles. The first nine are the same in substance as the first seven in the land laws of O'Reilly, and the subsequent twenty nine were either intended to explain the preceding ones, or to regulate the grants and concessions of lands in the Apalousas, Atakapas, Mobile, and Pensacola. They make no mention of Upper Louisiana.

It is believed, that these laws were never in force; certain it is, that they were never carried into effect. The reason for the first is, that the great clamor raised against them in all parts of the province induced the governor general and Cabildo to draw up a strong protest against them, and to lay it before the king. The consequence was, that Morales was removed from office; though he was afterwards reinstated merely to assist in transfering the possession of the country to the French republic. The reason for the second is, that the assessor died soon after they were promulgated, which totally deranged the tribunal of finance, and rendered it incapable of making or confirming land titles.

These land laws were exclaimed against as extortionate and oppresive; extortionate, because they made it necessary for a concession to pass through four, and in some instances, seven offices, before a complete title could be procured, in which the fees exacted, in consequence of the studied ambiguity of the thirtieth article, frequently amounted to more than the value of the conceded lands; oppressive, not only because the settler was deprived of his original papers, but because the twenty second article declared all concessions void, unless forwarded for confirmation within six months after the publication of the laws at the several posts. This was tantamount to a reunion of all the lands of settlers to the domain. Not one in fifty was able to transmit the evidences of his claim, and to defray the expenses of his title, within so short a period as six months. Besides, these laws reserved to the government the privileges of taxation, and nothing could render them more unpopular.

While the governor general was at the head of the finance, his legal representative in Upper Louisiana was the lieutenant governor, to whom was confided a discretionary power relative to the concession of lands, and the affairs of the Indians; though his proceedings were liable to revision and control. When the new department of finance was created in 1799, at the head of which was the intendant, the lieutenant governor became his sub-delegate, and was invested with the same discretionary power, though he acted with reluctance under his new superior.

The first laws passed by congress relative to the land titles in Louisiana, excited much alarm and apprehension among the people of that country. They contended, that the United States had no right to enquire, whether the Spanish authorities had exceeded their powers in the concession of lands; because such an enquiry would militate against the treaty, and against that full faith and credit, which one nation was bound to put in the official acts and proceedings of another. They also contended that, if the Spanish authorities exceeded their powers, and we chose to remedy the evils occasioned by it, the dispute rested between the two nations, and not between the claimants and the United States.

Suspicions have been entertained that, near the close of the Spanish government in Upper Louisiana, the property of the United States was attacked by ante-dated concessions. Before we proceed to enquire into the number and extent of these, it may be proper to observe, that many of these suspicions arose from other causes not difficult to explain. No sooner was it understood, that the country was ceded, than an extraordinary rise in the value of the lands was contemplated, and all those entitled to them solicited concessions and obtained them. Among these were most of the French inhabitants, who had hitherto contented themselves with house-lots, and had no disposition to resort to agriculture, at least so long as they were able to navigate the rivers, pursue the chase, or the Indian trade. What were called their head rights, added to the unextended concessions in the hands of English Americans, embraced about thirteen hundred thousand arpents. They deemed it expedient to extend their concessions, and to procure surveys; the consequence was, that near the close of 1803, every surveyor in the country was employed, and a much greater quantity would have been surveyed, had there existed a sufficient number of men capable of the business. Add to this, they extended their claims on the most valuable lands in the country, particularly on mineral lands; and to these circumstances may be traced many of the suspicions of ante-dated titles.

Other circumstances equally inauspicious contributed to these suspicions. The boundary marks fixed about some tracts of land, particularly about an extensive tract in the neighborhood of St. Louis, had become either defaced or destroyed. Just before the United States took possession of the country, a re-survey was directed, and new boundary marks established, in consequence of a proces verbal for the purpose; and this gave rise to injurious imputations. Most of the land included in the boundaries was conceded to various settlers by the French authorities; the remainder was conceded by the Spanish authorities soon after they were established in the country; the whole of which came into the hands of the present proprietor by purchase. Some unextended concessions also appeared about this period, bearing date several years before, and signed by the predecessor of the last lieutenant governor, which created a belief, that they were fraudulently obtained. The fact was, that a settler from the United States, designing to persuade ten of his old friends and neighbors to establish themselves about him, applied to the lieutenant governor for as many concessions, to whom he paid the customary fees of office; but he was unable to furnish him with the names. Soon after this, on the twenty ninth of August 1799, he was superceded in his office; on the same day he filed ten concessions for eight hundred arpents each in the office of the surveyor general, directed him to insert the names of such settlers as should be furnished him by their agent, who had originally applied for the concessions, and to deliver them accordingly. The settlers eventually applied for their concessions; but when they found them signed by a man, who had been several years out of office, they concluded them to be fraudulent, and a few only were accepted. The remainder of them were deposited in the office of the surveyor general. Another circumstance, equally pregnant with suspicions of fraud, must be here inserted. The land laws of Morales were deemed extremely rigorous, and it was readily conjectured that, if they applied to Upper Louisiana, the citizens of the United States would hesitate to become subjects of Spain on the conditions they prescribed. The lieutenant governor, therefore, resolved to evade them; which he did by inserting as a date in the concessions the latter part of 1799, or the early part of 1800, so as to bring them within the purview of those discretionary powers and privileges, which were derived from the governor general.

The above statement is the more necessary, as some of the circumstances contained in it, have been incorrectly stated to the government, published to the world, and relied on as instances of fraud. The reader will judge for himself.

It must be admitted, that some fraudulent and ante-dated concessions were issued just at the close of the Spanish government in Upper Louisiana; and we shall now proceed to enquire into the nature and extent of them. In the first place, it cannot be pretended, that any of these culpable concessions bear date prior to the twenty ninth of August 1799, when the last lieutenant governor entered on the duties of his office. In the second place, it is hardly necessary to include under this description any of those embracing small quantities of land only; because, if any such exist, they were generally given to actual settlers, who were entitled to head rights. Frauds therefore must be sought after in concessions, in which are included tracts of land of greater magnitude; and it is hardly probable, that the cupidity of speculators would be gratified with less than a league square. Twenty six concessions exist, derived from the last lieutenant governor, each of which embraces a league square, or more, of land. Thirteen of them bear date in 1799, nine in 1800, two in 1801, one in 1802, and one in 1803. They comprise two hundred and seventy one thousand seven hundred and fifty two arpents. Of this quantity, one hundred and twenty one thousand four hundred and forty eight arpents, contained in twelve concessions, were regularly surveyed. The remainder, one hundred and fifty thousand three hundred and four arpents contained in fourteen concessions, were in the hands of the several claimants at the time the United States took possession of the country. Such a number of extensive concessions, mostly bearing date in 1799 and 1800, when a few only of this description are to be found of prior or subsequent dates, certainly furnishes good ground to suspect their legitimacy. No doubt some of them are genuine, but it will be difficult to distinguish them from those of a spurious nature; partly because the claimants have no evidence of their actual dates, and partly because such evidence, if demanded, seems contrary to the rules of law: The record must prove itself.

OF LAND TITLES.   257

Of the quantity mentioned in the above unsurveyed concessions, fifty eight thousand two hundred and twenty four arpents, are included in those of a running or floating nature; and the remaining ninety two thousand and eighty arpents, are embraced by special concessions.

There is good reason to believe, that sixty two thousand and fifty six arpents of the surveyed lands, divided among four persons, as also eighty three thousand and fifty six arpents of the unsurveyed lands, divided among five persons, were conceded to them as compensations for long and faithful services. The Spanish government never gave any salaries to its provincial officers; nor any gratuities in money to those who, amid dangers and at a great expense, explored unknown regions, and made useful discoveries; but when compensations were solicited, it was usual to bestow tracts of land instead of money.

In addition to what is already stated, there exists three concessions of a less suspicious nature, embracing large tracts of land. The first is supposed to cover a valuable lead mine; but from the number of concessionaries mentioned in it, the shares are reduced to four hundred arpents each, most of whom are actual settlers, and had lands promised them on their first arrival in the country. The second is supposed to be of considerable extent; it is described by metes and bounds; but as the several courses and distances between them are not accurately defined, the quantity cannot be ascertained. The third, from the nature and extent of it, deserves a particular description. A tract of one hundred and two thousand eight hundred and ninety six arpents was conceded November the third 1799 to a catholic clergyman now in Upper Louisiana, who is an Irishman by birth. His petition states in substance, " that the duke of Alcadia, minister of state, and " of universal despatches for the Indies was desirous of " bringing from Ireland many catholic families to settle " in Upper Louisiana, as appeared by a letter of Don

" Thomas O'Ryan, almoner of honor to his catholic ma-
" jesty, and confessor to the queen, written in English,
" and addressed to the petitioner by the order of said mi-
" nister of state; wherein the government engaged to
" build a church on their arrival in the most suitable place
" for their settlement, leaving it with the petitioner to so-
" licit of the government the necessary domain lands;"
and therefore he prays, " that one hundred and two thou-
" sand eight hundred and ninety six arpents, between the
" black waters, and the branches which descend into White
" river, may be conceded for the causes mentioned." It
appears by the decree of the lieutenant governor, that the
letter of O'Ryan above referred to, and written by order
of the minister of state, had been presented to him by the
petitioner; in consequence of which, and in conformity to
the disposition of the governor general Gayoso, as appeared by his order of September the third, 1797, he " grants
" to the petitioner the quantity solicited, and in the place
" required ;" and then directs " the surveyor general to
" put him in possession of the said quantity, in the place
" mentioned, when those interested should make the de-
" mand ;" and that " after his operations he should form
" the figurative plan, and deliver it to the party, with his
" petition, so that it might serve him to solicit a title in
" form from the intendant general of these provinces."
This concession was never extended on the lands embraced by it; nor did any Irish catholics attempt to avail themselves of the pious and benevolent designs of his catholic
majesty.

During the time the author of these sketches was first
civil commandant of Upper Louisiana, the Spanish records were in his possession; and on them the preceding
statement is founded. Decisive and successful measures
were taken to ascertain the quantity of land comprehended in the unextended concessions, which were then in the
hands of the several claimants.

The mode of granting and conceding lands in Lower Louisiana was similar in all respects to the one already described; though incumbered with more conditions; and as the settlers were nearer the capital, and generally more wealthy, many of them in the first instance obtained complete titles.

The quantity of land actually granted and conceded in Lower Louisiana before we took possession of it, cannot be estimated with certainty, because under the Spanish government, individual claims were never recorded till after the surveys were made, and at the time alluded to a vast number of unextended concessions were scattered among the settlers. An idea of the quantity, however, may be formed from other data. The country on the Lower Mississippi is not open and champaign like that in Upper Louisiana, where settlers may fix themselves at pleasure, but the land capable of tillage is confined to narrow borders along the rivers and other streams, where most of the settlements are made. The plantations front these rivers and streams, and almost invariably extend one mile and an half back, each of which comprehends more or less of swamp. By ascertaining the extent of these borders, where lands were granted and conceded, the quantity claimed in Lower Louisiana under French and Spanish titles amounts to more than three millions of arpents, or French acres. In this quantity is comprehended the lands supposed to be claimed in the Atakapas, Apalousas, and on the Washita.

Will the United States permit the sale of the public lands in Louisiana, and by this measure encourage the settlement of that country? This question is of some importance in a national point of view; it particularly regards the interests of a growing people, and deserves a more critical examination than we are able to give it.

It has been suggested that, the more effectually to promote the national interests, we must first dispose of the public lands on the east side of the Mississippi; except, perhaps, some small tracts about the Washita and Red river, and between these and the gulf.

If such a measure be contemplated, it probably results from an apprehension, that such settlements will disperse our population, as also our capitals employed in commerce and manufactures, and at the same time lessen the value of the public domain. This apprehension seems to be grounded on the experience of foreign states engaged in colonization. Some of these states have wasted their strength on their foreign possessions, and if happily they survive them, it is to witness their own progressive imbecility, though their coffers may be filled with the wealth of Peru and the Indies. The situation of the United States with respect to Louisiana is materially different from that of the European nations with respect to their colonies; and therefore we have a right to calculate on very different results. Louisiana is not a distant colony divided from the United States by the ocean; it is no more separated from them than one state from another; it serves only to extend our boundaries, not to create a foreign possession; so that while colonization, in general, necessarily draws after it the wealth and strength of the mother country, the extension of our territory gives a greater activity to our capitals and population, without the least diminution of either. If this extension of territory renders the union less compact, its wealth and physical resources less combined, and not so easily drawn into active operation in times of public danger, it is an evil of a temporary nature, and it has a remedy in the rapid increase of wealth and population in the Atlantic States.

If our population be less than that of some of the states of Europe, it by no means follows, that a dispersion of it will have the same pernicious effect. The immense population of Great Britain, France, and Germany, (about one hundred and thirty souls to each square mile) is necessary to carry on their extensive commerce and manufactures, and to fill their armies and navies; and the more their population becomes dispersed, the more exposed they are to the inroads of their enemies, and the less able they are to extend their commerce and manufactures, by which some of them exist and are supported.

On the contrary, our army and navy, except in case of war, will employ but few of our citizens; our navigation only is considerable; manufactures to any considerable extent can never be introduced into the United States, because we can always purchase cheaper than we can make. Our vacant lands, obtained too on moderate conditions, will continue to keep up the price of labor. We are a nation of agriculturists, destined by providence to furnish Europe and the islands with provisions and raw materials; and no part of the world is better calculated for such supplies than the country on the Mississippi and its waters. Our manufactures must necessarily be limited to such coarse fabrics as are in common use among the people; to lead, salt, flour, iron, steel, and to such other articles as are of importance to navigation, and to the agricultural and mechanical professions. We cannot, therefore, draw any argument from the population of any given territory in Europe to prove the paucity of our own over a surface of the same extent; because *there* the wealth and strength of a nation depend on commerce and manufactures, and on a crowded population without land to supply it wholly with the means of subsistence; *here* our wealth and strength are mostly derived from the tillage of our fields, the raw materials we are able to furnish, and the extent of our landed possessions. The population of some of the eastern states (upwards of sixty to each square mile) is found too great for the quantity of land. This compels one part of the people to navigate the ocean, and no small proportion of the other to remove to less populous regions. They have settled large tracts of vacant lands in the upper part of the state of New York. They have also formed extensive settlements on th Ohio, and great numbers of them have penetrated to the Mississippi. All this proves that, when a given extent of territory furnishes a greater population than can be usefully employed in agriculture, it will dissipate, and gradually find its way to the western country, where the vacant lands are good and prolific in the extreme. We ought to avoid the evils incident to the laborious artisans of a manufacturing nation—ignorance, poverty, disease, and the premature waste of the human constitution.

Capitalists will naturally turn their attention to the Lower Mississippi. Agriculturists of moderate property will prefer a more northern situation, will plant themselves in Upper Louisiana rather than in the Illinois or Indiana territories. These territories, indeed, contain large bodies of excellent lands, especially on the Ohio, Wabash, and some other rivers; but they have their share of bad and indifferent lands. A small part only of that extensive tract between the Mississippi and Vincennes, extending along the post-road for nearly one hundred and fifty miles, will ever be settled. The scarcity of wood and water furnish insuperable objections to it. Hence it is, that settlers entertain a predilection for the lands in Upper Louisiana, where the same inconveniences do not exist, where the soil is of the first quality, and where they can be accommodated with numerous streams suitable for mills and other purposes. If the government makes no provision for the sale of lands in this quarter, it is to be feared, that trespasses will be frequent; and that, as the *squatters* increase in number, difficulties will arise between them and the United States.

Louisiana is particularly exposed to the inroads of the Indians. An immense number of tribes, and some of them powerful, inhabit the extensive regions on the west side of the Mississippi. Their depredations are frequent, and they entertain no fear of punishment; our ordinary force, especially in Upper Louisiana, including the militia, is not sufficient to create any alarm among them. They are extremely bold in their threats; and perhaps one reason why they hold us so cheap is, that they have never been at war with us, and were never beaten by the whites. They frequently committed hostilities under the Spanish government, though no regular war was carried on, and the Spanish authorities as often purchased a peace of them. This encouraged them to repeat their hostilities, and to ridicule the want of courage and dexterity in the whites. One instance, among many others, may be adduced to explain the character of the Missouri Indians. While a kind of predatory war raged in 1794 between one of their tribes and the whites, a peace was concluded in a singular manner: A war chief, with a party of his nation, boldly entered St. Louis, and demanded an interview with the lieutenant governor, to whom he said, " we have come " to offer you peace; we have been at war with you ma- " ny moons, and what have we done? Nothing. Our war- " riors have tried every means to meet your's in battle; " but you will not, you dare not fight us; you are a par- " cel of old women. What can be done with such a peo- " ple but to make peace, since you will not fight? I come, " therefore, to offer you peace, and to bury the hatchet; " to brighten the chain, and again to open the way be- " tween us." The Spanish government was obliged to bear this insult with patience, and to grant the desired peace. The faculty of ratiocination is denied to these sons of nature; they derive more conviction from what they actually experience and feel than from what they see and hear; and nothing but the exercise of superior power can restrain them from bloody deeds.

Hence results the policy of furnishing Louisiana with a population adequate to self-defence. The more effectually to accomplish this object, perhaps the settlers ought to be restricted to certain prescribed limits. If they be suffered to spread over a great extent of territory, their strength cannot easily be concentrated. Their divided and detached situations will serve to invite hostilities, and probably enable the Indians to destroy them in detail. Natural and prescribed boundaries already exist, within which the settlements should be formed.

The vacant lands in Lower Louisiana are mostly to be found in the Atakapas and Apalousas, on Red river and the Washita. These lands are, in general, of an excellent quality, and not encumbered with Indian or Spanish claims. No other incitement is necessary to a speedy settlement, than the passage of a law, authorizing the sale of them.

It would be well to restrict the settlements in Upper Louisiana to the following boundaries: Beginning at the mouth of the river St. Francis; thence up that river to the source of its main westerly branch; thence a short distance due north to the river Merimak; thence up that river to a line, which, drawn due west, shall intersect the mouth of the Gasconade, a branch of the Missouri; thence on the dividing line between the United States, and the Sacks and Foxes, as agreed on in the treaty of 1804, to the Jaffreon, a branch of the Mississippi. That part of the tract below the Merimak, and situated between the St. Francis and Mississippi, is about four hundred and sixty miles long, following the course of the latter river, and of various widths; about fifty five or sixty miles at St. Genevieve and cape Gerardeau, and between twenty and thirty miles at New-Madrid; and it gradually narrows as it approaches the confluence of the two rivers. The mouth of the Gasconade is about ninety miles up the Missouri; and the mouth of the Jaffreon, on the west bank of the Mississippi, about one hundred miles above the junction of these great rivers. These boundaries include all the white settlements, and a sufficient territory for a respectable population. The extent of this territory along the west bank of the Mississippi, is nearly six hundred miles. Nearly one half of it was conceded to settlers by the French and Spanish authorities. The remainder belongs to the United States, and is now at their disposal. The vacant lands are divided into a great variety of tracts, scattered here and there among the settlements, and if they remain unsold, a compact population cannot be formed. Were they granted to actual settlers, a strong cordon would soon be drawn across our extensive and exposed frontiers, the Indians kept in awe, and the necessity of a regular force in those regions, at least to any considerable extent, in a great measure cease to exist.

Louisiana possesses a variety of climates and soils, adapted to the views and circumstances of every class in society. The people can exchange commodities with each other to advantage. Those of the north already furnish provisions and raw materials, and those of the south are equally capacitated to remit the conveniences and luxuries of life. This mutual dependance serves to strengthen the bands of society, and to perpetuate national friendships. No doubt such ligamentous relations were designed by the Almighty for the most beneficent purposes, and it would be something worse than folly to oppose the arrangements he has made.

It is a well known fact, that the stream of population generally inclines to the north, and this may be accounted for on rational principles. Much the greatest proportion of mankind depend on manual labor for support. The heats of the south are supposed to forbid this occupation; while the pure atmosphere of the north strengthens and invigorates the human constitution. Lower Louisiana is adapted to the culture of cotton, rice, tobacco, and sugar ; and these require large capitals. All kinds of grain, meats, and vegetables, are the products of Upper Louisiana ; and settlers of moderate resources, who aim to acquire the substantials of life only, will naturally resort to it, where also a considerable traffic may be carried on in peltry, lead, and salt. The lands in many parts of the Atlantic states, perhaps by long culture, have become greatly impoverished, and some considerable slave holders, who now find it difficult to subsist, would soon with the same means accumulate fortunes on the Lower Mississippi. In no other part of the United States can each good slave yield his master from two hundred and fifty to three hundred dollars clear annual profit; and the expense of removing families to that quarter by way of the rivers would be inconsiderable. The same comparative advantages would result to agriculturists, were they to exchange their possessions on the east side of the Allegheny for lands of a more prolific nature in Upper Louisiana, where provisons of all sorts can be procured more abundantly, and with less labor.

When the United States first took possession of Louisiana, the lands had no fixed value; they cost actual settlers no more than the fees of office, and the expenses of surveys. About that period, large quantities of land were offered for sale at twenty five cents per acre; but as soon as it was understood that the United States would postpone the sale of public lands, the people began to estimate the value of their own more highly; and in less than three years after the cession, it was difficult to purchase good lands, in eligible situations, under two dollars per acre. In fine, the cession raised the general mass of property in Louisiana more than four hundred *per centum*.

On the subject of promoting the settlement of Louisiana, and indeed of the Mississippi territory, various considerations of a political nature present themselves. Among them, that of providing for the national defence, is certainly important. In case war be declared against us by any foreign power, (and in the present state of the world we have no right to claim exemption from that calamity) the blow will probably be directed to that quarter. We shall then experience the necessity of a strong population to sustain at least the first attack, and to furnish the means of successful opposition. As an inducement to emigration, perhaps it would be well to present each actual settler with a certain quantity of land. A wise and virtuous government will endeavor to anticipate events, and not postpone the preparation of suitable remedies for probable evils. In fine, we cannot populate Louisiana, particularly the lower Mississippi, too soon; and our interest requires, that this population should consist of men habituated to agriculture, and educated in the principles of our laws and constitution.

SKETCHES OF LOUISIANA.

CHAPTER VIII.

GOVERNMENT AND LAWS.

FROM what has been said in other parts of this work, a copious exposition of the government and laws of Louisiana, may be dispensed with in this place.

Spain, in acquiring new possessions in America, deemed it necessary to invest their colonial officers with civil and military powers. The numerous enemies the Spaniards had to combat, to conquer, and in some measure to extirpate, added to the refractory disposition of the colonists, served to perpetuate this union amid the various changes, revolutions, and storms, of more than three centuries. These powers though exercised by the same functionaries, were really distinct in their natures; and those to whom they were confided acted in different capacities in carrying them into effect. Hence the Spanish government in Louisiana was deemed (at least by those unacquainted with its structure) of a military nature, and extremely arbitrary in its principles. Most probably there were many aberrations in practice; but the Spanish colonial code contains a complete system of wise and unexceptionable rules, calculated to ensure justice, and to promote the happiness of the people.

The treaty of cession of 1762 was never published, and its stipulations remain unknown. When Spain came into possession of Louisiana under that treaty, she changed almost the whole of the French colonial jurisprudence, and only preserved the principles of *allodium* in their grants of lands, and in the settlement and distribution of estates *ab intestato*; and this was most probably done out of respect to the civil law. The substituted code varied in some particulars from the one adopted in the other Spanish provinces; and this variance was occasioned by a difference in their circumstances.

The several institutions, by which the Spanish provinces in America are governed, have been the work of much time and labor. These provinces or possessions were always regarded as domains of the crown; and hence their political and civil systems bear some analogy to those of the mother country. These were few and simple in their infancy, and accommodated only to small and detached societies. But when large cities and provinces were created, and population became numerous, they began to assume a more comprehensive and complex form; and hence has arisen by degrees an extraordinary and magnificent superstructure, duly proportioned in all its parts, and exhibiting the wisdom and ingenuity of the political artists of several centuries.

The provincial institutions of the Spaniards together with the municipal and other laws, have arrived to as much perfection as the policy of the government, and the circumstances of the people, will admit. These have been collected, examined, and digested with great care and labor; such only have been retained as experience dictated to be useful, and those of a different character were consigned to oblivion. This digest bears the stamp of authority in all the provinces, and is denominated *the code of the Indies*. In all cases where the code is silent, the general laws of Spain, called *the laws of the partidas*, prevail in all the tribunals. Many prominent features of the Roman jurisprudence are observed in all of them; and they appear much more conspicuously in the colonial system of Louisiana than in that of any other of the Spanish provinces.

The Roman code, indeed, may be said to have furnished laws for the government of Louisiana by adoption. These laws regulated the rates of interest among merchants, and on loans among other descriptions of people. They laid down precise rules for the fulfilment of the different species of contracts and obligations, and dictated the decisions to be given in contestations on the multiplicity of grounds incident to them.

These laws also regulated the formalities of executing wills and testaments, noncupatives, donations *inter vivos*, dispositions *mortis causa*, and revocations. They likewise sanctioned the principle of *implied revocations;* and perhaps this was carried to a greater extent in Louisiana than in any of the United States. It not only embraced those cases recognized by our common law, but it considered all those legacies and bequests as totally void, where the legatees treated the testators with ingratitude, or blackened their memories.

Bequests of whatever nature to collaterals, and particularly to strangers, in prejudice of the direct lines of descent or ascent, were much discouraged by the laws. This is one reason why, in testamentary dispositions, many formalities were required. In the first place, a will was of no validity, unless executed in the presence of a notary, or some other public officer. In the second place, no less than seven witnesses were requisite in some instances to give effect to bequests. The Spanish laws also regarded the sanity of testators, and the particular circumstances under which their wills were written and executed with more caution, perhaps, than those of other countries.

No parent could disinherit his child, except for causes expressly recognized by the laws; as where the latter struck, or raised his hand to strike, the former; or was cruel, and inflicted on him any grievous injury; or refused to take care of him when poor or insane; or to be his bail, or to redeem him from prison or captivity, when he had the means of doing it; or accused him of any capital offence, except that of treason. Nor could a legitimate child, who died without issue, disinherit his parents, or other ascendants, except for causes nearly similar to those just mentioned. Many other causes of disinherison were recognized; but those already enumerated will afford a sufficient idea of the nature of the Spanish laws on this point.

The succession of heirs, whether descendants, ascendants, or collaterals, on the principles of *allodium*, to estates *ab intestato*, was clearly defined; and it was predicated on nearly the same principles as those recognized by the laws of the several states in the union. The rights of primogeniture were never admitted into the laws of Louisiana. These laws allowed a reasonable alimony to illegitimates, both before and after the death of their parents. They paid a particular regard to the dowry of widows, and to whatever was secured in marriage contracts. They also defined the rights and privileges of infants and minors, provided for their subsistence and education, and for the security of their property.

Children were obliged to support their parents, and other ascendants, if they were in need; and the relations of the direct ascending line were likewise bound to maintain their needy descendants.

The laws provided for the partition and distribution of estates, and the assignment of dowry.

They also obliged either party to a suit to disclose on interrogatories such facts and papers as were material to the dispensation of justice; and in most respects the tribunals of Louisiana were guided by the same maxims as the chancery courts in England, and those of the same nature in the United States.

It would require the ability and industry of an able jurist to delineate even the leading traits of the laws, by which Louisiana was governed. These laws extended to all the ramifications of the various concerns in society, and afforded such rules as were calculated to direct a just decision, when properly applied, on all the points liable to be litigated among men. But the misfortune was, that very few of the public officers, except those attached to New Orleans, were acquainted with them. None of them were ever published, except one or two hereafter noticed; and those disposed to consult them were obliged to examine a voluminous digest. This obstacle to legal information made it necessary for many of the subordinate officers at a distance from the capital to decide according to their conceptions of equity, except where they were guided by the written instructions of their superiors, which generally contained some useful hints derived from the civil law, or the code of the Indies. No wonder, then, that the Spanish government in Louisiana was deemed arbitrary, and that it was put and kept in operation more by the military than by the civil power.

O'Reilly, the first Spanish governor general of Louisiana, (after he had imbued his hands in the best blood of the province) was active in providing for the administration of justice. He divided the colony into as many districts as were necessary to accommodate the inhabitants; in each of which a commandant was appointed, generally taken from the army or militia, and invested with powers, civil, criminal, and military, to such extent as was deemed proper. Their jurisdictions were subsequently extended or abridged as circumstances required.

The judicial power of the district commandants usually extended to the decision of all suits, where the damage claimed did not exceed one hundred dollars. An exact uniformity, however, was not observed in this particular: Some were invested with less, and others with greater authority. They executed the mandates of their superiors, arrested criminals and debtors, extended executions on real and personal estate, watched over the public peace, and superintended the internal police of their respective districts. They received no salaries from the crown, except one hundred dollars per annum to reimburse their expenses of stationery. If they belonged to the army, their pay, and the established fees of their offices, supported them comfortably. These fees were by no means exorbitant, except in the settlement of estates *ab intestato;* they were fixed by a tarif, which all public officers were obliged to keep posted up in some conspicuous place in their respective offices or houses.

New Orleans had its alcaids, whose jurisdiction was of considerable extent. Syndics, or justices of the peace, were placed over small detached settlements in the districts, the nature of whose powers was similar to that of the commandants. Notwithstanding their jurisdiction in civil causes was limited to twenty dollars; yet it was lawful to institute suits before them for the recovery of larger sums, and they were bound to receive and to record the testimony offered on both sides, and then to remit their proceedings to their superiors.

The Spanish government always encouraged summary proceedings. Of plain and incontested cases, a record was seldom made, unless the judgment or decree was followed by an execution. In cases of magnitude, where serious contestations took place, the proceedings were sometimes extremely voluminous.

Creditors presented their petitions, in which they stated the nature of their demands. The adverse parties were permitted to reply; and hence the written debates of the litigants, grounded both on the law and the fact, were often extended to great length.

Upper Louisiana was considered as a province in some measure distinct from the lower one, though dependant on it. An officer with the title of lieutenant-governor was placed over it, who, although he derived his appointment from the crown, was bound to conform to the orders of the governor and intendant generals in their respective departments. He was sub-delegate to the latter officer, and as such he superintended the affairs of the finances within his jurisdiction, in which was included every thing relating to the Indians, to commerce, to the levy and collection of the public revenue, and to the sale of lands. As the subordinate of the governor-general, he was at the head of the military; he appointed as many syndics as he pleased, and also nominated his own district commandants. His authority was without limitation in civil causes, and it extended to all criminal matters under the degree of capital, though his decisions of every kind were liable to be reversed on appeals.

The governor-general and intendant-general, were totally independent of each other in their several departments, and had an exclusive control over all suits, and other matters, which appertained to their respective jurisdictions.

Antecedent to 1799, the duties of both were confided to the governor-general; but in that year a department of finance was created, and an intendant general appointed.

Separate tribunals were constituted to assist these great officers of the crown in the adjudication of causes: But their decisions or opinions were of no effect unless sanctioned by their superiors; and indeed the heads of these departments often incurred the responsibility of deciding contrary to the opinions of the tribunals.

The governor-general was at the head of the military and judiciary departments. He decided on all criminal and civil suits, not appertaining to the revenue, which were instituted, or came before him by way of appeal. He was in some measure the legislator of the province. He gave occasional instructions to his subordinates, or promulgated ordinances for the benefit of the people at large, or for those of particular districts. These in most respects conformed either to the Roman law, or to the code of the Indies, and were generally digested and recommended by his advisory tribunals.

The department of finance was organised in a similar manner, at the head of which was the intendant-general. He had a number of dignified officers under him, who performed separate and distinct duties, independent of each other. He took cognizance of all admiralty and fiscal causes. The liquidation and settlement of all public accounts belonged to him; and no money could be drawn from the treasury without his order. It belonged to him to apportion, to levy, and to collect taxes, and to devise regulations for the interior government of the finances. He was assisted by a legal character, named an assessor, to whom all difficult and litigated points were referred, though the intendant was not bound to conform to his opinion. He regulated commerce and navigation, and repressed the abuses and disorders in the several branches of his department. He also regulated the affairs of the Indians, the admission of settlers into the province, and the sale of public lands.

Most of the great officers of the crown were appointed for five years only. Re-appointments were seldom made, except when cogent reasons rendered them necessary.

The subordinate tribunals, designed to assist the heads of the two great departments of the government, deserve more particular notice.

The alcaid-general was attached to the civil department, and had cognizance of all such criminal offences, under the degree of capital, as were committed without the limits of the city of New-Orleans.

The governor-general was assisted in all his deliberations by a tribunal of civil and military jurisdiction. No sentence of death pronounced against any criminal could be carried into execution before it was examined and ratified by a superior tribunal in the island of Cuba.

Each of the provincial tribunals had an auditor, and an assessor, who were doctors of the civil law, and whose duty it was to attend and to advise in all matters of importance.

The office of procureur general was deemed of the highest consequence. He acted not merely as solicitor for the crown, but was an officer peculiar to the civil law. He did not always prosecute; but after conviction he indicated the punishment awarded by the law, and on his suggestion it was often mitigated. He was also the curator of orphans, the expounder of the privileges of the city, and the public accuser of all public officers, who either infringed the laws, or omitted to perform the duties assigned them.

Cabildos are the most popular tribunals in the Spanish colonies, and the most discouraged by the government. They were originally placed over small detached villages and towns, in which they exercised civil and military powers. They devised municipal laws and held municipal courts, and were considered as the general and almost only conservators of the peace. They still exist in many of the cities; but their number is much reduced, and their powers greatly restricted. Superior tribunals have been constituted to receive and to decide on appeals made from their decisions. To the cabildos are usually attached a number of alcaids, regidors, syndics, and registers, who assist them in the administration, and in the execution of the laws. The powers of the cabildos in the several provinces and cities are not uniform; they are extended or limited as the circumstances of the people require; and they differ from those recognized by similar tribunals in Spain, where they are purely municipal.

The offices of the members of these tribunals are denominated *venal* by the Spaniards, because they are acquired by purchase; though no man can become a member in this manner without paying a certain sum into the public treasury, nor unless he be qualified in all respects to discharge his official trust. Notaries, attornies, assessors, tax-gatherers, and a variety of others, are obliged to purchase their respective offices, and to furnish ample security for the faithful discharge of them.

New-Orleans boasted of its cabildo, which consisted of twelve members, and the governor general presided in its deliberations. The judiciary powers of this tribunal were of a limited nature, and extended only to disputes and causes arising within the boundaries of the corporation. It derived its importance from the exercise of other and more extensive powers. The police of the city was confided to its discretion. It regulated the admission of physicians and surgeons to practice. The sheriff, alcaid provincial, procureur-general, and several other officers, were chosen by it, and generally from among its own members. By the nature of its constitution it was in some measure an *advisary* council for the several departments of the government, and authorised to deliberate on the general and complicated concerns of the province. It had a right to recommend the adoption of such measures as were deemed useful to the community, and solemnly to protest against all objectionable laws and regulations. This right was frequently exercised by it; and its protestations and demands were always treated with respect. The members of this tribunal obtained their offices in the *venal* manner already mentioned, and most probably this circumstance rendered them the less respectable.

The contador, treasurer, interventor, auditor, and assessor, were officers subordinate to the intendant, and particularly attached to the department of finance. They derived their appointments from the crown; and from the nature of their respective duties they served as checks on each other. A certain share or portion of every transaction devolved on each, and therefore in case of a vacancy the public business of the department was in a manner suspended till a new appointment took place. The first kept all the accounts and documents relative to the receipts and expenditures of the public revenue. The second was the receiver and keeper of all public monies. The third superintended all public purchases, as also the making of all public contracts. The fourth was solicitor for the crown, and obliged from the nature of his office to furnish the governor general with legal advice in all matters relating to the civil or military departments. The fifth was also solicitor for the crown; but his functions were limited to transactions of a fiscal nature. There was likewise an administrator attached to the same department, and the official drudgery of the custom-house was confided to his management. He was allowed several clerks, all of whom were commissioned by the crown.

In addition to these tribunals, an ecclesiastical one existed, which took cognizance of all matters appertaining to religion and the church. The inquisition was once attempted to be introduced into Louisiana; but the measure was so unpopular as to oblige the inquisitors to abandon the province.

The district commandants, and other inferior magistrates, usually held their offices during good behavior; though they were sometimes obliged to yield them to favorites, or to men of superior qualifications. Merit was generally consulted in all the appointments made by the crown, though other motives equally honorable sometimes prevailed; and the mention of one instance must suffice for the rest. The last lieutenant governor of Upper Louisiana was a Frenchman by birth, and an officer in the Spanish guards. His aged father and mother, educated in ease and affluence, had been despoiled of their property in the French revolution; they were even obliged to abandon their country, and to seek shelter in the wilds of Louisiana. Their son solicited an appointment of such a nature as to enable him to contribute to their support; and he solicited not in vain: By the avails of his office he in some measure rewarded parental affection, and soothed the last days of the two objects the most dear to him.

Notwithstanding the formalities observed by the judicial authorities in all litigated cases of consequence; yet justice on ordinary occasions was speedily administered. In processes on bonds it was common to obtain execution in four days, and on notes in the same time, if the promisers acknowledged them, or their signatures were proved. But these authorities by their judgments or decrees often suspended payments much longer than was consistent with the terms of specialties and other contracts, particularly when the creditors were able to wait without material injury, and the debtors not in a situation to cancel the demands against them without a great sacrifice of property. This indulgent maxim adorns the pages of the civil law.

Both real and personal estate were liable to be seized and sold on execution. It was allowable to expose them to sale in nine days after the levy, provided they were regularly advertized during that time at three conspicuous places in the neighborhood. It was, however, necessary to appraise both species of property taken in execution before it could be sold; and no sale was permitted, unless for a sum equal to half of the appraised value.

In Upper Louisiana the legal fees of office on notes and bonds, and other undisputed claims, even to judgment and execution, never exceeded four dollars.

The summary mode of justice created a much greater degree of punctuality in the payment of debts than is established in any part of the United States; and this was particularly useful in a country almost destitute of specie, where peltry was the medium of trade, and where credits were necessary and common. The change produced by the operation of the laws of the United States, the dilatory proceedings of our courts, the introduction of the trial by jury, and the expenses of legal contests, gave a temporary check to trade, and to the credit of merchants, particularly in Upper Louisiana. Experience led them to believe, that the Spanish mode of decision, grounded on equitable laws, was much the most wise and salutary; and they murmured at a system calculated to produce delays, and in many instances to create expenses equal in amount to the sums demanded. They preferred the judgment of one man to that of twelve; and it is but justice to observe, that their judicial officers were in most instances upright and impartial in their decisions.

Upper Louisiana was always destitute of a circulating medium: Specie, indeed, was a rare article in that country. This may be attributed to its distance from the sea board and the markets, to the low state of its agriculture; and to the nature of its trade. Remittances were made in peltry, lead, and some provisions; but as the value of these did not exceed that of the imports, no specie was put in circulation by commerce. The lead and salt sent up the Ohio and its waters were exchanged for castings, whiskey, iron, steel, and some other indispensable articles; and this barter trade, whatever were the benefits of it, served not to augment the quantity of specie. Even the public officers and troops received their pay of the traders, generally in foreign produce, in exchange for bills drawn on the treasury at New Orleans. This deficiency of money induced the government to consider peltry as the medium of trade, and as a legal tender in the payment of debts, except in cases where it infringed the express stipulation of the parties. The Spanish laws not only sanctioned, but coerced the *specific performance* of contracts, and on this principle all judicial determinations, at least in Upper Louisiana, were grounded. A note, for instance, of one hundred dollars was payable in peltry, unless it expressly stipulated, that the payment should be in *Spanish milled dollars*. The specification in contracts was the more necessary, as one silver dollar was always deemed equal to one dollar and twenty five cents in peltry. If a man bound himself to deliver certain articles, or to execute a certain work, the judiciary decreed the exact performance of the contract; and in case the debtor neglected or refused to comply with the decree, the creditor had a right to engage a third person to perform the contract at the expense of the original obligee or promiser, or to recover a sum equal to the damages sustained.

Perhaps in no country were aggravated crimes more rare than in Louisiana. The contrary of this might have been expected from the different languages, religions, and customs of the people: especially from the constant accession of various descriptions of new settlers. Two reasons may be assigned for this general exemption from crimes. The first is, that the Creole inhabitants were rather peaceable in their dispositions, perhaps the more so as they were educated in the habits of obedience to the laws, which seldom suffered the guilty to escape with impunity. Besides, the French attached much more disgrace to punishments than any other people; and perhaps this circumstance imposed some restraint on their actions. The second is, that the terrors of the magistrate, the frightful apprehension of the Mexican mines, and the dungeons of the Havanna, added to the supposed antipathy of the government to all strangers, awed the settlers from the United States into submission, and produced an uncommon degree of subordination among them.

Nor were punishments more rigorous than is consistent with the safety of governments, and the preservation of order in civil communities. For offences under the degree of capital the laws doomed the offenders to imprisonment, or to the stocks, and to the payment of costs, except when detected in carrying on a contraband trade, or in violating the revenue laws; and then they were liable to be put on board the gallies, in the mines, or on the public works, sometimes for life, but generally for a term of years. Treason, murder, arson, and the robbery of the public treasury, were pronounced by the laws to be capital offences. Many unhappy wretches convicted of these crimes remained in prison a long time after they received the sentence of death; probably in consequence of the tenderness or dilatory caution of the tribunal in the island of Cuba. Only four crimes were declared capital by the laws, and few states in the union can boast of so small a number of this description. The punishments already mentioned for offences under the degree of capital, were not much more rigorous than those experienced in our common prisons, penitentiaries, and other houses of correction.

The laws made ample provision for appeals both in civil and criminal cases. The party aggrieved had a right to appeal to the decision of a superior tribunal, if demanded within five days from the date of the objectionable decree or sentence. In Upper Louisiana, appeals lay from the decisions of the district commandants, and other inferior magistrates, to the lieutenant governor, and from thence to the governor general. This last mentioned officer received and decided all prosecutions and causes, which came before him by way of appeal from the inferior tribunals in Lower Louisiana. The intendant general and his sub-delegates exercised similar prerogatives in the department of finance. From the decisions of these two great officers of the government, appeals lay in the first instance to separate tribunals in the island of Cuba, and from thence to the council of the Indies in Spain.

This council, of so much dignity and consequence in the Spanish government, was founded as early as 1511. The conquest of America suggested the necessity of laws and regulations different from those of Spain, and particularly adapted to the circumstances of the new world; and the necessity of confiding the complicated concerns of the colonies to a separate and distinct administration was equally apparent. Hence the origin of the council of the Indies, generally composed of men who had faithfully discharged honorable trusts in America, or were well acquainted with American affairs. This council ever kept in view the union of the provinces with the mother country; and its wisdom was successfully directed to this end. The laws and regulations by which they were governed, emanated from it. The decisions of this tribunal were always held in the highest respect, and the whispers of complaint were never uttered against its integrity.

From this statement it is natural to conclude, that appeals, if carried to the tribunal of the last resort, were attended with great expense and delay. Most of the expense, however, arose in the first stages of litigated causes; and although some of them remained undecided for many years, yet this was more owing to the legal indulgence claimed by the parties, than to any disposition in the tribunals to postpone their decisions. Professional characters were seldom employed, except in preparing causes for trial. Forensic disputations were excluded from the Spanish tribunals; and their judicial determinations resulted wholly from the written evidence laid before them, and from the known laws of the kingdom.

In all civil causes where appeals were made from the decisions of the lieutenant governor of Upper Louisiana, the persons claiming them were obliged to pay the opposite parties the full amount of the sums decreed against them; and bonds were given to refund the sums thus paid in case the decrees were ultimately reversed. This regulation was partly intended to prevent litigious and vexatious appeals for the purposes of delay, and partly to shield the poor from the oppression of the rich; and it had the desired effect. Appeals were not common; and those who made them could have no other object in view than the reversal of erroneous judgments.

It was the policy of the Spanish government to discourage political enquiry, and to keep the people in a great measure ignorant of the laws by which they were governed. The governor and intendants general were authorized to devise and publish such ordinances and decrees, not inconsistent with the established policy of the provincial system, as were necessary in their respective departments. An ordinance relative to dowry, and the descent and distribution of estates *ab intestato*, and another relative to the grants and concessions of lands, prescribing the quantities allowed to settlers, and the formalities requisite to obtain complete titles, were almost the only ones of a general nature ever promulgated by them. If they now and then furnished their subordinates with written instructions, the effects produced by them were very inconsiderable, and not always conformable to the fundamental maxims of the laws.

The public revenue in Louisiana arose from several sources. The custom-house received a duty of six *per centum* on the value of all shipping transferred from one individual to another. Those who received legacies or inheritances from collaterals, of the value of two thousand dollars, were obliged to pay a tax of two *per centum;* and a tax of four *per centum* was assessed on all legacies or inheritances given to strangers. Those who received salaries from the government, exceeding three hundred dollars *per annum*, paid a tax; as also all those who acquired *venal offices.* All vessels of whatever size paid a pilotage of twenty dollars, seven of which went into the public treasury. Each person licenced to sell ardent spirits paid an annual tax or duty of forty dollars in Lower Louisiana, and thirty dollars in Upper Louisiana. The annual amount of these duties and taxes was only about six thousand dollars.

On all goods or other articles, either imported or exported, a duty of six *per centum* was charged; and the annual avails of this branch of the public revenue amounted to about one hundred and twenty thousand dollars. The annual expenses of the government may be computed at about six hundred and fifty thousand dollars; so that a deficiency arose of about five hundred and twenty four thousand dollars. This was in part supplied by an annual remittance of four hundred thousand dollars from La vera Cruz. The remainder was balanced by certificates, which became current in market, and which were usually purchased at a discount of twenty five or thirty *per centum;* and it is said on good authority, that some of the officers in the department of finance became the holders of them to a large amount. The public debt still due is estimated at about four hundred and fifty thousand dollars. Provision was made several years before the cession for the redemption of these certificates; but the funds appropriated for the purpose were ultimately applied to other and different objects.

These are some of the outlines of the Spanish government in Louisiana; only the prominent features of it have been attempted, and even those we have suggested are very imperfect. To form an adequate conception of its structure, its parts, and mutual relations, and to delineate all the forms and maxims established for the administration of the laws, would require more labor than is consistent with the nature of this work, or with the ability of the author.

We must not too severely condemn the provincial systems of the Spaniards, because they differ from our own, and because they appear to us defective and incongruous. We must remember, that all good governments are practical, not merely theoretic; and that we can only form a correct opinion of their fitness or inutility from the effects they produce. Our present government, both in practice and theory, is the best for us; but it does not from thence follow, that the same kind of government is calculated to promote the happiness of other nations. The difference among them is not less than that among the individuals of society; each labors under disadvantages peculiar to itself. No two of them correspond in their pursuits and wants; they vary still more in their educations, habits, manners, and dispositions; nor are they alike exposed to the same physical evils. Some are prone to war, to licentiousness, and to a contempt of all moral and legal restraints; who estimate no glory equal to that of conquest, and no riches equal in value to those obtained by plunder and rapine. These require governments essentially different from those, whose local situations protect them from foreign danger, and whose educations, tempers, habits, and pursuits, naturally incline them to seek repose in peace, and to yield obedience to equitable and necessary laws.

In fine, it is a fundamental truth in politics, though seldom regarded, that nations ought to exist under such governments, whatever be their forms, as are calculated to confer the greatest sum of general happiness on the people. If the views of statesmen and legislators were guided by this truth, we should witness almost as many forms of government as there are nations on the globe, and pregnant with all the various principles between the two extremes of liberty and despotism. The best and wisest governments are enumerated among the evils of our condition. These are endured, and even cherished and supported on the principle, that they serve to exempt mankind from those of greater magnitude.

Most of the celebrated writers on government were deceived by their own plausible theories, and this deception has multiplied the political errors of mankind. They labored more to define and illustrate abstract principles than to discover and suggest practical truths; more to frame general theories, applicable only to superior orders of intelligences, than to apply specific remedies to the particular evils incident to different societies. They considered mankind what they wished them to be, not what nature made them. Hence a wonderful mass of political error exists, and actual experiment only is capable of erasing it from the minds of men.

The United States framed a government for themselves in a time of profound peace. No jealous power existed, either within or without capable of obstructing their views, or of disturbing their deliberations. They were at liberty to pursue the dictates of their own wisdom, and to erect their political fabric on such foundations as appeared the most likely to render it permanent, and to afford the greatest sum of general happiness and prosperity to the nation. If the result of their joint wisdom and labors be a monarchy, as Dr. Priestley maintains, the experience of twenty years has not persuaded us to reject it.

The ancients had no adequate conception of representative governments. If they had their legislative and executive tribunals, both relative and hereditary, under the denomination of senates, tribunes, archons, ephori, cosmi, and the like; yet the duration of their offices, the fluctuation and undefined nature of their authority, and the want of co-ordinate branches to review, modify, and even to arrest the hasty and intemperate measures of each other, served only to nourish the seeds of perpetual discord, and to render public liberty insecure. The separation and distribution of governmental powers, as practised in modern times, were unknown to them. A cursory view of their history will convince us, that they were destitute of stability, virtue, and political knowledge, the most essential requisites in all representative governments, without which they cannot be framed or supported.

The Greeks and Romans were the most enlightened people of antiquity; yet during the many ages of their existence they never aimed at the establishment of regular governments. They exhibited a strange versatility of character. In times of public danger they rallied round their sages and heroes; they invested them with supreme authority; they implicitly yielded to their counsels; and perhaps they were never so happy and prosperous as when they submitted to the sovereign dictates of their rulers. The transitions from war to peace produced a change in their conduct. They became impatient of legal restraint; they were not disposed to yield a permanent obedience to the laws; they murmured at whatever obstructed the indulgence of their licentious passions; and they even incarcerated, banished, or immolated their best patriots and statesmen; so that the exercise of any description of power among them was always precarious, and often dangerous.

On a variety of occasions, particularly in time of peace, those ancient people were divided into parties and factions by their restless and ambitious demagogues. The wild and extravagant excesses exhibited by all classes, the murders, proscriptions, and other violences, to which they were led by the most brutal passions, were in some measure intenerated by their perfection in the arts, and by the blaze of their victories and triumphs. The fact appears to be, that they were totally destitute of political virtue and knowledge; and that governments of a strong texture, unshackled by representation, were the best calculated to promote their happiness.

The same remark will apply with equal force to many modern nations. Those in the north of Europe are incapable of any other than monarchic governments; and happy it is for them, if they find the extensive power of their monarchs tempered by mercy, and directed by wisdom. Even France, one of the most enlightened nations on the globe, struggled to establish a government on the broad basis of civil liberty, and failed in the experiment. The people of that country waded in blood to the throne; they were never able to find the object of their wishes; and, as if fatigued with the pursuit, they resolved to repose themselves under a military despotism. How much more enviable is their present condition than it was at any period of their disastrous revolution! Perhaps the Spanish provinces on our borders are still chained by the sentence of nature to the same melancholy grade, where they will probably repose, till some terrible convulsion elevates them amid seas of blood to the fruition of a more prosperous destiny. All this shews, that some nations derive the greatest sum of general happiness from the arbitrary dictates of their rulers; while others exist with more safety and prosperity under the wisdom and energies of derivative authority.

Let us not, then, pass judgment on the Spanish colonial systems, unless we found it on the situation and character of the people. Among these are Spaniards, Creoles, Aboriginals, a vast variety of mixed breeds, forming no less than seven distinct *casts*, and strangers from all parts of the world, from civilized as well as barbarous nations. Most of those who compose this crude and heterogeneous assemblage, are extemely ignorant, and capable only of a blind obedience. Yet they are apparently the happiest people on earth. The taxes and contributions levied on them are not exorbitant; very little labor supplies their wants; and most of them are unacquainted with those luxuries and expenses, which modern times have rendered fashionable. Their moral principles also are extremely debauched, and their intercourse with each other is marked by the most corrupt profligacy of manners. Those who believe these people capable of self-government are much deceived. They have a very inadequate conception of human nature as it is displayed in the Spanish colonies.

These observations are by no means applicable to the Louisianians. The French always preserved their integrity, their decency, and moral principles; though they lost most of their industry, and nearly all their knowledge. Hence the theory and administration of their government were in most respects as perfect as their situation and circumstances would allow. At any rate, they were satisfied with their allotment, and never sighed for a political change. This maxim cannot be too often repeated, that nothing *experimentally wrong* in politics, is true; and that every thing *practically injurious*, is politically false.

The French and Spaniards of the new world are much attached to their own forms of government, however radically defective they may be in principle. The laws of England were introduced into Canada in 1764. The trial by jury was established, and legislative assemblies, composed of the freeholders and planters, were chosen by the people to enact laws. This innovation was disagreeable to the Canadians, who petitioned against it in 1765, 1770, and 1773; so that in 1774 the parliament passed the Quebec act, by which all former laws and ordinances of the English were abolished, and " the laws and customs of " Canada" established. The Louisianians are mostly governed by the civil law. In the territory of Orleans the ancient forms of judicial proceeding, not incompatible with the change, are still retained.

SKETCHES OF LOUISIANA.

CHAPTER IX.

COMMERCE AND MANUFACTURES.

WHILE Louisiana was in the hands of the French, great exertions were made to introduce a spirit of commercial enterprise among the people; but they were not attended with the success they deserved. Agriculture and industry, by which wealth is at first accumulated in new regions, necessarily precede commerce, and are the foundations of it. To promote this desirable object the crown lavished large sums to promote the interest of the colony, expecting to derive abundance of provisions and raw materials in return for the benefits conferred on it. The exertions of Crozat and of the company, to whom the commerce of the province was successively granted, proved equally fruitless. The poverty of the settlers, their want of industry, and the trouble given them by the Indians and Spaniards, were insuperable obstacles to commerce, and these unfortunate impediments continued for a great length of time. Indeed, during the existence of the French colonial government, the Indian trade almost wholly occupied the attention of the people, who were more disposed to provide for present necessity than to discover the means of future good. Louisiana involved France in heavy expenditures; and perhaps the despair of remuneration was among the causes, which induced her so easily to cede the country to Spain.

When France first discovered Louisiana she was not in a condition to promote the settlement of it. The pressure of taxes, occasioned by complicated wars, deprived her of the means of colonization; and she was for some time allowed only to anticipate what she wished to realize. The distance too of the colony from the mother country, although it increased the prospects of wealth, served to check the spirit of emigration among the opulent, and to confine it almost exclusively to the poor; and even these embarked in the enterprise, not to obtain wealth by the slow process of agriculture, but to seize on rich mines, and to monopolize the Indian trade; the latter of which they fancied was not less valuable than the accumulated products of Potosi. They were not calculated to labor in the field: The climate was too warm, and proved injurious to health; and they were not able to procure a sufficient number of slaves to answer any valuable purpose. They soon found their expectations blasted, and regretted their destiny. Unable from extreme poverty to rejoin their connexions in Europe, and exposed to the vindictive rage of the Spaniards, and of some tribes of Indians, they mostly submitted themselves to indolence and fatuity. The little knowledge of agriculture they possessed was never reduced to experiment; it expired with the first generation, and was never fully revived while the country remained in the hands of France. Hence there was a radical defect in the first settlement of Louisiana, and it served to impede the prosperity of that colony through all the subsequent periods of its history. Had Indian commerce been wholly prohibited, or confided to a few exclusive traders only, and the settlers generally restricted to agriculture, and to the acquisition of raw materials for foreign markets, the power of France in America would have been much more formidable than it was.

The Spaniards, after they obtained Louisiana, experienced no great difficulty from the Indians: but they found a people who had lost all industry, and nearly all their knowledge of agriculture. O'Reilly, and some of his immediate successors in the government, endeavored to revive a spirit of industry, and to awaken the people to a sense of their interest. Their exertions, though in some degree successful, did not produce all the desired effects; and they saw with regret, that the inhabitants still retained their habitual indolence, and an unconquerable predilection for the Indian trade, which was always precarious and unprofitable, and did not increase the aggregate wealth of the colony. Their object was to create a revenue equal to the expenditures of the government. They well knew, that this depended on agriculture, which is the foundation of foreign commerce; and as they had exhausted every resource within themselves to promote it without effect, they resolved about the year 1787 to encourage the industrious citizens of the United States to remove into the colony, partly to increase the means of wealth, and partly to serve as a defence against the threatened invasions of two of the European powers. This gave a spring to agriculture and commerce; a spirit of foreign intercourse was diffused among all classes of the people; exertions were made to prepare raw materials for the West India and other markets; and the exports from Louisiana annually increased till the close of the Spanish government, though they never rose to the value of the imports.

The articles of export were sugar, cotton, indigo, rice, furs and peltry, lumber, tar, pitch, cattle, horses, lead, flour, beef, and pork. The annual exports from the province by way of the sea, the year before the cession to the United States, amounted to about two million one hundred and sixty thousand dollars, and the imports to about two million five hundred thousand dollars; but in this sum is included plantation utensils, slaves, and a variety of other articles of value not generally enumerated among those of commerce; so that the imports greatly exceeded the exports. Had the cession been deferred a few years only, the probability is, that the raw materials would have so much augmented in quantity and value as to have met the expenses of imported articles. This desirable occurrence has added new springs to population, commerce, and industry, and is already productive of individual and public wealth.

It is impossible to ascertain the value of the trade in Upper Louisiana; part of it was connected with New-Orleans, part with Canada, and no inconsiderable portion of it with the United States. This quarter alone furnished lead for the market, and also considerable quantities of salt, beef and pork, furs and peltries. The quantity and value of the two last articles may be estimated with some degree of certainty; but of the others conjectures only can be formed. The traders procured most of their Indian goods in Canada; the other goods consumed by the inhabitants were mostly purchased in Philadelphia and Baltimore, and the groceries and other heavy articles in New Orleans; iron, steel, nails, and castings, were boated from the Ohio and its waters. The furs and peltries were mostly exported to Canada. Considerable quantities of salt and lead found their way up the Ohio: Part of the latter article, all the surplus beef and pork, and some other articles, were sent to the New Orleans market.

The furs and peltries are susceptible of more accurate calculation. Accounts of these for fifteen successive years, ending in 1804, were kept by a gentleman of the first repute in Upper Louisiana; and their annual average quantity and value stand thus:

Castors——————*lbs*.	36,900 valued at	$66,820
Otters————————	8,000	37,100
Bear skins———————	5,100	14,200
Buffaloe skins————	850	4,750
Raccoon, wild Cat, Fox skins }	28,200	12,280
Martins———————	1,300	3,900
Lynx's———————	300	1,500
Deer skins——————	153,000	63,200
	Total	$203,750

The French and Spaniards extended the Indian trade a considerable distance up the Arkansas; along the whole extent of the St. Francis and White river, at least to the villages and hunting camps of the natives in those quarters; up the Mississippi to the falls of St. Anthony, and to the sources of all the westerly branches of it below that point; up the Missouri about nine hundred miles, as also most of its branches where Indians were to be found. A considerable trade was also carried on among the Indians to the eastward of the Mississippi, particularly with the Kickapoos near the head waters of the Kaskaskia river, and with the Piorias and other Indians on, and in the neighborhood of the Illinois river. The trade from the

Missouri was much more valuable than that of any other river, and perhaps of the whole of them united, owing to the great length of it, to the vast number of Indians on its waters, and to the excellent quality of the furs and skins obtained in those regions. The average value of the goods annually sent up the Missouri alone, during the fifteen years already mentioned, was sixty one thousand two hundred and fifty dollars. These were exchanged for furs and skins, which on an average yielded an annual profit of sixteen thousand seven hundred and twenty one dollars, exclusive of all expenses, or about twenty seven *per centum;* and by the same rule the annual profits of the whole Indian trade in Upper Louisiana amounted to upwards of fifty five thousand dollars; a sum of considerable magnitude when compared with the scanty population of that country. The prices of the several articles mentioned in this calculation were those of Upper Louisiana. Had they been rated according to those of London, to which place most of them found their way, the profits would have almost exceeded belief. Most of the traders were too poor to defray the expenses of freight, or to wait for the returns of an European market. They exchanged the avails of their trade for supplies of Indian goods, which were sold them at about one hundred, and sometimes at one hundred and thirty *per centum,* in advance of the original cost, and the expense of transporting them from Quebec to Michillimakinak, where they usually received them.

It is worthy of remark, that the Indian trade in this quarter was never liable to the same objection as that carried on in the Delta, and on the rivers flowing directly into it. The pursuit of it to the southward of the thirty second degree only impoverished the country, because it not only induced the inhabitants to neglect agriculture, but also because the furs and peltries obtained by them were of little comparative value. The trade in Upper-Louisiana was widely different, and susceptible of progressive improvement. The traders were always able to obtain suitable goods from Canada, and the furs and peltries given in exchange for them were of an excellent quality, and commanded a high price. The Indians were also numerous, and stood in need of greater supplies than those in warmer latitudes; they had it in their power from the multiplicity of game to make speedy returns for all the merchandise the traders were able to furnish them. Hence the ancient French in the Illinois country did not experience the poverty of their friends about the Delta, though they were equally inclined to indolent habits, and entertained nearly the same aversion to agriculture. The Spaniards seldom gave them any trouble, and they were mostly exempt from Indian hostilities.

The Indians are much more particular in the color and quality of their goods than is generally suspected. Most of the tribes or nations differ in their choice of goods; and indeed they are always known to each other by their dresses. Whatever be their wants they will seldom purchase strouding, blankets, or any other articles, unless they be of the size, color, and quality, to which they are accustomed. They sometimes carry their fancies to such extremes as to involve themselves in distress; for they will endure the rigors of winter rather than cover their bodies with a blanket too large or too small, or which is deficient in a border, or has one too many, or the color of which is not suited to their taste. The goods at present manufactured in the United States are in no estimation among them; and they have, at least in one instance, refused to accept an annuity of merchandise of this description. Were our manufacturers supplied with proper patterns, no doubt they might be able to gratify the delicacy of our own red neighbours, and at the same time afford suitable assortments. The manufacturers in England are well acquainted with the nature of the goods wanted in the various regions of the west and north-west: They also know how to apportion the different articles to the different nations, lakes, or rivers; so that an assortment put up by them will always be found to answer the wants of the Indians for whom it is designed. It is of importance to the trader, that the various articles of his cargo be exhausted at the same time; otherwise some items, and perhaps those of the most value, will remain unsold, and become mere remnants, because he has not others to match and accompany them: For if the Indians cannot obtain several different articles at the same time, so as to complete what may be called a suit, they will not purchase any, and frequently become offended. Hence their partiality for English merchandise is easily explained; and it is unfortunate, that our manufacturers are either unacquainted with these particulars, or are not sufficiently united in their endeavors to furnish the necessary supplies. If the labors of a certain number of gun-smiths, and of manufacturers of cutlery and cotton stuffs, were united and directed to the same end, it would certainly be in their power to supply our Indian traders; and the annual consumption of goods to the amount of more than two hundred thousand dollars, with the prospect of a gradual increase, ought to stimulate them to the experiment. Very few rifles are used by the Indians of Louisiana; they prefer light muskets, though of some length.

The United States have adopted a liberal policy in their intercourse with the Indians, situated on our borders. These Indians are not only supplied at a cheap rate with all the conveniences of which they stand in need, but they gradually acquire habits of industry, exchange the fruits of the chase for the more substantial avails of agriculture, and at the same time become more sensible of their inferiority, and of their dependence on us. Were the same policy extended to the Indians on the Missouri and the Upper Mississippi, no doubt the same effects would result.

The traders in these quarters put an enormous price on their commodities, though the profits of the trade are not very exorbitant, and this arises on the great advance charged on the goods obtained from Canada. The United States can supply the Indians at nearly one hundred *per centum* under what our traders now demand from them; and supplies in this way would serve to restrain the impositions at present practiced on them. Such a difference would soon be felt by the Indians; and the prospects of a successful issue seem fully to justify some further arrangements on the subject.

To carry such a plan into effect it may be necessary to establish several trading houses; perhaps one at the mouth of the Ouisconsing, or Prairie des Chiens, one at the mouth of the St. Pierre, one at the mouth of the Osage river, or near the Osage villages, one on or at the mouth of the river Platte, one on Red River, and also another on the Arkansas. These positions are not only calculated for the Indian trade, but trading houses at the two former would serve to obstruct the trade at present carried on from Canada, and secure it to ourselves. The Canadian traders must pass to the Upper Mississippi, at least to that part of it visited by our own traders, through lake Michigan, by way of the Illinois, or the Ouisconsing. The first is sufficiently guarded by the garrison at Chicago, and another at the mouth of the latter would interdict all improper communications between the Mississippi and Canada, except to the upper part of that river by way of Lake Superior. The Canadian traders annually rendezvous at *Prairie des Chiens*, where they have built a small village. From this place they dispatch their goods in various directions, particularly to the Rivers des Moins and St. Pierre, which fall into the Mississippi from the west, and no small proportion of them find their way across to the Missouri. If circumstances will not allow us to prohibit the Canadian trade at present carried on at the Mandan nation, and other Indians on the upper parts of these two great rivers, still we have it in our power to check them below the points just mentioned. These traders will endeavor to render public trading establishments unpopular, because they will in some measure deprive them of the trade, and force them either to lower their prices, or to withdraw their goods from market. They even contend that, since the cession of Louisiana, they have a right by subsisting treaty stipulations to extend the Indian trade into our territory on the west side of the Mississippi: But this claim is inadmissible.

On this subject, however, one difficulty presents itself, which, perhaps, cannot be easily removed. The merchants of Canada send their clerks and dependants to reside at Michillimakinak, within our territory, where they obtain naturalization. The trade is conducted in their name; but in fact they are no more than agents; and their principals, who belong to Quebec and Montreal, reap the fruits of their enterprise. To prohibit the exportation of merchandise from Canada would prove extremely injurious to our own citizens; but it would cure the evil.

The acquisition of the Indian trade by the English is the smallest evil we have to apprehend. While they engross the trade, the Indians, with whom they have an intercourse, will ever be under their control; and whenever they are prompted by interest or prejudice, they will be able to stimulate them to hostilities. By presents and misrepresentations they have caused some of our own traders to be either plundered of their property, or driven from their stations. They even prejudice the Indians against the citizens of the United States generally; represent them as disobedient and refractory children; as less numerous and less powerful than their red neighbours, whose objects are to encroach on them, and, under the appearance of friendship, to practice every species of treachery and deception; to take their lands from them, and finally to extirpate them. These topics, most of all others, alarm the fears and jealousies of weak minds, and serve to create a deadly enmity; especially as many of the Indians have long viewed with pain the rapid progress of the whites westward; their ancient domains in a degree usurped; their game destroyed by culture, and innumerable disorders introduced among them, unknown before the beams of civilization disfigured their horizon. Independent from nature, and the only legitimate proprietors of the soil, many of their wisest men view these things with regret, and lament the necessity, which obliged their ancestors to yield so much to the whites. They consider almost every treaty, especially if lands be granted away, as in a degree extorted from them, and therefore no longer obligatory than while their weakness prevents a reclamation of their rights. Such feelings and sentiments are excited in the minds of the Indians by those, who are inimical to the interest of our government and citizens; and they can only be softened or rendered useless by some firm and placable measures on the part of the United States, and by banishing from among them all those whose interets are disconnected with our national safety.

The boats used by the Indian traders are of various sizes; but those the most commonly preferred carry from fifteen to twenty-five thousand weight. Their sides are low, and their oars short, so that they may be navigated near the shore, where the counter currents or eddies accelerate their progress; their bottoms are nearly flat, so that they are enabled to pass in shoal water; they are also somewhat narrow, and their length is generally from forty-five to sixty feet. The boats employed between New-Orleans and the Illinois country are differently constructed; they are higher out of water, and sink deeper into it; of much greater width, and supplied with keels; hence they are called barges, and many of them will carry forty tons. The number of boatmen is usually designated by the weight of the cargo; one is required to every three thousand pounds. These are equal to any in the world; they generally consist of French whites, and French mulattoes; and as they are accustomed to the water from their childhood, they are capable of sustaining the greatest fatigue. They are seldom known to be impatient of labor, or to be affected by the heat; and on these accounts they are to be preferred to others. They are also accustomed to live on what would starve an English American. A small quantity of corn meal, and bear's grease, are all the articles of nourishment allowed them in Indian countries, except when they are so fortunate as to kill game: They are seldom furnished with salted meat, except when employed in the neighbourhood of the whites, where it can be occasionally obtained.

Very little can be said on the subject of domestic manufactures. At the time of the cession a small quantity of cotton was manufactured along the coast into quilts and cottonades. Most of the people in the neighbourhood of New-Orleans, and in the other settlements, especially at Point Coupeé, on Red River, and in the Atacapas, and Apalousas, spun and wove such articles of clothing as were necessary for their slaves; and these consisted of a mixture of cotton and wool. They find on experiment, that such domestic manufactures are of great importance, and begin pretty generally to metamorphose some of their female slaves into spinners and weavers, and some of their male slaves into smiths and carpenters. When we took possession of Louisiana, the Island of Orleans contained only one machine for spinning cotton; another was in operation in the Apalousas. In New-Orleans there was one manufactory of cordage, and several of shot and hair powder. In the neighbourhood of that city were also twelve distilleries for making taffia, a spirit somewhat similar to New-England rum, and likewise one sugar refinery.

The manufactures in Upper-Louisiana, especially in articles of clothing, were of a similar nature. The inhabitants generally cultivated a sufficient quantity of cotton for family purposes, and spun and wove it into cloth. They were not able to defray the expenses of foreign manufactured articles; the prices of which in these upper regions, were very exorbitant. They were, however, destitute of regular manufacturing machinery, except those of simple construction, generally used among the more indigent class in the states; these required much labor, and the process was slow. The manufacture of lead and salt is mentioned in another place. These articles, as well as iron in various forms, ship building, duck, and cordage, leather, and a variety of others, might be manufactured to a great extent, if the inhabitants were possessed of enterprise, and of capitals equal to the objects.

Luxury in every country treads closely on the heels of industry. The attention of people is usually drawn in the first instance to the manufacture of necessary articles, next to those of convenience, and then to those of voluptuousness. Thus it happened on the Mississippi, and indeed in all our western possessions. The manufacture of taffia at New-Orleans, and of whiskey in Upper Louisiana, was early introduced. It unfortunately happens, that men in our warm climates, especially of the laborious class, are attached to stimulating liquors, and this proves their destruction. They are guided more by their appetites than by their reason. Ashamed, however, to confess such a dereliction of principle, they have invented many ingenious arguments to prove the absolute necessity of a copious use of ardent spirits. One has the gout, and stimulating potions will drive it away. A second is cold, and they will warm him. A third is warm, and they will cool him. A fourth is disturbed in his mind, and they will obliterate his cares. A fifth complains of the foulness of the water, and they will purify it. A sixth, from long habit, has become habituated to them, and they alone will steady his nerves, and keep him in an equilibrious state. Such reasoning as this may be heard in every part of the western country, and is considered as conclusive against all the opposite sentiments of the divine, moralist, and philosopher. It may be safely doubted, whether, on the west side of the mountains, more have not fallen victims to intemperance, than to the tomahawks and scalping knives of the savages. A dangerous evil exists, calculated to destroy the morals and lives of the inhabitants; but, perhaps, a remedy is not within the reach of the civil power. It may be safely doubted, whether any measure calculated to remove, or even to lessen the evil, could be carried into effect. When men become debased in principle, their passions and appetites are not easily controled, and the pursuit of "treasons, stratagems, and spoils," excite no compunction or remorse in their bosoms.

SKETCHES OF LOUISIANA.

CHAPTER X.

LEARNING AND RELIGION.

THE Spanish authorities afforded but very little encouragement to learning. Whether it was their policy to keep men bound down in the chains of ignorance, or whether poverty and other imperious obstacles intervened to obstruct the progress of education, is not easily conjectured. It is certain, however, that the Spaniards were extremely solicitous to maintain the catholic faith. No doubt the prevalence of knowledge had a tendency to expose the absurdity of some of their religious creeds, and to weaken the ties, which connected them with the established church. Perhaps, too, they were of opinion, that a legalized religion, mixed with a variety of incomprehensible subtleties, was of more political advantage to a state, than the numerous divisions in society, occasioned by as many modes of faith.

The people of Louisiana are not to be censured for the want of more literature among them. Their natural capacities are good, and they learn whatever they undertake with remarkable facility. We here speak of the French and Spaniards, who were born and educated in the country; not of those who removed into it late in life. The want of a more general diffusion of knowledge must partly be attributed to the inattention of the government; the public treasury advanced but little money for the support of seminaries of learning; no law was ever made to compel the inhabitants to maintain schools. Even in New-Orleans, the capital of the province, two schools only were patronized by public authority. The preceptors of one of them were paid by the king, though they instructed their pupils in the Spanish language only, and in writing, and common arithmetic. The Ursuline Nuns also usually received six hundred dollars per annum from the public; and this sum, together with the avails of about one thousand acres of land belonging to the convent, enabled them to educate twelve female orphans. In addition to these they received young ladies as boarders, and instructed them in reading, writing, and needle work. There were also some private schools in the city; but they were of no great use. The settlements at a distance from the capital were still worse provided, and a person who could read and write was considered as a kind of prodigy among them.

In the early part of the last century, when the French in Upper Louisiana were at the apex of their glory, a college of priests was established at Kaskaskia. The practice of most other catholic countries obtained here; the poor were neglected, while some of the most wealthy and considerable were permitted to quaff at this literary fountain. The liberal and useful sciences, however, were but very little cultivated in this seminary. Scholastic divinity afforded almost the only subjects of investigation ; and instead of the noble works of Greek and Roman authors, their library was composed almost wholly of the huge folios of the holy fathers, and the pious reveries of more modern enthusiasts. Of what salutary use was such a seminary to the people at large ? It was in this quarter as at New-Orleans, no regulations were officially made on the subject of general education. The people now and then, sensible of the advantages of information, voluntarily contributed to the support of common schools among them ; in which some of their children were instructed in reading, writing, and counting-house arithmetic. But schools among the poor, without any other support than voluntary contributions, and not cherished by the government, either with money, or coercive sanctions, are generally of short duration, and produce no good or lasting effects in society. Hence we find, that the native French are extremely deficient in education ; multitudes of them cannot either read or write their names ; yet their manners are free and easy ; their conversation is pleasant, and often instructive, and many of them manifest extraordinary natural endowments. St. Louis and St. Genevieve were among the first villages to maintain private schools, and to open to the youth the treasures of knowledge. These schools, however, were only occasional ; and to obtain sufficient and speedy educations, some of the more opulent sent their sons to the seminaries in Canada. Upper Louisiana can boast of several native Frenchmen of education ; and also of many others of the same description from France and other countries.

The English Americans in that country, who compose at least three fifths of the population, are still more deficient in schools ; and this necessarily arises from their dispersed situation. They migrated from various quarters, and of course partake of all the varieties of character and acquirements found in the United States. Those from the eastern and middle states are the best educated. The remainder are from the back parts of the southern states, where less attention is paid to the diffusion of literature among the people.

In contemplating the character of the French people, the old observation, "that ignorance tends to happiness," seems in a degree to be verified among them. If we admit this observation to be correct, we degrade human nature; but of all the people on the globe the French in Louisiana appear to be the happiest. Their happiness, indeed, may be of the negative kind; but if the occurrences of the present moment, the reflections on the past, and the anticipations of the future, give them no painful sensations, we can hardly pronounce them miserable; their minds are passive, except when roused by insult or imposition, and they are exempt from those dreadful pangs, which attach themselves to the victims of sensibility. Indolence is prevalent among them; but they are honest in their dealings, and punctual in the performance of contracts. They obtain but little, and little satisfies their desires. They usually live within their incomes, and are never so uneasy as when in debt. While the English Americans are hard at labor, and sweat under the burning rays of a meridian sun, they will be seated in their houses, or under some cooling shade, amusing themselves with their pipes and tobacco, in drinking of coffee, and in repeating the incidents of their several perambulations over distant lakes and mountains. When occasion presses, however, they are not deficient in exertion. Many of them follow boating and the Indian trade; and these require much labor, activity, and circumspection. They are very patient under fatigues, and will subsist for months on such food as the woods afford without a murmur. They enjoy what they have, and are perfectly contented with it.

In fine, Upper Louisiana exhibits an assemblage of characters, manners, and customs, of greater variety than most other countries. Unless measures be taken to consolidate and assimilate them, the same variety will be apt to continue, and be productive of disunion, litigation, and unfriendly feelings. The sooner this heterogeneous mass is amalgamated, and attempts made to exterminate those prejudices, and varieties of character, which disfigure this frontier portion of the union, the better for the United States. In the event of success, the people would be more attached to the government, less liable to contemplate a separation, or resort to such foreign standards as may possibly be unfurled on the Mississippi. Indeed, few of the French, and part of the English Americans only, were at first reconciled to the change, though they never manifested any discontent. The former did not doubt the justice of the United States; but they seemed to feel as if they had been sold in open market, and by this means degraded; the treaty of 1762, and the change under it in 1769, rushed on their minds, and awakened all their apprehensions. The latter anticipated taxation, many of whom had abandoned their native country to avoid it, and voluntarily became the subjects of a government, careful not to impose any burthens on the agricultural part of the community. The best way to secure the affections of these people, is gradually to change their modes of thinking; and the only way to attach them to our republican systems, is to enlighten their minds by a more general diffusion of knowledge among them. An academy, under the direction of the government, seems the best calculated to effect these important purposes. This would gradually introduce the English language among the French, without the destruction of their own, and awaken a spirit of enquiry and investigation. The English Americans would also derive great advantages from it. At present they are not sufficiently opulent to send their children to seminaries out of the country, and they have none in it. If a liberal endowment of lands was made to aid the purposes of such an institution, the remainder of the expense would probably be defrayed by the people, who, on proper occasions, are not destitute of patriotism and public spirit. This portion of the country must one day form one or more states. Such a literary institution would gradually mould the rising generation into statesmen and legislators; produce a long list of Tullies and Chathams to preside over the destinies of Empire; give birth to useful designs, inventions, and discoveries; enable genius, at present buried in obscurity, " to ascend the brightest heaven of invention," and to reflect new rays of glory on the literary world.

With respect to the essentials of religion, mankind are generally agreed. They anciently disputed and wrangled about the mere forms and ceremonies of it; and in this dispute rivers of blood were spilt. Even our pious ancestors in the reign of Elizabeth, most of whom were rigid puritans, viewed all the rites and ceremonies of the catholics as badges of superstition; many things in the worship of the reformers were equally odious to them, particularly the ring in marriage, and the use of the surplice; these were considered by some as fundamental errors. At one time in some parts of Europe the real presence in the sacrament was maintained by many as necessary to salvation; while others, equally pertinacious, deemed it heterodox, and contended for a more liberal construction of the scriptures. This dispute, like an earthquake, shook the christian world, and served in the end to cover religion and its zealous professors with odium. Much less blameable were those who worshipped tangible objects as symbols of the divinity, such as blocks of wood and marble, vegetables and animals, and even the waters of rivers. Much more consistent and less culpable were those, who sacrificed to the manes of sainted impostors, and derived their religious creeds from the Alcaron of Mahomet, and the Vidam of Brumma. Modern professors of christianity differ almost as much among themselves as they do from those whom they stigmatize as pagans and infidels. Each sect has its particular notions, which must be supported, right or wrong. Sectarians reciprocally enter *viet armies* into the vineyards of each other; a contest ensues; mines and count r-mines are constructed; and at last it generally happens, that all, or the greater part, are destroyed or maimed by the explosion. If the scriptures in many particulars are obscure, why quarrel about the construction of them? Some contend for immersion in baptism, and others for sprinkling, as if on a right choice depended the happiness or misery of men in another world. It is improper to censure either formality, because it is possible, that both may be correct. No one ought to denounce his neighbor for the exercise of a privilege, which he deems of importance to himself. In fine, the quarrels among professed christians about religion, and the ceremonies of it, are so many evidences of their departure from the true spirit of the gospel.

Among the French and Spaniards in Louisiana, one form of religion only prevails. A variety of religious tenets are professed among the English Americans. These have removed into the country from various quarters, and therefore it cannot be expected, that their religious opinions are materially different from those prevalent in the several places where they were born and educated. They exhibit a mixture of baptists, methodists, calvinists, and episcopalians. They are not formed into religious societies, and the laws make no provision for the support of teachers; nor indeed are any teachers exclusively attached to any particular village or settlement. Those who occasionally expatiate on the truths of revelation in a public manner, are mere itinerants; and it is unfortunate that more of them do not exercise this sacred office. The benefits of this itinerancy are partial, and only now and then enjoyed by the people to any considerable extent. Under the Spanish government the Roman catholic faith was the only authorised religion, nor was the exercise of any other permitted. Those of other denominations were extremely embarrassed; they could not conscientiously worship in the catholic temple; nor were they allowed to receive the salutary exhortations of a public speaker of their own persuasion, or to partake of the sacramental feast in the way prescribed by their own devotional formulas. The human mind, when once liberated from the fetters of religious servitude, reflects with pleasure on the emancipation of itself, and views with a mixture of horror and satisfaction the prison from which it has escaped. The United States have restored the professors of all religions to liberty; but it cannot be expected, that all the advantages afforded by this liberty will be immediately enjoyed. The scattered situation of the people renders a speedy union impracticable; though it is presumed that, as the settlements increase in number and wealth, the public duties of religion will become more prevalent. The rising generation stand in need of them; and how degraded must men be, who are not instructed in the great principles of morality and religion! It is pleasing to observe the catholicism of those of different opinions and sects, and with what ardor they embrace every convenient opportunity to become acquainted with the sublime truths of revelation.

The French and Spaniards are uniformly of the Roman catholic persuasion, and great sticklers for their particular modes of worship; though they discover no disposition to alter or control those of other sects. The priests under the Spanish government were paid by the crown, and many of them, to retain their salaries, departed from the country when the change took place. The fact is, that these people, unaccustomed to contribute to the support of the clergy, were unwilling to set an example, which they considered as burthensome and unprecedented ; though, from the characters and talents of some of their priests, it is unfortunate, that they did not resolve on a different line of conduct. While the French were in possession of the country, they were not only furnished with missionaries from Europe, but were occasionally supplied with teachers from the college of priests at Kaskaskia. Of the labors of these missionaries, we may form some judgment from the accounts they have left us of their travels. They encountered the greatest hardships, and frequently exposed their lives to the merciless tomahawks of the savages. In propagating their religion they braved death in ten thousand shapes; they have left to their successors in the same vineyard, though few of this description now remain, examples of suffering and patience, which alone could result from an elevated faith, and a well grounded hope.

The policy of the French cabinet, in relation to the colonies in general, never extended to Louisiana. In Canada, the priests as early as 1663, procured the establishment of tithes; and these amounted to one thirteenth part of the products of labor, and of spontaneous growth. This, however, was deemed so exorbitant, and was so severely felt by the people, that the council of Quebec in 1667, reduced the tithes to one twenty-sixth part, and this reduction was soon after confirmed by an edict. No tithes were ever levied or claimed in Louisiana, either under the French or Spanish governments; and the people of that country were exempted from many other burthens of a similar nature, imposed on those of the other colonies.

The clergy at New-Orleans under the Spanish government consisted of a bishop, who never entered the province, two canons, and five curates. Twenty other curates were dispersed among the parishes in the country. The bishop was entitled to four thousand dollars per annum from a certain revenue established in Mexico and Cuba. The two canons were allowed six hundred dollars each; and each of the curates from three hundred and sixty-five to four hundred dollars per annum. These salaries were paid by the crown, as also those of the Sacristans, and some chapel expenses. Three of the curates resided in Upper Louisiana, one of whom acted as vicar. Burial and marriage fees were considerable; and these, added to their salaries, afforded the clergy a decent support.

Perhaps the levity displayed, and the amusements pursued, by the French people on Sundays, may be considered by some to border on licentiousness. They attend mass in the morning with great devotion; but, after the exercises of church are over, they usually collect in parties, and pass away their time in social and merry intercourse. They play at billiards and other games; and to balls and assemblies the Sundays are particularly devoted. To those educated in regular and pious habits, such parties and amusements appear unseasonable and strange, if not odious, and seem prophetic of some signal curse on the workers of iniquity. It must, however, be confessed, that the French people on those days avoid all intemperate and immoral excesses, and conduct themselves with apparent decorum. They are of opinion, that there is true and undefiled religion in their amusements; much more, indeed, than exists in certain night conferences, and obscure meetings, in various parts among the tombs. When questioned relative to their gaiety on Sundays, they will answer, that men were made for happiness, and that the more they are able to enjoy themselves, the more acceptable they are to their Creator. They are of opinion, that a sullen countenance, an attention to gloomy subjects, a set form of speech, and a stiff behaviour, are much more indicative of hypocrisy than of religion; and they have often remarked, that those who practise these singularities on Sundays will most assuredly cheat and defraud their neighbors during the rest of the week. Such are the religious sentiments of a people, void of superstition; of a people prone to hospitality, urbanity of manners, and innocent recreation; and who present their daily orisons at the throne of grace with as much confidence of success as the most devout puritans in christendom.

It is a truth not to be contested, that a pure and rational religion, such as is contained in the sublime pages of revelation, is of infinite use to mankind in a temporal sense. It is the foundation of integrity and moral rectitude; the link which unites societies and nations, and the best antidote to the belligerous passions. Those who practice it are more punctual in their engagements, and of course greater confidence is placed in them. In their intercourse with the world, whether as individuals or as nations, they enjoy many advantages and immunities, denied to those of an opposite character. They preserve an equanimity of temper and conduct, which gives a peculiar zest to their pleasures in prosperity; and they experience that inward sunshine of virtue, which enables them to sustain with fortitude the greatest calamities.

SKETCHES OF LOUISIANA.

CHAPTER XI.

CHARACTER OF THE LOUISIANIANS.

IT is the character of the Creoles, or natives of Louisiana only, of which we are to treat; and this embraces their manners and customs. Of these we have occasionally spoken in various parts of this work; but a more copious illustration is necessary, particularly as several publications have appeared on the subject, as different in their conclusions from each other, as from the genuine character of the people of Louisiana.

It is no easy task to place in its proper point of view the character of any people with all its discriminating features. None but those master spirits, the accurate observers of mankind, can excel in this species of writing. The most incurious observer may perceive a wide difference between the general character, manners and customs, of different societies; but the vast variety of minute shades, which are so arranged and combined as to produce a complete whole, are much less perceptible.

The Creole French are at least a century behind other civilized nations in the arts and sciences, if not in the amenities of life. Three causes have contributed to keep them stationary. The first is, that most of the original settlers were extremely illiterate, and this in some measure accounts for the same condition of their posterity: Their attention was almost wholly drawn to such laborious pursuits as were calculated to yield them a subsistence, and left them no time for the acquisition of learning. The second is, the inattention of the government, or, in other words, the defect of their social institutions. These were not of a nature to encourage literature, but rather to repress it; and the people had no ambition to excel, especially as the highest literary attainment was never considered as a passport to fame, except perhaps in the religious orders. The third is, that Louisiana was in a manner insulated from the rest of the world; the inhabitants seldom mixed with strangers; and strangers had no inducements to visit them; the trade of the country was either prohibited, or the products of its soil, till a late period, too unimportant to tempt their enterprise.

Notwithstanding these impediments, the people appear to much more advantage than others under like circumstances. Many of the most opulent planters along the Delta and Red River cannot either read or write; and yet they will converse fluently, and with much seeming confidence, on a variety of subjects, where mathematical learning is necessary to a solution. They will debate on complicated machines, the utility or defects of which cannot be determined without a knowledge of mechanics, and propose substitutes and experiments with as much apparent judgment as if they were complete masters of the principles of the art. This want of information cannot be imputed to all; for some of the Creoles possess real intelligence, and are well instructed in several branches of useful learning, though their number is too limited to afford, in this respect, a very favourable reputation to the country.

Perhaps these defects are less apparent from the native vivacity of the Louisianians. This vivacity, indeed, is peculiar to the French, and, in no situation does it wholly forsake them. To this may be ascribed their passion for social intercourse, which is always gratified when opportunities permit. They are particularly attached to the exercise of dancing, and carry it to an incredible excess. Neither the severity of the cold, nor the oppression of the heat, ever restrains them from this amusement, which usually commences early in the evening, and is seldom suspended till late the next morning. They even attend the balls not unfrequently for two or three days in succession, and without the least apparent fatigue. At this exercise the females, in particular, are extremely active, and those of the United States must submit to be called their inferiors.

The dancing assemblies of the *Quarterons*, or free people of color, in New-Orleans, are not the least interesting in point of beauty and dress. They enjoy much more consideration in that country than is usual in any other. They never associate with blacks; and as there is a strong barrier between them and the whites with respect to marriage, they may be said to form a distinct class. The females possess the most beautiful forms and features. If they are accustomed to bestow their favors on the higher orders of society, it is always for stipulated periods, and no depravation of manners is observable among them. Gentlemen of distinction resort to their ball-rooms, and other places of amusement, where decency and decorum maintain their empire.

To the social nature of the French may in part be attributed their fondness for games of hazard, and in part to occasional relaxations from toil and fatigue, when amusements become necessary to their active and volatile dispositions. The repetition of any one soon ceases to afford pleasure; what pleases them one day will disgust the next, and nothing short of a variety will satisfy them. Hence it is, that they escape from the ball-room to cards, from cards to billiards, from billiards to dice, from dice back again to the ball-room, or to some other pastime, and so on alternately. Gambling in New-Orleans is reduced to a profession, where members of the fraternity from the United States rendezvous in great numbers. It is not known in Upper Louisiana as a science, though it is becoming prevalent, especially among the English Americans. The loss of time is never considered by the French as an evil, because if it were not spent in this way, it would be wasted in some other, perhaps equally injurious, and more prejudicial to health. Indolence often induces them to seek repose on the sofa or mattress.

To what cause shall we impute the preservation of their ancient manners and customs? These have not varied in any great degree for two centuries, and are nearly the same among all classes. The poor country peasantry exhibit the polished exterior of the more wealthy villagers. Their manners indicate their origin too plainly to be mistaken; which serves as a proof, that the characteristic traits of a people, though severed from their country and nation, are not easily changed or obliterated. These have been preserved in more purity among the Creoles of Upper-Louisiana than among those along Red River and the Delta; perhaps because they have mixed less with Spaniards, Germans, and other strangers. They likewise have a greater share of education, at least those of the more wealthy class;

perhaps, because they had it more in their power, when young, to visit the literary institutions of Canada.

The French are prompted to marry early in life; the climate dictates this practice; and they are usually blessed with a numerous progeny. The women have more influence over their husbands than is common in most other countries. Perhaps this arises in part from the example of the parent state; in part from the respect, which the men entertain for their wives; and perhaps still more from the almost exclusive right, which the women have to the property, in consequence of marriage contracts. Matches are often made by the parents, and the affections and inclinations of the children are not always consulted.

A short acquaintance with the women might lead a prudish observer to believe, that there existed a laxity in their morals. Nothing would be more unjust than such a conclusion. If, in their manners and conversation, they are less guarded than their female neighbors on the east side of the Mississippi, it proceeds from a national habit, and from an unsuspicious temper, and not in the least degree from a corruption of principle or sentiment. To whom shall we appeal as the criterion of purity? Nations essentially differ in their conceptions of virtue and vice. This difference has been created by habit; and the French consider their women, (and they consider justly) as much exempt from impropriety as those of some other countries, who remain almost invisible during their lives.

It has been observed in another place, that the Creoles, or native inhabitants, are partly the descendants of the French Canadians, and partly of those who migrated under some of the first governors of Louisiana. These are intermixed with some natives of France, Spain, Germany, and the United States, and in many instances with the Aborigines.

Most of them are small in statue, and slender in their make, though their bodies and limbs are remarkably well proportioned, supple, and active. Their complexions are somewhat sallow, and exhibit a sickly aspect, though they experience a good degree of health, which results in a great measure from the nature of their food, (mostly of the vegetable kind) and their manner of dressing it. They usually possess a keen piercing eye, and retain their sight longer than most other people. They are almost strangers to the gout, consumption, the gravel and stone in the bladder, and in general to all chronic complaints. The hair of the old people in the Delta, and neighborhood of it, retains a dark brown color; while that of the old people in Upper Louisiana commonly becomes grey. The young men at this time manifest no great passion for long hair; not many years ago they were seen with queues dangling about their legs. Most of the laboring class disregard dress, and appear no better at home than on a trading voyage among the Indians.

The complexions of the women are, in general, much fairer than those of the men; perhaps because they are less exposed to the vicissitudes of the seasons, particularly the burning rays of the sun. They are usually handsome when young, but when arrived to the age of thirty-five or forty, their bloom mostly forsakes them, and they become wrinkled and withered. This observation is particularly applicable to those of the Low Country, about the Delta and Red River. They are extremely fond of dress; they possess ease, grace, and penetration; they are remarkably loquacious, and their manners are more polished than those of the men; they are hospitable, and manifest much pleasure in offering to their guests and visitors the best things they are able to furnish. They have one fault not easily extenuated; they are habitually cruel to their slaves.

If their manners be more polished than those of the men, it ought not to be wondered at. The estimation in which they are held, no doubt contributes to it. They mix more in society. The men, except along the Delta, are more or less engaged in trade among the Indians.

This is sufficient to give a peculiar cast to their manners; and the pride they take in filling the wardrobes of their family females, contributes in no small degree to the inequality between them. It is not uncommon to see thirty or forty charming females in a ball-room, dressed with taste and even elegance, suited to the most fashionable society, when perhaps the males of their own families appear in their blanket coats and moccasons. It is rare to see in such an assembly more than four or five young men, whose appearance is even tolerable. This strange diversity is prevalent in the detached settlements of the country, and it even appears in some of the villages.

The French Creoles are temperate; they mostly limit their desires to vegetables, soups, and coffee. They are great smokers of tobacco, and no doubt this gives a yellow tinge to the skin. Ardent spirits are seldom used, except by the most laborious classes of society. They even dislike white wines, because they possess too much spirit. No doubt the warmth of the climate is, in some measure, the cause of this aversion. Claret, and other light red wines, are common among them; and those who can afford it are not sparing of this beverage.

Great œconomy is displayed in their family meals. This is not the effect of a parsimonious disposition, nor always of the want of adequate means; it results from the nature of the climate, and from a conviction of what their constitutions require; they readily sacrifice what may be termed luxury for the preservation of health, and it is seldom they contract diseases from intemperate excesses. Naturally volatile in their dispositions, they sometimes precipitate themselves from one extreme to another. Hence it is, that, in making entertainments for their friends, especially for strangers of distinction, they study to render them sumptuous; their tables are covered with a great variety of dishes; almost every sort of food dressed in all manner of ways, is exhibited in profusion. The master of the house, out of respect to his guests, frequently waits on them himself. On such occasions no trouble or expense is spared in procuring the best wines, and other liquors, the country affords. Their deserts are no less plentiful, and there is no want of delicacy in their quality or variety. Many of these entertainments cost from two hundred and fifty to four hundred dollars, especially in Upper Louisiana, where the luxuries of the table are much more expensive than in the Delta.

This occasional display of luxury may be imputed by some to fastidious pride. The reputation of poverty is almost as dreadful to them as the reality; and even the appearance of wealth affords some satisfaction, if they are not worth a cent in the world. Pride, indeed, is a predominant feature in their character, and sometimes proves injurious to them, because it is the pride of appearing to as much advantage as their more wealthy neighbors, and of feeling the deep mortification of a disadvantageous comparison. For nearly eighty years after the first settlement of the country, there was no inequality of wealth to trouble their repose, or at least no invidious display of it. The most perfect equality in point of family expenditures seemed to reign among them. The sudden demand for the rich products of the country soon created opulent fortunes. The transition from competency to surplus wealth, introduced all the fashionable luxuries of commercial countries. Examples are contagious; and the less opulent precipitated themselves into extravagant expenses, which were useless, and which their circumstances by no means authorised; so that in the course of the last thirty or forty years, as great a desparity has arisen between the pecuniary means of each other, and consequently between the several conditions of life, as now exists in any part of the United States. It must likewise be admitted, that they possess no small share of vanity, which renders this desparity the more troublesome.

These qualities, however, are less culpable in them than in most other people; because they arise from purer principles, and are not so injurious to society. Their pride and vanity are of a nature to inspire them with a high sense of honor, to render them honest in their dealings, and to stimulate them to be as punctual in the payment of their debts as their abilities will admit. Punctuality, indeed, was inculcated as a duty under their colonial systems, and these systems rendered it habitual to them. These people have yet to learn, (and they will probably soon learn) the procrastinations, tricks, and impositions, so successfully practised in some other territories. The art of deception, when calculated to work an injury, is hardly known among them. In fine, they are never so uneasy as when in debt, and never more happy than when released from the apprehension of a legal process. They are by no means fond of litigation, and suits were rare among them under the Spanish government. These observations, however, must be admitted with some caution when applied to the people in the vicinity of the capital, who have mixed with strangers, and imbibed their vices.

The manners of all the Creoles sufficiently indicate, that they have been accustomed to a government very different from our own; and hence the truth of this observation, that in the features of every people may be discovered the features of their political systems. As a proof of this we need only refer to the extreme deference they pay to men in power, particularly to those of the military profession, and to the obedience they yield without a murmur to the official dictates of their superiors. Another proof is, that they apparently seek occasions to manifest their attentions; and if on their superiors they have an opportunity of conferring a favor, it is not from obsequious motives, or the expectation of pecuniary reward, but from habitual respect.

Notwithstanding they consider a spare diet as necessary to health, yet it is found, that the best livers enjoy the greatest share of it; not because they consume a greater quantity of food, but because they have it more in their power to exercise their discretion in the choice of it. A wholesome nutritive diet, and a considerable portion of indolence, produce many instances of obesity, particularly about New-Orleans, and along the coast of the Delta, which is less common among the men than women. These make a liberal use of the warm or tepid bath, which relaxes their systems, and serves to render them corpulent.

The Louisianians, particularly about the Delta, indulge, to some excess, one of the fashionable vices of older countries. Most of the married men lavish their attentions on dissolute females, whom they usually take under their protection. These, in most instances, are selected from the mixed breeds; except among the Spanish settlers, who prefer a fat black wench to any other female! It is not easy to account for this depravity of taste. The Spaniards carry their impure connexions to a much greater extent than any other description of inhabitants.

The Creoles in general are remarkably neat and cleanly in their houses. Their furniture, usually fabricated by the artizans of the country, is rough and misshapen; yet it is polished to a high degree. Their floors in many instances are waxed, and as smooth and bright as a mahogany dining table. This passion for cleanliness is particularly exhibited by the women, who frequently carry it to excess. All house affairs exclusively belong to them, and the men incur no small danger when they attempt to interfere with their prerogatives. Even in most instances of purchases and sales, the women are consulted; and they not unfrequently assume the management of property.

The mode of building, as practised by the first settlers, is still preserved. The houses are mostly built of wood, except in those villages situated in the neighborhood of stone quarries. The manufacture of brick is of recent date in Louisiana. Several houses in New-Orleans have been constructed of this material, and the inhabitants begin to appreciate its value. The houses in general are of one story high only, and either wholly or partly surrounded by arcades or piazzas, from eight to twelve feet broad. They usually have a spacious hall in the centre, which communicates with the rooms on each side of it. Houses of two stories high are less safe on account of the sudden and violent squalls of wind in that country. This mode of building is convenient in other respects. The arcades or piazzas afford agreeable shades, under which the inhabitants repose themselves during the heat of the day; they likewise serve to shelter them from the dews and rains; and many families eat and sleep under them in summer.

It has long been a question, whether the inhabitants of warm climates possess as vigorous intellects as those of cold ones? Were the labors of literary men taken as the criterion, perhaps it would be found, that the literary productions of warm climates contain more sprightliness and fancy; those of cold ones more solid erudition. The extremes of climate, however, have less effect on the intellectual powers than some are disposed to believe. If the literature of warm climates be less erudite than that of cold ones, it must be imputed in some measure to moral causes. In the former the human faculties arrive to maturity much sooner than in the latter: The passions are much stronger; they are less under the control of reason; and the opportunities of improper indulgence much more frequent. Hence impure connexions are early formed, which necessarily superinduce effiminacy both of body and mind. Slavery no doubt has an effect on the moral faculties; it is much more common in warm than in cold countries; it steels the mind to the sentiments of humanity; it is productive of idleness, and a variety of other maladies, which are hostile in their nature to literary pursuits. This general rule is liable to some exceptions, and we have to regret, that these exceptions are not more common.

It is said, that the French language in Louisiana has become considerably corrupted, especially among the lower classes. This need not be wondered at, as they are mostly the descendants of those, who settled in North America about two centuries ago; during which period no great intercourse subsisted between them and the mother country, nor were the migrations sufficiently numerous to afford a progressive improvement in the language. Many individuals, however, speak the French language in its purity; they have made it a point to acquire it, and to forget their provincial dialects.

It is hardly necessary to add, that the Creoles are obstinately attached to the Roman catholic religion. If health and prosperity in some measure divert their attention from it; yet in the hour of affliction, particularly when apprehensive of death, they cling to it as the only anchor of their hope. They are strict observers of the festivals prescribed by their religion, and of the days devoted to their favorite saints.

These people possess a variety of peculiar customs, wholly derived from their Canadian ancestors, such as relate to marriages, dancing assemblies, and the like; but as we aim to avoid prolixity, they will be passed over with this remark, that they are calculated to promote gaiety and good humour, and appear to be stamped with the features of innocence and simplicity.

SKETCHES OF LOUISIANA.

CHAPTER XII.

STATE OF SLAVERY.

WE have already seen, that Louisiana contains more than forty thousand slaves. The climate, the productive nature of the lands in that country, and the accumulation of wealth beyond all former example, seem to render it highly probable, that their number will soon exceed that of the whites.

It is an invidious task for a man, born and educated where slavery is unknown, to indulge any strictures on the municipal policy of respectable states and territories, or to arraign at the bar of public justice the flagitious conduct of their citizens; yet considerations of a higher nature than those resulting from local prejudices and habits, suggest the propriety of a few remarks. When we see the feelings of humanity outraged, the most odious tyranny exercised in a land of freedom, and hunger and nakedness prevail amid plenty, who but must lament the infraction of those universal moral obligations, which subsist between different nations, societies, and individuals, and which are inscribed on the heart of every man, and mistaken by none!

Experience has long since convinced the more intelligent planters, that the profits they derive from the labor of their slaves are in proportion to the good or bad treatment of them. But those planters of an opposite character are much the most numerous, perhaps they form nine tenths of the whole, especially among the French and Spanish settlers in Lower Louisiana. In no part of the world are slaves better treated than in the Mississippi Territory, where the planters generally allow them salted meat, as much corn meal as they can consume, cows to furnish milk for their families, land for gardens, and the privilege of raising fowls. They also allow them one suit of clothes for summer, and another for winter. Their slaves are active and robust, and enabled to perform their allotted portions of work with ease. Such treatment renders them contented and honest, and punishments are rare among them. Each good slave, well clothed and fed, will yield a yearly clear profit of two hundred and fifty or three hundred dollars. No small degree of satisfaction is derived from the performance of good actions; and happy is he, who is not accused by his conscience of aggravated wrongs done to the human species.

When we pass into Louisiana, we behold a different and more disgusting picture. The French and Spanish planters, in particular, treat their slaves with great rigor; and this has been uniformly the case from the first establishment of the colony. They were at first too poor to

supply their slaves with clothing and food : Add to this,
their families stood in need of the avails of their labor ;
and every expense incurred on account of their comfort
and support was viewed as a serious evil. Hence this o-
riginal defect in the system has been considered as a precedent by subsequent generations, not because they view
the examples of their ancestors with reverence, but because they conceive it redounds to their interest. These
planters are extremely ignorant of agricultural pursuits,
and of the quantum of labor in the power of a slave to
perform in a given time. Few of them allow any clothing to their slaves, or any kind of food, except a small
quantity of corn ; and even this they are obliged to pound,
or grind, while they ought to be at rest. The consequence
is, that the slaves are extremely debilitated, and incapable
of much labor. One well fed negro is nearly equal to
three of them. Their masters and overseers affect to believe, that their want of industry arises from laziness, and
a perverse disposition. Hence cruel and even unusual
punishments are daily inflicted on these wretched creatures, enfeebled, oppressed with hunger, labor, and the
lash. The scenes of misery and distress constantly witnessed along the coast of the Delta, the wounds and lace-
rations occasioned by demoralized masters and overseers,
most of whom exhibit a strange compound of ignorance
and depravity, torture the feelings of the passing stranger,
and wring blood from his heart. Good God! why sleeps
thy vengeance ! why permit those, who call themselves
christians, to trample on all the rights of humanity, to enslave and to degrade, the sons and daughters of Africa!

The evils of the slave system in Louisiana may, in a
great measure, be attributed either to the want of energy
or intelligence among the governors of that province. As
their appointments were limited to short periods, seldom
extending beyond five years, the accumulation of wealth
was the predominant motive of their actions, and some of

them did not hesitate at the means. They neglected the great concerns of the province; no attempts were made to populate it till since the American revolution; no encouragement was afforded to agriculture and commerce, nor to manufactures and the arts. An exception, however, must be made in favor of the Baron Carondelet, to whom the province is more indebted than to all his predecessors. He saw and lamented the deranged state of this portion of the dominions of Spain; and while he was devising and carrying into effect some salutary regulations for the improvement of the country, he was removed to another government: Yet, during his administration, he repaired the fortifications at New-Orleans, improved the commerce of the province, and greatly increased the population of Upper Louisiana. The wretched condition of the slaves, over whom their masters exercised an almost despotic power, did not escape his attention. But such were the inveterate prejudices and habits, and even customs, which he had to encounter, that he despaired of a complete renovation, and therefore aimed only to mitigate the wounds he was unable to heal.

In 1795 he published an ordinance on the subject, by which he established the monthly allowance of corn in the ear, to each slave, at one barrel. It was recommended to masters to assign waste lands to their slaves for the purpose of enabling them to raise the necessaries of life; and if this allowance was denied them, they were obliged to furnish each of them with a linen shirt and trowsers for summer, and a woollen great coat and trowsers for winter. Labor was to commence at the break of day, and to cease at the approach of night. Half an hour was allowed for breakfast, and two hours for dinner. Slaves were allowed on Sundays to rest, or to work for themselves, except in time of harvest, when their masters were authorised to employ them, paying them about thirty cents each *per diem.* Punishments at one time, under a penalty of fifty dollars, were not to exceed thirty lashes; but the stripes were allowed to be repeated after the interval of a day. It was permitted to fire on armed negroes, who had deserted their masters; also on those unarmed, if they refused to submit when required, or presumed to defend themselves against their masters or overseers; and likewise on those who entered a plantation with an intent to steal. Those who killed or wounded a negro, except in the above cases, were threatened with the severest penalties of the law. The amusements among slaves were restricted to Sundays; and the planters were forbidden, under a penalty of ten dollars, to suffer any strange negroes to visit their plantations after dark; and they were also forbidden, under a like penalty, to permit any intrigues or plots of escape to be formed on their plantations by negroes belonging to others. No slave was permitted to leave the plantation of his master without a written permission, under a penalty of twenty lashes; and if any slave was found riding the horse of his master without the like permission, he was liable to receive thirty lashes. Fire arms, powder, and lead, found in the possession of slaves, were liable to confiscation; and such slaves were adjudged to receive thirty lashes. No planter was allowed to employ more than two slaves to hunt for him at the same time; and on their return from the chase they were obliged to deliver up their arms. No slave was allowed to sell any thing, not even the productions of his own labor, without the permission of his master.

This picture, however dark and deformed it may appear, exhibits many favorable traits, when compared with the slave system in operation before the administration of the Baron: yet a man of reflection, unacquainted with slave policy, would be apt to consider even this as the production of some Goth or Vandal, designed to disfigure and to brutalize the image of the Creator. The labor imposed on slaves is equal to the powers of the most robust men; and yet for their subsistence they are tantalized with a small pittance of corn, which they are obliged to grind or pound for themselves, and also with the hard choice of a little waste land, which they have not time to cultivate, or a few rags to hide their nakedness, or to guard them against the severity of the weather. Hunger and labor render them feeble, and the calves of their legs are as flabby as the dulap of a cow. Those who have the greatest number of slaves, treat them the worst; avarice is the hydra of their cruelty.

Authors have remarked, that the bitterness of slavery is more severe in free than in arbitrary governments. According to this sentiment the slaves in the United States were always worse treated than those in Louisiana; but this was not the case, though the sentiment holds good with respect to the Spanish provinces, where, in consequence of a late revolution in their slave system, slaves are treated with kindness, and even live as well as their masters. If they acquire sufficient money to purchase their time, the law directs their ransom. Those treated improperly have a right to demand *letters of sale*, and are authorised to seek new masters for themselves. If they are refused this privilege, the magistrate of the place examines into the nature of the complaints, and, if well founded, grants the permission required, or disposes of the injured slaves at public vendue. Instances of the latter kind often occurred in Louisiana.

It is a stain on the character of civilized nations, that slavery was ever authorised among them; and how a christian people can reconcile it to their consciences, no one can determine, except it be on account of interest. Here then we find a motive for all our actions, much more powerful than the dictates of morality and religion. While we keep so many of our fellow creatures in bondage, let us cease to talk about liberty and the rights of man; let us not claim for ourselves what we deny to others. The slavery occasionally imposed on some of our citizens by the Barbary powers, has more than once excited the sympathy and indignation of the United States. Those the most clamorous for revenge, whether individuals or organized bodies, and the most forward to condemn the practice of those powers, seem not aware, that they stand self-convicted of the same offence; the censures they bestow on the pirates of the Mediterranean, are so many libels on their own conduct. Modesty dictates, that we be more reserved on the subject of personal liberty, at least till we emancipate those whom we retain in bondage. With what justice can we demand the enjoyment of a right, when at the same time we prohibit it to others?

We all know, that slavery is coeval with history, perhaps with the world. The sources of this system among the ancients were various; particularly the absolute power exercised by parents over their children, either to kill, or to sell them; and likewise that of disposing of their criminals and insolvent debtors, as well as their prisoners taken in time of war.

To the disgrace of America, and of human nature, negro slavery has its origin on our continent. The benevolent father De las Casas, the advocate of oppressed humanity in the new world, exclaimed against the slavery of the Indians; and, finding his efforts of no avail, proposed to Charles V, in 1517, the slavery of the Africans as a substitute. This proposal had the effect of lightening the chains of the natives, and of forging new ones for the inhabitants of another hemisphere. The Spaniards, however, from some religious scruples, refused at first to engage in the importation of slaves from Africa; though they eased their consciences by opening their ports to their admission, and by employing other nations to traffic for them. The Abbe Raynal says, that about nine millions of negroes were landed in the Spanish colonies, and that less than fifteen hundred thousand existed in his time.

Such an amazing diminution of the Africans must be attributed to barbarous cruelty. The example of the Spaniards was soon followed by the other European nations.

The most substantial argument in favor of slavery, is derived from the right of the strongest. The origin of this right may be traced to the dark ages of barbarism. Modern civilized nations do not sell their children, nor enslave their insolvent debtors, nor even their prisoners of war, to whose services they have some shadow of claim; but they depredate on the harmless and inoffensive Africans, merely to gratify their avarice, without the least provocation, and without any apprehended danger of their power. The laws of most European nations disclaim the right of slavery; and the great oracle of English jurisprudence declared some years ago from the bench, that, by the laws of that kingdom, a right of property could not exist in the human species. The common law of the United States recognizes the same doctrine. If slavery be maintained in some of the individual states and territories, it is by virtue of particular statutes, added to the mutual concessions inserted in the federal constitution.

Slave-holders pretend to justify negro slavery on two grounds. The first is, that other nations still continue the practice; and therefore to abandon it themselves would have no sensible effect on the general system. The second is, that the slaves they purchase were reduced to this condition in their own country; and therefore they are now in as eligible a situation as if they had never crossed the ocean.

This reasoning has no better foundation than avarice; and to this single quality of the mind must be attributed all the miseries of the many millions of human beings in bondage. Can the wickedness of other nations be justly adduced as an apology for our own? If precedent be allowed to sanctify crimes, why are robbers and murderers exposed to the vengeance of the laws? If other nations have done wrong, it becomes us to avoid the pernicious example. Were we to adopt some plan for the gradual abolition of slavery, it might possibly have some effect on the policy of others. We have prohibited the importation of slaves; Great Britain has done the same; and some other nations appear inclined to abandon the traffic. These prohibitions will induce slave holders either to treat their slaves with more kindness, and by this means enable them to preserve their number by propagation; or they will gradually waste away under the rigors of their fate, and eventually become extinct. However, none of the consequences of either case strike at the root of the evil.

To purchase Africans, who were reduced to bondage in their own country, is as criminal as to purchase those of a different description. The wars among the tribes of Africa are mostly fomented by slave merchants, and these merchants secure millions of prisoners merely for the purposes of traffic. Is it no crime to tear men from their country, families, and friends? The Africans are not destitute of sensibility, and they frequently manifest it in a manner, which does honor to human nature. The indignity and cruelty with which they are treated, often induce them to put a period to their existence, even in the presence of their masters and overseers; and shall we conclude, that this is the effect of insanity rather than of a greatness of soul! When the whites cease to purchase slaves, wars in a great measure will cease among the Africans, and their numerous tribes enjoy as much peace and harmony as other nations in the same circumstances. There are physical evils enough in the world without the addition of artificial ones; and it becomes us as men and as christians to provide against the asperities of the former, and to prohibit the creation of the latter.

Notwithstanding the guards placed on the slave system by the constitution and laws, and by the treaty of cession, which secures to the Louisianians the enjoyment and perpetuity of their rights, perhaps a way may be devised to remove this badge of our disgrace, without an infringement of either. It must be admitted, that the right of property in slaves cannot be invaded; yet doubts may arise as to the extent of this right, and it will be necessary to ascertain it with precision. The laws of some nations impose on the child the condition of the mother; the consequence is, that the children of freemen are often born slaves, and many of them drag out their existence in servitude under their own fathers. Louisiana presents at least one instance of melancholy depravity; the father disposed of several of his children as slaves, together with their mother. Among some nations the contrary principle obtains; the child born of a female slave follows the condition of the father. This principle is much more just than the other, though it is attended with one difficulty not easily removed; the father cannot be so readily ascertained as the mother. At any rate, this kind of right, from the very nature of things, is limited to actual slaves; it does not attach till they are in existence; it is not present and absolute, but contingent and future. If this position be correct, and it is supported by some good authorities, it seems to follow, that the legislature may provide for the emancipation of the children of slaves, at any age it pleases, born at some stipulated future period. Were such a measure adopted, it is easy to see, that a gradual abolition of slavery would take place among us. Perhaps this plan is less objectionable than some others, which have been frequently suggested; and it may be so modified and extended as to embrace a provision for the benefit of the objects of it.

The advocates of slavery not only contend, that the child ought to follow the condition of the female parent, but that the right of the master extends to the *possible* issue of the mother *ad infinitum*. The consequence of this doctrine is that slavery must continue as long as female slaves propagate their species; and that, to provide for the emancipation of future generations, would be illegal and unconstitutional. This doctrine obtains in many parts of the United States, particularly in the Indiana Territory; in which "slavery and involuntary servitude" are expressly prohibited by the ordinance of 1787. The obvious construction of this prohibition is, that the slaves at that period in existence were entitled to their freedom; or at least, that the children of female slaves, born after the adoption of the ordinance, were born free. If therefore the doctrine already mentioned be correct, they can claim no legal exemption from slavery, and of course the prohibition is a nullity. The practice in that territory seems to correspond with this strained and pernicious construction of the ordinance. Slave property, while it exists, ought not to be infringed; and if no legal means can be devised to abolish it, let it be perpetual.

It is difficult, even for men of moderate tempers, to suppress their indignation at one of the pretexts adduced in support of slavery, that the whites are unable to labor in some climates on account of the excessive heats! If we be allowed to consult our convenience without regard to the means; if each white is at liberty to make fifty or a hundred blacks wretched and miserable to promote his interest, and to gratify his avarice; then let us abandon our moral and political creeds, and study only to render our consciences inaccessible to remorse. The God of nature never intended, that one part of the human race should be governed by the whims and caprices of the other; nor that artificial evil should become a substitute for attainable good. The pretext is futile in every point of view. Nature has fitted men for labor in the climate where they are born and educated. A citizen of Georgia is as well qualified to labor in that state as a Yankee in New-England; the effects of heat and cold are about the same on both. Add to this, it so happens, that in the warm latitudes the lands are much more prolific, and much more easily cultivated, than in colder ones; of course less labor is required to gain subsistence. The native inhabitants of Lower Louisiana experience no inconvenience from the heats; and those employed in navigating the rivers are exposed to more fatigue than is common to any other class of our citizens. Besides, in that country, and in the Mississippi territory, hundreds of families from the middle and eastern states, have planted themselves. For several years after their arrival, their characteristic industry was evident; and they experienced no dangerous effects from the climate, except a troublesome lassitude for the two or three first years. The accumulation of wealth enabled them to purchase slaves; after which, like their neighbors, they contracted habits of indulgence. The heats, therefore, furnish no material obstruction to manual labor; and the effects of them in the southern states and territories are more than counterbalanced by the exuberant nature, and the valuable productions, of their lands. Much indeed is due to the people of slave states, to whom slavery has become familiar from long habit, and, perhaps, in their view, necessary to their prosperity, if not to their existence. Their feelings, and even prejudices, are entitled to respect; and a system of emancipation cannot be contrived with too much caution.

The fact is, that the people of the eastern states experience more inconvenience from the rigors of the seasons than those of the south. In New-England the mercury sometimes rises to one hundred degrees, and as often falls twenty degrees below *zero*. The extremes of heat are greater in New-England; but they are not of so long continuance, nor is the air so humid and unelastic as in the southern parts of the union, which are doubtless more or less prejudicial to health. Still these traits are more tolerable than the opposite extreme in New-England, where the country is covered with snow, and bound in icy chains for nearly six months in the year. Both men and beasts suffer from the rigors of winter; and the necessary subsistence for them, is obtained at a prodigious expense and labor. In Lower Louisiana the whites may labor nine months in the year, without experiencing any inconvenience from the heats; and three months labor in that quarter is productive of more real value than twelve months in New-England. Add to this, cattle and swine need no other food than what the earth spontaneously yields; and every planter has it in his power to supply himself with almost any number he pleases. In whatever light, therefore, we view the subject, the greatest advantages are attached to the southern states and territories.

The pernicious system of slavery deserves reprehension from another motive. No country can become populous where it prevails; and this truth is attested by numerous examples. We need cast our eyes only on the West-India Islands, and on the southern states of the union. No part of the country possesses a more happy climate, or a better soil, than the great state of Virginia; yet her white population is comparatively small. Kentucky is a slave state; and if her population be considerable, it must be attributed to accidental causes, which are not difficult to explain. The state of Ohio is now in its infancy: slavery is excluded from her bosom; and this very circumstance will induce a rapid population, augment her strength and resources, and soon enable her to rise superior to her neighbor.

SKETCHES OF LOUISIANA.

CHAPTER XIII.

ANTIQUITIES.

MANY antiquities worthy of notice cannot be supposed to exist in Louisiana. Indeed, all the monuments to be found of a hoary nature, may be traced to the ancient aboriginals of the country; and although they are not antiquities in the proper sense of the term, yet they deserve a place in history as worthy of the curious and inquisitive. Were it possible to present them in detail, and to give an accurate description of them, the philosopher might be assisted in his enquiries into their origin, and be able to gratify the curiosity of mankind relative to the early state of this part of the globe. Until the country be more explored, and accurate observers are enabled to investigate the remains of antiquity, we must be satisfied with partial accounts of them, perhaps in many respects erroneous, derived from various sources, and many of them of doubtful authority. All the historian at present can do is, to collect these accounts, to compare and weigh the authorities on which they are founded, and to form the best judgment in his power.

From the ancient fortifications and tumuli, and some other remains of antiquity, found in various parts of the western country, some have been led to believe, that they are the productions of a civilized people. Carver says, (and his accounts in general have been found correct) that he examined an ancient fortification near Lake Pepin on the Mississippi, of about a mile in circuit, the angles of which were distinguishable, and appeared to be fashioned with as much military skill as if constructed by Vauban himself. Probably this account is not exaggerated, as subsequent travellers have given a similar description of the same work, and as other works equally remarkable, if not of equal extent, are found in various parts. Some of those in the state of Ohio have been examined, and they manifest a degree of mathematical precision, not to be expected from illiterate savages, and it is extremely difficult to ascribe them to chance. It is admitted on all hands, that they have endured for centuries. The trees on their ramparts, from the number of their annulæ, or radii, indicate an age of more than four hundred years. Most of the ancient fortifications, of which we speak in general, are spacious, and surrounded by deep ditches, and are furnished in some instances with regular covered ways. The walls or parapets of earth still remain, and are generally from three to five feet high; so that the lines may be easily traced, in most instances covered with large trees, as old, perhaps, as any in the forest. Some of these works have regular bastions; and they are all well calculated to

ANTIQUITIES. 347

defend the places where they are situated. It is worthy of remark, that many ancient circular intrenchments are found in Ireland and Scotland, and in various other parts of Europe; but from the drawings made of them, they appear much less perfect in their construction than those in the western country.

Perhaps the most remarkable ancient fortification within the bounds of our territory, is situated in the neighborhood of Chilicothe. It has been accurately surveyed by an intelligent and skilful officer of our artillerists. It is a regular polygon of twenty-four sides, each of which is about fifty-five yards in length. It has four large, and four small gate ways, situated opposite to each other. About the centre of the work, the whole of which embraces upwards of twenty acres of ground, is a large mount of a conical figure, nearly seventeen feet high, on the summit of which are five or six large trees. Indeed, on all the lines of this extensive fortification, the trees are as large as those of the adjacent forest. This work manifests a degree of mathematical skill, not possessed by the aborigines, and by a few only, of those deemed intelligent whites. To suppose it the invention of any other than a skilful mathematician, requires a greater extent of credulity than is allowable among men of sense and reflection.

Perhaps it will never be known by whom, nor at what time, these fortifications were erected. Mankind are in the dark on this subject, and simple conjectures must supply the place of correct authorities. There is, however, some reason to believe, that they were constructed by a people much more civilized than the present race of savages. Till we are better informed, it seems fair to attribute them to the Welsh, particularly as there is some evidence to prove, that three small colonies of that nation landed in America more than three centuries before the days of Columbus. The science of fortification, as practised by the Romans, Saxons, Danes, and Normans, and generally by the other nations of Europe, was probably well understood in Wales long before Madoc and his people left it. This was probably the last of the arts to escape them, as no doubt they continually practised it in defending themselves against their enemies; and from their peculiar situation we have reason to conclude, that it was not wholly obliterated till after a lapse of several centuries.

On a subject of so much obscurity, no apology is necessary for the conjectures hinted at. If the origin of the numerous fortifications, dispersed over the western country, cannot be traced with any reasonable degree of certainty, it is not wholly superfluous and unpardonable, to indulge such conjectures as the obscure nature of it will afford.

The reader may attach what credit he pleases to the following story: Soon after the settlement of the French in the Illinois country, something like the cog-wheel of a mill, constructed in a rough manner, was found floating down the Missouri. The man who discovered this specimen of mechanic skill, lived to a great age; and there are now some old people on the Mississippi, who have often heard him relate the occurrence. The reader is requested to bear in mind what we have said in another place, relative to the existence of a white nation about the heads of that river.

Several publications have announced that, on opening a copper mine on the Mississippi, some distance below the falls of St. Anthony, the laborers found some tools adapted to the work, several fathoms below the surface of the earth; and that in digging a well, a furnace of brick work, with some coals and fire brands, were discovered thirty feet under ground. Of the great depth of these tools, coals, and fire brands, we have some doubt; but such a discovery is the more probable, as the French opened and worked some copper mines in that quarter more than a century ago, and they eventually abandoned them on account of the hostile disposition of the Indians.

The bones of the Mammoth, or of some other enormous animal, may at least be ranked among the curiosities, if not among the antiquities, of Louisiana. To what kind of animal they belonged, or at what time they were deposited in their present beds, is difficult to ascertain. Such accounts are given of their quantity and size, as almost to exceed belief. Some, (who have viewed them) pretend, that an entire skeleton may be formed, more than sixty feet long, and more than twenty-five feet high. This is not altogether a figure of rhetoric; for certain it is, that many bones of an uncommon size and length are found in various places, particularly on the Osage river, and beneath the surface of the ground. A square of several hundred yards in extent, situated in the vicinity of a salt spring, is filled with them; and what is still more extraordinary, they are intermixed with human bones. The ground, in which they are deposited, is of a spongy nature, and receives the substances rolled down by the rains from an adjoining hill. About the year 1796, a gentleman at St. Louis collected several sets of the teeth, some of which were but little decayed, and presented them to the Baron Carondelet at New-Orleans. They were compared with those of the elephant; and it was the opinion of the Baron, that they belonged to that animal. Some of the bones alluded to are petrified, and others much decayed; and the author of these sketches has frequently examined those of both descriptions.

Almost all parts of the western country, present us with pyramids or mounts of earth, which were doubtless intended either as works of defence, or as depositories of the dead. Hardly any part of Louisiana is destitute of them; and they mostly abound in those places the best adapted to culture. Many of them are from fifty to a hundred yards in length, and from ten to thirty feet high, terminating each way in a regular slope. Numbers of them have been penetrated in a horizontal direction. Some of them contain a multitude of arrow heads, fragments of pipes, and a rude kind of ware, made of clay. Others furnish several strata of a white glutinous substance, containing a considerable degree of moisture, and divided from each other by layers of common earth. This substance was no doubt produced from human bones, which time, and the operation of the elements, have converted into its present state. In some instances, indeed, the bones are found almost entire; whether this circumstance may be imputed to the qualities of the ground, or to recent burial, cannot well be determined.

No doubt some of these tumuli were the receptacles of the common dead; while others received the remains of chiefs, or of warriors who fell in battle. No less than five remarkable mounts are situated near the junction of the Washita, Acatahola, and Tenza, in an alluvial soil. They are enclosed by an embankment, or wall of earth, at this time ten feet high, and ten feet wide, which contains about two hundred acres of land. Four of these mounts are nearly of equal dimensions, about twenty feet high, one hundred feet broad, and three hundred feet long. The fifth seems to have been designed for a tower or turret; the base of it covers an acre of ground; it rises by two steps or stories; its circumference gradually diminishes as it is ascended, and its summit is crowned by a flatted cone. By an accurate admeasurement, the height of this tower or turret has been found to be eighty feet. Perhaps these works were designed in part for defence, and in part for the reception of the dead. Twenty-one of these tumuli or pyramids present themselves to view in a cluster just below Kahokia. There are several of them in the vicinity of St. Louis; two of which are of a large size, with an elevation of about twenty feet; one of them forms nearly a square, with a flat open space on the top. Many of them are found about the falls of St. Anthony, and at various other places in the country, mostly in the vicinity of water courses.

Many of the ancient nations buried their dead in this way, especially those of quality and consideration among them. Ireland still exhibits the remains of these tumuli; and according to the drawings made of them, they appear to resemble those on the Mississippi. Plutarch says, that Alexander, on the death of Demaratus, " made a " most magnificent funeral for him, his whole army " raising him a monument of earth eighty cubits high, " and of a vast circumference." The Scythians, according to Herodotus, " labored to raise as high a monument " of earth for their dead as possible." Semiramis endeavored to eternize the memory of Ninus, her husband, by raising a high and broad mount for his tomb. The same practice obtained among the Spartans and Thracians, and even among the Jews; for they raised a great heap of stones over the body of Acham, who had purloined the *accursed thing*. All rude and uncultivated nations have raised these pyramids of earth, either as mausoleums, or as cenotaphs to the memory of those they respected.

SKETCHES OF LOUISIANA.

CHAPTER XIV.

OF THE RIVERS OF LOUISIANA.

SOME of the rivers of Louisiana are incidentally noticed in various parts of this work, and care will now be taken to avoid repetition. No part of the world of the same extent seems to afford so great a number of rivers, and few indeed of equal magnitude. Had they been known to the ancients, with what raptures would their historians and poets have described them! The Achelous and Teliboas are insignificant rivers, when compared with the Mississippi and Missouri; and yet Thucydides and Xenophon exerted all their powers to render them immortal. Some of the moderns have distinguished themselves in the same field of description, particularly Mr. Orme, who has painted the Ganges in all the charms of a poetic and animated diction. The two great rivers of Louisiana furnish themes still more pregnant with the sublime and beautiful. The great length of them, the variety of scenes exhibited by them as they roll among the mountains, or over fertile and extensive plains, or along the alluvious spine of inundated regions, at once charm the senses, and warm the imagination. The facilities they yield to commerce, the superfluous wealth of several states and territories conveyed on their waters to the ocean, the variety of climates, soils, and productions on their borders, the mineral and other subterraneous riches ready to reward the toils of industry and enterprise, all seem to be designed by Heaven as significant tokens of two or more rising constellations in the west, not inferior in magnitud and brightness to any other in the American hemisphere.

Elaborate details and descriptions are inconsistent with the nature of this work; nor are sufficient data at hand to authorise the attempt.

Until within a very short period, the United States, and indeed the English and Spaniards, were totally ignorant of the sources of the Mississippi and Missouri. Their knowledge of the former was mostly limited to the falls of St. Anthony, and of the latter to the Mandan nation; and even below these points it was extremely defective. The voyage of Colonel Pike to the source of the Mississippi, and that of Messrs. Lewis and Clarke to the source of the Missouri, and from thence to the Pacific Ocean, will no doubt, when published, afford much information of our interior regions, and gratify the curiosity of the inquisitive enquirer. These gentlemen prosecuted their discoveries under the auspices of a liberal government; and their success is no less honorable to themselves than advantageous to the United States.

OF THE RIVERS OF LOUISIANA. 355

What is denominated the source of the Missouri is the junction of three rivers or branches, nearly of equal size, each of which is about sixty yards in breadth. This junction is formed in about north latitude forty five degrees twenty two minutes, in the rocky or shining mountains, which are spurs or prolongations of the Andes. Little is known of the two southern branches. The most northern one is navigable to near its source, two hundred and forty eight miles above the junction already mentioned. From this junction, in an opposite direction, to where the Missouri leaves the mountains is one hundred and eighty one miles; so that this great river flows four hundred and twenty nine miles in the mountains, and two thousand six hundred and sixty seven miles below them, before it unites with the Mississippi. Hence from its source to this union is three thousand and ninety six miles; from thence to the gulf of Mexico is about one thousand three hundred and sixty four miles; making the whole length of the Missouri four thousand four hundred and sixty miles! The general direction of it below the Mandans is nearly south east and north west; between the Mandans and the mountains its direction inclines more to the east and west; and within the mountains to the south west and north east.

There is some reason to believe, as is stated in another place, that a water passage may be found to the Pacific Ocean by means of the middle or southern branch of the Missouri. Such is the nature of the evidence on this subject, added to the great importance of such a water communication, that the fact ought to be ascertained. If a communication of this nature should be found to exist, though obstructed by falls and rapids, it requires no great penetration to perceive the immense advantages it is calculated to yield.

The rocky or shining mountains are several hundred miles in breadth. They are composed of several spurs or ridges, generally extending south west and north east, and alternately rising one above another. Some fruitful vallies are interpersed among them, especially along the water courses. They approach the river in a variety of instances; some of them, indeed, are in a manner suspended over it, and exhibit a prodigious elevation. They are mostly abrupt and barren, and their summits probably enveloped in perpetual winter, as they are known to be crowned with snow in the month of July.

Some of these mountains, particularly those situated to the eastward of the great chain, are composed of a fine white clay, which, when washed by the rains, is precipitated into the rivers and streams below; and hence the color of the water in the Missouri, and the unctuous impurities it contains, may be explained without a labored analysis. These qualities extend even to the sea. The gradual projection of the land into that element is owing to the deposition of these and other impurities. The formation of the numerous sand banks and islands, and the alluvious nature of the lands on the Missouri and lower Mississippi, may be ascribed to the same cause. The water is lively and soft, and the specific gravity of it about the same as that of rain or snow water. A common tumbler, filled with the Missouri water, and suffered to remain undisturbed for a few hours, will be about one third full of sediment. Notwithstanding this, the inhabitants drink it in preference to any other; partly indeed, because they deem it healthful, and in this particular they judge correctly. Some of them put it into large stone jars, and let it stand till the sediment has subsided. Others filtrate it through stone or sand, and others again render it clear and transparent, by putting into it a small quantity of alum, or the kernel of the peach stone, either of which precipitates the impurities to the bottom. The greatest number, however, use the water in its impure state, and experience no bad effects from it. The Missouri water is impregnated with sulphur and nitre, and those who drink of it pretend, that it is a remedy for cutaneous diseases. Certain it is, that it operates as a gentle cathartic on those unaccustomed to the use of it.

Among the mountains, and for a great distance below them, the navigation of the Missouri is either obstructed by falls and rapids, or by shoals and sand bars, and likewise by a strong current. On ascending the river, the first and most remarkable falls are seventy one miles below the mountains, and two thousand five hundred and seventy five miles from the Mississippi, in north latitude forty seven degress three minutes. These falls consist of four great pitches; the first is ninety eight feet, the second nineteen feet, the third nearly forty eight feet, and the fourth about twenty six feet, exclusive of others of less note. They extend up and down the river about eighteen miles, and the whole fall in this distance rather exceeds three hundred and sixty two feet. Small craft only can navigate the river above the Mandans, particularly in the season of low water. Between the Mandans and the Mississippi, boats of considerable size may navigate the river at all seasons; though above the river Platte the navigation is rendered tedious and troublesome by numerous sand banks and bars, which approach the channel in all directions. The channel contains water of sufficient depth at any season; but it is difficult to trace its meanders. When the water is high, generally from April to June, it moves at the rate of nearly five miles an hour; and yet a boat will ascend it at this season more easily, and with much greater speed, than when the freshets have subsided. The swell of the water renders the banks stable and safe; it covers the numerous trees and other drift stuff, which oppose the navigation in low water, and produces an eddy or counter current along shore, which is of great advantage; it also shortens the distance, because it enables boats to keep near the banks, and to avoid circuitous passages round islands; whereas in low water they are obliged to trace with great labor the zig-zag channel among sand banks and other obstructions, alternately extending from one shore to the other.

Few animals are found in the mountains, except beavers, and these are numerous. The want of game, added to the severity of the cold, has probably induced the Indians to prefer some other residence, as seldom any of them are to be met with in this quarter. Straggling parties from the Columbia, and other rivers of the west, sometimes make their appearance in these desolate regions; more to avoid their enemies than to seek subsistence.

Between Yellow Stone river and the mountains, (separated by a tract of about seven hundred and seventy nine miles in extent along the winding course of the Missouri) the country is steril and broken; the numerous hills scattered over it are mostly covered with pine and cedar, and the bottoms and other low grounds with cotton wood and willows. The banks of the river are thickly studded with high rocky cliffs. Game is plenty in this quarter; and among other animals incident to the country may be noticed the Ibex, or Antelope of California, called by the Spaniards mountain sheep; as also white bears and wolves of uncommon size, and of ferocious dispositions.

From Yellow Stone river to the river Platte is about twelve hundred and fifty eight miles,* and the Missouri along this tract is remarkably crooked. This portion of country may be considered as level, though at a distance from the water courses it is not destitute of hills and mountains, presenting arid plains and prairies of vast extent. The bottoms along the Missouri and other rivers are in many places of considerable breadth, and the natural growth does not materially vary from that among the settlements in Upper Louisiana. Plenty of salt is found on the waters of the Platte, and salt springs are

* From the source of the Kansas to that of Yellow Stone river, is only ten days ride over land.

frequently discovered above it along the banks of the Missouri. The beaver, martin, buffaloe, antelope, white wolf, porcupine's hare, the black-tailed or mule deer, are peculiar to this part of the country, as well as numerous other species of game. Here also are to be seen vestiges of several ancient fortifications, one of which has been measured, and found to be two hundred and fifty yards long. The Indians are numerous in this quarter, and some of them have made considerable progress in the agricultural arts, particularly the Ottos, Missouris, and Pawnes, on the river Platte, and likewise several bands of Scioux, and others, on the Missouri. They cultivate large quantities of corn, pumpkins, beans, and tobacco. These nations or tribes occupy a vast tract of country, and perhaps no part of the world produces game in greater abundance, or in greater variety. The English and Spanish traders occasionally approach this quarter; but it is in our power to paralize their influence, and to secure the trade to ourselves. Adequate supplies of goods, furnished either by the United States, or by individual merchants, would stimulate the industry of the Indians: The quantity and variety of peltries and furs, which they are able to deliver in return, would excite the surprise of those unacquainted with this traffic. The profits of the Missouri trade, under the Spanish government, have been stated in another place; and from the results there given may be inferred some satisfactory conclusions of what it is susceptible.*

* It is believed, that by way of the river Platte, or Yellow Stone river, perhaps by means of both, an easy communication may be had with the rio Colorado, of course with California. Certain it is, that the sources of these rivers are in the neighborhood of each other. It would be pleasing to examine and contemplate the country of the *Moqui*. These aborigines are still independent, and manifest extraordinary advances in civilization. In this quarter of the globe, also, may be seen the ruins of ancient *Aztec* cities and temples, little inferior in extent and grandeur to those of the elder world.

Some distance above the Mandans, and near the Missouri, a volcano has been discovered. Its eruptions are frequent; and this accounts for the pumice stones, so often found on that river, and on the lower Mississippi. Perhaps, too, it has some connexion with the earthquakes, which have so often agitated Upper Louisiana. The direction of these are known to be nearly from west to east.

From the mouth of the river Platte to that of the Missouri is about six hundred and thirty miles. The lands among the settlements have already been noticed; and the remainder along this tract are nearly similar in appearance and quality. It may be remarked, however, that along the Missouri are extensive bottoms, and that the high lands in the rear of them are of an excellent quality; except about the head waters of the Kansas, and between that river and the Arkansas, where the country is disfigured by knobs and other inequalities of surface, mostly destitute of wood, and presenting a barren soil. These are discouraging symptoms to agriculturists; but this vast tract is rendered valuable from the quantities of salt and lead it contains. Salt springs are numerous in the neighborhood of the whites, and they derive their supplies from them. Some extensive prairies appear about the Osage river; but these bear no proportion to the wood lands, which are calculated to sustain a numerous population. Mulberry trees are indigenous in this quarter, as also various other kinds of wild fruit trees. Grape vines grow in abundance along the water courses. Here are likewise many bluffs or ridges, almost wholly composed of iron ore.

Perhaps the country between the Missouri and Mississippi is not the least valuable part of Louisiana. It abounds in salt, lead, and other minerals, and the lands are generally covered with a good growth of timber. It is also intersected by a multitude of small rivers and streams, which are calculated for a variety of useful purposes.

It is difficult to estimate the average breadth of the Missouri. It is of very unequal breadths in different places; in some about nine hundred yards, and in others not more than three hundred yards. For eighteen or twenty miles above its mouth, it may be about half a mile in breadth, and in one or two instances, though for a short distance only, it probably exceeds three fourths of a mile. In some places, several hundred miles from the Mississippi, it is wider than near its mouth. It possesses two remarkable features, depth of channel and strength of current.

The tributary streams of this river, considering its long course, are not numerous; and those flowing from the south west, or west, are much the largest, and of the greatest length. Perhaps those from the opposite direction, though of inferior size and extent, are equally numerous, and no doubt will be highly useful to the future population of the country. This inferiority arises from the contracted space between the two great rivers, not calculated to give birth to any considerable navigable waters. The branches of the Missouri serve to fructify the regions washed by them, and to open ready communications in various directions; to establish an intercourse with the Indians, who inhabit them, and to place at our command such treasures as they possess. Those at present navigated by the whites, are the Osage, Kansas, and Platte. All of them are extensive. The waters of the latter, as well as those of the Yellow Stone river, interlock with some of the branches of the rio Bravo, which washes the eastern boundary of New Mexico. The names of the most considerable branches of the Missouri from the south west, or west, their breadth at their junction, their distance in miles from the Mississippi, and their respective latitudes, so far as they have been ascertained with any tolerable exactness, will be explained, among other objects, in the following table:

Names.	Yards in width.	Distance from the Mississippi.	N. Latitudes.			W. Longitudes from Greenwich.
			deg.	min.	sec.	min. deg.
The Gasconade	157	103	38	44	35	
Great Osage River	397	137	38	31	16	
Kansas River	230	364	39	5	25	
Big ne-ma-har River	80	510	39	55	56	
Bald pated Prairie		569	40	27	7	
River Platte	600	630	40	54	35	
Little Scioux River	80	763	41	42	34	
Rapid River	152	1026				
White River	300	1148				
Teton River	70	1280				
Shark River	400	1327	44	19	36	
We-ter-hoo River	120	1432	45	35	5	
Cannon-ball River	140	1511	46	39		
Mandan Indians		1610	47	21	47	101 25
Little Missouri		1700				
Yellow Stone River	858	1888				
Muscle-shell River	110	2270	47	0	24	
First great falls		2575	47	3	10	
Rocky mountains		2668				
Three great forks		2848	45	22	34	
Source of N. fork.		3096				

The junction of the two great rivers of Louisiana is in north latitude thirty eight degrees forty seconds, and forms an interesting spectacle. The two islands in the mouth of the Missouri oblige him to pay his tribute to what is denominated the father of rivers through one large, and two small channels. As if he disdained to unite himself with any other river, however respectable and dignified, he precipitates his waters nearly at right angles across the Mississippi, a distance of more than twenty five hundred yards. The line of separation between them, owing to the difference of their rapidity and colors, is visible from each shore, and still more so from the adjacent hills. The Mississippi, as if astonished at the boldness of an intruder, for a moment recoils and suspends his current, and views in silent majesty the progress of the stranger. They flow nearly twenty miles before their waters mingle with each other.

The Missouri is much larger, and affords more water, than the Mississippi. Geographers and other writers have considered it as a branch of the latter; whereas it is the main river, and the Mississippi a tributary stream only.

The obstructions in the navigation of the Missouri are similar to those in the lower Mississippi, which will be more particularly noticed in the sequel.

By the Indians the Mississippi was called *Meate Chassipi*, which in their language signifies the ancient father of rivers. This noble river has its source in upper red cedar lake in north latitude forty seven degrees forty two minutes, forty seconds, and longitude ninety five degrees eight minutes west from Greenwich. Six miles only from this lake are some of the waters which fall into Hudson's bay. The navigation of the upper part of the Mississippi is extremely difficult, owing in part to the scarcity of water, and in part to numerous shoals, rapids, and other obstructions; one of which is the great fall of Packagama.

The country above the falls of St. Anthony will never attract the attention of agriculturists. It is mostly of a cold and steril nature. The face of it presents sandy ridges, either covered with shrub oak, or pitch and other pine; some rich bottoms, covered with elm, cotton wood, ash, oak, and the sugar tree; prairies, covered with a long coarse grass; and swamps filled with hemlock. It is also chequered with numerous small lakes and rivers. Indigenous berries and fruit of various kinds, are common. The *zizania aquatica*, known by the name of wild rice, grows in this part of the country, as well as below the falls of St. Anthony, which affords the Indians a wholesome nutritive food. With the exception of one or two short portages, a navigable water communication exists between lake Superior and the heads of the Mississippi, and between the latter and the upper parts of the Missouri; and this communication is exclusively frequented by the Canadian traders.

Perhaps no part of Louisiana is better adapted to agriculture than that between the falls of St. Anthony and the mouth of the Missouri. This portion of it is of a rolling nature, and affords many charming and sublime views: The soil in general is rich, and calculated to yield all kinds of grain, grass, and vegetables, and the climate healthful. Prairies of any considerable extent seldom appear, except in the upper part of this tract. Timber of all kinds is plenty, as also calcareous and other rock. The richest lead mines in Louisiana are situated in this quarter, though only partially opened; as also a sufficient number of salines, or salt springs, to supply a crowded population with salt. The bottoms along the Mississippi are seldom inundated, and not less prolific than those on the Missouri. Among the trees common to the country may be noticed plenty of cedar and black walnut.

The falls of St. Anthony, according to the best calculations, are situated in about north latitude forty four degrees fifty minutes. The climate is as temperate here as in the heart of New England. The river below the falls is less than three hundred yards wide, and above them more than six hundred yards. The water is precipitated over a perpendicular rock of about eighteen or twenty feet, and then forms a rapid of more than two hundred and fifty yards below it. In the middle of the fall, and near the top of the rock, is an island of about fifteen yards long, and thirteen broad, bearing some shrubs, and a number of spruce and hemlock trees; and at the foot of the rapid is another small island, covered with a beautiful growth of oak: But it is almost inaccessible on account of the velocity of the current. The country about these falls is finely chequered with prairies and copses of wood; and these, together with a view of the distant hills, afford a prospect not only delightful, but in some degree sublime.

About sixty miles below the falls, there is a remarkable dilatation of the river, called Lake Pepin; on the borders of which are some ancient fortifications and tumuli.

The French more than a century ago opened some mines in this quarter, and procured no small quantity of virgin copper. The Indians, however, were troublesome, and obliged them to abandon their establishments, as well as their prospects of mineral wealth. They neglected to repeat the experiment, though there is good reason to believe, that abundance of copper may be obtained at no great distance from the banks of the Mississippi.

The navigation of this river, between the falls of St. Anthony and the mouth of the Missouri, is attended with no difficulty in the season of high water; but subsequent to about the first of July, the numerous islands, shoals, and rapids, obstruct the progress of boats, particularly above *Prairie des Chiens*, and in many places prove extremely dangerous to them; it requires experienced pilots to trace out the winding channel. The most remarkable rapids commence just above the mouth of the river *des Moins*, extending from twelve to fourteen miles up and down the Mississippi, at the head of which stands Fort Madison in about north latitude forty degrees thirty two minutes. These rapids are formed by successive ledges or shoals, which cross the bed of the river in a variety of places; and in passing them the greatest caution is requisite to avoid the numerous rocks amid the strong and irregular currents.

The banks of the Mississippi are in general stable, and for the most part exhibit plenty of rock and gravel. These materials, also, are spread over the bed of the river. The water is free from impurities, though rather insipid to the taste, and much less lively and agreeable than that of the Missouri. Plenty of excellent springs flow from the banks, and from the adjacent high grounds.

This part of the Mississippi is fed by numerous tributary streams; but the greatest number, particularly those of the largest size and extent, penetrate its left bank. This inequality is owing to the comparative narrow tract of country between the Mississippi and Missouri: Yet this tract contains some considerable rivers, and a vast number of other water courses, affording a boat navigation for some distance into the country; calculated in other respects to be of infinite advantage to an agricultural people.

The river St. Pierre joins the Mississippi from the west about ten miles below the falls of St. Anthony. At the junction of these rivers a fine site for a garrison presents itself, and the Indians have ceded to the United States nine miles square of land for that purpose. The St. Pierre is navigable to the lake, out of which it flows, situated about four hundred miles from its mouth. Several bands of the Scioux reside on this river and its waters, known under different names, and not always at peace with each other. The English from Canada carry on a profitable trade with them. It is no great distance (some say not more than seven miles) from one part of this river to the waters of the Missouri.

The river *des Moins* is of some note, and calculated to afford great facilities to internal commerce. It joins the Mississippi from the west about two hundred and thirty miles above the mouth of the Missouri, and in about north latitude forty degrees twenty minutes. The source of it is said to be within two days travel of the Mississippi; and as it is known to flow nearly parallel to the latter river, its length may be computed at about four hundred and fifty miles, though the Indian traders make it much longer. In its progress it is fed but by few streams; so that the size of it is nearly the same for several hundred miles. Part of the Iowas live on this branch; and they are neighbors to the Sacs and Foxes, who reside on, or near the west bank of the Mississippi.

Some of the other branches from the west, are, Salt river, the Buffaloe, the Jaffraon, the Wyaconda, the Turkey river, the Yellow river, the Iowa river, the Cannon river, the Rock river, together with a variety of others. All these afford an inland navigation, some of them from one hundred to two hundred and fifty miles, and their shores are bounded by large tracts of excellent land. Lead and salt, and probably copper, exist in great plenty on their borders.

The Ouisconsing is one of the easterly branches of the Mississippi; but as it is the great thorough-fare of trade between Canada and Louisiana, it is necessary to take some notice of it. Its confluence with that river is about six hundred miles above the mouth of the Missouri, and in north latitude forty two degrees forty minutes. About one hundred and seventy five miles from its mouth is the portage between it and Fox river, which is less than two miles over; and in the season of high water a good boat channel extends from one to the other. From the portage to Green bay, an arm of Lake Michigan, is about one hundred and eighty miles, and from thence to Michilimakinak about two hundred and thirty miles. A great proportion of the Canadian trade passes this way, especially in the dry season, as at that time the Illinois affords a much less safe navigation. The Ouisconsing forms the upper boundary of the lands ceded to the United States by the Sacs and Foxes in 1804. Those nations at that same time ceded a small tract on the right bank of the Mississippi, directly opposite to the mouth of the Ouisconsing, under the expectation that a garrison and factory would be erected on it.

On the left bank of the Mississippi, and three miles only above the junction just mentioned, is situated the village of *Prairie des Chiens*. This village, containing about twenty dwelling houses, is situated on what may be called an island, as it is separated from the main land by a ravine, which is connected both with the Mississippi and Ouisconsing, and which is filled with water in the time of the freshes. About twenty other houses are scattered about the neighborhood, and the whole population may be estimated at about three hundred souls. The habitual residents cultivate the land, and in some years dispose of about eighty thousand pounds of flour to the Indians and traders, exclusive of large quantities of beef and pork. The Canadian traders annually rendezvous at this place, where they divide their goods, and despatch them to their several stations; where also they receive their returns in peltries, which are sent to Canada. These circumstances draw an immense number of Indians to the village; from five to six hundred at a time : So that in the course of the summer from five to seven thousand of them visit that place. Here is a fine site for a garrison; and a factory, with a detachment of troops, would be able in some measure to regulate the trade of the Mississippi above it, and likewise that by way of the Ouisconsing.

The Illinois river joins the Mississippi from the north east about eighteen miles above the mouth of the Missouri. It is navigable to where it approximates to Lake Michigan, a distance of about four hundred and sixty miles. The isthmus between the Illinois and Chicago, is low and level, and eight miles in breadth : In the season of freshes a good boat navigation exists across the portage from one to the other; and from the head of the usual navigation on the Chicago down to Lake Michigan is four miles. Boats and their cargoes, in the dry season, are transported across the portage by teams, which are kept there for the purpose. Hence it is easy to perceive, that a good navigable canal may be constructed at this place, and at no great expense.

The length of the rivers in Louisiana is determined by estimation only. This estimation was made by the first explorers of them, and the distances established by them, which are uniformly over-rated, have been regarded by subsequent mercantile adventurers as sufficiently correct. Others again, who have paid more attention to the subject, and were better qualified to ascertain distances, have probably fallen into the opposite extreme; they were not careful to make proper allowances for the meanders of the rivers. From a comparison of the most correct itineraries, it appears probable that the source of the Mississippi is about seven hundred and fifty miles above the falls of St. Anthony, or one thousand six hundred and thirty five miles above the mouth of the Missouri; so that the whole length of this river may be computed at two thousand nine hundred and ninety nine miles. Hence it is perceived, that the Missouri is one thousand four hundred and sixty one miles longer than the Mississippi; or ninety seven miles longer than the latter river from its source to the gulf of Mexico!

The lower Mississippi presents a rugged aspect. The channel is crooked and deep, and often winds from one side of the river to the other. The annual changes in this great river are remarkable. New islands are formed, and old ones swept away; new channels opened, and old ones closed; the banks in many places either fall into the river and draw after them a multitude of trees, or are enlarged and strengthened by new accretions. The river often leaves its old bed, and assumes another at some distance from it. The vestiges of several derelictions of this nature present themselves to the traveller; particularly one near the Yazous, two between Natchez, and the mouth of Red river, and another at Point Coupeé. The one at the latter place has shortened the distance about thirty miles, and the one just above the mouth of Red river has proportionably increased it. Numerous points or tongues of land exist, which cause the river to form a circuit of twenty or thirty miles, when at their upper extremities or gorges, the channels above and below them are divided from each other by tracts of land of only a few hundred yards wide. Hence it may be easily conjectured, that this river forms many curvetures in its progress.

Perhaps the most dangerous obstructions in the Mississippi arise from the different and fixed positions of a multitude of large trees, which are constantly precipitated from the banks into the water. These, by means of their roots, become firmly fixed in the bed of the river. Some of them are called *planters*, because they are immoveable, and constantly expose their pointed shafts above the water. Others are denominated *sawyers*, because their elastic limbs, by the action of the current, alternately rise above, and fall below, the surface with great force. It is dangerous for boats to run on either of these; and the best way of avoiding them in descending the river is to keep in the channel, where they seldom make their appearance. The number of them visible to the eye is greater or less, according to the high or low state of the water. The Mississippi between the mouth of the Missouri and that of the Arkansas, is filled with these and other obstructions. Below the latter river they become less numerous and dangerous, and gradually diminish in both, the nearer the gulf is approached. In the season of high water the surface of the river is sometimes almost covered with floating trees of all dimensions: Thousands of them are vomited from the Missouri; some of them lodge on the islands, and the shores; others sink to the bottom of the river, and the remainder are precipitated into the sea.

In the season of low water, numerous banks of a kind of quick-sand appear in both the great rivers; and the beaches along the shores are sometimes composed of the same materials; which are, a very fine flinty sand, intermixed with a substance of an unctuous quality, precipitated from the Missouri. These banks and beaches are so hard as to resist the first pressure of almost any weight; but if a man remains stationary on either of them a few minutes only, the water will begin to ooze from the sand in a circle of six or eight feet round him, till at length the foundation under his feet trembles like a jelly, and soon absorbs whatever be placed on its surface. Some of these banks, as they yielded to the pressure on them, have drawn boats under water by the remarkable suction they occasion. Banks and beaches of this description, though numerous, are of small extent; and are usually attached to others of common sand, dry and compact in their texture.

The strength of the current in the Missouri is considerably greater than that in the lower Mississippi. Perhaps the velocity of the latter may in some measure be ascertained by the progress made by boats in descending it. When the water is low, a boat will float from forty five to fifty miles in twenty four hours; in a middle state from sixty to seventy miles; and in the season of freshes from ninety to one hundred miles in the same period of time. This statement applies only to that part of the Mississippi above the Arkansas; for below this, a small dilatation occurs, and the swamps also receive a vast body of water; by which means the current becomes less rapid. As soon as the river enters the Delta another check is evident; no doubt owing to the diffusion of its waters into various small channels. From this to New-Orleans no variation is perceived. Between the Arkansas and the Delta the velocity of the current is diminished nearly one third; from this to the sea about one half.

Perhaps the rivers in our western regions have a greater rise and fall than those of most other countries. The rise of the Ohio is frequently from forty to fifty feet;— the Cumberland sometimes ninety feet, as is attested by the inhabitants, who live on its banks. The swell of the Mississippi near the sea is only three feet; at New-Orleans twelve feet; at Baton Rouge twenty five feet; at Fort Adams, and generally between that place and the Ohio, about forty five feet; between this and the mouth of the Missouri thirty five feet; the upper Mississippi from eighteen to twenty two feet; and the lower part of the Missouri about forty feet. The swell is greater in the narrow parts of the river, than in places where it is broad.

It is difficult to ascertain the general width of the Mississippi. That part of it between the falls of St. Anthony and the Illinois varies from three hundred to nine hundred yards, and in some instances exceeds two thousand yards. At the mouth of the Missouri it is about two thousand five hundred yards; at St. Louis, eighteen miles below, one thousand four hundred and fifty seven yards; on an average between this and the Arkansas about fifteen hundred yards; from thence to the mouth of Red river about sixteen hundred yards, except at Fort Adams, where it is contracted to nine hundred yards; at New-Orleans rather less than fifteen hundred yards; though the general width of it along the Delta is somewhat less.

It is still more difficult to ascertain the average depth of the channel of the Mississippi. At New-Orleans and below it in dry seasons, it is about one hundred and twenty feet; it is said to be more than two hundred feet at the distance of one hundred miles above that city; from thence to the Arkansas it may average nearly fifty feet; and between that and the Missouri from twenty five to thirty five feet, in the lowest state of the water. The difference between this and high water is very great, especially above the mouth of Red river. The higher the Mississippi is ascended from Natchez, particularly from about the thirty third degree, the more winding and narrow the channel; and at the same time containing more obstructions to navigation. It is observable, that the freshes in the Ohio, and other tributary streams, have but little effect on the rise of the water in the lower Mississippi. The same observation applies to the Missouri. These great rivers seldom have any considerable rise, except in the months of May and June, when the waters from the vast mountains about their sources, are precipitated to the ocean.

Such is the rapidity of the current in the Mississippi, that no craft will be able to ascend it above Natchez by means of sails only. Most of our boats make use of sails, when the wind is favorable; but this is merely occasional. Owing to the zig-zag course of the river, and the great elevation of its banks, except in time of freshes, the wind is seldom favorable. Soon after the late Indian war, one of our gun boats was about eighteen months in ascending from Natchez to the Ohio. Many of the boats or barges concerned in the trade between New-Orleans and Upper Louisiana, and the settlements on some of the branches of the Mississippi, are from thirty to forty tons burthen: It is customary to employ one oarsman to every three thousand weight; so that the freight of goods to the upper settlements on our great rivers is very considerable. Attempts have been made, and are now making, to lessen the labor of this inland navigation by the substitution of machinery, worked by horses; but the success of them is at least problematical. To contrive an adequate substitute for manual labor, has now become a subject of enquiry; and the successful projector will be amply rewarded for his expense and trouble.

As the Missouri and Mississippi are extremely winding, the current is forced from one point of land to another, or rather from each successive point into each successive bend on the opposite side of the river. The greatest proportion of the water rushes into the bends, where also the channel winds its way, and where the current is always much more rapid than in any other part of the river; indeed it often presses so strongly on the islands and shores, that boats are only kept from them, and preserved from destruction, by means of oars. Most of the produce of the upper country is floated to market in what are called Kentucky flats, or arks. These are of various sizes, generally from forty to sixty feet long, and from twelve to fifteen broad, with roofs of thin boards to secure their cargoes from the water. They only require from three to five men each to navigate them. By means of oars the crews are generally able to avoid obstructions, and to bring their boats in safety to land. They are seldom suffered to float in the night time above the Arkansas, unless the moon affords a good light, the water be high, and the weather calm. These flats or arks are not calculated to live in rough water; and therefore when the wind blows hard, or a storm approaches, they are taken under some point, into the mouth of some creek, or safely moored among the willows. They are built of timber and plank; and on their arrival at the market, are dismantled and sold.

Boats of a different construction only, and calculated for a number of oars, can ascend the Mississippi and Missouri. A description of them is given in another place, and need not be repeated here. Keel boats, however strongly manned, cannot possibly ascend to any great distance in the middle of the current; in some places, indeed, they cannot make head against it. They are obliged not only to ply along the shore, where the water is less rapid, and where counter currents or eddies frequently prevail, but they also find it necessary to keep on the side opposite to the bends. Hence they cross the river at the lower extremity of every bend, which can seldom be done without falling down with the current about half a mile. It is said by old boatmen, that they are obliged to cross the Mississippi three hundred and ninety times on ascending from New-Orleans to St. Louis. If we admit the river to average three fourths of a mile in breadth, and the loss of half a mile at each traverse, on account of the velocity of the current, it is evident, that the track of the boat, between the two points just mentioned, exceeds in distance the direction of either shore, more than four hundred miles. These traverses are also necessary on other principles. Greater and more numerous obstructions appear in the bends than opposite to them. The banks likewise along the bends are generally concave, and constantly giving way in large masses, sometimes by several acres at once, which render a passage near them dangerous; while the banks on the opposite side project with a sloping beach, usually covered or fringed next the land with willows, and therefore safe of approach. It is universally the case that, where the banks cave in and waste away on one side, those on the other increase by the deposition of new matter. Boats usually ascend from fourteen to twenty miles in a day. The labor of propelling them is excessive; it requires great exertion to move them against the current; and boatmen find it necessary to rest every hour, at least at every traverse. The river is so winding, that the daily progress of boats to their destination, is very inconsiderable. In one instance they are obliged to stem the current for fifty four miles to gain five; in another thirty miles to gain one and a half; and similar instances, though of less magnitude, occur in the course of almost every fifteen or twenty miles.

A variety of branches join the lower Mississippi from the west; but five of them only are properly denominated rivers, and claim particular notice in this place.

The first is the Merimeg, which joins the Mississippi about fifteen miles below St. Louis. It is about sixty yards wide at its mouth; and in the season of high water affords a small craft navigation for nearly one hundred miles. It flows through a fine country, much of which is under cultivation. The salt works and mills on its borders are of great advantage to Upper Louisiana, and to the settlements in the Illinois territory.

The second is the river St. Francis, which is cursorily noticed in another place. It joins the Mississippi about three hundred and five miles below the Ohio, and is two hundred yards wide at its mouth. The source of it is about fifty five or sixty miles back of St. Genevieve. It first washes a rolling country, and then passes over a large tract of inundated land; and the whole length of it may be computed at about four hundred and sixty miles. Wealthy settlements are already formed about some of its head branches, as also on its borders in the districts of Cape Gerardeau and New Madrid. This river gradually converges to the Mississippi, and in some places flows at no great distance from it. Rafts and other obstructions abound in it; but it is not difficult to remove them. The period is at hand when our population will be so much increased as to render the navigation of it of the utmost importance.

The third is White river, which penetrates the right bank of the Mississippi about three hundred and ninety seven miles below the Ohio, by a mouth of three hundred and fifty yards wide. The source of this river is rather more than one hundred miles due west from that of the St. Francis; and indeed these two rivers flow nearly parallel to each other. The length of White river has never been accurately ascertained; it is probably about seven hundred miles: It has been navigated six hundred miles, and the distances carefully estimated by an intelligent officer of the Artillerists. This river is somewhat crooked; it rolls through an elevated country, which abounds in lead. The channel is deep, and generally free from obstructions. About three miles from its mouth, in the season of high water, a boat communication exists between it and the Arkansas, by means of a bayou or outlet, which intersects the latter river about twenty miles from the Mississippi. Boats on ascending to the upper country usually pass up the Arkansas, and through this bayou, where there is seldom any current, and thereby avoid twenty two miles of strong water in the Mississippi.

The fourth is the Arkansas, which flows into the Mississippi, about twenty two miles below White river, or four hundred and nineteen miles below the mouth of the Ohio, in north latitude thirty three degrees forty minutes. It is about four hundred yards wide at its mouth, and the length of it is found to be about fifteen hundred miles. The source of it is in the Mexican mountains in about north latitude forty degrees; and it is in the vicinity of the waters of the river Platte on the one hand, and of those of the *Rio del Norte*, or *Rio Bravo*, on the other. The general direction of it is nearly south east and north west. This river has a rocky bed, and the navigation of it in dry seasons is much obstructed by rapids and shoals. The extensive country through which it rolls is diversified by some mountains, numerous elevations, and fruitful vallies, especially along the water courses; by scattered groves and copses of wood, and by prairies or natural meadows of great extent, where immense flocks of various kinds of wild animals resort to graze. On this river, and the branches of it, lead, salt, and nitre, are common; and the water is so strongly impregnated with the two latter articles, that it is not potable at the Arkansas village, forty five miles only, from the Mississippi. No doubt the country about this river is pregnant with other treasures, which time and an industrious pursuit will disclose to our view. Some of the early French discovered both gold and silver in this quarter; but their ignorance of the mineral kingdom, more particularly the difficulty at that time of penetrating into the wild recesses of interior regions, cast a cloud over their prospects of speedy opulence. They were chained by poverty to an unprofitable drudgery, and all their time was necessarily devoted to the acquisition of a precarious subsistence.

The fifth is Rouge or Red river. It joins the Mississippi just below the thirty first degree, and two hundred and forty three miles above New Orleans. Near its mouth, it is about five hundred yards wide; but for many hundred miles, it seldom exceeds three hundred, and in some instances it is contracted to less than two hundred and fifty yards. The main branch of this noble river has its source in the Mexican mountains to the eastward of Santa Fé, and in about north latitude thirty six degrees. It runs nearly one hundred miles in a north east direction, when it unites itself with another large branch from the north west, and then makes a sweep round to the south east, pursuing this course to the Mississippi; the whole length of it must not be computed at more than one thousand four hundred and fifty miles. The country about the heads of this river has never been explored, except by Spanish and French hunters; and from their accounts, it very much resembles that about the upper parts of the Arkansas. It is almost destitute of wood, except along the various streams. Prairies or natural meadows spread over the greatest proportion of it, filled with wild horses, and every species of game incident to our western regions. There is also good reason to believe, that it abounds in silver. It certainly contains large bodies of mineral salt, as the Indians, and our hunters when in that quarter, easily collect what is necessary for their use; and an alum bank of considerable magnitude is known to exist on the river near the thirty third degree of north latitude. The water is so strongly impregnated with them, that it cannot be used at Nachitoches, especially in the dry season. Perhaps the saline quality of the water, not only in Red river, but in all the numerous lakes and bayous connected with it, contribute to the health of the inhabitants. At any rate, the climate on that river, above the Mississippi and black river swamps, is extremely healthful, though more than six tenths of the settled country, especially about Nachitoches, is constantly covered with water.

The country about the lower half of Red river has been pretty well explored, and it is found to be equal in fertility to any other portion of Louisiana of the same extent, except for about fifty miles near the Mississippi, which is annually deluged in water. The cotton and tobacco raised about Nachitoches and the rapids are of the first quality, and command the highest prices in the market. Corn, oats, and vegetables, are produced in abundance among the settlements; and at some distance above them, the lands are suitable for wheat and other grain. Cattle and swine find a plentiful subsistence, at all seasons of the year, along the rivers and lakes, and in the swamps; and multitudes of them are owned by the inhabitants.

In the season of high water, which is generally from February to June, loaded boats may ascend this river about nine hundred and fifty miles; but in the dry season, the channel is obstructed by rocks, banks of sand, and petrified trees, particularly above the great raft, a description of which we have given in another place.

Red river, by a division of its waters, forms several large islands, on which are to be found some of our most wealthy settlements. One branch leaves the main stream about four miles above Nachitoches, and flows to the left; it joins the river about seventy miles below. Just below that village another branch winds to the right, and joins the middle branch at the distance of about thirty three miles. The island formed by the two latter branches, was called Nachitoches, by the ancient Indians, and on it are formed the most wealthy settlements in this part of the country. The middle branch is usually navigated, though the distance is much greater than by either of the other, and the current extremely rapid; but the rafts and other obstructions in it are less numerous, and less difficult to pass.

It unfortunately happens on Red river, as on some parts of the lower Mississippi, that the best, and in some instances, the only lands suitable for tillage, are along the margins of the stream, and of an inconsiderable depth; they regularly descend from the river, and soon terminate in lakes and swamps. The high grounds on the opposite side of these, whatever be their quality, are of no great use to the planters; they prefer the rich bottoms, on which they build their houses, and which alone they cultivate. A cypress swamp usually intervenes, and obstructs the passage between the river and the hills.

It may appear almost incredible, and yet it is too true, that near seven tenths of Louisiana to the south of the parallel of Nachitoches and Natchez, is either constantly or periodically covered with water. No doubt a considerable proportion of this tract may eventually be redeemed, but not without more labor and expense than is in the power of the present generation to bestow.

The most frequented and ready communication between the Mississippi and the Mexican dominions, is by way of Nachitoches; and the period certainly approaches when a more frequent and sociable intercourse will be opened between the two empires.

The bed and banks of Red river are composed of a bright red sand, mixed with gravel and clay of the same color, and they communicate the like color to the water. The whole country about this river, particularly to the westward of it, whether elevated into hills, or depressed into vallies, exhibits the same complexion. The banks of the Chafalia are composed of the same materials; and this affords almost conclusive evidence, that the communication between Red river and the Mississippi is of no very ancient date; more particularly as the earth along the latter river, and its various other branches, is universally of a different color. The probability is, that the Chafalia is the old bed of Red river, and that the dereliction in question was wholly owing to the versatility of the Mississippi. This is confirmed by another circumstance. Just below Fort Adams, the Mississippi makes a sweep of many miles to the right, till it intersects Red river, and then suddenly inclines to the left, forming more than two thirds of a circle. An old bed of the Mississippi, covered with lofty willows, is at this time visible across the gorge or upper extremity of this bend, with one or two elevated islands in it; the length of which is only five miles; whereas by the course of the river it is fifty four miles. Hence Red river once found a much nearer way to the gulf than at present; and if the formidable obstructions in the Chafalia were removed, the Mississippi would be likely to pursue the same way, as it now presses its whole current into it, apparently in search of a passage. Such a change in the Mississippi is certainly among possible events; and the time may come when we may deem it necessary to accelerate it.

The Washita, although it may be deemed a branch of Red river, deserves notice. This river heads in the high country between the one just mentioned, and the Arkansas, and eventually unites with the Ocatahola and bayou Tenza; and from thence to Red river, a distance of seventy miles, this confluent stream is known by the name of Black river. The Washita has been explored five hundred and nine miles; and the probability is, that it may be ascended much further.

The right bank of the Mississippi from the district of Cape Gerardeau to the gulf, a distance of about twelve hundred miles, presents to the eye an immense level. No gentle elevations, nor any kind of stone or gravel, appear to diversify the scene. The whole of this tract, for some distance back of the river, is composed of alluvion, partly covered with cane breaks, and various kinds of trees. The left bank of that river affords a different aspect; alluvious regions, interspersed with hills and rocky clifts, alternately arrest attention, and excite pleasing emotions in the mind of the traveller.

This chain of hills and clifts commences near the Illinois river, and extends down the Mississippi (in some places a good distance from it) to the neighborhood of Baton Rouge. The iron and chalk banks, the four elevated clifts between them and the Chickasaw bluffs, where the United States have a garrison, the bluffs at what are called great and little gulfs, the one at Natchez, at the mouth of the river St. Catharine, at Fort Adams, and at Baton Rouge, successively rise and approach the river at some distance from each other, and relieve the mind from the dull monotony of an extensive level. The crests of these elevations are in some places seventy five, in others more than two hundred feet above the surface of the river. Some of them extend half a mile, and others more than double that distance, along the bank. Many of them exhibit the appearance of rock; but this substance, when carefully examined, is found to be extremely porous, and composed of a hard indurated sand, by no means strongly combined, easily broken, or crumbled in pieces. Others of them are solid banks of sand of various colors, intermixed with laminas of iron ore, ochre, and argillaceous earths. At the bases of some of them, numerous trees of various dimensions are found converted into stone, by the petrifying quality of the springs about them. It must be remarked that, in most instances, where these bluffs or ridges appear, the Mississippi approaches them with great force, nearly at right angles, as if in search of a passage more to the left. They cross the Ohio at a place called the Grand Chain, about twelve miles from its mouth.

Whoever reflects attentively on this great river, will be apt to suspect, that it has disrupted large portions of the country on each side of it, and even attempted in some of its capricious frolics to work a wonderful change in the face of nature. Large trees are often found from twenty to twenty five feet under ground in some of the extensive bottoms, and from four to six miles from the channel. Add to this, the trunks of large trees at the same depth appear in a horizontal position near the bases of the banks; also in the sides of the banks newly caved in, trees in a perpendicular position are constantly seen, whose shafts above their roots are sunk from twenty to twenty five feet below the surface of the ground. These facts afford conclusive proof, that the immense bottoms along the Mississippi have been formed by alluvion; that this river has occasionally changed its bed; and that it has washed in the course of time the whole of the extensive valley bounded by the distant high grounds on each side of it.

What alterations or revolutions have taken place in this valley in the course of ages, can only be conjectured; yet there are two or three facts of sufficient importance to attract the attention of philosophers.

The banks of the river are composed of alluvious strata, and in places where they newly cave in, the different layers are easily distinguished. The banks between the Ohio and Missouri have generally, in a low state of the water, an elevation of more than forty feet, and exhibit to the eye about nine hundred distinct layers. What conclusion results from this fact? Most certainly, that these alluvious banks have been accumulating during a period of nine hundred years; and probably much longer, as the freshes since the first discovery of the country have not risen over them more than once in about twenty years. No doubt the number of layers is precisely the same as that of the freshes. These freshes never occur *more* than once a year; they are wholly occasioned by the melting of the snows at the breaking up of winter about the sources of the great rivers; the rains have little or no effect on the Mississippi above the mouth of the Ohio.

Another fact is that, in the season of freshes, the water in many places is as deep in the centre of the swamps as in the channel of the river, particularly below New Madrid. This seems at first blush to give countenance to the conjecture, that the valley of the Mississippi was once a lake ; because, prior to the elevation or formation of the banks, there was nothing to prevent the expansion of the waters. But has not the bed of the river been gradually elevated as well as the banks ? The more the banks rose, the more the water was confined within them ; of course less alluvion was precipitated over them ; and of course also, the more of it, especially the heavy sandy particles, subsided to the bottom, and elevated the bed of the river. If this was the process, however, it would seem that, instead of nine hundred annual layers, as many thousand may exist. These hints are merely suggested to excite reflection.

Intelligent and speculative men have contended, that the valley of the Mississippi was once a lake, and that its waters were drained off by means of some convulsion of nature, or by a passage formed by gradual abrasion. If such a lake ever existed, where was its southern boundary ? One place only is known below the mouth of the Missouri, which seems to render the existence of a lake even possible, and it requires no small degree of credulity to attach any weight to the evidence it affords.

In the neighborhood of Kaskaskia, the gap or opening between the high grounds on each side of the Mississippi is not more than from four to six miles in breadth. Below this point the high grounds gradually diverge from the river, particularly on the west side of it, and leave a space between them of about forty miles in width. If ever the waters were so much obstructed at these narrows as to form a lake, still they must have had an outlet to the ocean, and a great river existed ; for it would be idle to suppose, that the copious and united streams of the Mississippi and Missouri above them were wasted by evaporation and absorption. The two rocky chains or ridges, which skirt the valley above the narrows, and whose crests are elevated about two hundred feet above the low country, exhibit regular horizontal lines, as if formed by the attrition of a strong current; and the advocates for the existence of such a lake adduce these as the strongest proof in favor of the hypothesis. As well might they contend, that the ocean once covered the Andes, because beds of petrified oysters, and other marine shells, have been found on their summits; that the Appennine mountains, the territories of Mantua, and the canton of Berne, were once immersed in the same element, because some parts of supposed petrified vessels, and even sea weeds, have been discovered enveloped in their rocky protuberances, or buried in their sandy plains; and that even Dalmatia was once a bed of the sea, because an anchor was once accidentally discovered ten feet under ground. Perhaps mountains, by some powerful agency of nature, have been elevated from the great deep; but that the valley of the Mississippi was ever a lake, cannot be supported by any rational proofs. Some indeed maintain, that a great lake, or inland sea, once existed, which covered the whole country between the Allegheny and Mexican mountains. This lake, then, must have been about two thousand two hundred miles in length, twelve hundred miles in breadth, and in the middle not less than five hundred fathoms in depth! It is needless to waste time on such a subject. Were they disposed to suggest, that the ocean at some former period extended several hundred miles more inland than at present, and that the apparent redemption of the Delta from the water is more owing to the gradual reflux of the sea than to the deposition of alluvious substances, they would not be destitute of arguments, at least plausible, to support and illustrate the hypothesis.

The Mississippi differs from all the other rivers known to us, except perhaps the Nile and Kian-ku, not only in its length, but particularly in the uniformity of its width and depth for many hundred miles. Neither of the three great rivers of South America appears to be of equal length, though each of them presents an estuary of one hundred and fifty miles in breadth. The breadth of one of them, the Oronoco, about one hundred and fifty miles above its mouth, is seven thousand yards; and yet the whole length of this river does not exceed fifteen hundred miles! Perhaps the Mississippi furnishes less than half the quantity of water; but its breadth and depth continue nearly the same to the mouth of the Missouri, a distance of about thirteen hundred and sixty four miles; so that a good boat navigation extends by way of the first more than twenty two hundred miles, and by way of the second more than four thousand miles; to which may be added several hundred miles of practicable navigation near the sources of each. These advantageous traits present themselves in no other rivers, with whose geography we are acquainted.

Maps never afford accurate data for the length of rivers; the intermediate windings and deviations are too minute to be delineated; and yet geographical writers seldom have any other materials to aid them in their calculations: The consequence is, that the length they allow to most great rivers in each of the hemispheres is much too limited. The Nile is said to be two thousand miles long; the Kian-ku two thousand two hundred miles; the Ganges fourteen hundred miles; the Burrampooter fourteen hundred miles; the Rio de la Plata nineteen hundred miles; and the Amazons, or rather Maranon, two thousand three hundred miles. Now it is well known, that the latter river, following its windings, is three thousand three hundred miles long; and it seems proper to allow a proportionable number of miles to the length of the others. Even after this allowance is made, it will be found, that the Mississippi, or rather Missouri, is much longer than either of them; probably longer than any other river on the globe.

In whatever light we view this majestic river, it appears of more real importance than any other known to us. Most of the different climates, soils, and productions, incident to the new world, are found on its borders; and it seems destined at some future period to form the boundary, if not the centre, of an extensive empire. It opens two or more communications with the Pacific on the one hand, and with Hudson's bay and Canada on the other; also with various territories and states in the union, affording to all the facilities of a ready and profitable commerce. By means of this river, and its tributary streams, the surplus produce of more than a million of industrious inhabitants is at this time carried to a ready market; and by the same means the valuable products of India, of Europe, and the islands, are received by them in return. What will be the increase of population and opulence at any future given period from this, would be presumptuous to conjecture: yet, if the United States remain for any considerable time at peace, and enjoy the freedom of the seas, the vast regions on the Mississippi will exhibit splendid tokens of industry and commerce; populous cities and towns will rise in the yet unexplored waste; the arts and sciences cherished; moral philosophy, civil and political liberty, diffused among numerous societies of human beings, disposed to cultivate harmony and social intercourse with each other, and with distant nations. It is not extravagant to suppose, that our population will eventually extend to the sources of the Missouri, and that such a communication will be opened between that river and the Pacific as to draw to it a portion of the wealth of the Indies. Neither the Nile, the Ganges, the Niger, nor the Gambia of the old world; nor any of those great rivers in the southern parts of our continent, yield so many natural advantages. It may be even safely doubted, whether any of them are calculated to afford a population equal to what may be expected to exist on the Mississippi and its waters. There is also this important difference between them: Most of the former are, and will long continue to be, inhabited by savage nations; the perpetual and bloody conflicts provoked and maintained among themselves, added to the cruel and disastrous policy of their more civilized neighbors, serve in a great measure to interdict inland navigation and commerce; whereas the regions about the latter are likely to be occupied by an enlightened race of men, peaceable and industrious in their pursuits, prone to enterprize and the acquisition of wealth, solicitous only to elevate the aborigines of the forests in the scale of human beings, and to make the best use of the advantages, which a kind and benevolent Providence has designed for them.

SKETCHES OF LOUISIANA.

CHAPTER XV.

MINERAL RICHES.

THE varieties of soil and climate, the numerous productions they afford, and the great and important facilities yielded to commerce, conspire to give Louisiana a place among the fairest portions of the globe. This country is doubtless equally valuable from the mineral riches it contains, which are gradually unfolded, in most instances rather by accident than labored research; and from their accessibility, where they are known to exist, we have a right to conclude, that industry and enterprise will be amply rewarded in pursuit of them. Our knowledge on this subject is extremely limited; especially when compared with the probable plenitude of the mineral kingdom. The discoveries already made are few in number; and in most instances the details of them are extremely confused, and partake of the marvellous: So that all we are able to do is, to select and arrange with caution the heterogeneous materials before us; not to admit as authority what appears to be spurious and incredible; nor to manifest too much incredulity where a great variety of circumstances unite to control it.

Most probably the bowels of the earth in Louisiana contain many articles of convenience and wealth, of which we are still, and shall long remain, ignorant. This we have the more right to expect, as symptoms of mineral wealth abound in various places. A considerable quantity of silver was obtained from a mine opened in 1719 on the borders of the Merimak; and the pursuit of it was abandoned, as it is said, more from want of skill in the workmen, than an apprehension of the scarcity of it. There is testimony to prove, that silver so pure as to be malleable has been found on the Arkansas. Silver mines, it is said, exist about the head waters of the Washita; more particularly about some of the head branches of Red river. Some French hunters and traders, near the close of the Spanish government, procured in that quarter, and produced to the Spanish authorities, several specimens of this metal; but on account of the known curiosity and enterprise of the English Americans, the pursuit of mineral riches on the rivers just mentioned was expressly prohibited, especially as they admitted of an easy access. An old French author and traveller declares, that he gathered a quantity of gold dust at the mouth of a rivulet on the Arkansas, which the rains precipitated from the mountains. The Spaniards have opened no mines in the neighborhood of our claims. The celebrated ones of Catorce are the nearest to them; but these are a long distance to the south west of Red river.

The source of the Washita is a considerable distance to the eastward of the Mexican mountains. On its borders are found beds of martial pyrites, large bodies of chrystalized spar, and hexagonal prisms, which are known to contain no small portion of the precious metals. Perhaps as our researches are multiplied and extended, new sources of wealth will present themselves; and the evidence of their existence is sufficient to awaken a spirit of enterprise, and to promise success.

On Red river in north latitude thirty three degrees, one hundred and forty six miles due west from the Mississippi, an alum bank has been recently discovered; which, from appearances, is calculated to yield large quantities of that article. Aluminous symptoms, indeed, abound in various places on that river; and these, together with the salt rolled from the numerous springs about the country, impregnate the water to such a degree as to render it unfit for use. Limestone abounds on this river, as likewise a sort of rock, from which the inhabitants manufacture good mill and grind-stones. Petrifactions are common; and above the great raft a multitude of trees are constantly seen wholly converted into stone. A metal exists on the west side of Red river, which exhibits the appearance, and seems to contain some of the properties of Platina; but no satisfactory experiments have been made on it. This metal possesses a shining appearance; it is known to receive a polish almost equal to that of a mirror, and vegetable and some other acids will not corrode it. The magnet, however, seems to have some power over it; but may not Platina contain a mixture of iron? It is ductile, though extremely hard, and infusible in a common furnace.

Stone or pit-coal is an article of some importance. It already begins to form in the Delta. A large body of it exists near the mouth of the Missouri, and it is found in various places on the east side of the Mississippi, particularly between Cahokia and Kaskaskia. It frequently makes its appearance on the Washita, the Sabine, and Red river, particularly on the borders of a lake in the neighborhood of Nachitoches. This article is of use to smiths even at this time, and its importance will increase as the country becomes more populous, and the villages enlarged; and the more so as various tracts, of great extent, are thinly covered with wood. To forges and furnaces it will be indispensible, and the inhabitants in some of the villages must eventually resort to it. Some of this coal, however, especially that on the Missouri, is said to contain such a quantity of sulphur as to render it less worthy of notice.

The western country, generally, furnishes plenty of salt petre; which is found, in some instances, almost pure in its native state. The banks of the Arkansas in many places are incrusted with it, and at some seasons exhibit a whiteness nearly equal to that of snow. What the adjacent country contains, is not ascertained; but from the quantity already discovered, and the places where it is produced, it is reasonable to conclude, that it yields an abundance of that article. Considerable quantities of it have been taken from the rocky caves and apertures, in the ridges and bluffs, along the Missouri and its waters. The powder-makers have used it in its crude state; and some of it by refining did not lose more than four *per centum*. This in time will become an article of exportation, and prove a source of wealth to the country.

Near Cape Gerardeau there is a substance, which, when ground in oil, affords an excellent brown paint, equal in beauty and durability to the imported Spanish brown. Many of the inhabitants on the Mississippi paint their buildings with it. This substance appears to be inexhaustible, and may eventually prove of great utility to the people of the western country.

On the rivers St. Pierre and *des Moins*, branches of
the Mississippi from the west, is found a singular species
of black hard clay; likewise a blue clay; a curious kind
of red soap stone of a very fine texture; and also an e-
qually curious fine white clay. From the first the Indians manufacture their household utensils; from the second
they make a sort of paint, which, when mixed with pul-
verized red-stone, affords a beautiful color, capable of many shades; from the third they construct the bowls of
their pipes and calumets; and it is conjectured by good
judges, that the last will produce a ware not much inferior
to that of China. The French, on their first arrival in
the country, collected a considerable quantity of this clay,
and sent it to France.

They also, about the same time, opened some copper
mines at no great distance below the falls of St. Anthony,
where they found virgin copper. It is even said by one
of their journalists, concerned in the transaction, that they
procured a piece of *native brass*, weighing sixty pounds;
but in what way the copper came to be united with zinc,
so as to produce this extraordinary mixture, is not easy to
conjecture; especially as that part of the country seems
not, as in some parts of South America, to have been agitated by subterranean fires. At any rate, the Indians drove
the French away, and the acquisition of mineral wealth
in this quarter has never been resumed.

It is doubted whether the lead mines in Louisiana, both
as to number and capacity, and the purity of their treasure, are not superior to those of any other country. No
mines of this nature, at least none of any consequence,
have been discovered below the Arkansas; those with
which we are acquainted, and which are worked, are situated in Upper Louisiana. In these regions various lead
mines have been discovered; but the number and value
of them cannot be ascertained with any degree of precision. Much of the inhabited part of the district of St.

Genevieve, is embraced by them. They are found along the Merimak, and its tributary streams, and on both sides of the Mississippi, more than four hundred miles above the mouth of the Missouri. They are numerous on the St. Francis and White river; some of them have been worked and proved productive. They discover themselves in the country of the Osages, and in the territories of several other Indian tribes. Mineral lead is in such plenty, that fragments of it are scattered about in some of their villages; and it is considered of no more value than the same quantity of coarse granite, or lime stone rock.

Some of these mines were opened and worked by the French more than a century ago; and, strange as it may appear, they were not ambitious, till a late period, of extending the manufacture of lead beyond their own consumption. Ten valuable mines in the neighborhood of St. Genevieve were worked in 1804, and several others have been opened since that period. The mineral is found in veins of various sizes, which generally extend in a horizontal direction, and usually from four, to six feet under ground. Some of them soon terminate; others are of great extent, and yield large quantities of mineral. Now and then, however, the veins take a direction downwards, and descend to a considerable depth. Wherever mineral exists, certain indications of it, vulgarly called blossoms, are found on the surface of the ground; so that those in pursuit of that article are at no loss where to dig for it.

An experiment, perhaps not altogether correct, was made on this mineral in 1804. The specific gravity of it was found to be 7. 50. The color of it is shining and brilliant; and it appears to be mixed with a small proportion of sulphur, and a still smaller proportion of the oxyd of iron. As the country abounds with calcareous rock, the matrix of these mineral veins appears to be mostly composed of the carbonate of lime. This mineral is by no means the richest in Upper Louisiana;

but it yields, when properly manufactured, about seventy *per centum*.

Such indeed is the quantity of mineral lead, that very little care is taken in the manufacture of it. It is the opinion of many, that regular machinery for the purpose is useless, and that the quantity of lead saved by it would never defray the expenses of it. They usually place the mineral on a confused heap of burning logs, and other wood, and in this way smelt it. The lead is precipitated among the ashes and dirt, where no small proportion of it is lost. Notwithstanding this singular and awkward process, the manufacturers are satisfied with the profits it yields them, and consider a machinery as an injury rather than a benefit.

This inattention to the regular manufacture of lead arises in part from the poverty of the manufacturers, who are not able to pursue an expensive process, but much more from the great quantity of mineral, the little labor required to obtain it, and the prolific nature of it. On account of the water the mineral is usually taken from the ground between the first of August, and the last of November; and during this period a great number of laborers, sometimes as many as three hundred, resort to the mines in the neighborhood of St. Genevieve. They dig and dispose of the mineral, and receive in payment goods and other articles for the support of their families. Some of them have been known to earn thirty dollars per day for several successive weeks; but such occurrences are rare, and never happen, unless the laborers are so lucky as to find veins of mineral of considerable size and extent; though the profits of procuring that article are undoubtedly great.

The dealers in lead, who are also in most instances the manufacturers of it, generally adopt two methods to obtain the mineral; they either purchase it, or hire laborers to dig it for them. The details of this pursuit were furnished the author of these sketches in 1803 by the owner of a mine in the district of St. Genevieve, and they stand thus: Were he to hire twenty five men to dig mineral during the four months already mentioned, they would furnish about two hundred thousand weight; and as it yields seventy *per centum*, the produce of the whole would be one hundred and forty thousand pounds for the market. The wages and food of twenty five laborers for the above time, and the expenses of transporting the lead from the mines to New-Orleans, would amount to three thousand six hundred and fifty dollars; and were it to sell in market for nine dollars per hundred, the proceeds would amout to twelve thousand six hundred dollars; so that, after deducting the expenses, the sum of eight thousand nine hundred and fifty dollars would be left for the proprietor or dealer, which may be considered as the net profits. These, however, wholly depend on the price in market, which varies according as commerce fluctuates, or as war or peace prevails in Europe. In time of peace, lead seldom sells for more than six dollars per hundred; during the European war it sometimes rises to twelve dollars, though the average price in market may be stated at nine dollars. Those dealers in lead, who receive mineral in exchange for goods, are supposed to make the greatest profits. They fix themselves about the mines, and purchase the mineral of the laborers at two dollars per hundred, and make their payments in merchandize at an enormous advance. They smelt the mineral, and carry the lead to market; and as they are not obliged to deal on credit, the profits of this barter-trade are very considerable.

The proprietor, to whom we have just alluded, planted himself among the lead mines in 1797, and obtained from the Spanish government a grant of a league square of land, most of which is impregnated with mineral. He is the owner of the only regular machinery in the country for making lead. He manufactures bar and sheet lead, as also great quantities of ball and shot: But it is doubted by some whether the more simple and awkward mode of manufacturing lead as practised by the itinerant pursuers of this metal, is not equally profitable; especially as they smelt the mineral on the ground where they obtain it, and are not at the trouble and expense of removing it to a distance for this operation.

The richest mineral known in the country is procured from two mines, situated on the west bank of the Mississippi, nearly five hundred miles above the mouth of the Missouri, which were opened some years ago by a Frenchman: one of them yields *eighty four*, and the other *nine-two* pounds of pure lead to each hundred weight of mineral; though from the manner of smelting, no more than seventy five is actually realized. The owner covered these, as well as other mines, in 1796, by a *complete grant* from the Spanish government, embracing a tract of one hundred and sixty nine thousand three hundred and forty four arpents, now recognized as valid by the laws of the United States. The mineral is found here, as in other places, in veins; but these generally descend at an angle of about thirty four degrees. Two of them have been pursued nearly two hundred and fifty feet beneath the base of a steep hill. At their extremity, in summer, the air moves with such rapidity, that a candle cannot be kept lighted, and is at the same time so cold as to prove uncomfortable to the workmen; but in winter a considerable degree of heat prevails, and a small portion of air only is found to be in circulation.

It is impossible to say what might be the avails of this article, were the manufacture of it carried to its full extent. It wants the hand of industry only, joined to a competent knowledge of the nature of lead, to prepare any quantity of it for market. Lead, while the European war lasts, will command a high price; and Upper-

Louisiana probably contains in its bosom a quantity, adequate to the consumption of all the belligerent powers in christendom. To those unacquainted with that country, this may seem an exaggeration; but when they are told, that the banks and beds of some of the small rivers present to the traveller large masses of mineral lead, and that extensive tracts of country exhibit it in plenty, they will not presume to set bounds to the quantity.

There is no way to ascertain the quantity of lead annually manufactured in Upper Louisiana; but it is much more considerable than a mere superficial observer would be willing to admit. The mines in this quarter supply several Indian tribes, as also the extensive settlements on both sides of the Mississippi, and those on the Ohio and its waters. In addition to this, large quantities of lead are sent to New-Orleans and Pittsburgh, where part of it is consumed; the remainder finds its way to the Atlantic and European markets. The want of capitals, and the still greater want of industry among the inhabitants on the Mississippi, especially the Creoles, operate as powerful checks to the manufacture of lead. When necessity compels them, they will labor with spirit till the means of a few months subsistence are obtained; they will then retire, and indulge their indolence, till necessity again urges them to resume their laborious occupations. Even the few capitalists in the country, who purchase mineral, and manufacture lead, complain of this as an obstacle to their success; they are obliged to wait for the moment when the victims of poverty and want deposit with them the fruits of their exertion.

Most nations, who own lead mines, derive a public revenue from them. How can the United States avail themselves of this advantage? If the country contained a given number of them only, and it required great labor, expense, and an intricate process, to obtain the lead, no difficulty of consequence would probably occur. But when mineral

MINERAL RICHES. 399

lead is found scattered here and there over the surface of an extensive territory, and also deposited in the bowels of the earth, at all times easy of access, it appears impossible to secure an exclusive privilege. If the people be prohibited from taking it in one or more places, they will resort to others. All the troops in service would not be able to guard this treasure; and those disposed to purloin it, would laugh at legal restraints. Some of the mines, indeed, are private property; but the number and extent of these bear no proportion to those included in the public domain. The discoverer of a mine, under the Spanish government, was entitled to a grant of land of sufficient extent to embrace it; or he was at liberty to occupy and work it, provided he rendered one tenth of the produce to the crown.

If the lead mines may be considered as productive of individual wealth, and at the same time of great national advantage, no less can be said of the mines or masses of salt found in almost every part of Louisiana. This article is even more general than that of lead, at least a wider extent of country is impregnated with it, and it is exhibited in a variety of forms; it appears in springs and other streams, in and on the earth, in thin strata, and in solid masses; it is likewise incorporated with vast bodies of rock found in the interior, and in some instances is easily separated from the useless substances connected with it.

The country about the Washita, and Red river, affords many instances of salt, where a sufficient quantity of that article may be obtained to supply a crowded population. Three salt pits or salines on the former river have been accurately examined. The specific gravity of the water in the first, when compared with that of the river, is 1.02720; that of the second 1.02104; that of the third 1.0176. The water of the two first, is of the same strength as that of the ocean along our coast; and double the strength of the water yielded by some of the best licks in Kentucky. Ten quarts of the water, taken from one of the first, will afford, by evaporation, eight ounces of good salt.

Several salt springs have been been discovered about the Sabine; and an excellent one is known to exist near the Ocatahola lake.

The saline in the vicinity of Nachitoches, and on the navigable waters of Red river, promises to be productive. Three wells only have been sunk; they furnish water for thirty kettles, whose contents are six hundred and sixty gallons; and as the water is nearly saturated, these kettles attended by seven laborers, produce about two hundred and forty barrels of salt per month, at an expense of one hundred and forty dollars. The salt is equal in goodness to that imported from Liverpool. To what extent this manufacture may be carried is uncertain; perhaps one hundred wells of equal value may be sunk. It is pretty evident, that the proprietors will soon be able to supply all the settlements about Red river, as also those in the Mississippi territory, at a cheaper rate than can be done by way of New Orleans.

The water in some of the branches of Red river is too strongly impregnated with salt to be potable. Hunters have discovered silver ore in many places about the head waters of Red river, as also great quantities of mineral or rock salt. This is likewise found on some parts of the Washita, together with several springs as salt as the ocean. The accounts, however, received of these several instances of salt, are extremely vague and indistinct; not calculated, indeed, to afford us any other than a confused idea of them. Cathartic salts, and magnesia, may be manufactured in the neighborhood of Nachitoches; articles of some consequence in a country, where certain diseases are endemical.

Salt springs exist on the Arkansas and Missouri, and are scattered over the country situated between them.

They afford salt in different proportions; in some it is hardly perceptible to the taste; while in others it is forced by the saturated water in small particles from the earth, which, as the water spreads, and the rapidity of it abates, are deposited in concrete masses on the ground. In the vicinity of one of them, the Osages have a hunting camp. No less than four tribes of Indians, who inhabit the waters of the Kansas and Platte rivers, derive their supplies in part from similar depositories, and in part from the salt springs with which the country abounds.

One spring of this nature, remarkable for its size, and for the productive quality of its water, deserves to be noticed in this place. It is situated on Grand river, which is an easterly branch of the Arkansas, and at a very little distance from the latter river. This spring forms a fountain or bason at its source of about forty feet diameter. It then suddenly disappears under a rock of about forty yards in extent, the top of which is flat and smooth, and great quantities of salt are formed on it, though it is not fit for use, as it is apparently mixed with sulphur, or some other offensive substance. The water is nearly saturated; the Indians and Indian traders procure their salt from it; and they say, that eight gallons of it will yield by evaporation one gallon of salt. About four hundred Osages, living near the mouth of Verdigris river, a short distance only from this spring, obtain their supplies of salt from it; and as it is situated on a navigable stream, it will probably very soon become of importance to the manufacturers of salt among the whites.

The salines just below St. Genevieve are productive. The inhabitants on both sides of the Mississippi derive most of their supplies from them; and no small proportion of the salt is boated up the Ohio. The salines on the Merimak are also valuable: They supply in part the settlers on the east side of the Mississippi; nearly all those of the district of St. Louis; and a proportion of those in the district of St. Charles. There are also some salines on what is called Salt river, in the neighborhood of the upper settlements on the Mississippi, which bid fair to be productive.

In addition to these springs and salines, Upper Louisiana furnishes some *extraordinary appearances* of salt, a description of which will now be attempted with as much accuracy as the materials before us will allow.

Near the source of one of the easterly branches of the Arkansas, and in a westerly direction from the Osage villages, is situated what is called the *salt prairie*. This is annually visited by some of our traders. Two of the most respectable characters in the country have repeatedly visited it, and made themselves fully acquainted with every particular concerning it. This prairie, according to them, is about twenty five miles diameter, (others say nearly forty) composed of a dark colored indurated sand, free from herbage, and surrounded by lofty hills. As soon as the heat of the sun begins to exhale the moisture of the sand, a thin coat of salt is gradually formed on the surface. The quantity of salt thus produced wholly depends on the degrees of heat; and frequently during the hottest days in summer, it accumulates to the thickness of nearly an inch and a half. In some places it has the appearance of fine table salt, and may be swept or gathered into heaps; in others it forms an incrustation, and resembles vast sheets of thin ice. The dews dissipate it. The rains occasionally precipitate large bodies of it into the branch alluded to, where part of it concretes, and is deposited along the shores. The author has several times seen salt taken from the prairie and branch: That from the first is free from impurities, very white, and sufficiently fine for table uses: That from the last is mixed with more or less sand, collected from the bed and sides of the stream, and exhibits the colors of the several strata of earth where it is deposited. No estimate can be made of the quantity of salt, which might be annually obtained from this prairie; but it would yield sufficient to excite our surprise and admiration. The branch, on which it is situated, is navigable at the season of high water : But no benefit can be expected from it at present, as the Indians claim the country, and generally prove troublesome to those of the whites, who venture to hunt or to reside in it.

About forty miles from this prairie, there are two mines of genuine fossil salt. This article is found in solid masses in the earth, and exhibits different colors : That taken from one of the mines approaches to a blue : That taken from the other is nearly red. The extent of them is unknown, though from a cursory examination they are supposed to be inexhaustible.

A little to the southward of these mines, and on a branch of the Arkansas, nature furnishes a singular phenomenon. On the side of a small hill five holes or basons may be seen sunk in a horizontal rock, which are always full of salt water, but never overflow. When water is taken from them, they instantly fill again. About ten feet below them a large spring of pure fresh water flows from the same hill.

There is another extraordinary appearance of salt, denominated by some the salt mountain, though its position and extent have been variously related : It is supposed to be situated at the head of one of the western branches of the Arkansas. This mountain, if it may be so called, has been visited by Indians only, and on them we are unfortunately obliged to rely for a description of it.

The Osages are well acquainted with this place. While the Spanish government existed they made frequent excursions to the borders of New Mexico, partly to obtain wild horses, and partly to depredate on the Indians in that quarter. From this mountain they obtained their supplies of salt, though it is situated about twenty five miles out of their common route. They uniformly describe a high bluff or mountain composed of a solid mass of fossil salt, and covered with a thin stratum of earth ; at the base of which issues a large salt spring, sufficient in size to be navigable soon after it reaches the plains ; and this, from the concurrent testimony of those Indians, appears to form one of the principal western branches of the Arkansas. They first remove the earth, and then break the salt into such fragments as are convenient to be carried on their horses. Of the extent of this saline mass they are totally ignorant ; nor are they able to state any other particulars concerning it. Salt rock, and salt springs are common in this country. In the winter season, the salt oozes from those rocks facing the sun, and forms an incrustation on them. Salt springs so hot as to boil fresh meat are sometimes found ; and for this purpose they are visited by the Indians and other hunters.

The existence of such a salt bluff or mountain as is mentioned is partly confirmed by the following facts. During the winters of 1771 and 1772 a gentleman now living at Vincennes pursued the peltry trade on the Arkansas. He ascended that river about eight hundred miles, and then entered what is called the western branch of it; the water of which was as red as vermillion, and as salt as the ocean. The freshes in the spring inundated the bottoms along the branch, and when the waters subsided the surface of the earth thus deluged, was found to be covered with a sheet of salt, from three to five inches in thickness! This relation, so far as it respects the color and saline qualities of the water, is fully attested by an officer, who, in the spring of 1806, explored the lower half of the Arkansas under the orders of the government. The fact is, that in the season of freshes, the water of that river is of a red color, and so salt as not to be potable at the settlements near its mouth. This saline quality is occasioned by several branches, which have their sources either in ground strongly impregnated with salt, or flow through a country where this article presents itself in more solid masses. Mineral salt, taken from the country about the Arkansas, has been seen among the Indians about nine hundred miles up the Missouri.*

Another extraordinary instance of salt remains to be mentioned. The adventurer, Philip Nolan, who visited the borders of New Mexico about the year 1796, where he eventually lost his life, constructed a map of one of his tours, on which he delineated a salt mountain, and beneath the delineation wrote " *here your friend encamped three* " *weeks.*" The gentleman, to whom he presented the map, questioned him relative to what appeared a phenomenon, and he declared with the strongest asseveration, that a mountain of fossil salt actually existed a little to the southward of the sources of Red river. This map has been inspected by the author of these sketches.

To those unacquainted with the existence of salt in a great variety of forms in other parts of the globe, the accounts of that article in Louisiana may appear incredible; perhaps some may be inclined to consider them as fabulous and without foundation. If, however, they will consult those authors, both ancient and modern, who have described the appearances of salt in general, their incredulity will vanish; they will even admit the probability, that Louisiana contains great quantities of that article. Pliny, the naturalist, has left us an account of the several examples and kinds of salt known in his time. Dr. Shaw speaks of several salt mountains in Barbary. Three scientific travellers, Watson, Townsend, and Kirman, have described a salt mountain in Spain, which is about five miles in circumference, and above five hundred feet in height: The depth of the salt below the surface of the adjacent country is not known; this article is transparent, and of

---

* A less copious account of the salt found in Louisiana was published by the author, in 1806, in the Medical Repository.

the rock kind, and extremely pure. Other mountains of salt are said by the same travellers to exist in Calabria, in the province of Astracan, and in the states of Tunis, and Algiers. In the isle of Ormus " *are mountains of salt* " *frightful to look at.*"

Sicard and Volney have described some remarkable instances of salt in Egypt to the west of the Delta. According to the last author, the whole continent of Africa is either composed of salt, or calculated to produce it.

Salt rock is found in England and France, from which vast quantities of salt are manufactured. Perhaps the Bosnia and Wiliska salt mines in Poland are the most remarkable of any on the globe*. Mines of a similar nature, and

---

* The mine of Bosnia was opened in 1251, and has been constantly worked since that period. The salt is taken from a vein or seam of ten thousand feet in length: The depth of this mass is unknown, though more than half a century ago it had been penetrated twelve hundred feet below the surface of the ground; the breadth of it at that time was seven hundred and fifty feet. The salt obtained here is dry, easily broken in pieces, and put into casks.—The mine at Wiliska is situated directly under the town, and the immense weight over it is supported by vast pillars of salt. This vein has been opened more than two thousand feet in length, upwards of six hundred feet in breadth, and eight hundred feet in depth; at least such was the progress made sixty years ago. This vast pit or mine contains a kind of subterranean commonwealth, and the members of it " are govern-" ed by their own policy and laws; many of those born in these dreary " abodes never see the light of the sun, and many of those who enter " them as laborers seldom return to the reat world again." Spacious galleries and chapels are excavated from the solid rock salt, as also store-houses and other buildings. They are constantly lighted, and the rays of light reflected from the luminous and various colored salt, afford to the eye a multitude of singular and pleasing images. The salt is procured here in large shapeless masses, from which blocks are cut, measuring in some instances more than one hundred square feet; it is of various kinds and colors, green and coarse, white and fine, and frequently crystallized; and when this last kind is taken from the rock it breaks into cubes and rectangular prisms. The annual produce of this mine is about six hundred thousand pounds, free from impurities. What is remarkable a spring of *fresh water* breaks out in this mine, and runs through it.

of equal magnitude, are said to exist in Moldavia and Wollachia.

Instances occur where salt is found on the surface of the ground, like that on the *salt prairie* already noticed. " Large tracts of country in California are occasionally " covered with fine salt, formed by the heat of the sun." Another singular instance of the kind occurs " on the con- " fines of Dancala and Tigra in Abyssinia, where there is " a large plain four days journey in extent; one side of " which is incrusted all over with a pure white salt in " such quantities, that some hundreds of camels, mules, " and asses, are constantly employed in fetching it from " thence." In Persia " whole plains, about ten leagues " long, and six or seven broad, are covered with a white " shining salt of good flavor."

South America, likewise, furnishes many extraordinary instances of salt. " That part of the Andes," says the Abbe Molina, " corresponding with the provinces of Ca- " piapo and Coquimbo (in Chili) contains *several moun-* " *tains of fossil salt*, dispersed in strata or layers, crystal- " lized in transparent cubes, frequently colored with yel- " low, blue, and red." This able writer was a native of Chili; and to men enjoying this advantage, we have the more right to look for faithful descriptions.

Those who give credit to these historical relations, need not wonder at the existence of similar instances of salt in Louisiana. Of their existence, indeed, we have sufficient evidence; but the nature and extent of them, as also the benefits to be expected from them, are much less accurately ascertained, and therefore to future discoveries we must look for a more competent knowledge of them.

SKETCHES OF LOUISIANA.

CHAPTER XVI.

OF THE ABORIGINES.

THE number of Indian nations in Louisiana, and the aggregate number of their inhabitants, cannot be ascertained with any degree of accuracy. Many of them have never been visited by the whites, and most of the accounts of those already known, are extremely defective. They are dispersed over an immense tract; they inhabit the rocky or shining mountains, the borders of North Mexico, the shores of the gulf, and the islands near the coast. Perhaps our western travellers may detail the number and situation of those on the Missouri and Columbia with sufficient certainty; but these, however numerous, form only a small proportion of the whole. Years must roll away, unless a greater spirit of enterprise is manifested, before any accurate account of the aborigines can be obtained. It cannot be expected, that the government will aid the exploration of all the parts of a wild and extensive country. The learned and curious in other countries project, and carry into execution, land and sea voyages of discovery, and derive no benefit from them, except what appertains to science in general. No doubt the interior regions of Louisiana contain objects of sufficient value to reward the labor of investigation. They would excite the ingenuity of the botanist, and chymist, particularly of the metallurgist and mineralogist; and the discoveries in the power of such men to make, would prove useful to mankind. The citizens of the United States are not deficient in enterprise; but this is excited among them more from the hopes of wealth, than from a disposition to extend the field of information. They voluntarily traverse the most distant seas and oceans, and mind not the hardships they suffer, nor the dangers to which they are exposed; but they appear solicitous to avoid land peregrinations, not because they want hardihood, courage, or perseverance, but because they expose themselves to certain expenses without any tempting prospects of remuneration. Under these circumstances, all that can be expected at present is, some brief relation of the most prominent traits in the character and manners of the Indians.

The Indians are now what they were when America was first discovered by the Spaniards, except those who have had any considerable intercourse with the whites, which has invariably tended to debase and corrupt them. In their manners and characters, the several nations differ from each other in some essential particulars. Perhaps this diversity is in a great measure occasioned by their different origins, and in some measure by the varieties of climate.

The peculiar circumstances of the Indians, in some degree, denote their character. Hunting and war constitute almost their only exercise. These require great caution and dexterity, particularly the latter. Hence they become grave and sedate, and seldom speak more than a few words on any occasion, except when awakened to it by considerations of magnitude. When the hunting season is over, and they have a stock of provisions on hand, and not engaged in war, they are weighed down by inactivity and lassitude. They indulge themselves in hardly any amusement, except that of dancing; and this exercise is usually pursued in the evening. An Indian conceives it beneath his dignity to labor in the field. This is almost invariably imposed on the women, who, on long marches, are also loaded like pack-horses, though they do not think themselves degraded; while the men walk at their ease with only their guns, or bows and arrows in their hands; and the greatest recommendation a wife can possess is, that she is healthy, strong and capable of bearing fatigue. Perhaps this is a dictate of nature; but the tyranny exercised by husbands over their wives, cannot be reconciled to any just or necessary principles. The women are the mere slaves of the men, not their companions; they must either submit to their whims and caprices, or be punished at the discretion of their vindictive and cruel masters. In some nations, the husband has an absolute power over his wife, and he either kills, or punishes her as he pleases. The exercise of this power, especially among the Ietans, has so reduced the number of females, that it bears no proportion to that of the other sex. Many of the women are disfigured; some appear without noses and ears; and others again without hands. The Scythians and Goths imposed heavy burdens on their women; but in other respects they treated them as equals. They exacted a fine from him who injured a man; and for the same injury done to a woman, a double fine was imposed.

Equality reigns among the Indians, and no one has any exclusive pre-eminence, except what arises from age, or from personal or mental endowments. Education and wealth never fail to create distinctions in civilized society; and even those possessed of the latter only, are frequently elevated to important offices in the state, without one virtue, or useful qualification to recommend them. Among the Indians the custom is different. They are destitute of what we call education; their lands are in common; what they separately acquire in the chase excites no envy or jealousy; the plunder obtained in war devolves on him who first seizes it, and he who acquires the most of it, is usually most applauded for his prowess and dexterity. In some instances, they have a kind of hereditary nobility: But in time of war and danger they take the advice of their old men, put themselves under the authority of their best military chiefs, elevated to office in consequence of their bravery and skill; and these in difficult times are implicitly obeyed, though during the existence of peace their authority is merely nominal, except in some rare instances.

The different nations of Indians are uniform at least in two particulars; innocence and simplicity prevail among them. To strangers they are humane and docile; every family is solicitous to welcome them, and to afford them protection. When a stranger enters one of their habitations, the best things it affords are set before him. If he visits all the habitations in the town, the same hospitality is successively repeated; and he must taste of the food set before him, or he is sure to give offence, as the Indians are led to believe that he despises them, and studiously slights their friendly offices. When a white man of rank visits them, they study to receive him with the greatest marks of respect. They usually meet him at some distance from the town, spread a buffaloe robe or other skin before him, in which he places himself; and in this manner is carried to their habitations. These are traits similar to those observed among many of the northern and eastern nations at this day.

Such indeed are the simple manners of the natives, and so unsuspicious in the common concerns of life, that they indulge many habits, which, to the more civilized and refined, appear to border on vice. Each dwelling or cabin, has seldom more than one room, and the size of it is in proportion to the number of individuals in the family. When an Indian marries his daughter, he usually takes her husband to his house; so that a family or lodge sometimes contains thirty or forty persons. The floor or ground is covered with mats or skins, and the members of the family repose themselves on them. If a stranger visits them, he sleeps among the rest; and instances have occurred where white visitors have reposed by the side of the unmarried daughters of their host, without the least suspicion, that they would indulge themselves to the dishonor of the family.

The ceremonies of courtship and marriage are by no means uniform; they are somewhat singular among the Indians on the east side of the Mississippi. When a young man is desirous of obtaining any particular female for his wife, he explains his intentions either to her real or adopted uncle. The bargain once completed, and the preliminaries settled, the groom builds himself a fire or hut separate from the rest; and in the evening commences playing on an instrument, something in the form of a whistle. The bride advances slowly behind him, and tickles his nose with a leaf or blade of grass. He starts as from a profound reverie, and manifests great surprise, while she leaps into the dark, and indulges a kind of tittering laugh. This farce is frequently repeated, till at length the groom wraps himself in his blanket, lays down, and pretends to be in a sound sleep. The bride silently approaches his feet, and tickles them, and he is again awaked to a seeming surprise. She makes her escape as before. This is also frequently repeated, till the fire becomes extinguished, and the Indians have retired to rest, when she silently lays herself down by the side of her husband.

If the Indians are humane and hospitable in peace, and practice some of the milder virtues, in time of war all their implacable passions appear to be awakened, and they excite terror and dismay among those unaccustomed to their modes of warfare. Considerable preparations are necessary before a war be undertaken. The old men are consulted on the propriety of it, and their advice taken in what manner to proceed; they at the same time endeavour to persuade other nations either to participate with them, or to maintain a perfect neutrality during the contest. They practise many superstitious and religious ceremonies; consult the eclipses and their jugglers or priests; and endeavour to discover some omens in their dreams, on which they place great hopes of victory, or despair of success.

These preparations are kept a profound secret; as their object is to surprise their enemy. When they are properly prepared, they march to the attack, not in the manner of the whites, but in the manner the best calculated to draw their enemy into ambuscades, and to destroy or cripple him before he is able to defend himself. Hence their warfare is rather predatory than systematic. They seldom keep in large bodies, except when opposed by an army of whites, but divide themselves into small bands; perhaps in some measure for the purpose of obtaining provision. In this way they depredate on each other. The weaker party usually makes a precipitate retreat. This draws after it no disgrace, as it enables them the better to practise the stratagems of war. If they happen to kill any of their enemies, they risk almost every danger to obtain their scalps, while the friends of the slain endeavour to prevent it; they conceive it a disgrace to let them fall into the hands of the victors; and on such occasions a furious and bloody combat frequently happens. All their onsets are accompanied with yells of defiance, sufficient to intimidate those not familiarised to such scenes.

During the continuance of the war, various modes of attack are concerted. Among others, for instance, is that contrived by some war chief; and to obtain warriors to carry it into execution, he proceeds thus: He erects a large post in some conspicuous place; proclamation is made for the warriors to attend, and he developes to them his plan. He then walks up to the post, and sticks his tommahawk into it; all those in favour of the measure, and disposed to share in the enterprise, follow his example. If there be a sufficient number of volunteers to promise success, they immediately move to the scene of action. The chief who proposed the expedition assumes the command. The one who stuck his tommahawk into the post next after him, is considered as the second officer, and so of the rest.

After the acquisition of a victory, however insignificant, the conquerors usually set out for their homes, with their prisoners, scalps, and articles of plunder. When arrived in sight of them, they commence a loud and mournful lamentation, which serves as a signal to the distant spectators, that some of their friends and relations have been killed. They are soon met by all the women, who set up loud cries, pluck out their hair, and even their flesh, in token of their undissembled sorrow. When arrived in the midst of the village or camp, an universal silence is proclaimed, when one of the warriors relates all the circumstances of the expedition. The women, who have lost any relations or kindred, again commence their melancholy wailing; and they sometimes work themselves into such a rage, that they fall on the prisoners, and massacre them on the spot. No one dares to interfere, or to plead in favor of the victims; for they consider this female sorrow as sacred, and the least interruption of it a crime of the deepest dye.

If however, the prisoners are not thus disposed of, another fate awaits them. The women have a right to take them, to supply, in part, the places of their lost friends, and in this case they are reduced to slavery. If this right be waved, the prisoners are doomed to a terrible death. They are usually conducted to an open plain, or some other suitable place, when they commence their death songs. They are either fastened to stakes, or placed on stages or scaffolds; and the most refined tortures are invented on the one hand, while on the other the most heroic fortitude is collected to sustain the terrors of the last scene. The nation assembles as on a festival, and both old and young, both male and female, feast with pleasure on the work of death before them. The nails of the unhappy victims are plucked out; their flesh is gradually torn from their bodies; hot irons are forced into them; matches of lighted wood are stuck about them; and sometimes the flesh taken from them is greedily devoured by the spectators. In this way they suffer five or six hours, and frequently for two or three days; and in these dreadful sacrifices the women act a more conspicuous part than the men. During all this time, not a groan escapes the victims, nor are their features distorted. They upbraid the conquerors for their ignorance; explain to them more exquisite modes of torture; repeat their exploits, and boast of the number they have killed, particularly of the victor nation. In this particular they resemble the ancient Cantabrians, who chanted their songs even at the moment they were dying by the hands of the Romans. Education and religion teach better things; and perhaps the time may come when the great family of mankind will be equally under their benign influence.

The Indians are not more implacable in their resentments than tender in their friendships; they carry both to an extraordinary excess. While they are friends they will omit no opportunity to serve you, and even risk their lives to protect you. The remembrance of a favor expires not with him who received it; it is frequently handed down from one generation to another, and if an opportunity occurs they will return it. A remarkable instance of this appears in the early history of one of the eastern states. The Indians attacked a village of whites, and were repulsed with considerable loss. Two or more of the wounded were secreted and protected by a poor widow, who eventually cured them of their wounds, and gave them instructions in what manner to return in safety to their nation. Nearly half a century afterwards, the same village was again attacked by the same nation of Indians, when they massacred all the whites they were able to secure; except the relations and descendants of the poor widow, who were treated with kindness, and none of them plundered of their property. Such instances of gratitude are not rare among them; and if the whites are more destitute of this noble quality, perhaps it is because their virtues are less founded on nature than on the dictates of a false education.

We must therefore, admire the stability of Indian friendships, and at the same time condemn the duration of their resentments. They will brood over them; no distance of time or place will obliterate them; they carefully conceal them; and when an opportunity offers they will exercise their vengeance. During all this time, even when filled with rage, they preserve their features unchanged; and no one can possibly suspect from their conduct, that they meditate any thing extraordinary. In fine, it is a characteristic trait among the Indians, never to be moved by accidents, or to manifest surprise at any sudden and unexpected event; except, perhaps, in time of war.

Let no one infer, from what has been said, that the Indians are really more passionate than the whites. The fact is, they are much less given to passion, and may be said to be almost destitute of it. The boisterous and vengeful spirit exhibited by them in time of war, cannot properly be called by this name. They perform many actions from principle, and in a dispassionate manner, at which the whites revolt with horror, and never attempt to achieve, except to gratify the most vindictive resentment.

Their lives are apparently wretched, yet, perhaps, they are the most happy people on earth. They exhibit in their manners a strong mixture of the fiercest and most gentle features; the imperfections of brutes, and the best qualities of human nature.

They appear to have no form of government, nor to acknowledge any law; yet they actually live under the first, and voluntarily submit to the latter. They have established principles and customs among them, from which they seldom depart. These are derived from their ancestors, and many of them appear to be founded in wisdom. The glorious prerogatives of independence and freedom, in a particular manner, belong to them, and they view with horror the exercise of despotic power. They are extremely impatient under any kind of restraint. Reason produces more subordination among them, than among civilized nations; and their almost total exemption from quarrels, factions, and discords, is a manifest proof of it.

They always respect a man whom they esteem; but this esteem is not easily imbibed. They rely much on physiognomy, and their conduct proves, that they are not wholly ignorant of the science.

No considerable number of people can be supposed to exist without some kind of government, and at the same time destitute of municipal regulations: Otherwise every man would be his own judge and avenger; the exercise of these dangerous prerogatives would soon disperse the members of the society. Hence it is, that all rude nations are governed by, at least, unwritten laws, preserved by tradition; and these are more or less certain in their operation, according to the personal authority of those appointed to carry them into effect, or according to the light in which crimes are viewed by the multitude. The ancient Irish had their Brehons, or heriditary judges, on whom devolved the preservation, interpretation, and execution of their traditionary laws, which remained in full vigor till the time of the conquest. Other nations in Europe had their Druids, and the Indians of America have their Priests and civil chiefs.

The rights of property among the Indians are not of a very complex nature, and few disputes occur concerning them. Contests of this description are generally adjusted and determined in a satisfactory manner, by the old men and chiefs, who are the customary judges on such occasions.

But the crimes and punishments among them are more complicated, and are so different among different nations, that the several grades of them are hardly susceptible of definition. With some the *lex talionis* prevails; while, with others, punishments for most offences are averted by composition.

They are also extremely ununiform with respect to their conception and definition of crimes. Among some a murder committed by a drunken man is not deemed criminal, but only a misfortune; they transfer the guilt from the man to the cause of his ebriety. Others admit of no excuse, except self defence and unavoidable necessity, and the destruction of the murderer ensues. Criminals of this description, in some nations, undergo a kind of trial and condemnation. In others they no sooner commit capital offences, than the laws are supposed to condemn them without trial, and it belongs to those the most concerned to carry the sentence into execution. If these neglect it, the chiefs will sometimes interpose their authority, and become the avengers of justice. Among some nations the murderer is delivered over to the nearest relation of the deceased, who has a right to kill him, or to compound with him, as was the case among the ancient Saxons. The same practice prevails in Turkey. In some other parts of the east, particularly in Abyssinia, the injured party has no power over the culprit till he is doomed to death by the judges, and then the right of pecuniary composition attaches.

It is wonderful with what fortitude, and even indifference, the Indians will face death; not only in presence of their enemies, but when doomed to it by their customs and laws. Most of them conceive it a disgrace to become the fugitives of justice, and therefore seldom attempt to escape. They will even present themselves to those they have injured, and impatiently solicit the fatal stroke. If these neglect or refuse to become their executioners, the misery they feel drives them almost to madness; and to release themselves from it they often provoke the hand of justice by the commission of new and aggravated crimes. The faithful monitor within tells them, that they have forfeited their lives, and hence they indignantly spurn the idea of existence. These sentiments are seemingly delicate and elevated, and it is difficult to account for them. Perhaps they may be traced in part to their religion, and in part to the veneration they entertain for their civil institutions.

In their last moments, when summoned to depart by sickness, or the infirmities of age, they call their family and friends about them, and impart their dying advice with as much serenity of mind as if uttered in health, and in a council of chiefs. Their patience never forsakes them; and perhaps this, as well as their intrepidity in the hour of danger, is derived from the expectation of a happy existence in another world.

The sick, when pronounced incurable by their physicians, are often put to death by their friends and relations; and even the old and infirm, when no longer able to support themselves, are doomed to share the same fate. The first preliminary to this tragedy is a feast. They usually kill a number of dogs, whom they instruct to proclaim to the spirits in the other world, that an addition will soon be made to their number. The carcases of the dogs are greedily devoured; after which they despatch their victims, generally by strangling them.

Perhaps even this practice, so repugnant to our feelings, as also that of massacreing prisoners taken in war, may find some excuse or alleviation in the peculiar circumstances of the Indians.

Almost their only sustenance is derived from the chase. None but the men are able to pursue it, and it often happens that six or eight women and children depend on the exertions of one man. This burden is still increased, if there be any sick or old to support. These, especially the latter, become tired of their lives when no longer able to share the fatigues of war, or to procure game for themselves. They therefore voluntarily submit to a premature death; and those who are bound by nature to nourish them while they live, are also doomed to become their executioners when unable to supply them with the means of living. Besides, as the Indians are almost always at war, they are obliged to move from place to place, and frequently with great precipitation; and in such an extremity, their sick and infirm old people must either prove an incumbrance, or fall into the hands of their enemies. Necessity therefore seems to dictate their destruction.

They are much more excusable in killing their prisoners. If they preserved their lives, who would support them? Were this difficulty removed, how could they spare their warriors to guard them? Situated as they are, vulnerable on every point, prisoners would be liable to make their escape, or snatched from captivity by the bold and successful exertions of their friends. They cannot with safety release their prisoners; such a step would increase the number and strength of their enemies; therefore to kill them is as much a dictate of self preservation as of ferocity. The tortures inflicted on them, are intended to familiarize the young to scenes of blood, and to make warriors of them.

It must be remarked, that an Indian cannot disgrace himself more than by suffering himself to be taken prisoner. If he ever returns to his nation, it is to experience, at least, a temporary degradation, to be habited like a slave, to be exposed to public ridicule and contempt; and the women and children are permitted to insult him as much as they please; he is even denied the rights of hospitality; his former acquaintance and friends avoid him, and he is obliged to herd and associate with domestic animals. His military conduct, however, is ultimately investigated in a council of chiefs; and if it be found that he manifested a suitable degree of courage and prudence at the time he was made prisoner, he is restored to his former station in life; though not without many solemn ceremonies, which in part appear to be derived from their religion. In some parts of Europe, a disgraced soldier is restored to his former respectability by passing under the flag of his regiment.

Perhaps this disgrace is somewhat aggravated by the notion, that eternal happiness awaits those who fall in a contest with their enemies. Such a sentiment unquestionably tends to make men brave. The Saracens never feared death on such occasions; because they believed, that all those who perished in battle were admitted to the joys of paradise. The Romans and Lacedæmonians entertained nearly the same notions. All those denominated priests among the Indians, inculcate this doctrine. This religious order is probably coeval with the first settlement of America; for Clavigero says, that at the time of the conquest of Mexico, about a million of this description of men existed in that empire.

Their religion, as may be supposed, is such as simple nature points out; though in some it appears much more rational than in others. A confused notion of a Supreme being, and of a future state of retribution, prevails among all of them, except those, perhaps, within the arctic circle. They all believe in the immortality of souls; but they have different ideas relative to their station and employment in the other world. Some conceive, that the good are whelmed in such pleasures as suited them in this life; while all admit, that the wicked are miserable. Others again seem to believe the existence of a purgatory, or middle state, for a longer or shorter time, and then are admitted to the fruitions prevalent in the abode of the great spirit. It is common with them to bury such things with the dead as they were pleased with before their departure. They also deposit with them their tommahawks, their bows and arrows, or muskets, and some venison; for they apprehend, that the journey is long and difficult, and that, without these articles, they will suffer by the way. Some nations, indeed, bury all the property of the dead with them, without regard to their debts, or the wants of their families. The ancient Canarians deposited jars of milk and wine with their dead, as necessary provisions for their journey. And Cesar says, that the Celts, or Celtæ, who burned their dead, placed such things, and even animals, on the funeral pile, as the deceased were most delighted with.

The general receptacles of the dead are not always in the vicinity of their villages and towns. Some bury their dead immediatelty after death, and leave them in their graves till the flesh falls from the bones, and then are taken from the ground. Others place their dead on scaffolds, erected for the purpose, till their bones are in a like condition. At stated periods all their bones are collected, and scraped and cleaned with great care. The whole nation assembles to bear them to the general magazine of corruption, and this ceremony is called the feast of souls. At these periods they open the tombs of their fathers and friends, and for a while indulge their tender pity and affection. The new collection of bones is carefully deposited, and the tombs closed; after which they return to their homes.

The Indians believe in the existence of good and evil spirits, which roam, unperceived, the regions of the air; and this belief is general from Greenland to Patagonia. Hence on occasions of importance, they endeavor to deprecate the wrath of the one, and to invoke the propitious smiles of the other. This ceremony is performed by their physicians, who are also their priests or jugglers; it consists of a variety of grimaces and contortions; and in their profound reveries, they are supposed to converse with the spirits. Almost the same methods are pursued by some in the cure of those diseases, which have baffled their medical skill. The more northern Indians practice incantations and charms; while those in more temperate climates much oftener trust to the efficacy of medicinal plants. In all these occult attempts, the jugglers are expert in their tricks, and usually perform them in a naked and exposed posture. Hearne saw one pretend to swallow a bayonet, the hilt of which only appeared out of the mouth. Another made an attempt to swallow a broad piece of wood, as large as a barrel stave, and shaped like it, one end of which was exposed in the same manner. Both of them walked about among the spectators with the articles apparently in their throats; nor was it in the power of Hearne to detect the deception. The author of these sketches has seen an Osage juggler swallow an arrow, eighteen inches long, and there was no deception in this instance.

The Indians have likewise much faith in dreams, by which they pretend to the knowledge of future events; nor are they less sanguine in their prognostications, grounded on certain occurrences in their wakeful moments. An Ioway chief who accompanied the author of these sketches to the seat of government in November 1805, was possessed of a very curious kind of shell, in which he carried his tobacco. In Kentucky a citizen took a fancy to it, and requested it of him. He readily parted with it; after which he turned round, and addressed his companions thus: " I have given away my tobacco shell, " and this circumstance puts me in mind that I shall die " in a few days." Four days afterwards he expired without any apparent previous indisposition, except a hard struggle for about an hour, while in the agonies of death.

These traits sufficiently discover, that the Indians are extremely superstitious. They behold eclipses with terror, and are apt to draw the most fatal prognostics from them. Columbus foretold an eclipse to the inhabitants of one of the islands who had refused him provisions, and threatened them with destruction unless they gratified him. The eclipse happened as predicted; which so terrified the Indians, that they furnished him with the provisions he wanted. Mango Capac founded the Peruvian empire, by means of superstition; and many hundred years afterwards, when Pizarro invaded that country, the Peruvians recollected an ancient prophesy relative to their fate, and submitted without opposition. Montezuma lost his throne and kingdom in the same manner.

The Indians in general have very imperfect ideas of the rights of property. This is the reason why some particular tribes are so much given to theft. They cannot conceive, that any one has an exclusive right to the goods of providence; and therefore believe it just to supply their wants from the stores of those, who are favored with a profusion.

The southern or Mexican Indians differ in their features and complexions from those of the northern tribes; in the first place they are more feminine, and in the second much fairer. They are also more moderate in their food, and more feeble in their frames, more timid and irresolute in their dispositions; with them the fatigues of the chase are generally exchanged for the cultivation of a few plants, and the avails of their manufactures, to which they have long been attached. They are likewise more refined in their manners; not, however, from any intercourse they have had with the whites. Perhaps rigorous climates are, in some degree incompatible with refinement, and the growth of the more amiable qualities. The Indians within the arctic and antarctic circles, resemble each other in their habits and manners; and this has led some to conclude, that the difference observable among the natives in different quarters, mostly arises from the effect of climate.

A perceptible difference exists, even among our western Indians. Those who inhabit the low grounds are known to be rather under size, and of swarthy complexions; while those who inhabit and range the elevated country, are of much larger forms, and their skins are not tinged with so dark a hue. Perhaps the effect of climate is here still more manifest.

In some instances the customs of the Indians on opposite sides of the Mississippi, differ from each other

Those to the eastward of it hunt, travel, and go to war, mostly on foot; while those to the westward of that river usually kill their game, and fight their battles on horseback. These own a prodigious number of horses; some they raise, and others are obtained wild from the woods. They are rather small, but fleet and hardy, and wholly subsist on the spontaneous productions of nature. Those who fight mounted, generally resort to the open grounds; while their brethren of the east prefer impenetrable woods and recesses, and take more advantage of circumstances to surprise their enemies. Perhaps this difference of warfare may be ascribed more to the nature of the country, than to any primitive custom among them. The country in the interior of Louisiana abounds in extensive prairies, which spread over at least two thirds of it: while on the east side of the Mississippi the grounds are more undulated, more rocky, and almost wholly covered with forests, except in the neighborhood of that river, and therefore not so well calculated for the use of horses.

Hence historians and other writers are mistaken when they contend, that there is a striking similitude in the form of their bodies, and in the qualities of their minds; that their color and features are the same; that they are small eaters; and that nature has denied them beards, as likewise hair on other parts of their bodies. From these supposed general traits they infer that all the Indians on our continent may be traced to one common origin. These errors were propagated by the early Spanish writers, whose information of the Indians was not only very limited, but whose object was to degrade them below the order of human beings.

Notwithstanding some of the traits before mentioned were produced by adventitious causes; yet it requires no great knowledge of the Indians to perceive, that they are radically as dissimilar in their features, complexions, size, and language, as the various nations on the other continents. Some are remarkably large in their frames, while others cannot boast the usual stature of men; some of them possess strong intellects, while those manifested by others are much less vigorous; some are prone to war, others are more peaceable; and they as little understand the different languages among themselves, as they do those of Europe. These are national traits: Perhaps part of them may be attributed to the influence of climate; for the powers of both body and mind are much less conspicuous in warm countries than in colder ones, in low marshy districts than in mountainous regions; but some of them are unquestionably primitive. If the Spaniards found a people of weak intellect in the islands, and in the Mexican dominions, they witnessed another in Chili of very extraordinary capacities.

The Auraucanians, though not numerous, proved a match for them in bravery, and in the fertility of invention; and they remain unsubdued to this day. It has been remarked in other parts of this work, that the complexions of the Indians are by no means the same; that some tribes or nations are much fairer than others, and that even some of them have red or sandy hair. We are assured by a native of Chili in a late valuable history of that country, " that the Boroanes, who live in the " midst of the Auraucanian provinces, in the thirty ninth " degree of south latitude, are fair and ruddy, have blue " eyes, and red hair, and are as well formed as the nor- " thern Europeans." The Auraucanians have long black hair, and their complexion is of a reddish or coppery brown. " Nothing (continues the same author) appears " to me more ridiculous than the assertion of several " writers, that all the Americans resemble each other, " and that from seeing one, you are able to judge of the " whole. A Chilian is as easily distinguished from a " Peruvian, as an Italian from a German. I have seen " natives of Cujo, of Paraguay, and of the straits of

" Magellan; and I can confidently affirm, that their " countenances present a very striking difference." If those in the same quarter of the country be thus distinguishable from each other, how much greater the difference between those inhabiting the various regions and climates on the continent! A wide difference exists between a Sac and an Osage, and a still greater difference between either and an Esquimaux.

Nothing is more unfounded than the assertion, that the Indians in general are small eaters. This is probably the case with those who live in warm climates, where vegitables, and the spontaneous productions of the earth, are usually preferred to animal food. The Indians in all parts of Louisiana, as also those on the east side of the Mississippi, are known to be voracious eaters; and this truth can be illustrated by a thousand examples, one of which follows: When the author of these sketches conducted about thirty Missouri chiefs to the seat of government in 1805, as before stated, the first three hundred miles of the way was too thinly inhabited to furnish them with regular meals; so that it became necessary to purchase fresh beef for them, of which they devoured on an average, three hundred and fifty pounds per day, or nearly twelve pounds per man!

Beards are as natural to the Indians as to any other people; and nature also furnishes their bodies with the usual proportion of hair; but, like the Tartars, they pluck them out as fast as they grow, because they deem it more cleanly; and by pursuing this method for a number of years, they appear as if nature had denied them these badges of puberty. They always carry about them a small looking glass and tweezers, which are very often employed, especially when they are about to receive, or to appear among strangers. The Tunisian women follow the practice of the squaws of America.

Among the differences manifested by the various Indian nations, that of intellect is not the least. Equally without education, blessed with the light of nature only, and exposed to the same physical evils, to what shall we ascribe this inequality? That there is a very great inequality, is evident to the most superficial observer. It is well known to travellers, that those Indians, who live in genial climates, particularly in mountainous countries, are much more vigorous in body and intellect, than the inhabitants of warm climates, who inhabit a less salubrious air. This distinction is manifested in their eloquence, in their hostile preparations and in their bloody rencountres; and it is evident, from a variety of considerations, that they are much less under the influence of moral than physical impulses.

If it be supposed, as some able men actually do suppose, that they have one common origin, on what principle shall we account for the great variety of languages among them? Had the European nations, like them, remained in their barbarous state, they would have preserved their ancient dialects. This sentence, written so late as the third Henry, " *He nees othes worthe that es enes gylty of oth broken,*" may be considered as a good specimen of the English language at that day. The gradual innovations it has experienced, is ascribable to the introduction of the arts and sciences. The Indians are probably now, what they were ten centuries ago; it is even difficult to assign plausible reasons for mutations in their dialects, except we admit occasional admixtures; and these most likely are not numerous, as in general they are scrupulously cautious to preserve their own, and to oppose the introduction of foreign idioms. It will, therefore, be difficult to trace the varieties in their languages, to this source: Those the best acquainted with them, perceive a radical difference between them. An Osage and a

Shawnee understand each other no better than an English American, and a Spaniard.

Some of the most reprehensible customs of the Indians, as they are so opposite to our moral sentiments, must not be omitted in a work of this nature. They permit and sanction polygamy among them. The men are at liberty to take as many wives as they can support, but not without the approbation of the old men and chiefs. Among some nations a husband has a right to repudiate his wife, or to sell or kill her as he pleases. Among others, neither of these steps can be taken without the sanction of public authority. Adultery and fornication are viewed in different lights by different nations. Among some it is customary for the chief to present his youngest wife to his stranger guest, and if he refuses to sleep with her, it is considered as an affront. Among others, the chief presents his daughter, or some other unmarried female relation. This custom is similar to one prevailing in Abyssinia and Arabia, where a stranger of distinction sleeps with the sister, daughter, or some other female relation of his host. In some nations of Indians, adultery is punishable with death, and fornication permitted. In others, fornication is a capital offence, and adultery is practised with impunity. But in some tribes, these crimes are not regarded. Mothers and daughters have been known to grant their favors in presence of each other; and they are always ready to prostitute themselves, particularly with the whites, whenever they are able to obtain a pecuniary reward for it.

Much has been said and written on the subject of Indian eloquence. They express themselves, especially in their public speeches, in a bold figurative style; and in this particular they resemble the orientals. Their gestures, though somewhat wild and extravagant, are rather graceful than awkward. They speak from nature, and not from education. They utter what their subject inspires, and never advert to approved models as their standard. Their language is barren; and hence they are obliged to resort to metaphor, or to use much circumlocution in the expression of their sentiments. This is doubtless the practice of all illiterate nations. All languages are figurative in proportion to their barrenness; and this is more pleasing and powerful than the smooth harmony of studied periods: Art will do much, but nature much more. Perhaps a profound knowledge of Roman and Grecian literature would have obscured the genius of Shakespeare. Who at this day, except the untutored sons of nature, can utter the language of Ossian and Homer? What man, trammeled with the forms of modern art, can speak like Logan, mentioned in the notes on Virginia? The language of nature can alone arrest attention, persuade, convince, and terrify; and such is the language of the Indians. They use many figures, which have an appropriate and technical meaning; and hence those unacquainted with their eloquence are apt, either to misapprehend them, or to consider them as destitue of sense.

Many instances of the sublime might be collected from their speeches; but one specimen only must suffice. A Miami chief in 1802, set out on a visit to the president. He called on the author of these sketches, at one of our western garrisons for money and horses; but as he was not furnished with a passport, these were denied him till the pleasure of the secretary of war was known on the subject. This was soon obtained, and it proved unfavourable. The chief then made a long speech on the importance of his mission, and concluded in this manner: " If I " could only see my great father, and obtain from him one " word declaratory of justice to my nation, it would be " like the beams of the sun breaking through a cloud af-" ter a storm." Classic erudition, connot invent a more apposite and sublime sentence than this. The speeches, indeed, of all the Indian orators are generally full of shining passages, which would have been applauded in the assemblies of Greece and Rome.

There is a wide difference in the sounds of the Indian languages. Some, as spoken by the tribes on both sides the Mississippi are full of guttural sounds; others are pregnant with a disgusting monotony. Some are harmony to the ear, while others are dissonant, and extremely disagreeable. The Huron language is said to have copiousness, energy, and sublimity; that of the Algonquins to have sweetness and elegance; and that of the Sioux, though harsh, to be very expressive. These are unquestionably radical languages. The two first are spoken about the upper lakes, and extend to the western ocean. The latter is prevalent between the Mississippi and Missouri, and has been traced westward to the rocky or shining mountains.

That the Indians were once much more numerous than at present, will not admit of a doubt; and it seems hardly credible, that the destruction occasioned by wars among themselves, and with the whites, though very great, should have made such a wonderful reduction in their number. Hennipin says, that when he first visited the Mississippi, (in 1680) the Osages had seventeen villages; that the Panimahas (probably the Mahas, at this time about nine hundred miles up the Missouri) had twenty two villages, the least of which contained two hundred cottages. If these numbers be correct, they must have contained about ninety thousand souls! This nation is now reduced to less than fifteen hundred. Many other nations were equally numerous, particularly the Panaossas, Panelogas, Matotantes, and Panas. The three first nations are unknown at this time, at least by the names given them by the early writers. Marquette states that (in 1674) the Chuoanous lived on the river Ouabouskigou (the Kaskaskias) in eighty eight villages. If he means the nation at this time known by the name of the Kaskaskias, which was very powerful when the French first settled in the country, it is now reduced to about sixty persons. Many other powerful nations, who inhabited the west bank of the Mississippi, have either become extinct, or now exist in some of the more interior regions. The Arkansas have endeavored to maintain their ground; but from a numerous nation they are now reduced to a few in number, and have exchanged their proud martial spirit for the most contemptible pusillanimity. War and ardent spirits have wasted the population of our continent.

When and by whom America was first peopled, has perplexed the learned for several centuries. Conjecture, in part, must supply the place of historical facts; and by a comparison of circumstances, and from the dim lights emitted by tradition, we must approach as near the truth as possible. That the Indians have different origins, is pretty evident from the dissimilarity of their features, language, and customs. Perhaps on enquiry it may be found probable, that we are indebted to all the other continents for our population.

It is remarked by travellers and voyagers, that the inhabitants of all the islands in the oriental seas, however widely dispersed, have a greater affinity with each other, than with the people of the continent, in their manners, customs, language, and features. Columbus found the the natives of all the West India islands to resemble each other in the same particulars, except that each island had a language of its own. The same cannot be said of the Indians on the continent; the difference between them, and those of the islands, is very considerable, but not greater than that among themselves. The inference is, that their intercourse with the other continents, and the islands we have mentioned, ceased at such a remote period as to give them the appearance of a distinct people.

The nations of Europe, in the days of Julius Cesar, resembled our Indians in many particulars, perhaps even in their color. They had the same confused notions of religion; they painted their bodies; the pursuit of game was their chief active employment; their modes of war, their civil regulations, their customs and manners, were similar in most respects to those of the aborigines of America. The conquests made by the Romans, though prolific of blood, served to introduce the arts and sciences, and to extend and to embellish the sociabilities of life. Even at this day, the Tartars and Russians, the progeny of the ancient Scythians, and other northern nations, cannot well be distinguished from some American tribes. They exhibit the same modes of life. They are divided into tribes or clans, under innumerable petty chiefs; their civil polity, and their warfare, bespeak a very great resemblance to those traits manifested on our borders. From these several agreements, it is reasonable to conclude, that the relationship between the inhabitants of the old and new world, is much less problematical, and indeed much nearer than some have conceived.

It is well known that several of the ancients circumnavigated Africa. It is even said that a colony of Phenicians passed into Ireland. Certain it is, that they built Cornwall in England, and *Gadez*, or Cadiz in Spain, where they carried on a considerable commerce in tin, and other articles. The Carthaginians discovered the Canary Islands. In the time of Plutarch the Fortunate Islands were inhabited, and much celebrated for their fertility. When Columbus first visited Guadaloupe, and some other islands in the West Indies, at that time uninhabited, he found the ruins of buildings, and the fragments of ships. The Egyptians and Phenicians were the first to make discoveries by sea. The Persians before the days of Alexander, on the authority of Herodotus, fitted out vessels, which navigated the river Indus, and even passed into the Red Sea. It is highly probable, therefore, that, in a course of ages, some of the Egyptian or Phenician vessels, were driven among the islands by the trade winds, which begin a little to the southward of the straits, and continue for at least nine months in the year. Most likely the vessels in those days, were not calculated for adverse winds, the mariners little skilled in the art of navigation, and perhaps still less acquainted with the nature and duration of the trade winds. If any of them were driven westward, they never returned; and that this actually happened in the course of time, is much more than probable. It is natural to conclude, that they first landed on some of the islands; and if they afterwards committed themselves to the waves, perhaps to pass from one island to another, the same winds necessarily forced them on our continent. In some of the first voyages of the Spaniards, a small colony of negroes was found in the gulf of Darien. No doubt these Africans arrived there in small craft; and this is as credible as the voyages made by the Indians in the tropical seas, as mentioned by Cook and other navigators.

The aborigines of America unquestionably derive their origin from some other country, and the claims on this point of the other three quarters of the world are nearly equal. Perhaps in early time the four continents were much nearer to each other than at present, but have since been more widely separated by some violent shock of nature, or by the evulsion of the winds and tides.

It may be proper to add here, that many of the Indians practise the rites and ceremonies of the ancient Jews. Some of them observe the feasts of the first fruits, regularly perform ablution, and occasionally separate seven days from their women. When Magellan first discovered the southern extremity of this continent, the Indians in that quarter made the sign of the cross at their meals, and on other occasions. Cortez remarked the same thing among the Mexicans when he seized on their empire. These traits, however, if they actually existed, were probably accidental, and no inference of weight can be drawn from them.

That a colony from Wales arrived in this country in 1170, is much more than probable: But this subject requires a copious detail, and must be reserved for a separate chapter.

Many of the Indians have a confused notion of their origin; though in the course of ages their traditional accounts have become obscured, and in most instances unintelligible. The Delawares have kept a register of the time since they first established themselves on the river of their name, and it amounts to upwards of four hundred years. This was done by putting a bead of wampum on a string, kept for the purpose, every year since that period; a circumstance to prove, that the Indians have the means of computing time, and of preserving the memory of events. The keeper of the Natchez temple was once asked, whether his nation was originally of the country it then inhabited? His reply was, that the Natchez once lived to the westward, when warriors of fire came among them from towards the rising sun, in floating villages, which caused the earth to tremble; that they were bearded white men, who carried arms that darted out fire with a great noise, and killed at a great distance. When questioned relative to the origin of the Natchez, he again replied, that their ancient speech did not point out the country, but that their fathers followed the sun, and came with him from the place where he now rises; that they were a long time on their journey, and suffered extreme hardships; and that they were brought into the country without their seeking it.

This clearly favours the idea, that they were of foreign origin. The Phenicians planted colonies on the coast of Africa, and were almost the only adventurers in early times, who passed the pillars of Hercules. They, and the Natchez, resembled each other in many respects.

Both worshipped the eternal fire; the custom of scalping their enemies was common to both; and the language of the Natchez, says Du Pratz, contained many figurative and bold Syriac expressions. There is also a passage in Diodorus Siculus, which is quoted by authors to prove that America was originally peopled from Africa; and it is thus translated.

"To the west of Africa is situated a very large island, "and distant many days sail from that part of our conti- "nent. Its fertile soil is partly plain and partly moun- "tainous. The plain country is sweet and pleasant, wa- "tered every where with rivulets, and navigable rivers; "it is beautified with many gardens, planted with all kinds "of trees, and the orchards are watered with many "streams. The villages are adorned with houses built "in a magificent style, with parterres, ornamented with "arbors, and covered with flowers. To these the inha- "bitants retire during the summer to enjoy the fruits, "furnished by the country in great abundance. The "mountainous part is covered with large woods, and "with a variety of fruit trees; the vallies are watered "with rivulets, where the inhabitants find every thing "calculated to render life agreeable. In a word, the "whole island, by its fertility, and the abundance of its "springs, furnishes the inhabitants with every thing ca- "pable of flattering their wishes, and of contributing to "their health, and strength of body. By hunting they "supply themselves with an infinite number of animals; "so that in their feasts they have nothing to wish for, in "regard either to plenty or delicacy. Besides, the sea, "which surrounds the island, supplies them plentifully "with all kinds of fish, and indeed the sea in general is "very abundant. The air of the island is so temperate, "that the trees bear leaves and fruit almost the whole "year round. In a word, this island is so delicious, that "it seems rather the abode of gods than of men.

" Anciently, on account of its remote situation, it was
" altogether unknown; but it was eventually discovered
" by accident. It is well known, that, from the earliest
" ages, the Phenicians undertook long voyages in order
" to extend their commerce, and that, in consequence of
" these voyages, they established several colonies in Af-
" rica and the western parts of Europe. Every thing
" succeeded to their wish; and, as they soon became
" powerful, they passed the pillars of Hercules, and en-
" tered the ocean. In the neighborhood of these pillars,
" and on a peninsula in Spain, they built a town, which
" they called Gadez. There, among the buildings proper
" for the place, they erected a temple to Hercules, to
" whom they instituted splendid sacrifices, after the man-
" ner of their country. This temple is held in great ve-
" neration at this day, and several Romans, who have
" rendered themselves illustrious by their exploits, have
" performed their vows to Hercules for the success of
" their enterprises.

" After the Phenecians had passed the straits of Spain,
" they sailed along Africa, when, by the violence of the
" winds, they were driven out to sea, and the storm con-
" tinuing several days, they were at length thrown on this
" island. They were the first who became acquainted
" with its fertility and beauty, and therefore published
" them to other nations. The Tuscans, when they were
" masters of the sea, designed to settle a colony on this
" island; but the Carthaginians found means to frustrate
" their object. In this they were influenced by two mo-
" tives. The first was, they were fearful that their citi-
" zens, tempted by the charms of the island, would pass
" over to it, and thereby weaken their own country.
" The second was, they considered it a secure asy-
" lum, for themselves, if ever their republic should expe-
" rience any terrible disaster."

Thus much of Diodoras Siculus, the Greek historian. He was contemporary with Julius Cesar, and flourished about sixty years before the christian era. If he had not said, that the place in question was *surrounded by the sea*, we should be tempted to conclude, that it was on some part of our continent, because it contained *navigable rivers*. The vessels of the ancients, however, cannot be supposed to have much exceeded in size some of our modern row boats.

Hanno mentions an island by the name of *Cerne*, situated to the west of Africa, on which he built a fort, and established a colony. It was the depot of the Carthaginians on the south of Africa. The situation of this island is not ascertained by ancient writers, nor is it known how long the Carthaginians maintained themselves on it. Whether this is the island described by Diodorus Siculus, may admit of question. It may be proper to remark, that the Carthaginians were of Phenician origin.

It is said and believed by many, that our western regions were once inhabited by a more civilized people than the present aborigines; and as an argument in favor of it, they ask, how is it possible for illiterate savages to construct fortifications on strict mathematical principles? It must be admitted that the old fortifications in the western country, where they can be sufficiently traced and identified, manifest in their angles and other particulars, a considerable degree of skill and precision. Many of them have regular bastions, and are constructed according to the rules of art. The figures or plans of the works are various; but in whatever shape they appear, they are always suited to the nature of the ground, and calculated for the best defence. Are they not the remains of the Welsh, who are said to have passed into America more than three hundred years before the days of Columbus? They serve at least, to illustrate and to countenance that idea. The fortifications successively erected in England and Wales, by the Romans, Saxons, Danes, and Normans, must have been familiar to the Welsh in 1170, and if they ever landed on our shores, the science of attack and defence, was probably the last to escape their remembrance: Their situation doubtless exposed them to war, and frequent practice enabled them to preserve for a long time, the arts of it. They must likewise have retained the science of building for a considerable time; perhaps this was never lost till after the conquest of Mexico by the Spaniards. What the Welsh were in the twelfth century, the Mexicans were in the fifteenth and sixteenth centuries; and these circumstances, together with some others soon to be mentioned, seem to support the conclusion attempted to be drawn in the next chapter.

When Columbus visited Cuba, he was surprised to find a wall of stone, which displayed skill and durability: In 1517, Valasquez landed on the continent, within the dominions of Montezuma, and was delighted with the traits of civilization found among the natives. They had made considerable progress in the useful arts; they lived in houses of stone, and their structure manifested skill and design. This indeed was the case in all the provinces under the jurisdiction of the Mexican monarch. The same was observed by the Spaniards when they entered the city of Mexico; the natives were remote from barbarism; they were refined in their manners, intelligent, and in some degree learned. Like the ancient Egyptians, they knew with precision the annual revolution of the sun; They fixed the year at three hundred and sixty five days, nearly, and divided it into eighteen parts. Their constitution was founded on the broad basis of religion and law. Their cities displayed magnificence in architecture, and opulence in their decorations. The palace of Montezuma had thirty gates, which communicated with as many streets. The front was composed of red, black, and white jasper, beautifully polished; and in a large shield over the gate were represented the arms of Montezuma, "*A Griffin with expanded wings, holding* "*a Tyger in its talons!*"

That an aboriginal king or chief, should have a regular coat of arms, appears rather singular; and it must be left to the learned to determine the origin of the one just mentioned. It may be proper, however, to remark, that coats of arms were used by the great in the early times of Europe, and that they, as well as crosses, served for signatures before writing became prevalent. There is the more ground to believe, that the one of Montezuma was of European origin, as the Mexicans reported, and the report was confirmed by him, that their rulers were descended from a STRANGE nation, which came among them from a *distant* country.

M. de Guignes is of opinion, that the Chinese in the seventh century extended their trafic to the north west coast of America, particularly as the promontory of Kamskatka, under the name of Ta-Shan, is mentioned in their books of travels. It is also said that California was known to them, because the Spaniards, when they first visited that part of the country, found the wrecks of Chinese vessels on various parts of the coast.

And Barrow says, that the natives of Brazil resemble the Chinese in their features, particularly in the conformation of the eye. The natives of Chili have a tradition among them, that some of their ancestors came from the west, perhaps from the south of Asia, and there are those who perceive evident traces of Maylayan and other Asiatic dialects, among them, as well as among the inhabitants of the islands in the Indian and Pacific oceans. One author has discovered upwards of twenty greek and latin words in the Auraucanian language, which is common to Chili.

It is admitted that Greenland was settled as early as 982, some say by the Norwegians; others by a colony from Ireland or England, as they were christians, and had among them some Irish books, bells and crosiers. Greenland is separated from America by a narrow strait only, nor is it certainly known that any such separation exists.

The north of Asia and America are divided by a strait of about forty miles in breadth; and the Indians in that quarter have a tradition among them, that, about two hundred years ago, this strait was much less dilitated than at present, and that the natives at low tides, were able to walk from one continent to the other.

It is now well known, that a chain of islands extends along the intermediate tract, over the Atlantic, between the coasts of Brazil and Africa, a distance of about fifteen hundred miles; and that another chain extends from some other parts of South America, across the ocean, to southern Asia. These islands are mostly inhabited; and who will venture to say, that they were not in former time much larger, and more numerous, than at present? Who is ready to pronounce, that an easy communication did not once exist between them and the continents? And lastly, who will deny the probability, that in ancient time the four continents were less divided from each other than they now appear to be?

It is therefore likely, that America derived its population from various sources; partly from the north and south of Asia; partly from Africa; and partly from the north, and perhaps from some other regions of Europe. The features, manners, and customs of the Indians, seem to resemble in many respects, those displayed on the other continents, the most contiguous to them; and certain it is, that they have several primitive languages among them.*
The Esquimaux and Greenlanders, exhibit the features

---

*INCA, among many tribes in Louisiana, is the word for father or chief.

and manners of the Laplanders of Europe, and the Samoides of Asia. Many animals are likewise common to America and Asia; the buffaloe of the former is the bison of the latter.

The exertions formerly made to civilize and christianize the Indians, produced no good effects. This was more owing to the wrong methods pursued, than to the untractable dispositions of the natives. The first settlers of New England, made great efforts to propagate their religion among the Indians; but they labored in vain. When Dartmouth college was founded by royal charter, in 1769, provision was made for the education and instruction of Indian youth. Several have been admitted to that seminary; but the moment they were liberated from it, they assumed the mode of living practised by their nations or tribes; and the knowledge they obtained served only to give them a keener relish for vice, and to enable them the more readily to invent ingenious expedients to gratify their propensities. In former times the French missionaries in Canada, and along the Mississippi, obtained and preserved an influence over the Indians, and persuaded many of them to embrace the catholic religion. The only permanent effect these missions had, was to reconcile the Indians to the French. In other respects they were more vicious and dishonest than those less acquainted with religion and civilization. Even to this day the French have an almost unbounded influence over them. The Indians still remember and speak of the old French government in Louisiana, and manifest a strong attachment to it. The French have been less at war with them, than either the English or Spaniards. Their mode of life, the long intercourse, and many intermarriages between them, have established a reciprocal friendship, and they consider each other as brethren. The house of a Frenchman is always open to an Indian, and they are ever ready to supply the wants of each other.

There is a striking difference between those Indians, who live in the neighborhood of the whites, and those who reside at a distance from them. The former, especially if accustomed to a long intercourse, have wonderfully degenerated. They have gradually imbibed all the vices of the whites, and forgotten their own virtues. They are drunkards and thieves, and act on all occasions with the most consummate duplicity. The traders and others, who are obliged to visit them, and to reside among them, never feel themselves safe, though they take the precaution to have their stores and dwellings strongly stockaded.

Traders are obliged to credit out their goods among them in winter, and wait till spring for their pay. It is usual for one or two chiefs to become responsible for the payment; but notwithstanding this, particularly in seasons unfavorable for the acquisition of skins and furs, many of the Indians cannot discharge their debts; others refuse to make any payment at all. Nothing so much offends an Indian as to be requested to pay his old debts. " If, says he, I deliver you my peltries to pay for the " goods I received last season, my family must suffer, and " perhaps starve."

The Indians who live at a distance from the whites, yield to the same principle, and for the same reason; but in other respects, they generally conduct themselves uprightly. If by accident any property of a stranger falls into their hands, they preserve it with the greatest care, and when an opportunity offers, readily restore it to the owner. Among them we discover the genuine simplicity of nature. Their countenances are noble, indicative of health, cheerfulness, hospitality, and friendship. When a white, especially one of note, arrives in their towns, he is received with marked attention. He is bidden welcome to every cabin, and each is emulous to have him for a guest, though in this particular the principal chief generally claims a priority of right. These Indians are large, and infinitely more active than those in the neighborhood of the whites. When employed on any particular business, they seldom prove treacherous; and to serve their employer they will encounter the greatest hardships. Their manners are simple, modest, and inoffensive; though when abused, and awakened to anger, they are not readily appeased.

As most of them believe in the existence of a supreme being, they easily comprehend the nature of an oath, some of the Missouri Indians when called to testify, *swear by the great spirit above, and by the earth beneath.* They are obstinately attached to their own religious opinions; and to depart from them would, in their view, trouble the repose of their fathers. In 1804, a pious christian in Philadelphia presented a large bible to a Missouri chief, and told him, that it contained the only true religion. The chief made him this acknowledgment: " Brother, I ac-
" cept of your book, because you offer it to me, and because
" the pictures in it will please my children and people.
" But I cannot promise to utter your words to them, or to
" explain to them your religion. We have a very good
" religion already, which our fathers handed down to us.
" We all believe in it, and it makes us happy and united.
" Now, were I to explain your religion to my people, per-
" haps some might be so foolish as to embrace it, which
" would create disputes and quarrels. Now a religion,
" which produces quarrels, and makes men unhappy, can-
" not be a good religion."—This is the language of nature; and were it adopted as a substitute for the fiery zeal of enthusiasts, perhaps mankind would be less disposed to disturb the peace of each other.

Few of the interior nations have any knowledge of ardent spirits, and it is not for the interest of the traders to carry any among them. In 1804, when a party of them was at St. Louis, one of them, on a visit among his acquaintance about the town, was persuaded to drink some spirits, which intoxicated him. On his return to his companions, he was supposed to be in a fit of madness, and therefore was seized, and tied fast to the ground all night: The next day, when the cause of his madness was known, the chief made a serious complaint to the civil authority, and demanded, that he who had misbehaved to one of his people should be punished. We are informed by Ulloa, that formerly inebriating liquors were carried among the Indians in Chili, which rendered them lazy and debauched, and precipitated them into crimes. This practice was finally abolished by the government; so that the Indians soon resumed their former habits of honesty, sobriety, and industry. A trader now is seldom defrauded; though he suddenly distributes all his goods among them in proportion to their wants, and means of payment; then gives them notice of the time of his intended departure, which seldom exceeds ten days, when all of them cheerfully cancel their debts agreeably to contract.

To judge from the past, we may safely pronounce, that all attempts to civilize and christianize the Indians on the principles formerly established, are illusive, and pregnant with evil. Instead of changing their moral or metaphysical sentiments and prejudices, we must change their occupations and modes of life, and then the end we have in view will result of course. But this important change, however desirable, can extend only to those nations, who are contiguous to the whites, and who can no longer subsist by the chase. They are better able to feel than to reason, and many of them already experience the want of game. If by this experience they can be made fully sensible of their wants, no doubt their attention will be drawn to agriculture and household manufactures, their natures in a manner changed, and their dispositions deprived of their ferocious qualities. The remains of the ancient Indians in some of our populous states, may be adduced in support of this declaration. Although they are incorrigible drunkards, yet they live in harmony among themselves, and with the whites, and their savage natures have long since left them. Nearly a century ago the Jesuits obtained permission to christianize the Indians in Paraguay, independent of the civil power, and no Spaniard or other white man was allowed to visit them without the consent of the fathers. The great object of these spiritual leaders was to change the occupations of the Indians, and to make them acquainted with agriculture, and the amenities of social life. They at first gathered into one place about fifty families; accessions were gradually made to their empire, and in the end, the amazing number of three hundred and forty thousand families were collected into towns and cities! The policy of the fathers was of a masterly kind. They unfolded to the Indians some of the plainest precepts of religion and morality; such indeed, and such only, as were of a practical nature, and easily comprehended. They explained to them the benefits of agriculture, manufactures, and an interior commerce. This vast number of Indians in a short time resembled the Europeans in their dress and pursuits, and many of them aspired to the elegant arts. The fathers infused a military spirit among them; they made them acquainted with the modern art of war, rendered them obedient to their officers, and subdued them to strict discipline. By these means an army of sixty thousand men was formed, armed after the European manner; and it more than once proved the salvation of the Spanish provinces in the south.

What these Jesuits actually accomplished in Paraguay, our government has attempted in part in the United States; and it is expected, that success will result from the measures in operation. The Creeks, Cherokees, Choctaws, Chickasaws, and some other nations within our jurisdiction, have already resorted to agriculture, and to the manufacture of many indispensable articles. Some of them have deserted their towns, planted themselves along the public roads, procured slaves, and turned their attention to the tillage of their fields, and the other usual occupations of husbandmen. Game is scarce among them; and they reflect with surprise on the little labor necessary to secure them from want, and even to increase their wealth: When they followed the chase, their subsistence was precarious, and this alone consisted of wild meat. They now raise poultry, corn, and garden vegetables in abundance. They also raise plenty of cattle and swine; so that many of them are real farmers, and seldom resort to the chase, except to supply themselves occasionally with skins for family use. Travellers find good entertainment among them; much better indeed than among the whites on the frontiers.

This change of life has a tendency to wipe away their savage manners, to restore them to the dignity of human nature, and to make them useful to themselves, and to the world. But this change, to be complete and permanent, must be gradual; it must be the effect of a steady policy. The Indians resemble children at school, whose manners must be formed before they can be graceful; they must become acquainted with language before they can understand the force of it; with the rudiments of science before they can attain to science itself.

The United States, however, will never fully realize their expectations, unless they review their present system of Indian intercourse, and provide some new remedies for the evils incident to it. The importance of the subject will authorize the cursory remarks we are about to make.

We certainly have it in view to improve the condition of the Indians; not simply from motives of charity and friendship to them, but from motives of security to ourselves; by obtaining a control over them, and rendering them dependant, we lessen the prospects of war. Other important advantages would result from it, and we are urged by many public considerations to extend and perfect the system we have adopted. The greatest obstacle to our success arises from the intercourse, which subsists and is carried on between the Indians, and the English and Spaniards; and until this be removed, the success of our exertions will be, in a great degree, partial and limited. Foreign traders of this description introduce themselves into our territory on the Mississippi, Missouri, and Red river; and perhaps it will be found on examination, that their trade may be greatly restricted, if not wholly interdicted.

The English of Canada visit the Indians about the source of the Mississippi, and also those high up on the Missouri, by means of lake Superior, and the waters connected with it. Perhaps it is not in our power wholly to prevent this intercourse; and indeed it is of the less importance, as the Indians with whom the English carry on a trade in those quarters, are too remote from our settlements to have any immediate or permanent connexion with us, or to afford us any trouble, except what results from the murders and depredations committed on our mercantile adventurers. The English likewise trafic on the Mississippi, and its tributary streams, below the falls of St. Anthony; and also on the Missouri, about the river Platte; and in the trade carried on at these two points, the United States are deeply interested. If they have a right to trade with the Indians in our territory on the east side of the Mississippi, and even to navigate that river, they cannot on any just pretence extend that trade to the Indians of Louisiana. The United States will find it necessary to prohibit this trade, and happily they possess the means of doing it with effect.

The Canadian traders, who visit this part of the Mississippi, are obliged to pass over lake Michigan. This lake affords only two communications with that river.

One of them is down the Illinois; but the most eligible one, and that most generally used, is by way of the Ouisconsing. The first joins the Mississippi about eighteen miles above the mouth of the Missouri, and the second about five hundred and eighty two miles still higher up. Each of these communications is obstructed by a short portage, except in the wet season, when the waters of lake Michigan mingle with those of the Illinois by means of the Chicago, at the mouth of which we have a garrison. The portage between the Ouisconsing, and Fox river, which flows into lake Michigan, is three miles.

These traders, in passing from lake Michigan, seldom descend the Illinois; because almost the only Indians below the Ouisconsing, and indeed below the falls of St. Anthony, are the Ioways, Sacs, and Foxes, who live on and near the river *Des moins*, in the neighborhood of whom we have lately established a factory and garrison. They will, therefore communicate with the Mississippi by way of the Ouisconsing, near the mouth of which they many years ago erected a small village called *Prairie des Chiens*, where they rendezvous at certain seasons, despatch their merchandize in various directions, but mostly up the river St. Pierre, and where also they ultimately receive the returns of them. The Sacs and Foxes ceded to the United States in 1804, a tract of land opposite to the mouth of the Ouisconsing, and on the right bank of the Mississippi, under an expectation, that a garrison and factory would be erected on it. This and *Prairie des Chiens* afford admirable sites for establishments of this nature; but neither of them would be fully sufficient to turn the current of trade, so long as the English are permitted to navigate the Mississippi. They would enter the river St. Pierre, the mouth of which is just below the falls of St. Anthony, in about forty four degrees north latitude, on whose banks are many bands of Indians, particularly the Naudowessies, and some others of the Scioux nation, whose trade is considerable. Some parts of the St. Pierre approach the waters of the Missouri; so that the English traders transport their goods to the latter with expedition and ease. An establishment, therefore, at the mouth of the St. Pierre would effectually destroy the English trade in this quarter: If foreign traders were excluded from that river, they would find it for their interest to abandon the country; because this affords the only communication with the Indians of Louisiana, inhabiting the country between St. Louis and the falls of St. Anthony, except the Missouri and river *Des moins;* and these are already sufficiently guarded. The mouth of the St. Pierre is about eight hundred and eighty five miles above the confluence of the Missouri and Mississippi, where the United States already own a considerable tract of land, which was voluntarily given them by the Indians.

The plan, however, just suggested, is attended with one difficulty, which is not easily surmounted. Many of those whom we denominate English traders, are invested with the rights and privileges of citizens of the United States, either by virtue of the treaty of 1783, or by subsequent naturalization. The merchants of Canada, to remove every obstacle to their intercourse with the Indians on the Mississippi, either formed connections, many years ago, with some of our citizens, or sent their clerks and others, in whom they could confide, to reside at Michilimakinak, within our jurisdiction. These are the English traders, of whom we speak; and the trade they carry on is ostensibly for themselves, though the interest they have in it, is really no other than that of agents or partners. At any rate, they derive all their supplies from English subjects, who are supposed, and not without foundation, to be almost exclusively benefited by their labor and enterprise. The duties paid at our custom-house on the Indian goods imported from Canada are of no value, when compared with the evils inflicted by this meretricious commerce. 'Taking into view the preceding circumstances, perhaps the only way to counteract or destroy it on the Mississippi, is to prohibit the importation of merchandize from the British provinces. This would probably inflict a temporary injury on some of our legitimate traders, particularly as they find it convenient to purchase their goods in Canada, where also they find the most ready and profitable market for their peltries. But as long as this intercourse is permitted, we have reason to conclude, that our views relative to the Indians will in a great measure be frustrated. Another conclusion is evident, that any competition in the Indian trade, either by our citizens, or by the United States, while they have the English for their competitors, cannot fail to terminate to their disadvantage: Yet a garrison and factory at the mouth of the St. Pierre, even if the Canadian trade was not prohibited on that river, would be of great public utility; because, in addition to the supplies we should be able to furnish the Indians, such an establishment would serve to restrain their depredations, and to render the intercourse of foreigners less pernicious.*

The English traders not only traffic with the Indians about the shining mountains, but they have extended it to the Mandans on the Missouri, and to several other tribes both above and below them. The Spaniards also from Santa Fé occasionally traffic with the Indians about the

---

* The Sacs, Foxes, and Iowas, have recently turned much of their attention to the manufacture of lead. In 1810 they procured four hundred thousand pounds of this article, which they exchanged for goods at our factories, or sold to our traders. The lead mines above them in the vicinity of the Scioux, and other tribes, are equally abundant. The manufacture of lead will probably become general among them, especially as they find it much more profitable than the chase. Such an occurrence would induce the Canadian traders to abandon the country; with them, in a commercial point of view, lead is of no importance.

waters of the Kansas, as likewise with those on the river Platte. These, and some others between them and the Mandans, stand in need of supplies, and they are able to furnish in return a vast quantity of valuable skins and furs. It is believed by good judges, that their trade, if once secured, would be more productive than that of all the other Indians, with whom we are connected. This renders it probable, that we should be more than indemnified for the extraordinary expenses of an establishment in that quarter; and such indeed are the advantages to be justly expected from it, that we ought to hazard the experiment.

The mouth of the river Platte seems to be a central position, both as to territory and Indian population; and in other respects it affords an eligible place for a garrison and factory. This is about six hundred and thirty miles above the mouth of the Missouri, according to the course of the river, and in north latitude forty degrees fifty four minutes. The Indians in this quarter procure merchandize both from the English and Spaniards, and in some instances from our own traders.

The garrison and factory recently established on the Missouri, is about three hundred and twenty five miles up that river, and just below the Kansas river. This establishment is too remote from the Indians on the river Platte to be of any material advantage to them; yet it is calculated to accommodate the Osages, as also occasional hunting parties from the east side of the Mississippi, and in some measure to obstruct the Canadian trade by way of the river St. Pierre; it is likewise of importance in several other points of view.

It is apprehended, that the factory at Nachitoches on Red river is of little importance to the United States, both in a pecuniary point of view, and as it relates to the convenience of the Indians. No nation or tribe rendezvous at that place, except the small band of Caddoques, and most of the peltries procured even by them are either disposed of to the upper settlers, or to the traders, who occasionally visit them. The Indians about the upper part of Red river, and between that and the Arkansas, find it convenient to carry their peltries to the Spanish settlements. Hence it happens, that the trade carried on by the factory at Nachitoches is almost wholly confined to straggling parties of Chickasaws and Choctaws, and to some parties belonging to nations or bands near the gulf in the Spanish province of Texas. An establishment made at such a distance from the Indian villages, and also from their hunting grounds, cannot be very profitable ; nor can it have any other tendency than to involve us in expense, and to increase the depravity of the Indians. Even the rations issued to them at Nachitoches authorize a considerable deduction from whatever profits may accrue from their trade. These, and other considerations, warn us to assume a new position.

All circumstances considered, perhaps the most eligible place for a garrison and factory is on the left bank of Red river in about north latitude thirty three degrees, which forms the divisional line between the territories of Orleans and Louisiana. The only obstruction to the navigation of the river is the great raft ; but in seasons of high water a good channel exists round it by means of bayous and lakes, connected with each other, and with the main stream ; and indeed it would require no great effort to remove such parts of the raft itself as at all times to afford a free communication. The Indians, who are now obliged to trade at Nachitoches, would be equally well, and perhaps better supplied at the proposed factory. In addition to this, the Pawnes * and Ietans, and some other Indians high up on Red river, and to the south west of it, might also obtain supplies from us, and thereby be pre-

* These are a different people from those of the same name on the river Platte.

vailed on to break their connexion with the Spaniards. The
Pawnes pursue no other game than the buffaloe, of which
they kill an immense number. They, however, attend to
agriculture, and raise more than double the quantity of
corn and vegetables than is necessary for their own consumption, and furnish their neighbors with the surplus in
exchange for peltries; so that their trade, which is now
engrossed by the Spaniards, is deemed of considerable
value. A very little exertion on our part would enable us
to secure not only this, but nearly the whole of the Indian
trade on and near Red river, particularly as we can afford greater supplies, and at a much cheaper rate, than
any of our Spanish neighbors. The Indians would soon
perceive the difference, and be induced to abandon their
former connexions, and to shield themselves under the protection of the United States.

The preceding remarks are mostly predicated on the
idea of profit. Other considerations of much greater
weight urge us to fix our trading establishments, protected by a competent number of troops, more in the vicinity
of the Indian villages, and at a distance from our population. The custom of inviting the Indians to some of our
large villages to receive their annuities, and to trade at our
factories, is extremely pernicious to them, and detrimental to the whites. While they remain among us, they are
exposed to temptations, which they cannot resist. Their
love of ardent spirits is well known; and they will gratify
this propensity at the expense of their present and future
good. Unfortunately, many of our citizens contribute to
their destruction, by an open evasion or violation of the
laws. The scenes of intoxication witnessed in most of
our frontier towns, furnish evidence of this melancholy
truth. The Indians readily part with their goods, and e-
ven with their ammunition, for ardent spirits. Their
drunkenness terminates only with the means of it. They
generally return to their homes without clothing for them-

selves or families, and without the necessary supplies of powder and lead. The privations they suffer in consequence of receiving their annuities and other goods in our settlements, are of a serious nature, and demand our interposition. Our citizens are often disturbed by their drunken revels, particularly those at Nachitoches, where the troops are frequently summoned to repress the riots and disorders occasioned by them. The only apparent remedy to these evils, is to remove the causes of them. Were our factories placed more immediately in the vicinity of the Indians, or at least in positions less accessible to the whites, our trade would be more profitable, the Indians more copiously supplied, their industry stimulated, and the avails of it more readily appropriated to the relief of themselves and families. This too would tend to facilitate the introduction of agriculture and manufactures among them, to excite their indifference to the English and Spaniards, and to make them friendly to the United States. No doubt the establishments recently made near the river *Des moins*, and on the Missouri, are parts of a comprehensive system, intended to afford security to our frontiers, and to improve the condition of the Indians. These objects will be attained with the less difficulty the further we extend our intercourse up Red river, the Missouri, and the Mississippi.

The effects of such extended arrangements would be sensibly felt. A competition at this time exists between our own and the Canadian traders on the Mississippi. The latter, in conjunction with those of the Spaniards, also contest the Indian trade with us on some parts of the Missouri; and the trade on Red river is almost exclusively possessed by our Mexican neighbors. These competitions are unfavorable to us; and the consequences of our neglect and inattention will become more serious the longer we delay to provide against them. The intercourse now carried on by the English and Spaniards with the Indians in our territory if suffered to continue, will become more firmly fixed, frequent, and extensive. Their influence, even at this time, is so considerable as to render the Indians unfriendly towards us: Our traders are sometimes murdered; often driven from their pursuits, and robbed of their property. If this influence be not counteracted, one effect will be, that numerous depredations will be committed on our frontiers, at least on our mercantile adventurers, which are the usual precursors of Indian hostility. A second effect will be, that we shall be wholly excluded from the upper parts of Red river, the Missouri, and the head waters of the Mississippi; for if the English and Spaniards once obtain the power, they will unquestionably prevail on the Indians to forbid us the navigation of those rivers; they have already made the attempt, and the Indians have been threatened with punishment for their seeming hesitation. A third, and a much more important effect will be, that the English and Spaniards will raise pretensions to the country about the heads of our great rivers, and these will be powerfully supported by the auxiliary aids of the Indians. Should such a crisis ever occur, and such a crisis is extremely probable, it will be difficult, and perhaps impossible, for us to adjust, and to maintain our territorial rights, or to guard our extensive frontiers against the hostile and bloody incursions of our predatory neighbors.

There is no position more true than this, that the Indians will readily yield their exclusive friendship to those whose power they dread, and who supply them the most liberally with goods, and on the best terms. Another position equally true is, that those who possess their friendship have it in their power to stimulate them to acts of aggression, or to give their dispositions and exertions any direction they please. This power, at present, is in some measure possessed by the English and Spaniards, and they endeavor to exercise it in a manner the best suited to their interests. The establishment of three or four additional garrisons and factories at the places we have mentioned, would probably transfer the same power into the hands of the United States, and effectually extinguish the rivalship and competition already noticed. It would also enable us the more easily to maintain our territorial rights, not simply by the advantages of actual possession, but by the assistance of the Indians. Besides, such a power in our hands would serve to weaken the expectations of the English and Spaniards, and probably induce them to abandon their pretensions without a struggle.

Other favorable consequences would result from such establishments. We should be able to introduce agriculture, and some of the household arts, among those Indians the most destitute of game; to make them acquainted with new and more convenient modes of life, calculated to mitigate the evils of their condition, to soften their manners, and the ferocity of their minds. Establishments on any of the great rivers would probably draw after them a considerable population, which would ultimately contribute to their support, and in other respects prove beneficial to the public. The Spaniards already carry considerable quantities of specie to Nachitoches, as also to the mouth of the river Platte on the Missouri, where they occasionally meet our traders, and exchange it with them for merchandize. Perhaps it would be good policy to encourage this traffic, particularly on the Missouri, and an establishment in that quarter would be likely to favor it. Upper Louisiana is nearly destitute of a circulating medium, and a moderate influx of specie from Santa Fè would be of advantage to it.

If, however, public factories among the more distant Indians be considered as drawing after them considerable expense, without the prospect of an adequate remuneration, perhaps nearly the same ends may be answered by instituting or tolerating trading companies. It would be impolitic for both to exist at the same time, in the same quarter; because these would produce an unprofitable competition, and the latter would ultimately prevail. They would disperse their merchandize over a wide extent of country, deposit it at all the Indian hunting camps, and by these means secure nearly all their trade. It would be better policy to encourage our traders to contend with those of Canada and the Spanish provinces, provided the latter be permitted to enter our territory; and were this trade carried on in the vicinity of our garrisons, no doubt the former would triumph over their rivals. These garrisons would repress the pyratic depredations of the Indians, and sufficiently bridle the unfriendly designs of the English and Spanish traders.

Grateful it is to the feelings of the philanthropist, and philosopher, to contemplate the improvements already made among the aborigines of our country, and to behold in prospect their final emancipation from the chains of ignorance and barbarity. The time, perhaps, is not remote, when this prospect will be realized; when moral philosophy and the arts will find a habitation in our western regions; when populous towns and cities will adorn the margins of our interior rivers and lakes; and when man shall no longer be the enemy of man.

The continued and augmented exertions of government will be necessary to assure these valuable effects. The vigorous and enlightened policy now in operation is calculated, if steadily pursued, to draw the attention of the Indians to the products of manual labor; and indeed this is the pivot on which rests the fate of our measures. To till the ground is odious to most of them. Labor of this kind imposes more restraint than is consistent with the turn of their minds. The French in early time took some of their children, and taught them the habits of industry; but no sooner were they able to discover a difference between their condition and that of their kindred, than they fled to the woods. The Tartars possess the same ideas of life. They conceive it a punishment to be confined to any particular village or district, or to be obliged to labor in the field for their support. The quantum of game among the Indians, who live in the vicinity of the whites, evidently decreases; but this is not sufficient of itself to alter their modes of life. Ancient prejudices and habits will still continue to govern them, unless they be convinced, by proofs adapted to their senses, that a change would be productive of advantages.

Many intelligent men are of opinion, that the gradual dimunition of game will precipitate our neighboring Indians to the wild regions of Louisiana. Two reasons may be urged against this opinion. In the first place, most of the hunting grounds on the west side of the Mississippi are claimed and occupied; so that were our more eastern Indians to enter on them, it would be considered as an act of aggression, and a war would probably ensue. They have sufficient foresight to calculate on such a result, and this will induce them to be extremely cautious in their movements. If such a movement be for the interest of the United States, it must be carried into effect under the auspices of the government. In the second place, the Indians are much more attached to their ancient districts and villages than is commonly supposed. Their veneration for the tombs of their fathers and friends, would induce them to suffer the greatest hardships rather than abandon these precious and pious remains. It may also be added, that these Indians gradually incline to agriculture, and the longer they pursue it, the less disposed will they be to hazard a removal to unknown regions.

It is difficult to relieve the Indians from two of the greatest scourges of the human race, war among themselves, and the use of ardent spirits. Perhaps these fatal propensities proceed less from their nature than from their peculiar situation.

An opinion prevails among them, that a nation is respected in proportion to the bravery of its warriors. With them the art of war is cultivated and preserved by experiment only. The chiefs of some of the nations in Louisiana have often expressed their regret to the author of these sketches, that their young men were arriving at manhood, and had no knowledge of war, and that it was necessary, for their instruction, to provoke hostilities. They also assigned their want of qualified chiefs as another reason in favor of war. It is a maxim with them to raise those to the rank of chiefs, who have most distinguished themselves in the stratagems of the field, or procured the greatest number of scalps. Perhaps those, with whom we have an established intercourse are so much under our control, as to enable us to appease their occasional differences.

Wise and salutary measures are devised by our laws to prevent the sale of ardent spirits to Indians; and it is extremely unfortunate that they are infracted with impunity. Under the Spanish government, a drunken Indian was seldom seen in the villages of Louisiana. The sale of ardent spirits to Indians and slaves was prohibited under severe penalties, and offenders had it not in their power to elude them. They were fined twenty five dollars for the first offence; fifty dollars for the second; and for the third they were sent to the capital, to be disposed of by the supreme tribunal of justice. No sooner were we in possession of the territory than the people either considered themselves liberated from all legal restraint, or they found it practicable to evade the laws of their country.

The habit of intoxication, like that of war, as we have already hinted, mostly results from their situation and pursuits. While engaged in the chase, or in a contest with their enemies, they are patient, temperate, hardy, and active; but when exempted from laborious exercises, they are almost destitute of entity; a fatal languor seizes them; their minds are inert; they experience a kind of intellectual vacuum; and hence they resort to the inflammable potion. They do not discern, that the remedy is more pernicious than the disease, and it is useless to reason with them on the subject. When the cause of intemperance be removed, a reformation may be expected.

SKETCHES OF LOUISIANA.

CHAPTER XVII.

A WELSH NATION IN AMERICA.

IT has long been a subject of enquiry, whether some part of this continent was not peopled from Wales. Authorities, indeed, are not wanting to prove their migration from that country more than three hundred years before the days of Columbus, and also their existence in America during the two last centuries. Their migration is recorded by three Welsh historians or bards, and the existence of one or more Welsh colonies among us is attested by various transient persons, on whom we are usually obliged to depend for such discoveries. It is morally impossible, that such a chain of testimony, as will soon be adduced, should be fabricated; nor can any reasonable motive be assigned for attempts to deceive the world by relations founded in fraud and imposture, particularly by so many different persons, and at such distant periods of time from each other.

Many of the learned, both in Europe and Ameicra, have endeavored to trace the origin of the aboriginals of our country. Some are of opinion, that they sprung from Asia, some from Africa, and others from the north of Europe. Perhaps they derive their origins from all of them; and why is it not as likely, that Wales furnished a population for America as some of the countries just named, particularly Africa, and the north of Europe? If the Phenicians or Carthaginians from Africa, or some of the rude nations from the north of Europe, ever planted colonies on our coasts, it was probably more owing to some unfortunate occurrences than design. It is indeed likely, that the Romans had some confused notions of the discoveries of the former people in the Atlantic, and that they imparted their knowledge on this subject to the Britons after they had made permanent establishments among them. The paucity of history furnishes no argument in favor of a contrary doctrine; the Welsh had few or no writers in the time of the Romans, and therefore were unable to hand down a history of events to posterity. Even so late as the days of Alfred, the clergy were unacquainted with Latin, and none of his lay subjects could either read or write; yet literature in those times was much more prevalent in England than in Wales.

The Welsh had as powerful motives for colonization as any other people. These ancient Britons have been celebrated for their bravery, and for the noble stand they made against several successive invaders. When the Romans laid waste the provinces of England by fire and sword, and resistance became vain, a portion of the inhabitants retired to the mountains of Wales, where they in some measure retained their liberty, though part of their country was bridled by garrisons. The Saxons and Danes inflicted the same injuries on the Welsh, and the former conquered two of their counties. Henry the first, in 1112, planted a strong colony of Flemings on the frontiers of Wales, as a barrier to England. He was succeeded by a prince of great military talents, and of powerful resources, under whose reign this migration of the Welsh is said to have happened, and during the long period he was seated on the throne, the Welsh trembled for their safety. But the conquest of Ireland, and other events of importance, most probably diverted the attention of Henry the second from an invasion of the last refuge of British liberty. Indeed the kings of the Norman race, were much more troublesome to Wales than their predecessors; and this country was often the theatre of bloody conflicts, till at last it was reduced to submission.

Besides, Wales was generally governed by a number of petty princes, and their interests or ambition frequently produced destructive wars between them. Invaded from without, and convulsed within, the Welsh had strong motives to abandon their country, and to hazard their lives in pursuit of another, especially at a time when they had nearly lost all hopes of maintaining their liberties. They were probably unacquainted with the difficulties they had to encounter; and the ordinary ones across the ocean from Wales are not much greater than those from Africa, and much less than those usually experienced from the north of Europe.

At any rate the subject is curious, and deserves investigation; and we shall now proceed to collect and arrange such materials as appear to throw the most light on it. Many of these materials have been already published at various times; but they seem not to have excited the attention which is due to their importance.

In the history of Wales, written by Caradoc, in the Welsh language, translated into English by Llwyd, and published by Dr. David Powel, in 1584, the voyages of Madoc, a Welsh prince, in 1170, are particularly related. On the death of Owen Gwyneth, prince of North Wales, his sons quarrelled about the succession. After stating the particulars of this quarrel, the historian proceeds thus:——

"MADOC, another of Owen Gwyneth his sonnes, left the land in contention betwixt his brethren, and prepared certain shipps, with men and munition, and sought adventures by seas, sailing west, and leaving the coast of Ireland so farre north, that he came to land unknown, where he saw many strange things. This land must needs be some part of that country, of which the Spanyards affirme themselves to be the first founders since Haunoes time; for, by reason and order of cosmographie, this land to which Madoc came, must needs be some part of Nova Hispania, or Florida.* Whereupon it is manifest that that country was long before by Bretons discovered, afore either Columbus or Americus Vesputius led any Spanyard thither. Of the voyage and return of Madoc there be many fables fained, as the common people do use in distance of place and length of time, rather to augment than diminish; but sure it is that there he was. And after he had returned home, and declared the pleasant and fruitfulle countryes that he had seen without inhabitants, and upon the contrary part, for what barren and wilde ground his brethren and nephues did murther one another, he prepared a number of shipps, and got with him such men and women as were desirous to live in quietnesse, and taking leave of his friends, took his journey thitherward again. There-

---

* At this period all North America was known by the name of Florida.

A WELSH NATION IN AMERICA.

" fore it was to be presupposed, that he and his people
" inhabited part of those countryes; for it appeareth by
" Francis Lopez de Gomara, that in Acuzamil, and other
" places, the people honoreth the crosse: Whereby it may
" be gathered, that christians had been there before the
" coming of the Spanyards. But because this people
" were not many, they followed the manners of the land,
" and used the language found there. This Madoc ariv-
" ing in the countrey, into the which he came in the year
" 1170, left most of his people there, and returning back
" for more of his own nation, acquaintance, and friends
" to inhabit that fayre and large countrey, went thither a-
" gain with ten sails, as I find noted by Gutyn Owen. I
" am of opinion that the land whereunto he came was
" some part of Mexico. The causes which make me to
" think so, be these. 1 The common report of the inha-
" bitants of that countrey, which affirme that theyr rulers
" descended from a strange nation that came thither from
" a farre countrey: which thing is confessed by Montezu-
" ma, king of that countrey, in an oration made for qui-
" eting his people, at his submission to the king of Cas-
" tile, Hernando Cortez being present, which is laid down
" in the Spanish chronicles of the conquest of the West
" Indies. 2. The British words and names of places
" used in that country, even to this day do argue the
" same, as when they talk together they use the word
" *Gwrando*, which is hearken, or listen. Also they have
" a certain bird with a white head, which they call *Pen-
" guin*, that is, white head. But the island of *Corroceo*,
" the river *Guyndor*, and the white rock of *Penguin*, which
" be all British (or Welsh) words, do manifestly show,
" that it was that country Madoc and his people inha-
" bited.'

This historical passage is quoted and preserved by Hakluyt in his voyages and discoveries of the Britons, published in 1589. Several historians have mentioned the voyages of Madoc, and seem to consider them as indisputable. Dr. Warrington, in his late history of Wales, has carefully examined the original Welsh authorities on which the above passage is founded: They are the poems of Meredyth ap Rhys, Guytin Owen, and Cynfryg ap Grenw; the first flourished in 1470, the second in 1480, and the third about the same period. These bards, or historians composed their works antecedent to the expeditions of Columbus, and they relate or allude to the voyages of Madoc, as events well known in their time, and universally believed to have happened three hundred years before.

Dr. Belknap seems to discredit the truth of the historical passage before quoted, because it appears to him " confused and contradictory; the country discovered by " Madoc is said to be *without inhabitants*, and yet the peo- " ple whom he carried thither *followed the manners of the* " *land, and used the language found there,*"

In making this objection, the doctor evidently departed from his usual accuracy of discrimination. Madoc is said to have made three voyages. During the first he discovered *unknown land*. The second presented him with pleasant and fruitful countries *without inhabitants*. What he discovered on his third voyage no one knows. That the Welsh *followed the manners of the land, and used the language found there*, were the mere suggestions of Caradoc and Hakluyt, made more than four centuries subsequent to the migration, to which they allude. Their design was to prove, that the Mexicans derived their origin from the Welsh; yet, to account for the difference of language, it was necessary to infer the loss of their own, and the adoption of the prevalent one of the country. The accounts given by Madoc himself on his return from his two first voyages, as preserved by the three original authors already mentioned, are perfectly natural and consistent; all the confusion and contradiction in the narrative must be wholly ascribed to their commentators, who wrote after the conquest of Mexico. It is worthy of remark, that Dr. Belknap has quoted only one of the original authorities, which attest the adventures of Madoc, and which gave birth to the historical passage before quoted. His partiality, too, for Columbus, and his zealous endeavors to render ample justice to the memory of that celebrated man, no doubt made him less disposed to admit the possibility of a competitor.

The art of navigation was little known in those days; yet it pretty plainly appears, that Madoc united his two first colonies at the point of destination. Of the fate of the third, which sailed in ten ships, we have no account. If by some unfortunate occurrence, such as shipwreck, adverse winds, or the want of a more accurate knowledge of navigation, it happened to make land at a great distance from the other two colonies, probably they remained disunited and unknown to each other; and this accounts in part, for the apparent confusion in some of the subsequent proofs of their dispersed situation on this continent.

It appears that Madoc committed himself to the sea, sailing *west* to the *north* of Ireland, and finally came to land unknown. The question is, to what unknown land does he allude? Every reader must be ready to pronounce, that the land he discovered was either among the islands, or on the continent of America.

Dr. John Williams, in " an enquiry concerning the " first discovery of America by the Europeans," has quoted the Welsh authorities already mentioned, and illustrated them by references to some subsequent writers, whom we shall endeavor to follow.

In 1620, " a brief description of the whole world" was published in London. The writer makes several remarks on the supposed voyages and discoveries of king Arthur, and justifies queen Elizabeth in not claiming them by de-

scent, " imagining them to be grounded on fabulous foun-
" dations," and adds, " only this doth convey some shew
" with it, that now, some hundred years, *there was a*
" *knight of Wales, who, with shipping, and some petty*
" *company* did go to discover these parts, (America)
" whereof, as there is some *record of reasonable credit* a-
" mongst the monuments of Wales, so there is nothing
" which giveth more frequent shew thereunto than that,
" in the late navigations of some of our *monta Norumbe-*
" *ga*,* and some other parts of America, they found
" some tokens of civility and christian religion."

One of the most remarkable documents on this subject is the narrative of Morgan Jones, (who, it seems, was a clergyman) dated March the tenth, 1686, and published in the gentleman's magazine for 1740; the substance of which is as follows: He certifies that, in the year 1660, while he was an inhabitant of Virginia, and chaplain to major general Bennet, he accompanied two ships to Carolina as their minister, and landed at Oyster Point, where they continued eight months. The want of provisions induced him and five others to travel back to Virginia over land. The Tuscaroras, who were settled on Pontigo river, seized them as prisoners, and gave them to understand that they must die. On this intelligence, Jones, (who was a Welshman) exclaimed in the Welsh tongue, " have I escaped so many dangers, and must I " now be knocked on the head like a dog!" A war chief then came to him, and embraced him by the middle, and told him in the same language, that he should not die! He and his men were then received with welcome into the Tuscarora town, where they were entertained for four months; during which time a conversation was carried on in the Welsh language, and Jones preached to them

---

* The first discoverers of the New England coast, gave this name to the bay of Penobscot, or to the country about it.

three times a week: They could confer together on the most difficult subjects. He declares, among other things, his readiness to conduct any Welshman, or others to the country. This account written by Jones himself, and addressed to Dr. Thomas Lloyd of New York, was finally deposited in the Ashmolean museum, where it now remains.

This narrative of Jones is strongly supported by several others. Dr. Williams mentions, that another clergyman was taken prisoner by the Indians in Virginia, soon after the settlement of it, and that he saved his life by the knowledge he had of their language, which was Welsh. " They produced a book, which he found to be the bible, " but which they could not read !" Were it not for this remarkable circumstance, we should be inclined to believe, that the discovery of the last mentioned clergyman, has been mistaken for that of Jones.

In the " British Remains," published in 1777, appeared a letter written by Charles Lloyd, bearing date about the same period with the narrative of Jones, which serves to confirm the two preceding statements. It alleges that one Stedman, about thirty years before the date of the letter, was on the coast of America in a Dutch bottom, and that when he was about to land, the natives strongly opposed him. He understood their language, which was Welsh, and spoke to them; after which they were very courteous, and supplied him with the best things they had. They told Stedman, that their ancestors came from a country called *Gwynedd*, (North Wales) in *Prydain fawr*, (Great Britain.) This discovery is supposed to have been somewhere between Virginia and Florida. It is also stated in addition to this, that one Oliver Humphreys, a merchant of Surinam, informed the same Charles Lloyd, that the master of an English privateer or pirate, in repairing his vessel near Florida, became acquainted with the Indian tongue spoken there, which was afterwards found to be Welsh.

Some authorities of a more recent date are now to be stated, relative to the existence of the Welsh in another quarter. Father Charlevoix possessed talents and an inquisitive turn of mind, though he has been deemed somewhat credulous. He was a French missionary, and travelled from Canada to the Mississippi in 1721; he took much pains to inform himself of the history, religion, language, customs, and manners, of the different Indian nations. Some Indians, whom he calls the Aiouaz, (probably the Iowas) informed him, " that the Omans,* three " days journey from them, *had white skins and fair hair*, " especially the women." They further alleged, that the Pawnes, and other distant nations to the west, had often told them, " that there was a great lake, very far from " their country, on the borders of which were people resembling the French, with buttons (leather) on their " clothes, living in cities, and using horses in hunting the " buffaloe, and clothed with the skins of that animal, but " destitute of any arms, except the bow and arrow." In another part of the same work the good father thus expresses himself; " I met in the bay (in lake Michigan) " some Scioux, of whom I made many enquiries about " the countries which are to the west and northwest of Canada; and though I know we must not entirely depend " on what the savages say, yet by comparing what I have " heard from them, with that which I have heard from " many others, I have great reason to believe, *that there " are on this continent some Spaniards, or European colonies, much more north than any we know of in Mexico " or California.*" Carver spent the winter of 1766, among the Scioux on the river St. Pierre. They told him, that

---

* No nation by this name is known at the present day.

about the heads of the Missouri lived " a nation rather " smaller and *whiter* than the neighbouring tribes, who " cultivated the ground;" and from various intimations it appeared evident, that they were in some measure acquainted with the arts.

A Welshman by the name of Griffith was taken prisoner by the Shawnee Indians about the year 1764, and conducted to their towns. His adventures* were made public in 1804, from which the following particulars are abridged.

Two years after the captivity of Griffith, five Shawnees resolved to penetrate to the source of the Missouri, and they admitted him of the party. They had a long and laborious journey to the shining mountains, through which the Missouri finds its way. In these mountains they accidentally met with three *white men* in the Indian dress, with whom they travelled for some time, when they arrived at their village, and found the whole nation of the same complexion. A council was soon assembled, and the question was debated for three days, What shall be done with the strangers? It was finally concluded to put them to death, especially as they appeared to belong to a warlike nation, and were probably exploring the country to find out a suitable place for the future residence of their friends. Griffith, whose presence created no suspicion, could remain silent no longer. He addressed the council in Welsh, and explained the motives of their journey. It is needless to say, that full confidence was restored, and the strangers treated with kindness. Nothing could be ascertained of their history, except that their forefathers came up the Missouri from a very distant country. There was not a black man

* These were detailed by him to a man now living in Kentucky, and published by Harry Toulmin, esquire, at present one of the Judges of the Missisippi Territory.

in the nation, which was pretty numerous. The party returned to the Shawnee towns, after an absence of two years and six months. Griffith soon made his escape, and joined his friends in the back part of Virginia.

The subsequent narrative, corroborative of the one just mentioned, was given to the author of these sketches in May, 1805, by a Frenchman in upper Louisiana. This man had been several years employed in the north west by the English traders. His usual station was at the factory or trading house on the Assinniboine, a few days travel only from the Mandans on the Missouri. The conductor of that establishment aimed to extend the trade, and for this purpose selected a party, of which the informant was one, to explore the Missouri. In ascending that river they were obliged to pass one or two cataracts or falls in the shining mountains, as also several rapids, and much *hard water*. On the summit of these mountains they entered a large lake, from which the Missouri flows; and from the opposite extremity another river issued towards the west, down which the informant descended for some distance, and spent eleven days on it. The publication of the narrative of Griffith suggested the propriety of some enquiry relative to the Indians about the head of the Missouri. The informant declared, (and he sustains the character of a man of truth) " that there " was a numerous and singular nation of Indians about " the lake, who were not in the least tawny, but rather of a " yellowish complexion; that they wear their beards, and " that great numbers of them had red hair on their " heads." This is almost literally the statement furnished by the Frenchman.

This account is strongly supported by two others. Vancouver found a people in the vicinity of Columbia river, *speaking a language different from that of their neighbors, and in features resembling the northern Europeans*. Captains Lewis and Clark discovered some people near the mouth of the same river, who had *red or sandy hair on their heads*.

That the Welsh once existed on our coast between the gulf of Mexico and the Potomac, and also on the upper Mississippi, particularly about the head of the Missouri, is at least probable from the preceding proofs. That they more recently resided on Red river, is rendered as probable from the proofs now to be adduced.

In the year 1766, an Indian missionary by the name of Beatty, travelled into the western country, where he met with several persons, who had lived with the Indians from their youth, among whom were Benjamin Sutton, and Levi Hicks.

Sutton informed him, that when he was with the Chocktaw nation on the Mississippi, he went to an Indian town " a very considerable distance above New Orleans, whose " inhabitants were of different complexions, not so taw- " ny as those of the other Indians, and who spoke Welsh." He saw a book among them, which he supposed was the Welsh bible; " they kept it carefully wrapped up in a " skin, but they could not read it." After this he heard some Indians among the Shawnees speak Welsh with a native of Wales by the name of Lewis. " This Welsh " tribe, now (1766,) live on the west side of the Missis- " sippi river, a great way above New Orleans." He also alleged that both men and women observed the rites and ceremonies prescribed by the Mosaic law; the former " observed the feasts of the first fruits," and the latter occasionally " separated seven days from the men."

Hicks told the Missionary, " that he once attended an " embassy in a town of Indians on the west side of the " Mississippi river, who talked Welsh;" and the Indian interpreter of this missionary added, " that he saw some " Indians, whom he supposed to be of the same tribe, who " talked Welsh;" and he repeated some words in their language, which were found to be Welsh.

About the year 1764, captain Isaac Stewart, with some others, was taken prisoner by the Indians, and conducted to the Wabash. Subsequent to his liberation from captivity he published the following narrative in England.

"After remaining two years in bondage among the In-
" dians, a Spaniard came to the nation, having been sent
" from Mexico on discoveries. He made application to
" the chiefs for redeeming me, and another white man,
" who was in a like situation, named John David, which
" they complied with. And we took our departure in
" company with the Spaniard to the westward, crossing
" the Mississippi near Rouge, or Red river, up which
" we travelled seven hundred miles, when we came to a
" nation of Indians remarkably white, and whose hair
" was of a reddish color, at least mostly so. They lived
" on the banks of a small river, which is called the *River*
" *Post*. In the morning of the day after our arrival, the
" Welshman, (David) informed me, that he was deter-
" mined to remain with them, giving as a reason, that he
" understood their language, it being very little different
" from the Welsh. My curiosity was excited very much
" by this information; and I went with my companion to
" the chief men of the town, who informed him, (in a
" language that I had no knowledge of, and which had no
" affinity to that of other Indian tongues that I ever heard)
" that their forefathers in this nation, came from *a foreign*
" *country*, and landed on the east side of the Mississippi,
" describing particularly the country called Florida, and
" that *on the Spaniards taking possession of Mexico*, they
" fled to their then abode. And as a proof of what he
" advanced, he brought forth rolls of parchment, which
" were carefully tied up in otter skins, on which were
" large characters written with blue ink. The characters
" I did not understand, and the Welshman being unac-
" quainted with letters, I was not able to know the mean-
" ing of the writing. They are a bold, hardy, and intre-

" pid people, very warlike, and the women beautiful, " when compared with other Indians."

Some other proofs of a similar nature, recorded in works of celebrity, are intentionally omitted; and those inserted in this chapter are considerably abridged, except the passages included in inverted commas: More attention has been paid to the substance they contain than to the multiplicity of words and conjectures, with which they abound.

Against these authorities several plausible objections may be urged, calculated at first blush to weaken their validity. In the first place it may be said that, if they prove any thing, they prove too much; because they allude to a Welsh tribe in Virginia, to a second in Florida, to a third on Red river, to a fourth on the Mississippi, to a fifth on the Missouri, and perhaps to a sixth on the Wabash; whereas it is hardly to be expected that they ever became so numerous, or so much dispersed, as to occupy these different and distant regions. In the second place it may be said, that there are no Indians within our knowledge, whose appearance indicates an European origin: That Morgan Jones, and the other clergyman, already noticed, made no such discoveries about the year 1660, as they pretend; because if the Tuscaroras were of Welsh extraction, and spoke the Welsh language at that period, their origin must have been subsequently discovered, and some traces of the Welsh dialect found among them at the present day. These and several other objections naturally arise from a view of the subject, and suggest the propriety of a few cursory remarks.

The number of people drawn from Wales by Madoc, cannot be easily conjectured; the only data we have for calculation are, that he made three voyages, and that he sailed with ten ships on the last voyage. If we estimate the whole number at twenty, perhaps we shall be within the bounds of probability; and if we suppose each to have carried fifty five colonists, (a number about equal to the size of the vessels in those days) the whole number would be eleven hundred. From the time of their migration, to that of their discovery in 1660, was nearly five hundred years; and if we allow them to double once in every fifty years, (an increase of population a little more than half only to that generally admitted among civilized nations) the whole number at the period of discovery was nearly one million, one hundred twenty six thousand, four hundred; and by the same rule of calculation their number at this time rather exceeds eight millions. But the sanguinary warfare of European christians on this great continent, has thinned it of its ancient inhabitants, and many, once numerous and powerful nations are consigned to oblivion. Several nations of this description formerly inhabited Red river, the Arkansas, and the Mississippi; and to the moderns they are known only in the records of the first settlers of Louisiana.

Perhaps the third colony never joined the other two; and this is partly to be inferred from a circumstance soon to be mentioned. At any rate, it is natural to conclude, that Madoc, in whatever part of the world he was cast, exercised the supreme authority over those with him till his death; his rank and enterprise gave him a claim to this distinction. If they planted themselves contiguous to other nations, wars most probably ensued; and as the tactics of the Welsh were doubtless superior to those of their enemies, the issue must have been in their favor. Their knowledge likewise of fortification served to secure them from danger, while it proved destructive to those less acquainted with it. Hence we are led to believe, that population was rapid among them; and perhaps the more so as they had exchanged a foggy and barren country, for one of a serene atmosphere, and more prolific in the necessaries of life, both vegetable and animal. No doubt they preserved many of the useful arts for a long time, particularly the art of war, which enabled them to reside in regions of their choice, and to multiply in security. It seems fair to attribute to them the numerous monuments of art and skill found about the country. If the Tuscaroras are of Welsh extraction, they probably built the subterraneous wall discovered a few years ago in North Carolina. This indeed, is the more likely, as they inhabited that part of the country till about a century ago, when they incorporated themselves with the Oneidas; because, from an affinity in their language, they believed the two tribes to be branches of the same common stock.* The wall alluded to is of unquestionable antiquity. It is wholly buried beneath the earth, which has been rolled from the circumjacent high grounds. One hundred and sixty feet of its length was recently uncovered, as likewise nearly thirty feet of its depth. It is built of stone, and well cemented. It is uniformly two feet thick, and both sides of it are smooth. In fine, in the construction of this wall may be discovered a people considerably advanced in the arts. This specimen of regular masonry, however, is less to be admired than the instances of the art discovered by Columbus on the island of Cuba, and by his successors on the continent. The perfection of the arts was more particularly witnessed in the city and valley of Mexico. The arms of Montezuma, suspended in a broad shield over the front gate of his palace, (a griffin with expanded wings, holding a tyger in his talons) appear to be derived from the heraldry of Europe. Yet we must not yield lightly to the idea, that the ancient Mexicans were the descendants of the Welsh. The investigations of able historians have rendered it pretty certain, that some of the most polished nations of Anahuac

---

* This serves as proof, that the last colony never joined the other two, or that an early separation took place, and the bands or tribes remained disunited, probably for centuries.

were of Asiatic origin, and arrived there from the north west coast of America, as early as the seventh century. Therefore, before we can presume the Welsh to have penetrated into Mexico, we must prove a gross anachronism in the details of historians.

No doubt the death of Madoc, and the augmented population of the Welsh, served to create divisions among them, which ended in their dispersion under different chiefs. These evils, indeed, afflicted Wales before and at the time of the migration; and it seems just to conclude, that the example of the mother country had some influence over the colonists in this country. The temper and disposition of the Welsh in those days created a succession of wars and divisions among them; and hence the dispersion of the migrated bands, was probably attended with a waste of blood.

That such discoveries as we have mentioned were actually made, seem the more probable, as there is a remarkable coincidence and agreement, between the several accounts of them. The existence of a Welsh tribe in Virginia, said to be the Tuscaroras, is attested by two clergymen, both of whom saved their lives by the knowledge they had of their language. The testimony also of Stedman and Humphreys, though somewhat apocryphal, proves the existence of the Welsh in or near Florida; and the former declares they told him, " that their fa- " thers came from a country called North Wales, in Great " Britain!" There is likewise the testimony of three persons to prove the existence of the Welsh bible among at least two tribes of them; and it is worthy of remark, that these three persons lived at different eras, and indeed in different centuries, and were wholly unconnected and unknown to each other. On what ground shall we consider their testimony, as well as that of many other persons, as the result of artifice, or fraud; especially as it illustrates the same points, grows out of different occasione, and was published nearly at the same time? Most of the great events recorded in ancient history, and even those in the history of modern Europe, are supported by evidence much less certain and conclusive.

That a white people recently inhabited some part of the country near the head of the Missouri, we learn from Charlevoix and the other French traveller, already noticed; and that these white people were Welsh, is rendered almost certain from the testimony of Griffith. This man more than intimates, that they were settled along the banks of the Missouri within the shining mountains. The French traveller, and the authorities produced by Charlevoix, place them about a lake. The former indeed alleges, that he found such a people about the lake, which forms the source of the Missouri. No doubt they all refer to the same place, and to the same people. The different accounts of these men support each other; they serve at least as collateral proofs, and create a violent presumption, that the Welsh, or some other white people, inhabit the country about one of the head branches of the Missouri.*

---

* As another proof, that the Welsh once lived in or near Florida, and also on the Missouri, the following interesting letter, (received since this chapter was prepared for the press) from his excellency, John Sevier, dated, Knoxville, Tennessee, October 9th, 1810, is here introduced.

"I shall with pleasure, give you the information required, so far as my memory will now serve me, and the help of a memorandum I hastily took on the subject, of a nation of people called the Welsh Indians. In the year 1782, I was on a campaign against the Cherokees, and during my route, discovered traces of very ancient fortifications. Some time after the expedition, I had occasion to enter into a negotiation with the Cherokee chiefs, for the purpose of exchanging prisoners. After the exchange had been settled, I took an opportunity of enquiring of a venerable old chief, named Oconostoto, (then, and for nearly sixty years had been, a ruling chief of the Cherokee nation,) if he could inform me of the people that had left such signs of fortifications in their country? and particularly the one on the bank of the

If indeed there be a Welsh or white people in that quarter, as the authorities indicate, why were they not discovered by captains Lewis and Clark on their way to, or return from the Pacific ocean? This question admits of a satisfactory answer.

Highwassee river? The old warrior briefly answered me as follows: "It is handed down by our forefathers, that the works were made by "*white people*, who had formerly inhabited the country, while "the Cherokees lived lower down in the country, now called "South Carolina, and that a war existed between the two nations for "many years. At length, it was discovered, that the *whites* were ma- "king a number of large boats, which induced the Cherokees to sup- "pose, that they intended to descend the Tennessee river. They then "collected their whole band of warriors, and took the shortest and "most convenient route to the muscle shoals in order to intercept them "down the river. In a few days, the boats hove in sight, and a warm "combat ensued, with various success for several days. At length "the *whites* proposed to the Indians, that if they would exchange "prisoners, and cease hostilities, they would leave the country, and "never more return; which was acceded to, and, after the exchange, "parted in friendship. The *whites* then descended the Tennessee to "the Ohio, and then down to the big river, (Mississippi) then up it "to the muddy river, (Missouri) then up that river to a very great "distance. They are now on some of it's branches: But they are no "longer a *white people*; they are now all become Indians; and look "like the other red people of the country". I then asked him, if he had ever heard any of his ancestors say what nation of people those white people belonged to? He answered: "I have heard my "grandfather and other old people say, that they were a people cal- "led *Welsh*; that they had crossed the *great water*, and landed near "the mouth of Alabama river, and were finally driven to the heads of "its waters, and even to Highwassee river, by the Mexican Indians, "who had been driven out of their own country by the Spaniards." Many years past I happened in company with a Frenchman, who lived with the Cherokees, and had been a great explorer of the country west of the Mississippi. He informed me, "that he had been high up "the Missouri, and traded several months with the *Welsh tribe*; that "they spoke much of the *Welsh dialect*, and although their customs "were savage and wild, yet many of them, particularly the females "were very *fair* and *white*, and frequently told him, they had sprung "from a *white nation* of people; also stated they had yet some small "scraps of books remaining among them, but in such tattered and "destructive order, that nothing intelligible remained." He observed

A WELSH NATION IN AMERICA. 48

Those gentlemen found that the Missouri within the shining mountains, and more than two hundred miles below its source, was divided into three branches, nearly of an equal size. They pursued their route up the most northern one, and returned the same way. It is therefore likely, that two of the travellers we have named, ascended one of the other branches. The account of one of them derives some support from the discoveries of captains Lewis and Clark. On descending the Columbia, they found several tributary rivers, flowing into it from the left, one of which was nearly five hundred yards wide. If a river flows from the lake to the west, as has already been stated, it must join the Columbia from the left below the point where those gentlemen intersected it; and it possibly affords a much shorter, and more safe and expeditious communication with the Pacific ocean, than is to be found by the head of the northern branch. It must not be forgotten, that they discovered some straggling Indians near the mouth of the Columbia, similiar in appearance to those mentioned by Vancouver, and resembling those also said to reside on one of the branches of the Missouri.

Of the existence of a people on Red river, speaking the Welsh language, forty or fifty years ago, as has been mentioned, seems difficult to doubt. On what ground

that their settlement was in a very obscure part of the Missouri, surrounded with innumerable lofty mountains. The Frenchman's name has escaped my memory, but I believe it was something like Duroque. In my conversation with the old chief Oconostoto, he informed me, that an old woman in his nation named Peg, had some part of an old book given her by an Indian living high up the Missouri, and thought he was one of the *Welsh tribe*. Unfortunately before I had an opportunity of seeing the book, the old woman's house, and its contents, were consumed by fire. I have conversed with several persons, who saw and examined the book, but it was so worn and disfigured, that nothing intelligible remained; neither did any one of them understand any language but their own, and even that, very imperfectly."

shall we invalidate the testimony of captain Stewart? This is strongly supported by the narratives of Sutton and Hicks. The presumption is violent that they all allude to the same people.

The Ietans or Alitans, are the only Indians in that quarter known to us, who in any great degree answer the description given of the supposed Welsh. About sixty of them, for the first and only time, visited Nachitoches in 1807; and it was particularly observed, that the women were comparatively handsome, and that the hair of many of the men was of a sandy complexion. The customs and manners of these people indicate them to be of an origin different from that of their neighbors. Their lives are pastoral. Their movements are mostly confined to the Mexican mountains, particularly to the regions about the sources of Red river, the Arkansas, and some of the westerly branches of the Missouri; they follow the buffaloe and other game, which alternately inhabit the north, and the south, the high and the low country. They are the hereditary enemies of the Spaniards, and a predatory warfare has long existed between them and some of the Indian tribes of Louisiana. These people are divided into a great number of bands, and some of them were discovered by captains Lewis and Clark in the neighborhood of the shining mountains. They uniformly live in tents of a conical figure, fabricated from skins, and so disposed as to resemble the streets and squares of a city. They are cleanly in their persons and dress, particularly in their cookery, and obesity is common among those advanced in years. Their language widely differs from all others in the country, and few are disposed to encounter the difficulty of acquiring it.

Some enquiry ought to be made into the origin and language of this singular nation, and the trouble and expense of making them a visit, if properly managed, would be inconsiderable. If they spoke the Welsh language forty or fifty years ago, it no doubt still prevails among them. The lapse of more than six centuries, the occasional admission of strange idioms, the revolutions in dress, pursuits, and modes of life, are sufficient to change, and even destroy, the vernacular dialect, not only of the Welsh colonists, but of every nation on the globe. It must, however, be remembered, that the Indians, more than any civilized people, endeavor to preserve their language in its purity; it is much more liable to fluctuation and change among those in a state of progressive improvement.

Were it once satisfactorily ascertained, that the Welsh ever established themselves on this continent, a multitude of difficulties would be solved, which at present perplex the learned. In case of such a discovery, the ancient fortifications and other works of art, the traits of civilization, and the many tokens of christianity, discovered by the Spaniards and others at various times and places, ought in some measure to be ascribed to them. To them and to others, most probably of European descent, must likewise be ascribed the confused notion of an universal deluge, entertained by several tribes, apparently of different origins. Christianity spread in Wales many centuries before Madoc is supposed to have left it, and the scriptures were prevalent in that country; both indeed made their way into the north of Europe soon after their introduction into the southern parts of it. Hence the scripture account of the deluge was unquestionably known to Madoc and his people. It is therefore natural to conclude, that they brought the scriptures with them to this country, though all knowledge of them long since perished, except what tradition has preserved. In fine, most or all of the traditionary accounts among the aboriginals, which are founded on biblical history, must be traced to the early migrations from Europe and Africa.

Travellers describe certain private societies among the Indians, which apparently resemble our lodges of Freemasons. Their rules of government, and the admission of members, are said to be nearly the same. No one can be received as a member of the fraternity, except by ballot, and the concurrence of the whole is necessary to a choice. They have different degrees in the order. The ceremonies of initiation, and the mode of passing from one degree to another, would create astonishment in the mind of an *enlightened* spectator. Is not this practice of European origin? In the early periods of English history, the knowledge of freemasonry was mostly confined to the druids; and Wales was more fruitful of this description of men, than any other part of Europe. They were almost the only men of learning in those days: They executed the functions of priests, historians, and legislators. Those in Wales, in particular, animated their countrymen to a noble defence of their liberties, and afforded so much trouble to the first Edward, that he ordered them to be barbarously massacred. This inhuman order, the lineament of a ferocious tyrant, was carried into effect about the year 1282; and a few only of the bards survived to weep over the miseries of their country.

One principal aim of this chapter is to excite a spirit of enquiry. The subject is particularly interesting to the learned, at least of sufficient importance to awaken their curiosity, and to stimulate their enterprise; it cannot be too often revived, nor too strictly investigated.

FINIS.

CPSIA information can be obtained
at www.ICGtesting.com
Printed in the USA
LVHW042046010523
745797LV00019B/138